the Interpretation
of
dialogue

the Interpretation of dialogue

Edited by Tullio Maranhão

The University of Chicago Press • Chicago and London

Tullio Maranhão, associate professor of anthropology at Rice University, is the author of *Therapeutic Discourse and Socratic Dialogue*.

The University of Chicago Press, Chicago 60637
The University of Chicago Press, Ltd., London

© 1990 by the University of Chicago
All rights reserved. Published 1990
Printed in the United States of America

99 98 97 96 95 94 93 92 91 90   5 4 3 2 1

Library of Congress Cataloging-in-Publication Data
The Interpretation of dialogue / edited by Tullio Maranhão.
    p.   cm.
    Includes index.
    ISBN 0–226–50433–6 (alk. paper). — ISBN 0–226–50434–4 (pbk:
alk. paper)
    1. Dialogue.   2. Communication.   I. Maranhão, Tullio.
P95.455.I5   1990
401'.41–dc20   89-5074
                                                     CIP

⊗The paper used in this publication meets the minimum requirements of the American National Standard for Information Sciences—Permanence of Paper for Printed Library Materials, ANSI Z39.48-1984

contents

Acknowledgments

This anthology is not a work of circumstance but resulted from several years of discussions involving many colleagues in the United States, Europe, and South America. I am thankful to all those who participated in the dialogue. I owe special gratitute to Dennis Tedlock, Vincent Crapanzano, Stephen Tyler, Bradford Keeney, Jan Swearingen, Steven Crowell, and Lane Kauffmann for their participation in our conference in Philadelphia in 1986. A work as long in the making as this one becomes possible only with the goodwill and perseverance of those who undertake it. These qualities were abundant in Sylvia Louie and in Elizabeth Cummings, who helped me with the manuscript preparation. Provost Neal Lane and the Office of the Dean of Social Sciences at Rice University provided me with the financial means to produce the manuscript. A compilation of dialogue of such a scope lies beyond the capacity of the individual— my deepest appreciation goes to Richard Wolin, Stephen Tyler, Steven Crowell, and Lane Kauffmann for their help in keeping the thread of dialogue from being severed by the sharp blades of domineering speech and passive listening.

Some of the contributions in this volume have already appeared in print. The following articles are reprinted, in some cases with modifications, with the permission of the publishers: Richard McKeon's "Dialogue and Controversy in Philosophy" appeared in *Philosophy and Phenomenological Research* 17(1956): 143–63; I am especially grateful to Zahava K. McKeon. Werner Kelber's "Narrative as Interpretation and Interpretation of Narrative" appeared in *Semeia* 39(1986): 107–33. Greg Urban's "Ceremonial Dialogues in South America" appeared in *American Anthropologist* 88, 2(1986): 371–86. R. Lane Kauffmann's "The Other in Question" is based on an argument partially developed in his "Julio Cortázar y la Narración del Otro," which appeared in *Revista de Literatura Hispanica* 22–23(1986): 317–26. Alessandro Ferrara's "A Critique of Habermas's *Diskursethik*" appeared in *Telos* 64(1985): 45–74.

Introduction

Tullio Maranhão

In traditional epistemology the clash between two ideas and the triumph of one over another are explained as a consequence of the prevailing idea's being more right or true. From this point of view knowledge is more important than any of the processes helping to generate, shape, or change it. Even when the outcome of the debate is determined by the arguments, these are perceived as natural extensions of the idea proved right or true and not as appendages attached to the theses in discussion. In dialogical understanding, on the contrary, the debate follows the logic of dialogue, that is, the turns of stating and questioning, and the synthesizing in consensual agreement. The result of the dialogical operation may reinforce epistemology, but it may also reflect accommodations having little to do with categories of knowledge regarded as true and right. The present plea for dialogue presents it as the antipode of epistemology. Thus, arguments can be legitimized only in particular contexts of dialogue, not by virtue of claims to universality.

Evidently, dialogical hermeneutics undermines the stability of the categories of knowledge by taking away the axis of decision from ideas and entrusting it to the rhetoric of argumentation. Dialogical knowledge is a game of instances of understanding conditioned not by the logic of the categories of knowledge, but by shifts along a spiral line traced through the subject-speakers. Knowledge thus produced is shrouded in skepticism and emphasizes process over essence. The question of how the discussants arrive at a certain conclusion becomes more important than what that conclusion is. This encourages negative knowledge as opposed to positive, in which certain categories precede the process of discussion and are held as necessary foundations if the debate is to unfold. Whereas in positive knowledge underscored by epistemology conceptual categories are relatively inexpungable, in dialogue they are exposed to questioning and to criticism. These operations tend to replace the categories as corner-stones in the edifice of knowledge.

The essays in this anthology constitute an effort to interpret and understand the antiepistemology of dialogue as a framework for rethinking knowledge. The book is divided into six sections repre-senting different perspectives on the nature of dialogue. It opens with the discussion of the context of emergence of the interest in dialogue in classical philosophy. Although claimed as belonging to the Western heritage, the culture of ancient Greece invites us to think whether dialogue may be something different in every cultural and historical context. If, like the epistemology it debunks, dialogue lays claim to universality, it must be found behind every cultural and historical expression. The next section of the book helps illuminate this topic with discussions about dialogue in early Christianity, among South American Indian tribes, and in Islam. The recent awakening of interest in dialogue was spawned by hermeneutics and by literary criticism. The third section of the anthology turns to experiments with the identities of author, character, and reader in works of fiction. Whereas literature experiments with representations of dialogue, other disciplines seem to depend directly on represen-tations of dialogue in order to unravel their scientific inquiry. This is the case for psychotherapy and anthropology, the objects of our next two sections. Psychotherapeutic theory can be regarded as a reflec-tion on the dialogue between the roles of therapist and client, and anthropology, of ethnographer and native. The opening article in the collection, McKeon's "Dialogue and Controversy in Philosophy," introduces the question of the transformation of the quest for dialogue from an ontological to an ethical endeavor. If the attempts to grasp the essence of dialogue unfailingly frustrate the interpreter, perhaps instead of asking what dialogue is we should ask whether it promotes rightness and truth, thereby subordinating it to classical epistemology. However, there are other alternatives in the character-ization of dialogue that constitute the aim of our collective reflection in this anthology. The final section of the book turns precisely to the discussion of dialogue as a noumenon free from the confining space created by the opposition between truth and rhetoric. This issue surfaces in many articles and constitutes the backbone of our reflection.

Our discussion is cast within the parameters of the postmodern debate outlined by poststructuralist philosophers such as Foucault, Derrida, and Lyotard in their unsparing critique of the intellectual products of modernity, by neopragmatists like Apel, Habermas, and Rorty who, despite being critical of modernist thinking, oppose its uncompromising denial, and by the philosophical hermeneutics of Gadamer. The work of Bakhtin and the phenomenological tradition from Husserl to Levinas are also of central importance to our discussion. Dialogue is given prominence in the work of Apel (1986) and of Habermas (1984, 1987) as they attribute an important role to the communicative competence of the speakers of natural languages in deliberating about private and public life, or about how the individual and the collectivity should conduct themselves. For Habermas, in spite of the fact that communicative competence has evolved throughout history and that it may vary from one cultural setting to the next, human communication is fundamentally the same, and it is through ordinary communicative actions that mankind can find solutions to its problems of survival and coexistence. Consequently the history of controversy is regarded as the great conversation of mankind, as Rorty puts it (1979). However, whereas for Rorty the edifying role of philosophy stops there, for Habermas and for Gadamer the conversation has a telos—emancipation for the former author and understanding for the latter.

It is significant that the postmodern French philosophers have not emphasized dialogue and communication, because in their view all representations of ontological and ethical issues are always already caught in the web of power games (Foucault 1972) or of logocentrism (Derrida 1974). Lyotard (1979) characterizes the postmodern condition as a crisis in the narrative tradition brought about by science and technology. The traditional master narratives *(récits)* lose legitimacy, while the technoscientific explanations either dispense with the need for legitimation or seek it in the paralogism and fragmentation of its discourse. The only reason the postmodern sociocultural world does not collapse together with its self-reflecting and self-devouring discourse is that legitimation does not require consistency anymore but lives on in the proliferation and dissemination of language games or, in Lyotard's words, in the paralogism of overgrown performativity (1979, 105).

In addition to postmodern criticism and universal neopragmatism (universal because of its claim for the universality of certain fundamental categories of knowledge), philosophical anthropology in its search for an answer to the question What is man? has also turned to dialogue as a fruitful domain of inquiry. Whereas in neopragmatism the subject in dialogue is taken for granted as the psycholinguistic individual who reasons and speaks, and in postmodern criticism it is dismissed as a product of representation, in philosophical anthropology the subject is examined as an entity that turns to the Other (Buber 1970; Gadamer 1975; Bakhtin 1981; Levinas 1969, 1987). In the act of turning to the Other the subject gains identity, that is, meaning. Thus the question of philosophical anthropology becomes, Who turns, and who is the Other? In the gesture of turning to the Other the subject is an interpreter and dialogue is hermeneutics.

Bakhtin's dialogical principle unfolds from the notions of Self and Other as mutually constituting. The subject's "conceptual horizon" represents the circle of one's vision, that is, the refractions imposed upon reality and at the same time constitutive of reality from the point of view of a Self addressing an Other. In his neo-Kantian trajectory the Russian thinker moved away from a philosophy centered on the subject, toward the analysis of speech genres and worldviews that are ultimately responsible for the constitution of the subject himself, proposing an architectonics of the mind that arises out of the choreography to which Self and Other dance.

Bakhtin emphasized the precedence of the social over the individual and explained the generation of meaning in terms of the relation between utterances (intertextuality), of the prevalence of context over text (heteroglossia), and of the hybrid nature of language (polyglossia). He also called attention to the presence of meaning as something lying outside the subject's sphere of consciousness. Casting his glance upon literary works, Bakhtin reasoned in terms of the vitriolic effects stemming from the author as a novel writer and as a speaker within the novel. The subject/author/speaker is successively enfeebled, first, by his lack of autonomy in the face of his addressees, who also participate in the production of meaning; second, by the dilution of his identity behind the characters, who start speaking for him and soon speak as independent voices; third, by the characters themselves' having their roles attenuated by the polyphony reigning in the novel, a dialogical situation that is typical of ordinary life or of "real-life dialogue" (1986, 75). The utterances in dialogue do not proceed from the subject's will. The inclinations of individual speakers constitute "speech genres" (or discourse formations, as we would say after Foucault) that can be better understood by a linguistics aware of speech and utterances (and not of sentences alone) than by psychology.

For Gadamer the Other is the text of tradition. Dialogue does not begin by accident but is initiated when certain elements in the historical horizon of the interpreter called his attention to particular constellations of meaning. In his critique of Kantian aesthetics Gadamer remarks that "the 'subject' of the experience of art, that which remains and endures, is not the subjectivity of the person who experiences it, but the work itself" (1975, 92). Like the aesthetic play, interpretation is not an action, nor does it begin with the subject. The text of tradition does not precede interpretation but is itself already interpretation. Like the aesthetic experience, the hermeneutic endeavor is discontinuous and permanently confronted by its limitations. The "experience of human finitude" (p. 320) is surely disappointing for consciousness, but at the same time it contains the seed of hope of mastering historical experience (or, mutatis mutandis, the object of art). Gadamer places hope on a par with language as a guide to experience (p. 313), the spearhead of dialogue. Thus Gadamer's position represents a step away from the notion of subject as center of dialogue, bringing him closer to postmodern criticism than to the philosophical anthropology of phenomenological heritage that nevertheless constitutes his intellectual background.

Throughout the twenty-five centuries of reflection on dialogue (ever since Socrates and the Sophist philosophers), the differences between *description* and *ideal* have not always been made clear. As something describable, dialogue can be the object of study of empirical science, but as an ideal it is a topic of discussion in moral philosophy. If dialogue can be described, its fulfillment is accomplished by the unfolding of life, whereas if it is an ideal its fulfillment can only be contemplated on the horizon, but never realized. The components of dialogue as either an empirical reality amenable to description or an unfulfilled ideal are nominally the same: dwelling, subject, language, and meaning. But these components are defined rather differently as description and as ideal. In the descriptive model dialogue is represented as communication between two individuals (subjects) who share a common background of sociocultural tradition and immediate interests (dwelling), who talk to one another by means of a common language, and whose conversation sometimes presupposes and at other times, in addition to that, aims at a consensual understanding of meaning. In dialogue as an ideal the subject's identity is disclosed when he expresses himself, and consequently it cannot precede dialogue as it is assumed in the descriptive model; the dwelling itself is built in the process (it is the outcome of dialogue); language is a mode of expression very broadly defined; and meaning cannot be understood apart from happiness and satisfaction.

From the point of view of the descriptive model, dialogue depends not only on the stability of its conceptual components, but also on the resolution of problems cropping up in the intermediary zones between dwelling and subject, subject and language, and language and meaning. Both components and intermediary areas have been the province of studies of empirical disciplines. The social and historical sciences—that is, anthropology, history, ideology critique, or sociology—have thematized dwelling through concepts such as "culture," "period," "ideology," and "society." Psychology has studied the subject as a unique personage in his adaptation to the sociocultural background. Linguistics and pragmatics have created definitions for language and hypothesized the relation between speaker and language. Dialectic and analytic philosophy, semantics and semiotics have focused on the connections between language and meaning. But can a clear notion of dialogue emerge from the combination of all these disciplines as Habermas proposes (1984, 1987)? Despite all the agreement on basic concepts, in the world of empirical sciences the objects constituted by the discourses based on methodological regularity are not stable. In each discipline discourse is kaleidoscopic, pervaded by dialogical rather than monological processes. Contemporary anthropology, for example, has realized that cultural description is always conditioned by the spiral effects of the encounter between two dwellings (two cultural traditions), underscored by conflicting political interests, two subjects (ethnographer and native), and two languages. The meaning of the ethnographic description reflects more the encounter than the observation of the Other. The inconclusiveness of the descriptive project of the empirical disciplines makes one wonder whether the endeavor is merely unfinished or in fact impossible.

The descriptive model of dialogue resulting from the scientific disciplines is a monstrosity: a split subject relating to a fugitive dwelling, often homeless in his communicative pilgrimage, speaking a limited and deceitful language to an Other who is a projection of himself (the psychoanalytic hypothesis) in pursuance of a diaphanous meaning that he can never entirely grasp as a lonely subject. Interestingly, the descriptive model—an offspring of modernity—yields a postmodern picture of dialogue. Its flaw lies in its pronouncing the end of knowledge before the realization of what can be known, for if dialogue can be described the meanings produced can be seized. However, dialogue is always open to reinterpretation, and consequently no description is able to pin down ultimate meanings. Aware of this daunting limitation of description, Socrates and Plato cast dialogue as an ideal.

Socrates subordinated speech to man and steered his dialogues as encounters among souls. For him the aim of philosophy—the new discourse embodied in the dialogues—was to unearth knowledge in a practice qualified as ethical. In his diatribe against the poets, or against the Sophist philosophers, he argued that they had estranged themselves from truth by their choice of inadequate means to express meaning in poetry and in rhetoric. Truth was uncovered neither by poetics nor by eloquence, but by the sincere and dialectic analysis of ideas. It resided in the human soul and blossomed in speech as knowledge with the aid of the midwife-philosopher. Thus, although dependent on the efficacy of words, and consequently on poetics and rhetoric, truth emanated from the soul, not from language.

Reading Plato's dialogues in the present times of strong individualism, we are inevitably struck by the power of the individual and his voice, his logical maneuvers revealing the workings of his reason and his passions (desire, jealousy, spite, or pride), thereby subordinating the content of the communication to the speaker's personage. In Plato's dramas of knowledge, the meaning-content being discussed is also expressed in the speakers' attitudes in such a way that, for example, in a discussion about the meaning of love, the defenders of the opinion that lovers will be better off by loving less than they are loved have a selfish conduct in the dialogue; in turn, those who advocate love beyond a theory of supply and demand make a greater contribution to the conversation, often becoming the thread that keeps the dialogue flowing (Socrates' role). Albeit contemporaneously read with an emphasis on the individual's personality, the Socratic leadership was not personal. It was based on the ideal of a democratic communication in which social hierarchies should be displaced, making room for pure argument. Asymmetries such as those between guest and host, famous and obscure, known and unknown, wise and ignorant, rich and poor, or handsome and ugly should not influence the evaluation of arguments. The best argument should be determined by reason, which was independent of those values from which social asymmetries sprang.

Aristotle crystallized the sense of reason in dialectic. The logic of dialectic was akin to predication and other grammatical operations involved in describing sentence construction. Since grammatical operations were an offshoot of literacy, the logic of dialectic was closer to the grammar of writing, whereas the logic of dialogue was steeped in speech procedures. In the absence of a psychology of the individual, the science of dialectic (sorting out concepts and making sense of them) developed with a focus on language rather than on the subject. Indeed, dialectic dispensed with the speaker and with the context of the argument. It consisted in the possibility of splintering concepts through analysis toward a definition of essence. Exacting definitions made ideas appear more detailed and closer to essence than in their state before analysis, so that in retrospect they seemed blurred, general, and coarse. Dialectic followed the premise of the ancient atomists, who thought that dividing things up into their smaler parts (atoms) brought one closer to constitutive essence. Dialectic appropriated the method and premise of atomism and applied them to words. Therefore, in its beginnings, it was a sort of scientific and historical philology. As with antomism, the inspiration of dialectical reasoning came from geometric notions of space, for the meaning of words is rendered clearer when the relations among them are mapped out. Although for Aristotle the categories of knowledge remained vulnerable to the unpredictability of life, essence was definitely the loftiest entity in his cosmology of Being.

From Socrates to Gadamer, symmetry of participation and goodwill have been regarded as indispensable conditions for the ideal of dialogue. However, the equality among subjects refers not to their physical, linguistic, psychological, social, cultural, or political characteristics, but to the participation in the process of dialogue itself, which should overshadow all traces of individuation. Likewise, the goodwill is not that of the good Samaritan, but that of the listener. The totality of meaning to be grasped is given in the structure of preunderstanding (cf. knowledge by recollection for Socrates and Gadamer's rehabilitation of prejudice [1975]). Grasping the totality of meaning is another ideal purpose that is based on the hope of completing interpretation and reaching understanding. In the absence of that hope, dialogue cannot be. Nevertheless, the ideals of equality of participation, of goodwill, and of totalization of meaning are never concretely fulfilled, because no sooner is knowledge submitted to the scrutiny of the Socratic maieutic than it is revealed as ignorance, and no sooner is seriousness confronted by irony than its face of arrogance is unveiled. Pari passu, in Gadamerian language, unraveling the totality of the human experience is an undertaking mediated by the prejudices in which knowledge is steeped, by languages, and finally by the infinite dialogue that is the closer approximation to "the truth that we are" (Gadamer 1976, 16).

The contemporary assessment produces a picture of dialogue very different from that of classical philosophy, or from that of any other historical context in which it surfaced as a major philosophical issue. Although at first sight dialogue seems to be a flow of meaningful expressions between two subjects with unequivocal identities, several undercurrents are simultaneously taking place in such a way that the actual transaction may turn out to be something very different from what was initially perceived. In his contribution to this anthology Crapanzano presents dialogue as a complex weaving of meaning, as a congeries of levels of discourse, types of language, and moments of assertion flowing into one another, often at cross-purposes. The role of interpretation in dialogue is to build bridges among subjects, languages, and meanings. Dialogue is not carried out willfully by any of the participants.

The participant in dialogue is himself split (the many parts of self, or the dubious identity of words between Self and Other), and his interlocutor may be a projection of himself—compare Kauffmann's questioning of the status of the Other in literature in this anthology—and may not even be the addressed Other, but may be a "third" or "shadow" figure in dialogue with the speaker (cf. Tyler and Crapanzano, respectively). The scenario resulting from the contemporary representation of dialogue is characterized by images of free-floating languages and speechless subjects, of disconnected meanings, and of ambiguity beyond intentions.

Undaunted by this acute criticism of dialogue, the descriptive undertaking proceeds contemporaneously in the study of the modes of communication such as speaking, writing, and electronic broadcasting. The current sensibilities to the dynamics of orality and literacy have constituted a provoking template for the reflection on dialogue. The works of Albert Lord and Milman Parry on epic narrative, those of Eric Havelock on the consequences of the invention of the alphabet and the adoption of literacy in ancient Greece, and Walter Ong's studies of the implications of prevalent modes of communication stand out prominently in this movement (cf. contributions by Kelber and by Fischer and Abedi in this anthology). Even those thinkers who regard dialogue as an ideal, such as Plato and Gadamer, employ the language of empirical description to develop their arguments. Thus Plato writes about dialogue through the metaphor of oral exchanges between two speakers, whereas Gadamer carries out his reflection through the metaphor of the reader's interpretive effort before the text.

Treating dialogue as an ideal evidently has an ethical implication. Furthermore, when a particular mode of communication is chosen as the model of dialogue, it becomes identified with the sense of goodness or rightness inhering in the ideal to the exclusion of other modes of communication. Plato's time was characterized by a cultural struggle between writing and speaking; in ours the battle is between electronics and writing. Is speaking more ethical than writing, and writing more ethical than the electronic processing and broadcasting of information? There is no easy equation between ethics and modes of communication, and neither Plato nor Gadamer attempted that equation (cf. Kelber's essay).

Nevertheless, the expressivity of talking or of writing continues to have a gripping power over the representations of dialogue. The reason is that every mode of communication displays a phenomenal dimension of dialogue present in *logos* that, however, is not reducible to the technologies involved in speaking, writing, or broadcasting. *Logos* in the ancient Greek usage means sentence, count, tell, say, speak, phrase, account, definition, reason, reasonable, rational, language, talking, speech, argument, and proposition (cf. Swearingen); and in the age of television and computers we might want to add to that list notions such as bits, watts, bytes, and digits. Therefore the phenomenal dimension of *logos* underlies every form of communication, and its isolation constitutes the first important step in the interpretation of dialogue.

As an antiepistemology, dialogue must at least share the ground with epistemology and be an ontology or first philosophy, that is, the basic principle from which knowledge begins. Or, putting it the other way round, dialogue must have an ontology to which all knowledge can be traced back. This ontological base is not found in the empirical manifestations of dialogue. The first domain where it can be encountered is that of *logos*. Ever since Socrates and the Sophist philosophers, it has been tempting to separate form and content and to uncover the meaning of dialogue independent of the meaning-content flowing through its channels. But the separation between form and content produces disconcerting effects. No sooner is dialogue thus divided than form dissolves into either subject identity or meaning-content. The form becomes the framework constituted by the speakers, or by the dialectic of the meaning-content, and dialogue returns to the state of an empirical expression that can be described as a mode of communication. Thinking of dialogue in terms of subject (dwelling and speakers) and of meaning-content (language and meaning) is already a way of separating form and content and of taking the empirical description of oral communication for dialogue. Dialogue is change rather than repetition, but in order for a category of knowledge to change the backdrop constituted by the subject must remain immutable; otherwise there will be no contrast for the change of meaning to be perceived as such. Thus change of meaning-content is a correlate of subject continuity. Perhaps it is for this reason that the subject was taken for granted until the advent of the psychology of the individual. But the more recent focus on the analysis of the subject has tipped the scale to the other side, making the subject emerge essentially as a changing entity. Mutatis mutandis, changes in subject identity lead the categories of knowledge to repeat themselves, thereby establishing the contrast necessary for the subject to be perceived as shifting identity. The separation of form and content creates a polarization between two sides mutually necessary to one another: one is permanently changing while the other is permanently repeating itself.

Kierkegaard noticed the opposition between the ancient Greek concept of knowledge by recollection and the category of repetition in modern philosophy. The Greek argument that knowledge is recollection is problematic, because recollection looks at the past and knowledge thus unveiled has nothing to do with the present. Knowledge would always be taking place in the past, and the present would be a deviation from the past. Repetition, on the contrary, emphasizes present and future, linking them to the past, for it ensures the knowledge of what is to come as well as of what was (cf. Kierkegaard 1983). Two kinds of repetition can be distinguished: reproductive and differential. Reproductive is the repetition exhausted in regularity. Differential, although following a pattern, defeats all efforts to explain its logic through laws derived from the pattern (cf. Deleuze 1968).

Freud established the "compulsion to repeat" as the nucleus of neurotic behavior and the symptom to treat in psychoanalysis. His notion of repetition (like that of drive or instinct) is challenging because it is presented both as a characteristic of the subject and as a philosophical concept. Initially, like the ancient Greeks, Freud (1963) defined repetition as the patient's *acting out* (as opposed to remembering) the traumatic events of his biography. Transference itself would be a link in the chain of repetition. The analyst could comprehend the content of repetition only when transference ran deep. He would then help the patient *work through* the repressed motives of his conduct by restoring the flow of memory and thereby stopping its substitution by the repetitive acting out. In his initial approach, Freud understood repetition as a trait of behavior to be explained in the context of biography—as a negative and repressive reaction to be removed in psychoanalytic treatment. Later (1961, 1969) he linked repetition to the death instinct. Like the organism, the psyche would wish to return to a state of undifferentiated stability. The flow of life would aim not at opposing death, but at preventing it from occurring in a nonnatural way by trying to control it through a compulsive retention. As such, repetition cannot be regarded as aberrant conduct to be treated. Freud's last conception of repetition is more philosophical, in the tradition of thinking of Hegel, Nietzsche, Heidegger, and Derrida.

If repetition is the staple of life, as Kierkegaard and Freud indicate, there would be no difficulty in fathoming the totality of meaning. But there is a surplus meaning that results from the refraction effect of repetition. Nietzsche's metaphor of dice throwing (1968) is helpful here. At the time of the throwing there is suspense; no one knows exactly which face of the die will show up. When the die stops rolling, the face shown becomes known, but it comes as no surprise since everyone knew what all six possibilities were. However, the number shown picks a new winner each time, and although it is the same old number, each time the die is thrown it creates a new situation with a new winner and a new loser. The meaning of language in dialogue is like the numbers on the die, while dialogue is like the dice throwing, capable of exacting a meaning surplus from every familiar occurrence.

The reflection about dialogue as a systematic form and the search for its possible meanings is carried out in several contributions to this anthology. Swearingen discusses the atemporal and liminal character of dialogue; Urban focuses on ceremonial dialogues among South American Indians who ritualistically enact social solidarity; and Keeney proposes a cybernetic model to describe dialogue in family therapy. Although in all three essays the content and form of dialogue are not entirely severed, by putting the emphasis on form these authors subordinate the meaning of the issues discussed in dialogue to the meaning of the very action of debating. This approach stands in diametric opposition to epistemology, which puts meaning on the content of the ideas being debated. Dialogue as form and epistemology as content are indeed two extreme positions that do not exhaust the universe of possibilities of interpretation. The articles by those contributors who privilege the meaning of form over that of content already present too many nuances, ranging from the neopragmatism of Habermas (cf. Ferrara) to postmodern criticism (cf. Mecke).

Other traditions in the interpretation of dialogue find form and content inextricable. This is the case with classical philosophy as discussed by McKeon and also by Swearingen, early Christianity (cf. Kelber), Islam (cf. Fischer and Abedi), literature (cf. Kauffmann), psychoanalysis (cf. Daelemans and Maranhão), and philosophical hermeneutics (cf. Crowell).

The combination of the meaning of the saying with the meaning of the said is central to the psychoanalytic project for the restoration of dialogue. The Freudian assumption that existential malaise is revealed when Self talks to the Other suggests that there is a healthy and happy communication and that the psychoanalytic treatment is an exercise in the restoration of distorted communication. Instead of focusing on the process of verbal communication to attribute meaning to dialogue, Freud turned to different spheres such as the relations between the conscious and the unconscious and the transferential bonding between analyst and analysand. However, like the Socratic dialogue, the interaction between therapist and patient follows the road of the meanings under discussion—that is, the history of relational and representational difficulties experienced by the patient. In psychoanalytic interpretation transference cannot be unraveled outside the meaning of the patient's biography, and this meaning in turn is opaque in the absence of concepts such as transference, resistance, defense, repression, and interpretation. The transparency necessary for interpretation is a product of braiding together the definitions of the psychoanalytic encounter as formulated in the metapsychology and of the biographic experience of each patient. The psychoanalytic dialogue is kept alive as long as neither one of these two poles sways the interaction.

Literature is another area where the interpreter feels lured to separate form and content and to attribute meaning to dialogue by contrasting these two angles. In the work of fiction dialogue surfaces in two venues: as communication between reader and writer and as dialogical situations among characters in the story. In the latter capacity dialogue is identical to narrative. Instead of the usual paratextual features of narrative—temporal clauses, commentaries on the narrated events, and instruction for the reader to understand the story—represented dialogue draws on characteristics of actual dialogue. But since the verbatim copy of its model produces a riddled text, because actual dialogue often is inconclusive, represented dialogue introduces new elements in order to guide the reader: a convergence between words and deeds embodied in the exemplary attitude of a dialogue leader. This central speaker appears in every manifestation of represented dialogue and can be illustrated by the Socratic philosopher, the psychoanalyst, or the main character in the novel. Represented dialogue is not only that one that is committed to text, but also dialogue springing from a textual blueprint. Thus the dialogue leader performs the functions of the paratextual elements in narrative in guiding the reader's understanding of the text and is a creation neither of narrative nor actual, but of represented dialogue (cf. Tyler's contribution for a discussion of represented dialogue in the Renaissance).

In contrast to the logic of narrative, which is temporal, sequential, and mimetic (speech events describing actual events), represented dialogue is characterized by atemporality, by the logic of argument and counterargument, and by the central speaker who weaves coherence into the text for the reader. Also mimetic, instead of describing, represented dialogue simulates actual events. The effort to control the reader's interpretation discloses another central character: the author who, concealed behind the text, is perceived as a speaker/writer endowed with an infinite capacity to invent/discover meaning. As in the case of narrative, in which the narrated story was composed by someone else or was present in the collective memory of the tradition, represented dialogue also depends on a deus ex machina: the author as superspeaker. But are the omniscience and omnipresence (or omniabsence) of author and of central speaker not identical? In relation to narrative, represented dialogue opens an additional fold in the fan of representation by adding the character of the leader to that of the author.

This point is discussed in Mecke's article as he writes that in addition to being an invention of the literary tradition, the author is always inside the text, not outside. Basing his argument on Lyotard, he contends that the narrative universe is dominated by master narratives, that is, the Enlightenment's metanarrative with its tale of intellectual progress, the Marxist's with its tale of emancipation from exploited and alienated work, and the capitalist's with its tale of emancipation from poverty through the accumulation of capital and technoscientific progress. Narrative and represented dialogue are two sides of the same coin. The identity between the two is revealed not only in their structural resemblance (description and simulacrum, temporality and logic of argumentation, paratextual features and exemplary speaker), but also in the unrelenting vocation of represented dialogue to repeat the stories in the master narratives. Internally it has a telos and a conclusion. Externally it falls within the folds of social history. Chronicling this history, Lyotard (1979) writes that master narratives have been rendered obsolete in postmodern times, being replaced with the proliferation of language games. The fragments resulting from this explosion of meaning have lost contact with totality and constitute a new universe. In this scenario universal claims are untenable, and the meaning of dialogue becomes confined to the boundaries of community and of historical time.

Commenting on Habermas's thesis that ethics inheres in communicative actions, Ferrara points out the difficulties of sustaining the claim when one turns to the discourse of the individual. He proposes that the ethical considerations about public discourse do not hold for the issues of private life and that the political-philosophical discourse addressing issues of collective interest should run parallel, without intersecting the discourse of the individual. Writing within a tradition that favors totality over fragmentation, Ferrara finds in the Aristotelian category of *phronesis* (prudence), as reinterpreted by Gadamer, a bridge capable of reestablishing the connection between individual and collective interests. The standards for moral conduct in society would be maintained in democratic dialogue, while the happiness of the individual would be protected by his freedom to act autonomously and authentically. Public liberties would be the guarantor of individual freedom, and both would be inspired by the prudence stemming from communicative competence and from the memory of the history of social conflict.

If the empirical model of dialogue welcomes description and makes the separation between form and content attractive to the interpreter, the model of dialogue as an ideal appeals to consciousness. The ideals of equality of participation, of goodwill, and of completing the interpretation with the totality of meaning establish a stark contrast with the practices of dialogue characterized by the asymmetries among participants, by conflicts of interest, and by incompleteness of interpretation. In the wake of this contrast a critical consciousness arises. The conflation of the empirical process with the ideal has often led to placing consciousness within the mind of the individual. This has been particularly true ever since the Cartesian claim that knowledge rests on the subject, and it became even more common after Freud's theory of the mind and psyche of the individual.

However, the consciousness that counterpoints the ideal of dialogue is not a psychological function. It is attention awakened in the interpreter by particular constellations of meaning. According to the empirical and descriptive imagination, dialogue is portrayed as an effort by the subject to decipher the meaning of signifiers. Alternatively, insofar as consciousness is concerned, the surplus meaning emerging out of repetition pricks the ears of attention, establishing subject identity. The subject does not precede the process of dialogue, and consequently, from the point of view of consciousness, it is not only the hermeneutic direction of interpretation that is reversed—from subject-to-meaning to meaning-to-subject—but also the phenomenological maxim according to which consciousness is always the consciousness of something; contrarily, surplus meaning always is the meaning of a particular consciousness.

In the work of Bakhtin, Buber, and Levinas dialogue is an ethics of answerability, of respect to otherness and of disclosure of identity. Thus, from an ethical point of view the heart of dialogue lies in the relation between Self and Other, not in particular manifestations or in consciousness. In dialogical hermeneutics, Self and Other are an extension of the ontological difference, that is, the difference between a category and the instances capable of fulfilling it. Is Self the Being of dialogue and Other its fulfillment, or are Self and Other together unfulfilled promises of Being?

Although prima facie Self and Other are variations of speaker and listener, their appearance as main elements in dialogue as ethics comes from sources of inspiration different from the descriptive model of communication. For Bakhtin (1984), for example, the heterology of selfness and otherness resides in the fundamental need Self has for the Other in order to exist. In a Kantian fashion, the Russian thinker realizes that the differences of perspectives in the world are the consequence of a process of differentiation introduced into knowledge by time and space. Each position or view (Bakhtin draws heavily on visual metaphors) can be reduced to a point in space and in time. Each outlook establishes an I-here-now that bestows sense on the Thou-there-then. The Bakhtinian model of the dialogical principle clearly takes shelter under the umbrella of consciousness, which allows for shifts in perspective, because the recognition of different I-here-now(s) prevents any position in this chronotopic centrality from seceding from the whole and pursuing its self-perpetuation. Undoubtedly, for Bakhtin it is consciousness that remains stable and is perpetual. However, the Bakhtinian conscious-ness is not a psychological function of the individual, but the arena where the clash of meanings takes place, that is, the domain of heteroglossia (Bakhtin 1981).

One of the chapters in Heidegger's *Being and Time* is entitled "Being-in-the-World as Being-with and Being-One's-Self: The They" (1962, 149). In a chapter with such a mysterious title, he addresses the question of who is *Dasein* or, as he puts it, of the who of *Dasein* (section 25) and argues that *Dasein* is the "They," the Being-with-others that constitutes the existential environment of everydayness. The separation between mind and world, Self and Other, or subject and object is supplanted by a thought in which these polarizations, welded together, become constituents of the environment of "*Dasein*'s primordial spatiality" (1962, 155–56). *Dasein* acquires mean-ing not in opposition to an Other, but in Being-with among others, which is a form of Being-in-the-world. Hence, consciousness is no longer a source for the legitimation of meaning. As Levinas (1982, 179) puts it, Heidegger offers an alternative to Husserl's transcenden-tal idealism by presenting intentionality not exclusively as the consciousness of something; Heidegger reverses the equation and shows that what was perceived as the object of consciousness is indeed the fulcrum of meaning, the stirrer of thought and conscious-ness. The object, the thing, cannot be the privileged possession of Self.

Heidegger noticed that in the history of metaphysics Being was always something in an Other, in the Thing, in God, or in the Subject. But Being cannot be in the Other, for it cannot be an object for Self; it must be a form of presentation free from the need of a legitimizing observer. Thus the ontological difference consists in the impossibility of equating Being with concrete beings and with thought and language. From a historical point of view it unfolded first as the difference between Being and beings (Parmenides' One and Many), second as the difference between Being and *logos* (cf. Heidegger 1975), and third as the difference between Self and Other. At the present intellectual juncture, with the development of Gadamer's hermeneutics and of postmodern criticism, consciousness has been removed from its pedestal and put among the other elements—

dwelling, Self, Other, language, and meaning. Consciousness itself is subject to interpretation, for it is historical and, in such a bondage, fallible.

The transformation of the ontological difference into the question of identity between Self and Other marks the passage in the interpretation of dialogue from ontology to ethics, that is, the replacement of the inquiry about what dialogue is with the inquiry about whether dialogue promotes truth and justice. The argument for dialogue as an ethical endeavor has been forwarded from two angles. First, dialogue promotes truth and justice by extricating good arguments from bad, making the former prevail. But what in dialogue or about dialogue would do this? The answer is its dialectical nature, which brings into confrontation all arguments, sifting the good ones out of the bad ones in a process similar to the Darwinian selection of the fittest. Along this line of reasoning, the arena where the process takes place is consciousness. Socrates already claims that goodness lies in the human soul, which is therefore the seat of just reasoning. Throughout the Western heritage the argument has been made that consciousness is the ultimate instance of deciding between right and wrong, true and false, and just and unjust, irrespective of whether it is placed in the faith in God or in the Cartesian *Cogito*, in reason or in the transparency of the individual's self-examination.

The second angle through which the ethics of dialogue is approached is the relation between Self and Other. The question here is the complementarity of subject identities. Dialogue is ethical in the sense of the Self's turning to the Other. But is the invitation for the Other to speak not a great risk to Self? It seems to come at the price of self-denial. However, from this perspective ethics resides precisely in listening, since the subject is not at the center of dialogue as a source of meaning. Indeed, speaking is not the oxygen of his life, and listening marks his presence in the world.

The psycholinguistic individual can still be a subject in dialogue, though not by virtue of his psychological and linguistic capabilities alone. Like any other subject, he enters the process as someone chosen by a constellation of meanings that breathes identity into him as a speaker endowed with a face, with linguistic competence, and with a particular personality structure. These traits of his identity, however, do not precede dialogue; they are bestowed upon him as he speaks and listens. The subject comes into being together with dialogue and is as much a meaning-content in the process as are the things talked about.

In his essay in this collection Crowell argues that Derrida's reservations to dialogue are cautions already present in Gadamer's reflections. The Gadamerian homecoming to genuine dialogue, in addition to being a search for ontology, constitutes a plea for dialogue as ethics. However, ethics lies beyond politics, beyond the psychology of individuals, beyond the structures of language, beyond the metaphors of oral and written communication, in a realm that, although intimated by Gadamer, Crowell finds better explained in the work of Emmanuel Levinas. In Crowell's words, "Levinas seeks to reverse the traditional hierarchy which subordinates ethics to ontology, justice to truth." For Levinas, "dialogue is neither a fusion of horizons, nor a site of endless deferrals," Crowell proceeds, "but the creation of commonplaces governed by justice." The contours of dialogue are faces not of individual identity but of living presence.

The face of living presence does not have a lonely existence. It exists only insofar as it finds another face, but the truth of its encounter with the Other does not reside in the possibility of consensus and agreement or in its dissolution through a fusion with the expression of the Other. Contrary to Plato, Levinas argues that desire is opposed to need. Desire is the predicate of the Other, of the object that animates the subject, "whereas need is a void of the soul, it proceeds from the subject" (Levinas 1969, 62). Truth resides in otherness, not in narrativity. Consequently, the alternative to the abandonment of master narratives is not the infinite dissemination of dialogue (or of language games), with the ensuing destruction of meaning, but the realization of the truth of the irreconcilability of Self and Other, or the irreducible character of the face-to-face encounter between living presences. The ethical ground of dialogue is thus constituted by a symmetry that, according to Crowell based on Levinas, poses a demand to Self to "relinquish [his] anarchic autonomy."

The current notion of individual identity is defined in terms of biography whose continuity is proved by connections deriving from the logic of emotions. To generate this identity the individual resorts to self-reflection, not to conversation with others, and as a result he creates myriad representations of self or combines them all into a highly allegorical picture. The coherent individual—that is, the individual fully explained—is alienated from the world. In contrast, the subject in dialogue has his identity always shaped anew by every new utterance and therefore is embedded in the world of language.

The currently conceived psycholinguistic individual cannot meet the conditions imposed on the subject of dialogue and at the same time preserve the criteria of psychological and linguistic coherence through which he is defined.

If the autonomous individual cannot be considered the privileged subject of dialogue anymore, his consciousness has been rendered obsolete as a locus for ethical decisions. Is the postmodern scenario of dialogue an axiological desert of consciousness, or are there new forms of consciousness (e.g., collective, communal, historical, cultural, textual) independent of the individual? The idea that persons are bonded to one another by social solidarity and by the affective links of love and friendship so deeply fastened to contemporary culture (since Durkheim and Freud), but introduced in ancient Greece and developed by Christianity, cannot be reconciled with the erstwhile ideal of a decionistic *technē* founded on the reason of arguments and on the symmetry of participation. Indeed, throughout the Western tradition, reason on the one hand and social interests and emotions on the other have been cast as antipodes. Thus, in reaching the epilogue of the critique of the Enlightenment, we are confronted with the gaping hole opened between the public and the private, or between totality and part, teleology (transcendence) and immanence, and so on, in such a way that dialogue is either trivialized as the myriad verbal exchanges between individuals or criticized as the mechanical recitation of the master narratives. Postmodern critical thinking does not recognize the primacy of reason over other faculties or of any particular reasons over others. Among the several consequences entailed by the relativization of reason, two must be singled out as importantly disturbing: that bad or evil arguments may prevail over good ones, and that the classification of arguments itself can be the object of a constant reframing, thereby making the evil of today seem the good of tomorrow.

The flow of meaning in dialogue runs from expression to subject, not the other way around. Constituted by the meaning-content of dialogue, the subject is deferred together with the totality of meaning, and therefore interpretation remains incomplete. Opposed to the epistemological focus on positive knowledge, whether ideal or practical, dialogue remains as the hope of overcoming the dogmatic dominance of certain meanings over others, a dominance spawned by rigid conceptions of dwelling, subject, language, and meaning. The hope lives on in the gesture of turning to the Other with goodwill. In this spirit I invite the reader to turn to the essays in this anthology in their difference, for the language of dialogue consists in the acceptance of dissent.

References

Apel, Karl-Otto. 1986. *Understanding and explanation: A transcendental pragmatic perspective*. Cambridge: MIT Press.

Bakhtin, Mikhail. 1981. *The dialogic imagination*. Austin: University of Texas Press.

———. 1984. *Problems of Dostoevsky's poetics*. Minneapolis: University of Minnesota Press.

Buber, Martin. 1970. *I and Thou*. Trans. Walter Kaufmann. New York: Scribner's.

Deleuze, Giles. 1968. *Différence et répétition*. Paris: Presses Universitaires de France.

Derrida, Jacques. 1973. *Speech and phenomena*. Evanston, Ill.: Northwestern University Press.

———. 1974. *Of grammatology*. Baltimore: Johns Hopkins University Press.

Foucault, Michel. 1972. *The archeology of knowledge*. New York: Harper Colophon.

Freud, Sigmund. 1961. *Beyond the pleasure principle*. New York: Norton. Originally published 1920.

———. 1963. Further recommendations in the technique of psychoanalysis: Recollection, repetition and working through. In *Therapy and technique*. New York: Collier Books. Originally published 1914.

———. 1969. *Inhibitions, symptoms, and anxiety*. New York: Norton. Originally published 1926.

Gadamer, Hans-Georg. 1975. *Truth and method*. New York: Continuum.

———. 1976. *Philosophical hermeneutics*. Berkeley: University of California Press.

———. 1980. *Dialogue and dialectic*. New Haven: Yale University Press.

———. 1986. Text und Interpretation. In *Gesammelte Werke*, vol. 2. Tübingen: J. C. B. Mohr.

Habermas, Jürgen. 1984. *The theory of communicative action*. Vol. 1. *Reason and the rationalization of society*. Boston: Beacon Press.

———. 1987. *The theory of communicative action*. Vol. 2. *Lifeworld and system: A critique of functionalist reason*. Boston: Beacon Press.

Heidegger, Martin. 1962. *Being and time*. New York: Harper and Row.

———. 1975. *Early Greek thinking*. New York: Harper and Row.

Kierkegaard, Soren. 1983. *Kierkegaard writing*. Vol. 6. Princeton: Princeton University Press.

Levinas, Emmanuel. 1969. *Totality and infinity*. Pittsburgh: Duquesne University Press.

———. 1982. *En découvrant l'existence avec Husserl et Heidegger*. Paris: Vrin.

_____. 1987. *Hors sujet*. Paris: Fata Morgana.

Lyotard, J. F. 1979. *The postmodern condition*. Minneapolis: University of Minnesota Press.

Nietzsche, F. 1968. *Thus spoke Zarathustra*. Portable Nietzsche. New York: Penguin.

Plato. 1961. *The collected dialogues*. Princeton: Princeton University Press.

Rorty, Richard. 1979. *Philosophy and the mirror of nature*. Princeton: Princeton University Press.

part 1

Dialogue in Classical Philosophy

1

Dialogue and Controversy in Philosophy

Richard McKeon

Philosophers have always welcomed dialogue, if one is to credit the interest they profess in the interplay of arguments; and treatises on philosophy would be shorter, and probably less intelligible, if all references to other positions were deleted from them. This happy expectation that the restatement of distinctions and arguments will lead to agreement on principles and conclusions and contribute to the advancement of knowledge has nonetheless been thwarted when-ever two voices have entered the dialogue. Controversy takes the place of dialogue when the philosopher whose position is reported and adjusted bursts into the conversation to restate what has been attributed to him and rescue it from distortion. The recriminations, which form as large a part of the history of philosophy as the open-minded professions of willingness to consider other assump-tions and approaches, suggest that it is no less difficult—if indeed it is even possible—for one philosopher to restate the position of another when he appropriates it to his own uses as a truth he expresses somewhat differently, or even when he defends it as the doctrine of a beloved master who has been misinterpreted, than when he sets it forth starkly in all its weakness as the construction of an opponent to be refuted out of hand.

Many plausible reasons can be alleged to account for this failure of dialogue. Most of them have no direct bearing on the truth or falsity of the philosphical conclusions they account for. They are for the most part themselves intrusions into the dialogue that brusquely turn it into a jurisdictional controversy concerning the ultimate authority in treating philosophic questions: whether relations among the sciences should be explored on philosophic assumptions concern-ing logical and dialectical proof, forms of experience or reason, or characteristics of phenomena or being, or whether, on the contrary, philosophic problems should be explained away on assumptions drawn from psychology, sociology, economics, history, the conditioning of man, or the claims of society. The nature of the failure of dialogue, even in its large reductive and pseudoscientific forms, is clarified, on the other hand, if the task the philosopher undertakes is considered in general before failures in communication are accounted for as failures in proof. Like inquirers in other fields, the philosopher not only seeks truth, but also constructs arguments to relate the truths he finds to warrantable or defensible grounds, and he addresses his arguments to minds not yet enlightened or convinced. Unlike other disciplines, however, philosophy is synoptic and inclusive by design, not by occasional extension, and philosophic differences tend to focus on basic considerations about objects, arguments, and other minds.

Most of the extreme controversies in which philosophers abandon all pretense of dialogue and turn their backs on arguments can be traced to differences concerning the structure of arguments and their relation to objects and to minds. There have been, and still are, philosophers who argue that these three tasks are inseparable, and that the discovery of truth, the construction of arguments, and the clarification of minds proceed pace by pace; methods that separate them fall into the error of constructing formal or subjective arguments unrelated to reality or into the error of constructing mechanical or partial conceptions unrelated to real processes or scientific principles. There have been philosophers, no less numerous and no less confident of their scientific pretensions and venerable antecedents, who argue that man is the measure of all things, that truth is discovered only in the free clash of opinions, and that plausible arguments can be found to support the contradictory of any proposition or doctrine; dialogue explores the plurality of positions, and it is transformed into controversy by dogmatisms that must therefore be refuted. At the other extreme throughout the long history of the opposition of dialecticians and skeptics, other philosophers have sought a method to construct arguments based on the nature of things without intrusion of imagination, emotion, or opinion; methods that fail to make this separation must be shown to be unsound and unscientific, since they do not penetrate to the nature of things but weave verbal arguments to support meaningless statements pertinent only to unreal problems—although, it should be added, the verbal statements do express emotions, the groundless arguments are often persuasive, and the unreal problems are consequences of artificial tensions, unexamined complexes, or persistent traditions. There remains a fourth possibility, which was developed by philosophers in antiquity and was further extended and applied at later stages of history; that each of these tasks presents a separate problem of method; that a logic should be elaborated for formal arguments, a method of inquiry for the discovery of truth, and a rhetoric and dialectic for communication among men; and that the use of these methods requires a metaphysics to explore the principles and organization of knowledge, a psychology or epistemology to explore the functions and powers of man, and a sociopolitical theory to explore the diversity of communities and circumstances. Confusions among these methods must then be sought out and corrected.

As Plato conceived dialectic, it is the unique method of philosophy and science, precisely because it is suited to carry out all three tasks of philosophy simultaneously—the discovery of truth, the construction of arguments, and the clarification of minds. All other arts and methods are incomplete and dangerous unless transformed by dialectic. The dialectician is the true poet and interpreter of poetry, the best rhetorician and linguist, and the only sure mathematician, moral guide, and political ruler. Dialectic is a method of definition and argument, of division and collection; but far from being satisfied with verbal formulations, Plato is suspicious of the written word, which is dead and cannot answer back when questioned, and he seeks instead living words, which are planted and grow in living minds. The influence of dialectic on the mind, moreover, is due to the fact that it divides and collects real classes; dialectic divides at the joints of reality, and to accomplish that purpose it assembles an intellectual alphabet for argument whose letters, like those of ordinary alphabets, cannot be combined arbitrarily but only as they form syllables and words. Even in the *Cratylus*, where the subject of discussion is the nature of language, the proponents of the opposed theories of natural and conventional language come to agree in dialogue that they must give up seeking in words a knowledge of things and instead turn their attention not to names but to things themselves, acknowledging the dialectician to be superior to the maker of language.

In order to form arguments and to treat things, dialectic must prepare minds. Socrates compares his art to that of a midwife, since it merely assists in bringing knowledge to birth, and he compares its effect to that of a torpedo-fish, since it shocks the mind free from unexamined attractions or polarities. The development of knowledge is a detachment, a reminiscence, an initiation that may have a divine or apparently accidental origin but may also be occasioned by method in discussion. The determining factor is not the concatenation of phenomena, the nature of mind, or the structure of argument, but the common source from which they all derive and to which they owe their interrelations. Education consists in turning the attention of the mind and enlarging the scope of its contemplation to a synoptic vision. Dialectic is the method of achieving this threefold purpose—it is a dialogue by which men come to agreement by means of argument concerning the nature and divisions of things.

The method of dialectic is dialogue in the sense that two or more speakers or two or more positions are brought into relations in which it becomes apparent that each position is incomplete and inconclusive unless assimilated to a higher truth. Phenomena may become the stages of history, and minds may become spirit, without affecting the character of the argument as it operates in development of the dialogue. The processes of development of things, the levels of formation of knowledge, and the steps of synthesis of proof are fundamentally the same. Dialecticians, for the most part, do not refute, but rather assimilate other philosophers. Plato apparently found no need to differentiate his method from the method of Socrates or from the methods of the Eleatics, the Pythagoreans, the Heracliteans, or even at times the Sophists, who appear in his dialogues. Historians and scholars have not always been happy with the consequences of this assimilation of methods in dialectic, and they have constructed the Socratic Question and the Platonic Question to recover distinctions Plato failed to make from the indications he does give. For no one speaker expresses the truth, and all methods, even that of Socrates, show their weakness and incompleteness in some regions and on some questions.

Plotinus, using a similar dialectic, later adjusted the categories of Aristotle and of the Stoics to the Platonic categories, discovering that both have some basis in truth but that Aristotle's errors arose from seeking the categories of being in sensible rather than intelligible things and the Stoic errors from materialism. Porphyry transformed Aristotle's logic into a dialectic by writing an introduction, an *Isagoge*, to the *Categories*, borrowing the "predicables" from Aristotle's *Topics*, in which the commonplaces of dialectic are treated, to loosen up the literal distinctions and univocal definitions of the Aristotelian logic, and the long line of Greek commentators labored further to make

Aristotle an acceptable, though imperfect, Neoplatonic dialectician. Saint Bonaventura found the formula of synthesis in the discovery that Aristotle spoke the language of science, Plato spoke the language of wisdom, and Saint Augustine, illuminated by the Holy Ghost, used both languages. Hegel could trace the whole sequence of the history of philosophy evolving to its assimilation in his own philosophy; and Erdmann, who argued that Hegel's assertion that his system had assimilated all earlier systems was confirmed even by his opponents, is constrained by the passage of time and the continuation of the inevitable dialectic of history to add a final volume on the dissolution of the Hegelian system as an appendix to his *History of Philosophy*.

This complex process of synthesizing is interrupted—and dialogue becomes controversy—whenever dialectic degenerates into sophistic or skepticism by neglecting content or into subjectivism and mechanism by neglecting argument. Socrates frequently notes the transition from dialectic to sophistic or eristic. " 'What a grand thing, Glaucon,' said I, 'is the power of the art of contradiction [*antilogiche*].' 'Why so?' 'Because,' said I, 'many appear to fall into it even against their wills, and to suppose that they are not wrangling [*erisein*], but arguing [*dialegesthai*], owing to their inability to apply the proper divisions and distinctions to the subject under consideration. They pursue merely verbal oppositions, practising eristic, not dialectic on one another" (*Republic* 453E–454A).

The other form of controversy, due to neglect rather than misuse of argument and leading to partial conceptions of subject matter, may take two forms. One is exemplified in the battle of the giants in which the aggressors break bodies and what they call truth into small fragments and talk about a kind of generation by motion rather than being, while the defenders proceed very cautiously with weapons derived from the invisible world above, maintaining that true being consists of certain ideas that are conceived only by the mind and have no body (*Sophist* 246b–c). The other is the pragmatic empiricism that neglects scientific analysis to concentrate on sensible effects and practical applications—as calculation or logistic (logistiche) is adapted to commercial purposes but not, like arithmetic, to knowledge (*Gorgias* 451B–C; *Republic* 525D).

Dialectic became the method of Christian theology and philosophy until the translation of Aristotle in the thirteenth century suggested the possibility of two methods and two ways; dialectic was also opposed during the Middle Ages because it is a purely verbal art and because it applies reason to matters that transcend reason. During the Renaissance the choice of methods lay between dialectic and rhetoric, and medieval logic was dropped out of the dialogue as verbal and as concerned with nonexistent entities like universals and transcendentals. The grounds of controversy are the same during the nineteenth century after the revival of dialectic attributed to Kant. According to Hegel, three attitudes toward objectivity are found in logic and the formal doctrine of logic has three sides. The first attitude toward objectivity leads to metaphysics; the second is expressed in empiricism and the critical philosophy; the third is immediate or intuitive knowledge. The second of these attitudes was adopted by Hume and Kant. Thought is subjective, and its most effective operation depends on abstract universality according to this attitude, but the logical development of empiricism is materialism (matter being an abstraction), whereas the critical philosophy of Kant sepa-rates the world of sensible appearances from the world of self-apprehending thought. The second of the three forms of logical doctrine is dialectic, which must be carefully separated from sophistry and skepticism. Modern skepticism partly precedes the Critical philosophy, partly springs out of it; it consists solely in denying the truth and certitude of the supersensible and in pointing to the facts of sense and of immediate sensations as ultimate (cf. Hegel 1959, part 1, chaps. 3–6). Engels is able to fit Hegel into this classification when he borrows and transforms the Hegelian dialectic. Philosophers are split into two great camps, idealists and materialists, on the paramount question of the relation of thinking to being, of spirit to nature. But the question of the relation of thinking to being has another side that separates Hegel, who asserts the identity of thinking and being, from Hume and Kant, who question the possibility of any cognition of the world. These distinctions form the foundation of Lenin's philosoph-ical argument (Lenin 1927, 74–77), but he traces the beginnings of immaterialism to Berkeley's arguments against matter and encounters at every turn a variegated progeny descended from the "Humean agnosticism"—not only Kant, but also Mill, Mach, Huxley, Cohen, Renouvier, Poincaré, Duhem, and James.

The dogmatisms of dialectical history tend to overshadow the equally plausible—and in the context of twentieth century dogma-tisms more attractive—version of the relations among philosophies set forth by the defenders of the antilogism and contradiction, the adherents of skepticism and sophistry, who find the method of philosophy in the interplay of doctrines and opinions and who expose the consequences of dogmatism concerning the ultimate principles of knowledge and reality. Discrimination, not assimilation or reduction, is the method of philosophy, and dialogue proceeds by exploring the varieties of arguments and doctrines and testing assertions by their contradiction, not by adjusting all doctrines to a preferred position and refuting those that will not fit. In the course of controversy with dialectical and logistic philosophers, all the names assumed by philosophers of this tradition have been given a pejorative sense: they are sophists who were concerned with wisdom, skeptics who developed reflective thought and inquiry, rhetoricians who were skilled in the arts of communication, and academics who employed the method of Socrates and Plato.

Sophistic and rhetoric provided the counterpart, and a phase of the context, for the development of Plato's dialectic. They had themselves developed as practical instrumentalities in the democratic Greek city-states, and they provided arts by which opposed opinions might be brought into relation and confrontation. Plato gives Protagoras's aphorism, that man is the measure of all things, a relativist and sensualist interpretation that accords with the criticism attributed to Democritus as well as Plato in opposition to the doctrine ascribed to Protagoras, that all sensations are equally true for all sentient subjects (*Theaetetus* 151e–152E; Sextus Empiricus [1958, 388–90]). Isocrates criticized speculative philosophers, who are in total disagreement concerning the nature of things and in even more confusing disagreement when they profess to attain scientific knowledge of moral questions. Philosophy is concerned to impart all the forms of discourse in which the mind expresses itself—not in abstract but in particular statements—and should therefore bring the student into contact with the variety of opinions rather than inculcate a pretended or useless science.

Skepticism grew out of the exigences of dialogue at the very center of dialectic. Skeptics were prominent among the "Socratics" who set forth their philosophic positions in "Socratic dialogues." The Academy defended the position of Plato against the dogmatism and materialism of the Stoics by means of the skepticism elaborated by Arcesilas and the probabilism evolved by Carneades. Cicero, as a follower of the New Academy, interprets all the great philosophers as exponents of an identical truth to which they only give verbally variant expression, and he reserves controversy for the refutation of the materialism of the Epicureans and the dogmatism of philosophers who conceive truth to be susceptible only of a unique expression. Sextus Empiricus marshals an encyclopedic refutation of all dogmatisms, idealistic and materialistic, empirical and rationalistic. John of Salisbury in the twelfth century labels himself an Academic, and John Duns Scotus at the end of the thirteenth century elaborates subtle arguments to refute the Academics. The revived dialectic of the Renaissance is a battleground between Neoplatonists and Skeptics. Hume acknowledges the attraction the academic philosophy had for him, and when Kant returned to dialectic he called it an art of semblance and disputation, an *ars sophistica disputatoria*, and derives the method he practices from the skeptics (cf. McKeon 1954, 12). The moderm exponents of the skeptical position tend, as Hegel pointed out, to be less thorough than the ancients and to favor one of the forms of dogmatism—empiricism—in their search for the useful and the practical among opinions.

Sophistic or the skeptical dialectic is an operational method. As expounded by Cicero it consists of two parts, a method of discovery and a method of judgment or proof, as contrasted to the dialectic of the Stoics, which wholly neglects the method of discovery. This method is also called rhetoric, the art of discovering arguments and of organizing them in exposition. Properly employed it results in wisdom, and it should be employed only in conjunction with wisdom. In the history of philosophy, as Cicero recounts it, early philosophers combined eloquence and wisdom. Socrates unfortunately separated them, and thereafter rhetoric and philosophy followed independent courses until the New Academy again undertook to join them. If men will equip themselves with the art of discovering and stating arguments a dialogue is possible, since philosophers will come to recognize that truth is acquired not by a private and mysterious insight into reality, but by understanding the arguments by which truth may be distinguished from error in a given situation and application or an identical truth may be discovered by different means and be stated in different terms. Controversy results from inability to follow an argument and from dogmatic attachment to positions that are thought to be unique.

This conception of the relation between method and knowledge, between rhetoric and wisdom, has served as the basis for histories of philosophy. Philostratus wrote of philosophy in this sense in his *Lives of the Sophists:* "We must regard the ancient sophistic art as philosophical rhetoric. For it discusses the themes that philosophers treat of, but whereas they [the philosophers], by their method of questioning, set snares for knowledge and advance step by step as they confirm the minor points of their investigations, the sophist of the old school assumes a knowledge of that whereof he speaks" (Philostratus 1922, 480). A few philosophers who were renowned for eloquence, like Carneades, Dio Chrysostom, and Favorinus, figure in Philostratus' history along with the older Sophists from Gorgias to Isocrates; but the New Sophistic applied rhetoric to a wisdom that had little in common with the subjects treated by the philosophers, in spite of the interest the philospher-emperor Marcus Aurelius took in it. Eunapius's *Lives of the Philosophers*, on the other hand, begins with Porphyry, who is presented as skilled in rhetoric and in all branches of knowledge, and moves from the Neoplatonists to the sophists, pagan and Christian, to culminate in the iatrosophists, the healing sophists. Zeno of Cyprus was expert in both oratory and medicine, and his disciples were trained in one or both. The latter included Magnus, who was so able in rhetoric that he "used to demonstrate that those whom other doctors cured were still ill" (Eunapius 1922, 408), Ionicus, Oribasius, and Chrysanthius, who was in turn Eunapius's master. The two traits the Sophists should cultivate— ability to discover and present arguments and willingness to listen to arguments—are found in a marked degree in the portrait Eunapius draws of his master, who possessed this disposition, according to Eunapius, either because the Platonic Socrates had come to life again in him or because his effort to imitate Socrates had led him to form himself from boyhood on the model of Socrates.

> But it was not easy to rouse him to philosophical discussions [*dialexis*] or competitions [*philoneichia*,] because he perceived that it is especially in those contests that men become embittered. Nor would anyone readily have heard him showing off his own erudition or inflated because of it, or insolvent and arrogant toward others; rather he used to admire whatever they said, even though their remarks were worthless, and would applaud even incorrect conclusions, just as though he had not even heard the premises, but was naturally inclined to assent, lest he should inflict pain on any one. And if in an assembly of those most distinguished for learning any discussion arose, and he thought fit to take part in the discussion, the place became hushed in silence as though no one were there. So unwilling were they to face his questions and definitions and power of quoting from memory, but they would retire from discussion and contradiction, lest their failure should be too evident. (Eunapius 1922, 502)

The revival of the study of the history of philosophy in the Renaissance followed rhetorical rather than dialectical lines: exemplary uses of doctrines, aphorisms, and arguments rather than epochal successions of systems are emphasized in the lives of philosophers and the compendia of arts that followed the model of Hellenistic histories and Roman treatises and that showed a rhetorical tendency to refute dogmatisms and to seek the causes for the decline of the arts.

The importance of dialogue to the modern "skeptics," who are derived from Hume's agnosticism by their dialectical critics, is precisely in its encouragement and development of arguments. The advancement of science, the cultivation of values, and the resolution of practical problems all depend on the confrontation of arguments, the test of opinion by opinion, and the open possibility of innovation moderated by the stabilizing influence of tradition. Like the ancient Skeptics and Academics, John Stuart Mill bases the practical use of the free interplay of opposed arguments on the example of the theoretic use of the methods of rhetoric to advance toward truth in the natural sciences.

> The peculiarity of the evidence of mathematical truths is that all the arguments is on one side. There are no objections and no answers to objections. But in every subject on which difference of opinion is possible, the truth depends on a balance to be struck between two sets of conflicting reasons. Even in natural philosophy, there is always some other explanation possible of the same facts. . . . But when we turn to subjects infinitely more complicated, to morals, religion, politics, social relations, and the business of life, three fourths of the arguments for every disputed opinion consist in dispelling the appearance which favors some opinion different from it. The greatest orator, save one, of antiquity, has left it on record that he always studied his adversary's case with as great, if not greater, intensity than even his own. What Cicero practised as the means of forensic success requires to be imitated by all who study any subject in order to arrive at the truth. He who knows only his own side of the case, knows little of that. His reasons may be good, and no one may have been able to refute them. But he is equally unable to refute the reasons on the opposite side; if he does not so much as know what they are, he has no ground for preferring either opinion. The rational position for him would be suspension of judgment, and unless he contends himself with that, he is either led by authority or adopts like the generality of the world, the side to which he feels most inclination. (Mill 1908, chap. 2)

There are more proponents of this view than can be tabulated under any of the shining names—sophistic, skepticism, academicism, rhetoric, utilitarianism, liberalism—that have been attached to it and that have been tarnished by the contempt for "opinion," "sense experience," and "utility" expressed by its opponents. It underlies Justice Oliver Wendell Holmes's vision of the free competition of ideas, James's pluralism, Bridgman's operationalism. Dialogue is statement and counterstatement, based on ordinary ways of life and ordinary uses of language, with no possible appeal to a reality beyond opposed opinions except through opinions about reality. Truth is perceived in perspective, and perspectives can be compared, but there is no overarching inclusive perspective. Meanings are defined in action and measurement, and there is no theory apart from practice. Method is the art of seizing and interpreting the opinions of others and of constructing and defending one's own. Virtue is method translated into intelligent self-interest and respect for others.

The Sophists used a method so similar to dialectic that Socrates could complain in the *Apology* that his critics mistook him for a Sophist, and yet they denied dialectical absolutes beyond the relativities of perception and reduced dialectical certainties to opinions in the interchange of rhetorical argument. The ancient physicists and atomists, on the other hand, appealed to a truth based on reality so similar to the Ideas of Socrates that Socrates thought his position had been confused with that of Anaxagoras, although the physicists made no use of dialectic. Democritus's objection to Protagoras's sensationism is so like Plato's that the two were lumped together in antiquity. The special senses are false, since there is no counterpart to sensation outside the sentient subject. Trueborn knowledge, as opposed to the bastard knowledge of sensation, is scientific knowledge of the atoms, and Democritus uses the same word as Plato— "Ideas"—to designate these ultimate nonsensible realities. Aristotle judges the methods of Plato and Democritus to be balanced evenly in achievement and failure: Plato developed a theory of method in his dialectic but failed to apply it successfully to account for phenomena; Democritus developed a method that was faithful to phenomena, but he failed to formulate his method and overgeneralized it as a result of his misconception of definition and cause. The method of scientific knowledge is distinct from verbal logic or dialectic, and knowledge of atoms and their motions is distinct from the relativities of secondary qualities. Dialectic, in its transcendental no less than in its skeptical form, seemed to later atomists to be verbal and inapplicable to this scientific task, while the calculation of motions and combinations of elements was of so little interest to dialecticians that Plato's silence concerning Democritus was a scandal in antiquity. Dialecticians who came after him found modest historical places for mechanistic materialists.

As later skeptics found it desirable to temper their doubts with some confidence in empirical aspects of experience and in the tautologies of thought and expression, so too later atomists provided a place in their rational methods for sensations and feelings. According to Epicurus there are three criteria of truth: sensations, anticipations, and feelings. The external world is known by perception. Sextus Empiricus (1958, 9) reports the equivalence of truth and reality in sensation: "Epicurus said that all objects of perception are true and real: for it was the same thing to call a thing true and to call it existing. True then means that which is as it is said to be, and false that which is not as it is said to be." But the method Epicurus expounds in the *Canonic* has no place for dialectic or verbal arguments, and his critics are distressed by the contempt he expresses for logic, which he criticizes as misleading. Cicero (1914, 22) is shocked because "he abolishes definitions, he has no teaching about division and distribution, he does not tell how reasoning is conducted or brought to conclusions, he does not show by what means sophisms may be exposed, and ambiguities resolved." The central problem of developing a method to construct truths from simple elements and their relations was, however, to receive impressive and suggestive embodiment in a field ignored by Epicurus. The long chains of proof Euclid organized in his *Elements* were to provide inspiration for philosophers and scientists attracted by the hope of deriving all truths from combinations and constructions, whether they begin with simple bodies, simple ideas, or even simple terms.

The geometric method has no necessary philosophic implications when it is employed to construct figures from their "elements" or even when it is used to make a transition from geometric solids to physical bodies and motions. It is made into a philosophical method when it is generalized to cover all conceivable phenomena and all realities and when it is made to provide the test for truth and reality. When philosophers adopt the geometric or deductive method as the method of philosophy and construct deductive demonstrations (with or without recourse to the forms of geometric proof), they face a choice of starting point and subject: they may find their elements in things and make the world geometric, if primary qualities are distinguished from secondary; or they may begin with common notions or simple ideas and distinguish the combinations that yield knowledge of reality from fantasy and error; or they may start with symbols and their relations to atomic facts and separate the noncognitive from the cognitive uses of symbols. They find themselves opposed in this effort to free philosophy of meaningless questions by philosophers (like Plato, Nicholas of Cusa, and Whitehead) who give mathematics a dialectical development, by philosophers (like Poincaré and Russell) who make the method of mathematics arbitrary and its subject matter indeterminate, and by philosophers (like Aristotle, Mill, and Dewey) who distinguish the methods of mathematics from the methods appropriate to other fields.

The geometric method has had many imitators in philosophy. Alan of Lille and Nicholas of Amiens used a mathematical deduction from "common notions" and "maxims" to rid theology of controversy in the twelfth century. Bishop Bradwardine used a geometric method to organize the sequence of proof from common notions in his *De causa Dei* in the fourteenth century, and Richard Swineshead laid the foundations of a logistic philosophy in his *Calculator* by an exploration of variables homogeneous with the verbal logic in which his contemporaries engaged. But the great efflorescence of the geometric method came in the seventeenth century, when treatises on mechanics, optics, astronomy, and all sciences that pretended to precision were thrown into the form of deductions from axiom sets, and the hope that psychology, ethics, and politics might also be made scientific was attached to the endeavor to deduce them from a few simple definitions and principles. Descartes's confidence in the long chains of mathematical reasoning contributed to this tendency by providing an analysis to justify it, for simple ideas cannot be erroneous since error arises in the combination of ideas, and if one could proceed from indivisible ideas by indivisible connections, one could encompass the whole of human knowledge and achieve certainty in all sciences by avoiding the intrusions of imagination, emotion, and opinion that impede the development of science and philosophy. Spinoza used the geometric order in his *Ethics* to provide scientific demonstration of propositions that established morality and freedom on adequate ideas and on minimizing the effects of the passions. Although his learning in Greek philosophy was slight, he confessed an attraction to Democritus, Epicurus, and Lucretius as opposed to Socrates, Plato, and Aristotle. In the nineteenth and twentieth centuries the philosophic use of the geometric method moved slowly and indecisively from laws of thought to constructions built from simple sentences and atomic facts or from the elements of language and what they designate, for the vestiges of epistemology were attached to the symbolism borrowed from mathematics— science is the "cognitive" use of language as contrasted to a host of opposed uses, "emotive," "persuasive," "ejaculatory," "hortatory," evocative"—and new commitments to the theses of empiricism and physicalism seemed necessary if the cognitive was to be preserved from its old epistemological rivals.

The logistic or geometric method is better suited to controversy than to dialogue. What other philosophers conclude on other grounds can rarely pass as "cognitive." When it does, appropriate restatement is needed to make it precise. Much of traditional philosophy is found, therefore, to be devoted to the consideration of unreal problems, and the history of philosophy is a cumulative sequence in which sciences were separated one by one from the disorderly mass of conjecture, superstition, and insight until only logic and the theory of values stood in need of like reformulation for philosophy to be assimilated wholly to the sciences. The larger region of philosophic discussion is best treated by considering not the content of propositions but the state of mind of those who enunciate them. As dialogue it is noncognitive. It may be brought to a conclusion by the discovery of truth, and the contribution of science to questions that involve only emotions is to remove superstition and fear, as the Epicureans put it, or to cure tensions and complexes and promote mental health, as the program is formulated in more modern terms. Discussion contributes to the discovery of truth and is cognitive when it takes the form of interchanges between men of different backgrounds and technical skill assembled in research teams. Controversy is a symptom of confusion, mental disorder, and drives to power.

In the historical context in which dialogue concerning basic philosophic issues takes many forms—such as the synthesis of contraries and the assimilation of divergent views, the development of differences and all the examination of unresolved oppositions, and the reduction of all views to a basic thesis about the nature of physical reality and sense experience and the abandonment, as meaningless and noncognitive, of statements that resist reduction—the desirability of making a series of literal distinctions among methods and meanings has appealed to philosophers repeatedly. It has seemed plausible that a method of formal proof common to all inference might be discovered and formulated; that this method might be distinguished from the method of examining the hypotheses and principles from which inference proceeds; that a dialectical method might be devised to treat opinions concerning particular matters and problems when agreement in statement is desirable and that it might be supplemented by a rhetorical method of constructing arguments to influence audiences when agreement is sought in attitude and action; that a method of solving sophistical arguments might be a useful adjunct to detect apparent inferences or apparent principles employed to reach demonstrably false conclusions; that a method of analyzing objects of art might be employed to separate aesthetic characteristics from moral and political influences and doctrines adumbrated; and that, finally, methods of inquiry might be developed to treat the problems and matters particular to different fields.

The most obvious mark by which this effort to distinguish a plurality of methods may be recognized in its many employments and manifestations is a concern to apply a scientific method to all fields and yet to differentiate the use of science in three large areas—the theoretic, the practical, and the poetic or productive. Aristotle first made this differentiation, recognizing the need—if methods are to be developed appropriate to the various tasks to which they are applied—of three master or architectonic sciences: metaphysics to treat the first principles of the sciences and to provide the grounds for a theoretical organization of knowledge, including not only natural sciences but also sciences of action and production; politics to treat the first principles of human actions and associations and to provide the grounds for a practical organization of common activities, including those that affect the advance of science and the cultivation of art as well as morals and politics; and poetics to treat the first principles of human production and to provide the grounds for an aesthetic organization of the products of arts, including those that set forth knowledge or affect action as well as the fine arts. Thomas Aquinas employed the same distinctions to rectify the controversies and confusions of medieval dialecticians and to separate philosophy and natural theology from the dialectic of the Augustinian formulation of revealed theology. John Dewey sought to extend the use of scientific method or the method of reflective thinking to the resolution of all problems, but he saw danger in applying the method of the physical sciences to practical problems, and he treated philosophy itself as an art concerned with meanings rather than with truth and falsity.

The principles employed by philosophers in the development of other methods often lead them to differentiations similar to those based on the method of inquiry into problems and into problematic situations. Spinoza employed the geometric method in his *Ethics*, but since the principles from which his deduction flowed led to the conclusion that even the wise man does not live always according to the dictates of reason and that most men rarely do, an ethics based on adequate ideas must be separated sharply from a politics based on power and a religion based on piety. Kant was awakened from his dogmatic slumbers by a skeptical dialectic and separated the realms of pure reason, practical reason, and judgment with the aid of distinctions between general logic, transcendental logic, the uses of logic as organon and as canon. Aristotle's rejection of Plato's reduction of different forms of human association by the analogy between state and family finds echo in Locke's refutation of Filmer's use of a like analogy and in Montesquieu's study of the circumstances that determine the variety of systems of positive law.

Dialogue has a place in this distinction of methods according to the problems to which they are addressed. The problematic method, like the dialectical method, provides a place for each of the tasks of philosophy, but the methods proper to inquiry, proof, and persuasion are found to be different when their respective problems are distinguished. Like the logistic method, the problematic method requires univocal definitions and undemonstrable first principles, but there are many sets of such basic propositions, and they are not used to organize all knowledge in a single body of deductively derived propositions. Rhetoric has an important independent place in the development of the problematic method, but is not, as in the skeptical or operational method, the whole method of science. Dialogue is preliminary and propaedeutic to the treatment of theoretic questions; other philosophic theories are studied in order to avoid errors already tried and exposed and to adapt truths already discovered and established. The treatment of practical questions does not permit like precision, and their resolution depends on attitudes and communication bearing on what is best in various circumstances. The production of artificial objects must relate their proper perfections to the natural objects they imitate and the proper pleasures they occasion. Politics and poetics, like metaphysics, employ a dialectical method in inquiry concerning principles that are applied demonstratively in deduction and induction. But it is a limited dialectic, concerned with specific questions, such as the nature of cause or sensation, earthquakes or the source of the Nile, property or slavery, rather than with large questions of philosophic systematization. On most questions numerous imperfect anticipations of the correct solution can be brought together. Neglect of method or the improper use or extension of methods, however, leads to outright error: Democritus is betrayed into innumerable inconsistencies and absurdities by his failure to examine the method he used successfully; the Sophists practice verbal trickery when they ignore the requirements of substantive fact and formal argument to extend methods derived from rhetoric; Plato attributes being to separated objects constructed to provide grounds for dialectical analogies among things and dialectical extensions of reason and understanding. Controversy results no less from restatements of doctrine with partial approval than from refutations.

The methods elaborated by philosophers to treat materials and meanings fall into patterns that determine the forms of dialogue and controversy. The large forms of these opposed methods are easily recognized, and philosophers express their attitudes toward dialogue and betray their proneness to turn dialogue into controversy in ways that those methods can explain.

In significant senses dialogue is an inseparable part of dialectical or operational methods. Both methods use opposed opinions or hypotheses directly as means of resolving substantive problems, but despite occasional overlaps and some consequent confusion of the two methods by philosophers committed to other methods, the two uses of dialogue and their characteristic excursions into controversy are different. In the large forms assumed by philosophies that employ the dialectical method, oppositions are found in fact as well as in opinion; and the processes of nature, history, and thought are identical or strictly comparable, since they all assimilate contraries to higher unities and syntheses; for the dialectician any doctrine is both true (in one sense and at one stage) and false (in many senses and at many states). The dialogue may have either positive or negative results without falling into controversy; it is interrupted in controversy by the intrusion of a verbal or skeptical method that separates thought from its object or by a partial conception of thought or its object that makes thinking subjective or nature mechanical. In the large forms assumed by philosophies that employ the operational method, on the other hand, the oppositions are found only in opinion, hypothesis, perspective, or measurements, and their basic irreducibility is itself an important trait to be observed in the methodological acquisition of theoretic knowledge and in the resolution of practical problems. Two possibilities are open to the operationalist—one of the opposed hypotheses may be inapplicable and the decision may be in favor of one of the opposed parties, or both hypotheses may account for or measure the same facts in different ways, and different reasons based on opposed policies may be adduced for the same course of action. Dialogue is interrupted in controversy only by dogmatisms that refuse to submit opinions about ultimate reality or the compelling evidence of experience or thought to the test of other opinions and hypotheses.

Dialogue is not an essential part of logistic or problematic methods. Both methods use opposed opinions or hypotheses only indirectly in the solution of substantive problems, since both separate questions of opinion formation and communication from questions of inquiry and proof. In the use of the problematic method dialogue is relevant to proof, and there is even place for a restricted form of dialectic to resolve differences of opinion and belief. Dialectic is a stage in the search for truth, but its methods are sharply separated from those of inquiry and proof. The examination of other theories and doctrines has a heuristic value in the treatment of any problem, for the assemblage of what has been said previously makes available existing knowledge at the start of investigations, but the balance of opinions does not contribute directly to the examination of data or the construction of suitable hypotheses concerning them. On the other hand, dialectic is the only method applicable to fundamental metaphysical questions. Controversy is directed against dialecticians (who invent fictive entities to make their propositions true), against sophists (who advance propositions that are indifferently true or false), and against methodless thinkers (who have no proof for their propositions even when they happen to be true). In the use of the logistic method dialogue is avoided, since the truth is one, and the effort of science and philosophy is to achieve knowledge of truth. Dialogue enters into that effort when truth is not available and knowledge ceases in the balance of probabilities, preferences, and emotions and in the preparation for decision and persuasion. Acquisition of knowledge depends on exclusion of emotion, imagination, and opinion, and consequently of dialogue; and although none of these can be eliminated wholly from the lives of the many, science can control their deleterious effects by exposing substitutes for knowledge. Controversy is directed against philosophers who consider unreal questions, make meaningless statements, or construct proofs unsusceptible of empirical verification.

The primary purpose of philosophy is to discover and demonstrate truth. But "truth" is differently conceived according to the principles of different philosophies, and philosophical methods are constructed to form and justify bodies of doctrines that express truths so conceived and so justified. Dialogue is part of all such methods, since the justification of a philosophic conclusion must take into account other proposed analyses, yet the attempted dialogue does not extend beyond the limits of those who agree in method, and controversy arises both because the tenets of each method predestine certain methods to error and because the restatement that conclusions receive in the dialogue constructed by philosophers is seldom adequate or satisfactory to those who hold those conclusions. Differences of methods are seldom remarked, however, even in the case of philosophers who place great store on the novelty of their methods and explain and illustrate them in detail. In spite of the obvious differences in the large forms philosophies take as a result of the methods employed in their construction—the massive progressions and syntheses of dialectic, the long chains of reasoning from primitive propositions of logistic, the skeptical pluralism of opinions and perspectives, the problematic pluralism of methods and principles—efforts at philosophical dialogue usually take the form of extracting isolated statements from the system of arguments by which they are justified to try them in the context of other principles and methods. Like the Cartesian "good sense," a sense of method is apparently thought to be equally distributed, for everyone thinks himself so well supplied with it that critics rarely pause to examine another method or to consider its possible cogency or validity before announcing the discovery of simple inconsistencies and fantastic absurdities, such as are seldom encountered in casual conversation, in the works of philosophers who base their statements on methods and principles they have scrutinized meticulously.

Controversy has so far outrun dialogue in contemporary philosophical discussions that dialogue has all but disappeared except among the sects that have formed within particular philosophical traditions. This is no new phenomenon in the history of philosophy, and in a fundamental sense it is a natural consequence of the oppositions of philosophic methods. It has, however, taken on unusual importance today—as it did in the Roman Empire and again during the Renaissance—since the failure of communication and understanding in philosophy is a symptom of what is happening in larger communications in cultural relations and political negotiations. It might be argued equally plausibly that philosophy has come into new responsibilities and uses, since the practical problems of our times may be traced back to an ideological conflict that is fundamentally philosophic, or that the integrity and effectiveness of the search for truth are destroyed by differences of philosophic tradition that simply reflect differences of culture and interest. In much the same fashion, historians of Roman and Renaissance philosophy have argued equally plausibly that philosophy was freed from dogmas and superstitions in those periods, that philosophers differed only verbally, and that philosophy disappeared wholly into the barren verbalism of rhetoric and the discouraged ineffectiveness of skepticism.

It is improbable that invitations to dialogue will lead to philosophic agreement or cultural uniformity, and it is doubtful that such agreement or uniformity would be desirable if it were possible. But if controversy arises from the radical differences among the methods by which philosophers have sought truth, the possibility of dialogue is to be found in the similarities among the methods by which they have sought intelligibility and consensus. It is impossible to avoid controversy concerning what is true or probable, but controversy might be avoided without abandoning problems of the relation of arguments to the exploration of reality by turning attention to problems of the relation of arguments to elucidation of minds. Problems of communication are not wholly independent of problems of proof, but there are large regions of coincidence in the methods by which philosophers take into account the audiences their arguments address. The controversies that grow out of differences of method are crucial precisely because they concern issues in which it is difficult to separate substantive differences concerning the nature and relations of things from verbal differences due to shifts of meanings of terms defined according to opposed methods and principles. Formal analysis of what is accepted as inference and what is accepted as principle not only should clarify meanings by separating fact from form of statement, but it should also have material implications by giving objective grounds to the study of attitudes and audiences that has taken a skeptical and relationistic turn in comparative psychology, the sociology of knowledge, and the variety of studies in which the relations of cultures are treated. This large region is the field of what has often in the history of thought been called rhetoric, and since the four methods enumerated above have been described by considering four possible positions concerning the relation of proof to persuasion, the possibility of cooperative study and mutual understanding of arguments of the second kind may be judged by considering the place of rhetoric in each of the methods.

The methods of rhetoric constitute the whole of philosophic method in the operational or skeptical method. Many of the efforts to reduce controversy and advance truth in the history of modern philosophy from Francis Bacon and Vico to Mill and some contemporary analytical philosophers have made more or less conscious appeal to the commonplaces of rhetoric. Chaïm Perelman has urged a return to rhetorical considerations for a theory of philosophical argumentation (Perelman and Olbrechts-Tyteca 1952). The preceding analysis of dialogue and controversy was made from the point of view of the rhetorical or skeptical tradition in which the fundamental assumptions are that knowledge is best advanced by the free opposition of arguments, that a common truth may be given a variety of statements from different perspectives, and that there is an element of truth in all philosophic positions. In problematic inquiry, rhetoric or its counterpart, dialectic, is a methodological stage antecedent to the resolution of philosophic problems; it is not the method of philosophy, but any philosophical argument may be examined rhetorically or dialectically to disclose its assumptions and form. In the context of a dialectical philosophy, rhetoric is imperfect dialectic limited to subjective distinctions, but such distinctions and principles are susceptible of dialectical expansion and examination such as they received in the "inconclusive" dialogues of Plato. In a logistic philosophy, rhetoric has no place as a cognitive method, but rhetorical arguments possess a structure that can be analyzed in logistic semantics and compared in structure to cognitive arguments.

Analyses of arguments for communication, separated from analyses of arguments for demonstration, may provide not merely the method by which to advance dialogue in philosophy but also materials by which to lessen tensions and oppositions between cultures. It is not to be anticipated that there will be agreement in the treatment of this common region of philosophy, since the approaches to it are affected by differences of method as much as by the substantive problems of truth that are the center of philosophic controversy. But the different treatments will be comparable approaches to problems of communication—rhetorical enumerations of modes of expression adapting opinions or positions to audiences, problematic enumerations of methods adapting concepts to circumstances, logistic enumerations of constructions in which terms are defined and combined, dialectical enumerations of systems adapting principles to arguments—and they should make it possible to focus attention on the different structures of argument and the different presuppositions employed in different traditions and forms of philosophy. The basic problems of dialogue are, first, to find ways to make certain there is agreement concerning what is in question and, second, to understand what is conceived to constitute a satisfactory answer to the question. Only when these problems have been resolved is it possible to decide whether proposed solutions are in agreement or opposed. Mutual understanding in the sense of agreement concerning what the question is and what is required in a satisfactory solution is necessary if philosophers are to resume their dialogue or even continue their efforts to convince each other of the truth of their respective positions, and it is essential also to the solution of social and political problems—to make possible agreement on common courses of action for different reasons, appreciation of alien values, and confidence based on understanding.

References

Cicero, Marcus Tullius. 1914. *De finibus bonorum et malorum*. Latin text with English translation by H. Rackham. Loeb Classical Library. London: Heinemann.

Engels, Frederick. 1935. *Ludwig Feuerbach and the outcome of classical German philosophy*. New York: International Publishers.

Eunapius. 1922. *Lives of the philosophers*. In Philostratus and Eunapius, *Lives of the Sophists*. Greek text with English translation by Wilmer Cave Wright. Loeb Classical Library. London: Heinemann.

Hegel, G. W. F. 1959. *The encyclopaedia of the philosophical sciences in outline*. Transl. Gustav Emil Mueller. Philosophical Library. New York: Macmillan.

Lenin, V. I. 1927. *Materialism and empirio-criticism: Critical notes concerning a reactionary philosophy*. New York: International Publishers.

McKeon, Richard. 1954. Dialectic and political thought and action. *Ethics* 65: 1–37.

Mill, John Stuart. 1908. *On liberty*. London: Longmans.

Perelman, C., and L. Olbrechts-Tyteca. 1952. *Rhétorique et philosophie: Pour une théorie de l'argumentation en philosphie*. Paris: Presses Universitaires de France.

Philostratus, Flavius. 1922. *Lives of the Sophists*. Greek text with English translation by Wilmer Cave Wright. Loeb Classical Library. London: Heinemann.

Plato. 1961. *The collected dialogues*. Ed. Edith Hamilton and Huntington Cairns, Bollingen series 71. Princeton: Princeton University Press.

Sextus Empiricus. 1958. *Sexti Empirici opera*. vol. 3, *Adversus mathematicus*. Trans. Hermanus Mutschmann. Leipzig: Teubner.

2

Dialogue and Dialectic:
The Logic of Conversation
and the Interpretation of Logic

C. Jan Swearingen

The interpretation of dialogue may be located as a subset of the analysis and interpretation of oral interlocutionary discourse, as one of a family of oral and interlocutionary modes: conversation; "controversy," argument, and similar modes used for negotiating conflicts or differences; nonnarrative modes of speaking to a live audience, such as oratory, rhetoric, and sermons; and "routines" in which some structure dictates the patterns and substance of alternation among two or more individuals: playing the dozens, word games among children, antiphonal liturgical responses. Studies of oral literature (Parry and Lord 1954; Ong 1982; Finnegan 1977), oral cultures (Goody 1982; Goody and Watt 1968; Havelock 1986; Ong 1982), and the patterns of cognition they seem to share (e.g., Havelock 1986; Ong 1982; Olson 1986; Scribner and Cole 1981) are undergoing extensive revision (Finnegan 1977; Geertz 1988; Tannen 1982a; Havelock 1986), problematizing the project of interpreting narrative and dialogue. In particular, with the dispersion of notions of universals in language, thought, and culture (Geertz 1988), dialogue and narrative alike are being reconceived, not only as objects of study but as ways of defining discourse. What makes something a dialogue? The spirit of its participants or the form its utterances take?

In what follows I propose that from its inception in Plato, dialogue has always been and continues to be programmatically liminal: interstructural, between two states or conditions, essentially unstructured rather than structured by contradictions; because of its deliberate avoidance of closure and finality, it serves perpetually as a vehicle for reformulating old elements into new patterns (Turner 1967, 97–98). Dialogue provides a meeting ground, *communitas*, and manifests itself in a variety of spontaneous and ritual modes of discourse in which nature and structure meet (Turner 1969, 140). I will further suggest that in its classical, German romantic, and modern hermeneutic manifestations dialogue has served important functions not only as a kind of discourse but also as a way of viewing discourse. Understood as a conceptualization of a kind of discourse and also as a way of viewing and interpreting discourse, dialogue shares with narrative the characteristic of being atemporal, existing in many times and places. As discourse phenomena, however, dialogues differ from narratives in that they are internally atemporal. They do not tell about events in time; instead, dialogues span a "dialectic of event (i.e., discourse event) and meaning" (Ricoeur 1976); they present utterances, ideas, and understandings in nonlinear, recursive, diaeretical, and synthesizing sequences.

Today "dialogue" evokes the modern hermeneutic tradition represented by Gadamer and Ricoeur, and Bakhtin's celebration of the dialogic, polyphonic voices in the novel as well as in all modern "speech genres" (1986). For Gadamer, Ricoeur, and Bakhtin all speech is speech in and through others, intertextual, intervocal. It is ironic that the modern conception of dialogue as a hermeneutics of all discourse coincides with the anti-"Platonist" rejection of the idea that there are common patterns to be "found" out there. The instigator of dialogue is now a villainous totalitarian. In the—up to now—resoundingly empirical fields of cognitive psychology, linguistics, and anthropology, methodological revisionists claim that in research there is no meaning to what you say apart from how you say it, that "empirical" studies of all kinds, as well as interpretations of data, are well-told tales, that there are no ethnographic realities independent of the literary versions constructed by the ethnographer (Geertz 1988; Brown 1987). Like philosophy (Rorty 1979), all ethnography is now being re-viewed as storytelling. Given the anti-Platonism and anti-positivism of the new ethnography, however, this credo cannot be meant to be taken literally. The recent universalization of "storytelling" functions as a synechdoche, I suspect, for broadly "literary" and "poetic" (e.g., Friedrich 1986) aspects of language long eschewed by social scientists. To designate as "storytelling" what social scientists do, though unsettling to many social scientists, marks a return to the "literary" fabric and polyvocalities (Bakhtin) of virtually all nonpositivist, nontechnical *uses* of language. This shift in focus toward texture and voice also restores common ground between Western and non-Western understandings of language, permitting a context in which analyst and subject can talk together as equals. Recently, cultural anthropologists have styled this democratization a "dialogue" with the cultures who are the objects of their study. Through cultural dialogue they seek to replace "colonial" anthropology with an egalitarian community of peers that will allow the culture being "studied" to share in defining the objectives and social uses of research.

The anti-"Platonist" and antipositivist agenda of those redirecting the social sciences toward the rhetoric of their own inquiry (e.g., Nelson, Megill, and McCloskey 1987) compounds the difficulty of interpreting dialogue by problematizing dialogue as a stable, knowable genre or phenomenon. Instead of What is dialogue? or How do we productively interpret and understand dialogue? the questions become What assumptions are we making in interpreting dialogue? or How have we conceived and "told the story" of dialogue in the past? Further complicating the study of dialogue within the social sciences is its deployment to denote ethical and political goals of egalitarianism and cultural symbiosis, a notion of democratic and familial relationships evocative of what Victor Turner calls "communitas" (1969, 128–76). Dialogue within a newly defined communitas of "the West and the rest" (Goody 1977, 41) and dialogue conceived of as fundamentally a ritual of communitas round off a circle, for dialogue as a ritual of communal philosophizing and philosophy as a way of knowing that can only be conducted dialogically were among the several definitions Plato gave to dialogue. Within this hermeneutic circle surrounding dialogue, however, are many other points of context, reference, and approach.

As a "genre" and as a way of viewing language and thought, dialogue is of ancient and mixed lineage. Within literary and philosophical studies dialogue has long been apprehended as interestingly anomalous in the senses anthropologists now express as marginal and liminal (Douglas 1966; Turner 1967, 1969). When Plato wrote, dialogue was neither an already ancient literary tradition nor the simple transcription of natural conversation. Instead, dialogue was unprecedented and was inaugurated by Plato's hybrid of oral and written conventions, oral genres, and philosophical modes, a blend he termed *dialegesthai*, not just two but many voices "crossing speakings" or speaking across one another, or "spanning" or "comprehending" each other's statements. Plato's dialogue was unlike the contemporary ethnographic practice of transcribing previously oral discourse whether narrative or conversational, a practice only in this century conjectured to be Homer's technique, but widely used since the nineteenth century by folklorists to preserve previously oral "literature" (cf. Ricoeur 1976). Since in Plato's time little philosophy—or literature for that matter—had yet been written down, it is difficult to conceive of the earliest dialogues as "simple transcriptions" or even as literary compositions purporting to be simple transcriptions, since neither "simple" transcription nor "literary composition" as yet had any rules, predictable shape, or purposes.

What is written down and what *can* be written down, as ethnographers well know, are different but enormously powerful determinants of any written record. This point is one of the recurring subjects of Plato's dialogues. Like Gregory Bateson's "metalogues," Plato's dialogues are shaped by and as what they are about. They deal with "some aspect of a mental process in which ideally the interaction exemplifies the subject matter" (Bateson and Bateson 1986, 210). A different warp and woof weave the fabric of each dialogue according to its thematic, structural, and epistemological concerns. The recent emphasis on Plato's dogmatic idealism favors an aspect of Plato's thought that fluctuates in its prominence from work to work. Defined with astonishing variety, Plato's "idealism" has waxed and waned in the attention it has been given by scholars. It may be the modern association of Plato with idealism that has led to neglect of the great variety of forms he adopts, mixes, mingles, varies, and calls into question. He uses the narrative frame of the storyteller to introduce a dramatic script whose speakers remain independent of the narrative frame and, in some cases, subsume or consume it. In this they serve as propaedeutics for the "divine madness" defined in the *Phaedrus* as an "escape" from custom and convention.

Though drawing on the conventions used for writing dramatic scripts, Plato's dialogues are very unlike other dramatic scripts of the same period in terms of "plot" (*muthos*)—a concept of thematic organization that was not defined as such before Aristotle's *Poetics*. Plato's dialogue scripts place ideas, concepts, and statements alongside persons as interlocutors, entities, for consideration as real or unreal beings. The questions are not What happened? and Why? and Was justice done? but rather What is? How do we talk about it? and How can we better understand what is the good, justice, truth? Unlike Aristotle's conception of dramatic plot, organized around a theme (*ktema*) and mimetic of events in temporal sequence, Plato's definitions of dialogue, like the process of the dialogues as a whole, are neither systematic nor conclusive. On many matters Socrates contradicts himself within and across the dialogues, further exemplifying the notion of dialogues as crossing and blending voices rather than as settling arguments, as evolving coknowledge rather than as the "testing of propositions"—Aristotle's definition of dialectic. The dialogues are atemporal; within and across dialogues the "same" question recurs, and each time it has a different force and a different answer depending on context. "Where we have gotten to," in Socrates' recapitulations, is nearly always a subtle version of "back to where we started," a return that in the most shining cases brings with it an improved, but never a final understanding.

On several counts, then, Plato's "theory" and practice of dialogue, which are given joint exposition in the dialogues may be viewed as structural rituals of role reversal, status reversal, humiliation, and metamorphosis. In them, individuals as well as concepts are rendered liminars along the lines suggested by Victor Turner (1969, 143). This is true not only of the textual "evidence," Plato's dialogues, but is borne out as well in the diversity of explanations and emulations of their elusive, chameleonesque character. Cicero's *Academica* and Diogenes Laertius's *Vitae* record the unfamiliar view held in antiquity of Plato as standing aginst Socrates, who together with Aristotle was held responsible for undermining "the forms," positive knowledge, and criteria of truth. The work of Mikhail Bakhtin provides a modern antidote to the problems of narrowness and disciplinary specialization that have hampered studies of Plato's dialogue as well as modern hermeneutic conceptions of dialogue. Bakhtin provides a linguistic methodology for defining an essentially extraformalist nature and meaning of dialogue:

> *Dialogic relations* have a specific nature: they can be reduced neither to the purely logical (even if dialectical) nor to the purely linguistic (compositional-syntactic). They are possible only between complete utterances of various speaking subjects. . . . Where there is no word and no language, there can be no dialogic relations; they cannot exist among objects or logical quantities (concepts, judgments, and so forth). Dialogic relations presuppose a language, but they do not reside within the system of language. They are impossible among elements of a language. (1986, 117)

An integrated and explained methodology for examining "logics" of oral discourse as well as the orality of Plato's dialogical logic will help uncover assumptions implicit in ostensibly objective descriptions of oral discourse, dialogue, and logic alike. I will advance the argument that unlike predicational logic, and unlike informal conversation, dialogue is both topicalized and "field dependent"; its structure and

meaning are woven through interlocution taking place among already
related individuals who voluntarily enter a collective pursuit of
understanding and who are able to do so only because they "know"
one another. These very qualities, contained within each dialogue,
spring it free from the constraints of ordinary context and temporality. An underemphasized, explicit condition of Plato's dialogue
dialectic is that its participants, much like initiates (Harrison 1962,
507–13) or liminars (Turner 1969, 143), are willing to be denuded of
and to reverse their usual "dress," that is, to have their preconcep-
tions, beliefs, understandings, and language questioned, tested, and
stripped away. In this ritual "time" and space the ordinary temporal
lines of epic, drama, rhetoric, and logic alike are suspended.
Paradoxically, the dialogues are rendered out of time precisely
because they are self-contained, carrying within text and context a
network of relationships that the reader cannot avoid entering. For
this reason I propose there continue to be debates about the literary
or nonliterary, serious or jesting sense in which we are to take a great
many of Socrates' and other interlocutors' utterances.

German romantic (Schleiermacher 1959; Schlegel 1968) and
modern hermeneutic (e.g., Gadamer 1975; Ricoeur 1976) resuscita-
tions of Plato's conception of dialogue have diverged from Anglo-
American analytic and speech-act approaches to "ordinary language." Within Anglo-American philosophy and linguistics, a
cacophonous array of terms is used to define and distinguish formal,
logical, interlocutionary, conversational, natural, "everyday," oral,
literate, rhetorical, narrative, and poetic uses of language. Given this
diversity of cognates, apples and oranges, it is not surprising that
there are debates about how to approach different forms and uses of
language. Dialogue finds itself grouped with conversation and
analyzed as speech, discourse, everyday language, practical language, argument, and logic. To further complicate the hermeneutic
phenomenon, any one of these kinds of discourse may be examined
as shaped by culture, nature, nurture, accident, evolution, adaptive
value, social transaction, aesthetics, or ethical considerations. Linguists, drawing primarily on the analytic, ordinary language, and
speech-act methods of Anglo-American philosophy, have ended up
in the somewhat curious predicament of analyzing the formal
structures of speech with little machinery available for dealing with
meaning, and particularly meaning within interlocution, outside a
narrowly defined syntactical semantics. Semiotics and other kinds of
descriptive linguistics have superseded many understandings of

meaning and thereby many understandings of understanding itself. There is growing consensus that dialogue and dialogic relations cannot be reduced to the purely logical, even if dialectical, or to the purely linguistic. The relationship among speaking subjects that is the body of dialogue cannot be described exclusively in terms of concepts or logical entities as content, as statements, arguments, views, and positions. "Dialogic relations presuppose a language, but they do not reside within the system of language. They are impossible among elements of a language" (Bakhtin 1986, 117).

The transcription and analysis of oral discourse, and particularly of conversation, being conducted in ethnography and linguistics (e.g., Heath, Tannen, Chafe, Michaels, and Collins) is giving us extensive information about the structure or logic of conversation in different settings, but the analysis sometimes suffers, I propose, from the restriction of meaning to semantics and of semantics to narrowly defined concepts of topic and logic, traceable finally to the narrow predicational logic used to analyze the pre-Socratics' and Plato's "arguments" as if they were essentially of a kind with any other samples of logic and argument. These assumptions and the resulting interpretations nicely illustrate the atemporality of logic and, more broadly, of philosophy since their inception. Like philosophers during the reign of idealism, linguists have sought to make statements that would be always true, or true in all cases, and have defined their role as scientists as the discovery of such truths. In the following section I will examine in more detail how the predication-alist bias of modern interpretations of Plato's dialogues has tended to reduce dialogue to conversation and both to a kind of informal topicalized logic. This procedure has obscured the considerable dissimilarities between dialogue and conversation not only in the case of Plato studies, but in linguistic analysis of oral discourse as well.

The Interpretation of Logic

The history of predicational logic is part of a larger whole of Western logical and literate patterns, but it is a singularly important part because its assumptions continue to form the backbone of philosophical and linguistic analysis in analytic philosophy, speech-act theory, linguistics, anthropological linguistics, and ethnography. As a kind of logic, and as a way of looking at and for logic, predication provides a sharp contrast to dialogue and helps define the delicate lines that form the boundary between dialogue and dialectic (cf. Gadamer

1980). Often, as has been the case with modern analytic philosophy since the thirties, the conception of logic has been so narrowly restricted to predicate logic and set theory that other forms of discourse have been regarded as unlogical or as logically unanalyzable. In speech-act theory this assumption lurks in the distinctions between constative and performative, illocutionary and perlocutionary. The narrow predicational definition of logic has led to a restrictive descriptivism in linguistic analysis as well, resulting in the denial of analyzable content to discourse that cannot be translated into topical or predicational form: nontopical conversation, anecdotes, associative and metaphorically organized discourse. In this classification Aristotle's definitive division of logic from "rhetoric, poetry, and prayer" is replicated. Of these discourse modes, says Aristotle, only logic can be true or false. Outside analytic traditions that have restricted logic to predication, alternate logics have been defined, including semiotics, structuralism, speech-act theory, and— I will propose slightly later—dialogue as it has been defined in the modern hermeneutic tradition. These methods and approaches constitute diverse meanings of logic, ranging in conception from a characteristic of language or texts or mind to procedures used first and foremost, and in some cases always, to interpret language, texts, and mind.

It is virtually impossible to examine the history of predicational logic without also looking at its ties to Western literacy, ties that link it very closely and narrowly to the forms of metalinguistic analysis that coincided with the emergence of a parts-of-speech grammar of the kind exemplified, indeed in large part inaugurated, by Aristotle's *Categories (Kategoriae)* and *On Interpretation (Peri hermeneias)*. Conjugating a verb, or learning verbs through conjugation, requires a written grammar, one that has itself probably depended on the analysis of written texts. However, it is becoming increasingly clear that grammars and texts have little intrinsic relation to how the mind works. Modern linguistics and developmental psychology have demonstrated that such grammars are not the most obvious way to describe, define, learn, or teach a language. Classical commentators from Plato through Augustine noted that rote grammar bears little resemblance to the way children learn language. Nor do parts-of-speech grammars occur with any particular frequency in literate cultures untouched by Western influence. Phonetic writing systems, perhaps more than others, encourage the analysis of speech into parts, a form of analysis that is much more difficult without a phonetically accurate means of transcribing "pure" sounds independent of meaning. Parts-of-speech grammars, then, can be seen as prompted by linear conceptions of syntax that resulted from a "sounds-in-sequence" phonetic writing system (de Kerckhove 1986).

The phonetic alphabet's representation of sounds in sequence, which may have prompted the conceptualization of words as "parts" in linear syntax, is only one form of linearity. However, it is not at all at odds with logical patterns of predication and subordination that in the philosophies of the pre-Socratics became hallmarks of logic and grammar alike. Reinterpreting the history of logic, and reviewing that mode of interpreting logic that we know as predication, uncovers early identities between grammar, literacy, and logic. The earliest grammars, many of them titled, as Aristotle's was, *Peri hermeneias* were also composed as logical treatises. Conversely, the earliest logical treatises functioned as guides for the construction of grammars. Without Parmenides' "Being" there might not have developed an independent copula, and yet until recently it has been unusual to think of ontology and the syntax of predication as part of a whole. Syntax itself is an analytic conceptualization of small parts (*tagmai*) within sentences; sentences first went by the term *logoi*. Logic conceived of as a systematic science for making true statements-about requires analysis within the sentence, an analysis that in turn requires a taxonomical nomenclature for "kinds" of words, precisely the list provided by Aristotle's *Categories*. In order to make statements-about, and in order to predicate qualities of subjects, subjects and statements must be isolatable from one another, and a means must be devised for assessing the properties of the constructed links. These procedures for linking statements to one another and for linking units within statements remain essential elements of predicate and set theory and more broadly of philosophical and linguistic analysis.

Not surprisingly, the characteristics of "literate," "standard," "formal," and "logical" discourse defined by empirical linguists are cognate with the categories of logic and grammar evolved by the philosophers of Attic Greece. "Integrated" written discourse is characterized by Wallace Chafe (1982) as having the following features:

(a) Nominalizations.
(b) Increased use of participles.
(c) Attributive adjectives.
(d) Conjoined phrases and series of phrases.
(e) Sequences of propositional phrases.
(f) Relative clauses. (Tannen 1982b)

This list is doubly analytic. Not only does it "find" in "integrated formal written discourse" the features that have long been assigned to—indeed, required by—predicational logic, but it also seeks a componential characterization of such language. An alternate kind of discourse, defined as "spoken language," is characterized in a strikingly different fashion:

(a) Devices by which the speaker monitors the communication channel (intonation, pauses, requests for back-channel responses).
(b) Concreteness and imageability through specific details.
(c) A more personal quality; use of 1st person pronouns.
(d) Emphasis on people and their relationships.
(e) Emphasis on action and agents rather than states and objects.
(f) Direct quotation.
(g) Reports of speaker's mental processes.
(h) Fuzziness.
(i) Emphatic particles. (Tannen 1982b)

Here syntactic structure and logical relationships within sentences such as "attributive adjectives" in the first list are almost entirely missing. Instead, interpersonal relationships, talk about persons and events, dependence on shared contexts, and "fuzziness," presumably measured by the standards of "formal written discourse," are among the characteristics found in the genre "spoken language." As characterized here, "spoken language" seems to have more of the characteristics of dialogue than "planned written language." Or is it that spoken language is here being described in dialogical terms while planned written language is not? How can the phenomenon of a given kind of discourse be separated from the countless assumptions and descriptive nomenclatures brought to bear on it by any number of modes of linguistic analysis? Item 3 in the second list above, "Reports of speaker's mental processes," could, for example, describe one of the methods of formal written discourse, expository self-reference. Is not "I found it plausible to contend that . . ." the "formal written" equivalent of "I think . . ."?

The conundrum of distinguishing linguistic phenomena from description pervades histories of predicational logic. Logical analysis, as well as methodologies of empirical linguistic analysis, requires texts. Creating a text out of philosophies such as the pre-Socratics' that were first "published" orally (Havelock 1983) distorts such philosophies at the outset, obscuring the complexity of the contexts of

oral transmission. Modern analytic philosophy has further com-
pounded the distortions in translations that impose predicative
syntax on philosphers up through Plato. Centuries of doxographical
interpretation stretching from modern times back to Plato's dialogues
and Aristotle's account of "the Milesian school" reformulated—or in
some cases invented—earlier philosophies (Havelock 1983). Textual-
izing and quoting earlier oral traditions, doxographers attributed
predicative, syllogistic, or argumentative form to philosophies not
initially articulated in those forms. An essential element in restoring
the original syntax of early Greek thought has been the recovery of
original texts not filtered through doxographical citation. A second
important element has been a chronology of the emergence of a fully
iterated and independent copula in the syntax of philosophy, the "is"
statement used to assert an attribute of a subject (Havelock 1986;
Rosen 1983; Derrida 1979; Owen 1986; Kahn 1966; Moravsik 1962;
Ackrill 1957; Shorey 1933). Not only philosophers but the Greek
dramas as well have been rendered in predicate syntax by many
modern translations. The opening lines of *Oedipus rex*, for example,
are rendered in the patterns of modern literate prose by one widely
used translation: "The town is heavy with a mingled burden of
sounds and smells" (Grene 1954). The copular "is" makes this a
definition of the town, completed with modifying prepositional
phrase. The original Greek says something more like "The city
altogether bulges with incense burnings" (Havelock 1986, 95). More
striking perhaps is the degree to which modern translators feel
compelled to supply copular syntax to passages in Aristotle, where
predicate syntax is much less common than might be expected. Here
are the opening lines of the *Politics* in a literal translation.

> From these [considerations] it is evident that the city is [one] of the
> things-by-nature, and that man [*anthropos*] by nature is a city-animal,
> and that the non-city man [*apolis*] due to nature not some vicissitude is
> surely either a worthless [person] or a superman—like the one reviled
> by Homer: "clanless, lawless, hearthless" [*anestios*]. . . . Man alone
> of all animals possesses discourse. . . . As man is best of the animals
> [*beltison zoion*], so also sundered from law and justice he [is] worst of all.
> (Havelock 1986, 105)

There is much debate about whether Plato used a predicate
syntax. Is it warranted to infer that a copular structure was "meant"
if the structure is not there? Increasingly, the consensus is that it is

distorting to draw such inferences (Stokes 1988; Rosen 1983). Instead, recent commentaries are recovering the interestingly varied and unfamiliar verb structures of Plato's logic. It has been common to translate Plato's verb forms "is a," "blends with," and "combines with" as predicative. "Motion blends with existence"; becomes the predicative "Motion exists." This hypostatization of the "to be" verb along the lines it assumed only after Aristotle creates not only a copula but also predicates that are not in the original. A translation of "motion blends with existence" that provides an even sharper contrast with the predicative "motion exists" is "The form change combines with the form being" (Rosen 1983, 33). Modern predicationalists have not understood what such "combination" means and so have taken it to mean predication; the later Platonic dialogues—the *Theaetetus* and *Sophist* in particular—have been ransacked for evidence that there is a "doctrine" of predication in Plato (Ackrill 1957; Rosen 1983). But there has been for some time an alternate view advanced, that the relation of ideas as they are preserved in the lexicon and syntax of the dialogues is one of "implication or compatibility and its opposite, not that of principle and derivative or whole and part" (Cherniss 1944, 46). Alternatively, the theory of forms as it is developed in the dialogues has been termed "a theory of predication without predicates" (Allen 1967, 46).

It is unfortunate for considerations of predicate logic in Plato that the English "form" has become the preferred translation for Plato's *eide* and *idia*. "Form" evokes ideal chairs floating in the sky; "idea" and "concept" do not. Plato's lexicon is rich in ideals, ideas, and concepts, but it is not at all clear that he fashions predicates out of them. A related development important to the formalization of logic, indeed constitutive of it in many ways, was the development of abstract nouns, among them Plato's *idia* and the *incipit* metalinguistic consciousness it brought with it: the concept of a concept. Plato's later work defines "five great kinds" of the *megista gene:* being, change, otherness, rest, and sameness. These are the "classes" or ideas whose combination, compatibility, and implication of one another are tested in the diaeresis of the dialogues. But it is not until the list constructed by Aristotle in the *Categories* that these undergo the logical and grammatical metamorphosis into "kinds of terms," that is, restrictively defined linguistic counters that can be combined syntactically. At this point a parts-of-speech grammar and predicational logic are created simultaneously, each defining the other. The objective of logic subsequently becomes to make statements that are valid according to the rules of statement making. Dialectic throughout Aristotle's work carries the meaning of probabilistic syllogism that can prove the negative or the affirmative of the same propositions. Earlier, and up through Plato, dialectic had denoted a discussion that proceeds by question and answer.

Like modern analytic philosophers, Aristotle tends to view earlier philosophers as incipient predicationalists. He implies that Parmenides had a mistaken idea of the physical concept of Being that cannot represent anything because it cannot be fitted into a logical proposition (Cherniss 1944, 73). Heidegger's analysis of Heraclitus's *logos* and of the full range of Being terms before Aristotle is an extended nonpredicational estimation of pre-Socratic philosophical discourse and ontology (1975, 13–58). His appraisal of the interdependence of logos and Being is particularly illuminating on the question of logic as one among many possible ontologies of language. With Aristotle, logos becomes logic and is restricted to "statement," "proposition," "argument," "sentence," or "account." Among the pre-Socratics, logos denotes the very principle by which things are being thought and said, the "principle" or "law" or "essential order" that permits and validates statement making, discoursing, and philosophizing. "That which is," the very principle of Being, will later be elided and domesticated as the predicative copula. Heidegger asks what would have happened if *ta onto* (beings), *ta polla* (the many), *ta panta* (the totality of being), *on* (Being), and *einai* (to be) had remained the essential foci of consciousness. Instead, these became nouns and verbs and plurals and singulars and essential as opposed to existential uses of the copula.

Heidegger repeats like a refrain, "As it reveals itself in beings, Being withdraws" (1975, 26). And "Error is the space in which history unfolds" (p. 26). Only with full exposition—history, argument, fiction—is error brought into being, by the fragmentation and loss of the all, the one, the whole. As it becomes beings, infinitely numerous substantive nouns, the subjects of sentences, Being withdraws. With the concept of logos as "presencing the present" or bringing into being, *ho logos to legein* ("the laying that gathers"), Heidegger forges a link between nonpredicational senses of "isness" and discourse itself (pp. 39–77). Very much like contemporary speech-act theorists and proponents of dialogue hermeneutics, Heidegger emphasizes the conception of logos as willful choice, as intentional, as attention to, as mental action in his appraisal of the Heraclitan uses of the term. *"Legein* [to speak] always means for the Greeks to lay before, to exhibit, to tell, to say. *Ho logos* then would be the Greek name for speaking, saying, and language. . . . But, say. *Ho logos* then would be the Greek name for speaking, saying, and language. . . . But, Heraclitus included, they never think the essence of language expressly as the *Logos*." If they had, he proposes, they would have "thought the essence of language from the essence of Being—indeed as this itself." "Instead," he asserts, "language came to be represented as vocalization, *phone*, as sound and voice, . . . *phone semantike*, a vocalization that signifies. . . . This correct but extremely contrived representation of language, language as 'expression,' remains definitive." Modern linguistic categories of phonology, morphology, pitch, and inflection perpetuate the phonological materialism.

In words about words and in their use lies a record of Western conceptions not only of language but of thought as well and, most particularly, of logic. The difficulties of understanding logos are illustrated in a daunting list of no fewer than sixteen words used to translate *logos* in Aristotle's work alone: sentence, count, tell, say, speak, phrase, account, definition, reason, reasonable, rational, language, talking, speech, argument, proposition (Aristotle 1963, 124n). Heraclitus's use of logos, as Heidegger's analysis suggests, is closer to the roots "picking out," "selecting," "stringing together' (as in "log" or "account"), "gathering." This usage emphasizes what an active knower does, mentally (Heraclitus 1954, 33–73). As order, or ration, or "true-meaning- statement," logos also comes to denote the statement about what is, about what increasingly comes to be thought of as the static and unchanging "content" of what is, and finally, the logically certified proposition.

In the earliest senses of logic as logos, then, are two complementary meanings. Logos is a consciously constructed, intended, assembled, ordered, ratio-giving statement or discourse about what is. It is meant to be *about*, and it is made to be accurate, reliable, true. Once made, the logical statement itself becomes conceived of as a matter of discussion, generating the juxtaposition of reliable and unreliable, true and false, valid and invalid *logoi* that are the object and vehicle of dialogue dialectic in Plato.

Plato's Dialogue: Betwixt and Between

Plato's conception and practice of dialogue preceded the emergence of predicational logic and was arguably an attempt to avert it.

Approaching Plato's dialogues as something other than a logic of propositions, or group of positions and arguments, requires abandoning the idea that philosophy is a long march toward mathematical precision, "from the opaque to the clear, from the vestigially metaphorical to the purely logical" (Ryle 1966, 271). To review the dialogical in the dialogues as programmatic rather than as vestigially "oral" or "literary," it is worthwhile to dispense with the following predicationalist conceptions of Plato's dialogue: (1) that it represents a middle stage in an evolution toward the syllogistic dialectic "finally" achieved by Aristotle; (2) that Plato is developing arguments and doctrines building toward a systematic philosophy; (3) that the choice of the dialogue form is quaint but cumbersome—that the literary and dramatic contours of the dialogues distort and cast into disarray otherwise sensible arguments; and (4) that the propositional content of any single statement in the dialogues may be examined without reference to its immediate context within the dialogues and can instead be collated with statements on similar subjects across the dialogues in order to form a "unified" understanding of Plato's theory of language, of knowledge, and of other "topics."

It is impossible to retrieve the original "Plato's dialogue" in any absolute sense, an insight about the relationship between "original" and "image" that is one of the lessons of the dialogues (Rosen 1980, 115–81). But it is possible to renew attention to the diversities and discontinuities within the dialogue form developed by Plato. Restoring to Plato's dialogue its diverse contexts, its asystematic suspension of ranges of views, and its preservation of maieutic interlocution permits a sharper definition of the limits of modern analytic interpretations and reveals the illusory substance of descriptive techniques that have been used to define the features of discourse modes. There is method in Plato's madness once it is reviewed, deliberateness and delight in the disorderly uses of polyvocality, discontinuity, precipitous reversals and changes of subject, myth, and metaphor. This "disarray"—Plato's dialectic as distinct from Aristotle's—has been obscured by the habit of using the model of mathematics in Plato scholarship, a reductive application that "dissolves the philosophical intelligence of the scholar. . . . The dialogue-form is already a step toward dialectical logic. However, it preserves the distinction between mathematics and poetry or tries to display each in its separate identity as well as in its relation to the other. Dialectical logic crosses this bar" (Rosen 1980, 179).

The harmonics of image and idea, myth and concept, story and statement as they evolve within each dialogue cannot be separated from one another, as kernel from chaff. The conceptual mutilation that is necessary to align Plato's dialogues with post-Platonic conceptions of logic distorts the novelty of his invention, pervasive and characteristic blending of genres, lexicons, and levels of abstraction that are varied within and across the dialogues. To say these "elements" are "blended" is itself a distortion, because Plato's multiplicity and "poly" vocality take shape before the isolation of genres, sciences, and voices from one another. On several counts, then, Plato's dialogue dialectic and Aristotle's syllogistic dialectic are different in more than degree. Although both kinds of dialectic "test and perfect" propositions—Aristotle's definition—the similarity stops there and is quite superficial in the end.

When modern philosophers are not being mathematically analytic, they have styled what they do as argumentation, as controversy when the lines of argument become dogmatic, as dialogue when through "ordinary" uses of language and opinion synthesis and communication are achieved, and as a scientific logistic when the discovery of truths and the furthering of knowledge are at issue. Dialogue, in the context of controversy and argument within modern philosophical traditions, has been defined as based on "ordinary" ways of life and language, as noncontroversial, and as concerned with opinion rather than reality. If modern conceptions of argument could be given a more dialogical turn and devoted to "the elucidation of minds" rather than to exploring reality, controversy within philosophy might be minimized (McKeon, this volume). Along similar lines, philosophy has been conceived as a great conversation that unfortunately degenerates into "mere" inquiry, a contentious exchange of views, when reigning dogmatisms ossify (Rorty 1979, 371–78).

The "elucidation of minds"—maieutics—has been a hallmark of dialogue philosophy since Plato, most familiarly through the Socratic method in teaching. The modern Anglo-American tendency to equate dialogue with "ordinary" ways of life and uses of language is as distorting as regarding the dialogues as failed logical treatises oddly marred by "mere" dramatic and literary conventions. In both cases, a kind of willful ignorance brought about by oversimplification obstructs the grappling with complicated, substantive, and deliberate levels of thought and conceptual interaction involved in dialogue philosophy. At best, the virtues of dialogue as simultaneously dialectic and conversation can restore some of the impasses reached by modern philosophy, a restoration that revives philosophy's role as genetrix: "To see wisdom as consisting in the ability to sustain a conversation, is to see human beings as generators of new descriptions rather than as beings one hopes to be able to describe accurately" (Rorty 1979, 378).

One limitation in construing philosophy as "the great conversation" lies within the modern understanding of "conversation," an understanding that too often leads to its use as a quasi-metaphor, and one that skirts detailed understanding of dialogue. The essence of "conversation" is informality and structurelessness, total openness, whereas dialogue is far from amiable rambling. Existentialism and the other edifying philosophies, for example, have been depicted as "inherently reactive," a role defined as "restoring the conversation" and sending it off in new directions. But many edifying philosophers never see or want to see the other side of the Jordan; though their role may be to restart the conversation, they often avoid participating in it. Traditionally, such philosophers have been iconoclastic, antisystematic, opposed to the notions of objective knowledge and stable truths, and opposed to the definition of philosophy as a finder of essences and producer of representations of those essences: Kierkegaard, Nietzsche, Heidegger, Santayana, William James, Wittgenstein, the ubiquitous Derrida. These philosophers are exponents of a negative dialectic, not of dialogue. The greatest difficulty these philosophers have is "to decry the very notion of having a view, while avoiding having a view about having views" (Rorty 1979, 371). Rorty shares with McKeon the notion that philosophy as a whole is at best a conversation rather than systematic, or is mere inquiry, limited analysis, or at worst is divided by rigid dogma and pitched controversy among sects, each group decrying the others as "not really philosophers." For both McKeon and Rorty tolerant pluralism, practical extra- or prelogical views, and an investigative spirit are the hallmarks of philosophy as conversation.

In Plato's use of the dialogue form, as well as subsequent uses, edifying conversation is only one among several intricately interwoven threads. Another of these threads is dialectic, understood as a logic of question, answer, and reformulation. After Plato dialectic became technologized in two forms: a method for discovering and forming arguments or propositions, and a method of testing, judging, or providing those arguments and propositions (cf. McKeon, this volume). Yet Plato and Cicero, among other practitioners of dialogue, continued to regard dialectic as irreducibly dialogical: as a "dialogue by which agreement is arrived at through argument concerning the nature and division of things" (McKeon). No single person or argument expresses the truth, the "correct" view, or the "final" point. No one has the last word because there is no last word. Thus defined and practiced, and as a way of viewing discourse as well, dialogue allows for alternation and simultaneity of intuitive and discursive understanding, for working back and forth between the exercise of self-consciousness and the analysis of concepts.

Agreement among persons and the agreement of views are inseparable in dialogue, which is not to say that the views can be dispensed with, yielding a subjectivism in which everything becomes "just your opinion." Degeneracies of dialogue are prominently featured in Plato's dialogues, an inclusion that marks this form as a form of forms, as an examination of the contexts of philosophy, a metalogical recursiveness that should warn us against taking any single statement or segment within a dialogue at face value. The dialogue form evades any final interpretation as view, or reduction to "mere" drama. In examples ranging from Plato to More to Diderot to Kierkegaard, dialogue carries within it its own context and counterpoint, in ways that defy resolution rather than promoting it. Its polyvocality and polysemy force, as it were, interlocution on the part of the reader and thereby defy some of the canons that divide textual from oral discourse. Dialogue involves and teaches; it cannot be taught.

For all these reasons, dialogue is a truly liminal mode of discourse, quite possibly intended as such and intended to remain as such. In Plato's practice, dialogue emerged between and subsumed pre-Socratic, sophistic, and epic-dramatic modes of discourse and drew on them as well as on the more ancient narrative epic oral tradition. Dialogue is written orality in a sense, but it is not narrative epic or, as linear logic would come to be, "one" statement. It is often about the notion of one, or whole, or wholeness, about the possibilities of certain statements, their range and distribution and limits. *Dia* means across, spanning; the most frequent verbs used throughout the dialogues are "blending, weaving, mixing, sharing, participating in."

Dialogue is essentially and irreducibly interlocutionary, but it is not informal conversation. It was at its inception an unprecedented interlocutionary procedure. In Plato's case, dialogue carries within it parallel proscriptions on writing, on monologue discourse, and on self-contained predicational dialectic. Though he speaks of dialectic as an instrument for testing and analyzing statements by juxtaposing them through question and answer, Plato never proposes that either dialectic or analytical logic per se become the final fulfillment or objective of what he conceives of as philosophy. Instead, he presents dialogue as the vehicle that can contain and help direct as well as comprehend the many modes of discourse that are already and always in use. One solution to the problem of why Plato wrote the dialogues, in which he objects to writing, lies in the lack of finality in the views juxtaposed within the dialogues. The critique of "writing" developed in the *Phaedrus* and *Letter VII* can without too much difficulty be interpreted as specifically directed at the logographers, who compiled ostensibly final digests, or accounts of a philosopher's view or of other teachings. In *Letter VII* a student of Plato's is chided for publishing a treatise summarizing Plato's teachings. The point is that Plato's teachings cannot be summarized; they are the product of a lifelong process, not a quantity of information. In the *Phaedrus* the objection to "writing" is that it will lead to the confusion of memory with "mere" recollection and of wisdom with "a quantity of information." As early as Heraclitus such compilations were questioned and condemned: "Pythagoras, son of Mnesarchus, practised research . . . , making abstracts from these treatises he compiled a wisdom of his own, an accumulation of learning, a harmful craft" (B129 in Freeman 1983). Unlike compilations and hoards of collected information, the dialogues themselves must be completed at each reading by the active participation and judgment of the reader or, in their original settings, by the "reader's theater."

Victor Turner's depiction of liminality provides a way of looking at dialogue in a cultural context that illuminates ritual aspects of language practice often ignored or eschewed in philosophical analysis. Turner notes Plato's indebtedness to the Eleusinian and Orphic initiation rites of Attica (1967, 97). Turner is not the first to examine Plato's dialogue in terms of ritual forms and meanings. Jane Ellen Harrison (1962) remarked on the similarities between Plato's presentation of interlocutors as taking on views they did not agree with, or of being forced to say something they didn't mean, and the Eleusinian rites in which males dressed as females (p. 507). Transformation and transcendence are effected through deliberate reversal. Harrison asserts that "Plato's whole scheme alike of education and philosophy is but an attempted rationalization of the primitive mysticism of initiation" (p. 513).

Though not a rite of passage in the sense of marking physical and cultural role transition, dialogue as defined by Plato bears many of the marks of such a rite. It is an apprenticeship; it requires lifelong participation in a group of initiates; it cleanses raw youth of some of its more contentious discourse habits. But as a form of discourse dialogue is itself betwixt and between. Turner remarks, "We are not dealing with structural contradiction when we discuss liminality, but with the essentially unstructured (which is at once destructured and prestructured) and often the people themselves see this in terms of bringing neophytes into close connection with deity or with super-human power, with what is, in fact, often regarded as the un-bounded, the infinite, the limitless" (1967, 98).

It is the deliberate and explicit structuring by *contradictions*, or logical opposites, that Plato objects to as a mechanistic and divisive mode of analysis, an infinite regress of no value. Although such deliberate contradictions will be central to Aristotle's dialectic, they are shunned by Plato, whose concept of dialectical juxtaposition of propositions is part of a larger whole: context, understanding among "lifelong friends." Thus dialogue as defined by Plato avoids, perhaps deliberately, some of the already existing logical machinery that could put ideas or statements through various sausage grinders. Yet he objects to the traditional epic narrative as well, the songs of the poets mindlessly absorbed by the "sightseers" looking at the shadows on the wall of the cave rather than thinking for themselves.

Liminal processes are often regarded as analogous to those of gestation, parturition, and suckling. Undoing, dissolution, and decomposition are united with growth, transformation, and reformu-lation of old elements (Turner 1967, 99). In this regard it is striking how atypically, for his own era and its philosophical argot, Plato likens the role of Socrates to that of midwife and even has Socrates define a fairly lengthy parallelism between himself and his mother, who was a midwife. Similarly, in the *Phaedrus*, writings are likened to abandoned children who, without their parent to guide them, will wander forever without understanding, incomprehensible ciphers to all but those who know the context they came from. The context is multiple, not only of meanings, but of relationships, trusts, under-standings, and the several genres or understandings of discourse itself that always form a backdrop. "Oral societies have commonly assigned responsibility for preserved speech to a partnership between poetry, music, and dance. It is arguable that in all its guises rhythm [and might we not here include the interlocutionary rhythm of conversation?] is the foundation of all biological pleasures—all the natural ones, sex included—and possibly of the intellectual ones as well" (Havelock 1986, 72). Conceiving of discourse itself as participating in such elementary biological patterns is both strange and not so strange. Parmenides claims that through the pursuit of the One, of Being, "Coming into Being is quenched and Destruction also into the unseen. Becoming and Destruction have been driven very far away, and true conviction has rejected them" (B7, 8, in Freeman 1983). There is a war of sorts suggested here—traditional notions of coming into being and disintegration are triumphantly rejected by "true conviction." In Plato's dialogue these are mixed and mingled, in varying degrees, with truth, which is itself presented as elusive, always in process.

Plato's concept of dialogue was and is a sturdy innovation, an officially liminal discourse mode designed to unstructure what had preceded it and to prestructure what would follow. Dialogue as defined by Plato is a vast experiment in mixing and mingling discourse conventions in order to bring about optimum understanding, partaking of extant patterns but altering them to fit new objectives. It can, I think, be productively applied to transitional discourses, logics, and literacies today. As discourse becomes conceptual, abstract, about ideas and their relationship to one another, it becomes less narrative. Or to put it another way, narrative paradigms do not always prepare people for contact with conceptual discourse. As it becomes more conceptual and less narrative, discourse needs rules for its use, rules that typically take the form of metalinguistic terms and instructions. One less than happy solution to this problem is to provide a reductive protocol for the use of the new terminology; thesis and proof, hypothesis and verification, the five-paragraph essay, the outlines for speeches and letters provided by classical rhetoric. Plato proposed an alternative, an antiprotocol, a meetinghouse of sorts, by narrating presentations of dialogue that function as antidotes to the tendencies toward closure and conclusion, toward "discourse under the conditions of inscription" (Ricoeur 1976).

The Logic of Interpretation

It is dangerously misleading to say, as I just have, that discourse "becomes less narrative and more conceptual" in certain settings or under certain conditions. The very concepts of narrative, dialogue, and logic are themselves highly abstract and variously defined technical terms used almost exclusively by Western academicians. This is not to say that narrative, dialogue, and logic do not lurk beneath the surfaces of much language. Even the notion of the "surface" confirms the persistence of the Greek conceptions of truth (*aletheia*) the unrevealed, the hidden; and of interpretation (*hermeneias*) as uncovering or unlocking the hidden. Narrative, dialogue, and logic are among the modern logics of interpretation that permit *under*standing, the comprehension of those meanings and structures that are beneath the appearances of things. Yet these logics are ways of seeing, lenses rather than windows. "What is structually 'visible' to a trained anthropological observer is psychologically 'unconscious' to the individual member of the observed society. . . . But rituals of status reversal make visible in their symbolic and behavioral patterns social categories and forms of grouping that are considered to be axiomatic and unchanging both in essence and in relationships to one another" (Turner 1969, 176). Here lurks a doubling—of the rituals of the observed with those of the observer. It has become axiomatic to claim logical structures for discourse, mind, and finally culture itself. Historians of discourse, and particulary of oral literature, discover universalities for story and storytelling—Because they are storytellers themselves or because they are looking for stories? In hermeneutic circles, it has become similarly axiomatic to posit all discourse, truth, and understanding as interlocutionary, as dialogical.

　　　Three "moments" of dialogue ascendant in Western tradition mark periods of loosening boundaries, transitional reform, and a conceptual alchemy replacing knowledge as content with truth as interlocutionary process. Plato's dialogue transcended earlier "story," that of epic and drama, with a protocol for conceptual interlocution that was designed to frustrate the technification of thought (Gadamer 1980). Schleiermacher's translation of Plato's dialogues into German came to be the headwater of a massive reform in the theory and practice of both philosophy and literature, a reform that emphasized natural voices, living speech, union between minds rather than understanding of texts, polyphony, deliberately unsystematic philosophizing in spoken and written dialogues (e.g., Schleiermacher 1959; Schlegel 1968). The modern hermeneutic tradition represented by Heidegger, Ricoeur, Gadamer, and Bakhtin has revived and extended the German romantic template to emphasize the irreducibly polyvocal, interlocutionary elements in all language. These need not be seen as outside narrative and logic; though they

direct attention to elements other than linearity they do not—
necessarily—contradict the linearity of logic or of narrative. Instead,
they reintroduce the presence of storyteller and audience, the
interlocutionary elements involved even in logic. Dialogue persists in
evoking the quasi-religious because even when it is not being used in
the hermeneutics of sacred texts it invokes the presence of the author,
a presence that is undergoing ontological interrogation in many
critical contexts. Nonetheless, dialogical models persist and prolifer-
ate in unsuspected places. If the author is banished, a new locus for
dialogue is emergent in the notion of the reader's control of the text
and the parallel notion of the ethnographic storyteller's control over,
even invention of, the culture being described. In either case, story
and dialogue, "account" and interlocution, work together in various
ways, ways whose diversities will no doubt ossify and be transformed
again. Story and dialogue have their reductive technified forms and
their transformative, ritual, and creative forms. To oppose them to
one another as enemies, or even as opposites, itself exemplifies a
reductively technical abuse of dialectic.

> He imposes orders as he thinks of them
> As the fox and snake do. It is a grave affair.
> > But to impose is not
> To discover.
> > Wallace Stevens, "Notes towards a Supreme Fiction"

References

Ackrill, J. L. 1957. Plato and the copula: Sophist 251–259. In *Plato I:
    Metaphysics and epistemology*, ed. G. Vlastos, pp. 210–22. New York:
    Doubleday Anchor.
Allen, R. E., ed. 1967. *Studies in Plato's metaphysics*. London: Routledge and
    Kegan Paul.
Aristotle. 1963. *Categories* and *On interpretation*. Trans. J. L. Ackrill. Loeb
    Classical Library. Cambridge: Harvard University Press.
Bakhtin, M. 1986. *Speech genres*. Austin: University of Texas Press.
Bateson, G. 1979. *Mind and nature*. New York: Dutton.
Bateson, G., and M. C. Bateson. 1986. *Angels fear*. New York: Macmillan.
Brown, R. H. 1987. *Society as text*. Chicago: University of Chicago Press.
Chafe, W. L. 1982. Integration and involvement in speaking, writing, and
    oral literature. In *Spoken and written language: Exploring orality and
    literacy*, ed. D. Tannen, 35–54. Norwood, N. J.: Ablex.
Cherniss, H. 1944. *Aristotle's criticism of Plato and the Academy*. Baltimore:
    Johns Hopkins University Press.

Derrida, J. 1979. The supplement of the copula: Philosophy before linguistics. In *Textual strategies*, ed. J. Harari, 82–120. Baltimore: Johns Hopkins University Press.

Douglas, M. 1966. *Purity and danger*. London: Routledge and Kegan Paul.

Finnegan, R. 1977. *Oral poetry: Its nature, significance and social context*. Cambridge: Cambridge University Press.

Freeman, K. 1983. *Ancilla to the Presocratic philosophers*. Cambridge: Harvard University Press. Originally published 1948.

Friedrich, P. 1986. *The language parallax*. Austin: University of Texas Press.

Gadamer, H.-G. 1975. *Truth and method*. New York: Continuum.

———. 1980. *Dialogue and dialectic*. New Haven: Yale University Press.

Geertz, C. 1988. *The anthropologist as author*. Palo Alto: Stanford University Press.

Goody, J. 1977. *The domestication of the savage mind*. New York: Cambridge University Press.

———. 1982. Alternate paths to knowledge in oral and literate cultures. In *Spoken and written language: Exploring orality and literacy*, ed. D. Tannen, 201–16. Norwood, N. J.: Ablex.

Goody, J., and I. Watt. 1968. The consequences of literacy. In *Literacy in traditional societies*, ed. J. Goody, 27–68. Cambridge: Cambridge University Press.

Grene, D., ed. 1954. *The complete Greek tragedies: Sophocles I*. Chicago: University of Chicago Press.

Griswold, C. L. 1987. *Self knowledge in Plato's "Phaedrus."* New Haven: Yale University Press.

Harrison, J. E. 1962. *Epilegomena* and *Themis*. New York: University Books. Originally published 1927.

Havelock, E. A. 1983. The linguistic task of the Presocratics. In *Language and thought in early Greek philosophy*, ed. K. Robb, 7–83. LaSalle, Ind.: Monist Library of Philosophy.

———. 1986. *The muse learns to write*. New Haven: Yale University Press.

Heath, S. B. 1982. Protean shapes in literacy events: Ever-shifting oral and literate traditions. In *Spoken and written language: Exploring orality and literacy*, ed. D. Tannen, 91–118. Norwood, N. J.: Ablex.

Heidegger, M. 1975. *Early Greek thinking*. New York: Harper and Row. Originally published 1933.

Heraclitus. 1954. *The cosmic fragments*. Ed. G. S. Kirk. New York: Cambridge University Press.

Kahn, C. 1966. The Greek verb "to be" and the concept of being. *Foundations of Language* 2:245–65.

Kerckhove, D. de. 1981. A theory of Greek tragedy. *Sub-Stance* 29:23–36.

———. 1986. Alphabetic literacy and brain processes. *Visible Language* 22(3): 274–93.

Kirk, G. S., and J. E. Raven. 1957. *The Presocratic philosophers*. New York: Cambridge University Press.

Mates, B. 1967. *Stoic logic.* Berkeley: University of California Press.

Michaels, S., and J. Collins. 1984. Oral discourse styles: Classroom interaction and the acquisition of literacy. In *Coherence in spoken and written discourse,* ed. D. Tannen, 219–44. Norwood, N. J.: Ablex.

Moravcsik, J. M. E. 1962. Being and meaning in the *Sophist. Acta Philosophica Fennica* 14:23–78.

Nelson, J. S., A. Megill, and D. N. McCloskey, eds. 1987. *The rhetoric of the human sciences.* Madison: University of Wisconsin Press.

Olson, D. 1986. The cognitive consequences of literacy. *Canadian Psychology* 272: 109–21.

Ong, W. 1982. *Orality and literacy.* New York: Methuen.

Owen, G. E. L. 1986. Plato on not being. In Logic, science, and dialectic, ed. M. Nussbaum, 104–37. Ithaca: Cornell University Press. Originally published 1967.

Parry, M., and A. Lord. 1954. *Serbocroation heroic songs,* Vol. 1. Cambridge: Harvard University Press.

Plato. 1973. *Phaedrus* and *Letter VII.* Trans. W. Hamilton. Loeb Classical Library. Cambridge: Harvard University Press.

———. 1977. *Theaetetus* and *Sophist.* Trans. H. N. Fowler. Loeb Classical Library. Cambridge: Harvard University Press.

Ricoeur, P. 1976. *Interpretation theory: Discourse and the surplus of meaning.* Fort Worth: Texas Christian University Press.

Robinson, R. 1953. *Plato's earlier dialectic.* Oxford: Clarendon.

Rorty, R. 1979. *Philosophy and the mirror of nature.* Princeton: Princeton University Press.

Rosen, S. 1980. *The limits of analysis.* New Haven: Yale University Press.

———. 1983. *Plato's "Sophist."* New Haven: Yale University Press.

Ryle, G. 1966. *Plato's progress.* Cambridge: Harvard University Press.

Schlegel, F. von. 1968. *Dialogue in poetry and literary aphorisms.* Trans E. Behler and R. Strue. University Park: Pennsylvania State University Press. Originally published 1789.

Schleiermacher, F. 1959. *Hermeneutik.* Trans. H. Kimmerie. Heidelberg: Karl Winter.

Scribner, S., and Cole, M. 1981. *The psychology of literacy.* Cambridge: Harvard University Press.

Shorey, P. 1933. *What Plato said.* Chicago: University of Chicago Press.

Stokes, M. C. 1988. *Plato's Socratic conversations.* London: Athlone.

Tannen, D. 1982a. The myth of orality and literacy. In *Linguistics and literacy,* ed. W. Frawley, 37–50. New York: Plenum.

———. 1982b. Oral and literate strategies in spoken and written narratives. *Language* 58(1): 1–21.

———. 1982c. The oral literate continuum in discourse. In *Spoken and written language: Exploring orality and literacy,* ed. D. Tannen, 1–16. Norwood, N. J.: Ablex.

Turner, V. 1967. *The forest of symbols.* Ithaca: Cornell University Press.

———. 1969. *The ritual process.* Ithaca: Cornell University Press.

part 11

Cultural and Historical Contexts of Dialogue

3

Narrative as Interpretation and Interpretation of Narrative: Hermeneutical Reflections on the Gospels

Werner H. Kelber

The art of telling stories has faithfully accompanied the human race from preliterate to postmodern times. So "natural" appears to be the impulse to narrate that one is hard put to imagine a language or culture devoid of narrative elements. The need to make scraps of life cohere in the imagination and to plot events so as to give them a semblance of coherence and sequentiality may thus reasonably be counted among the human universals. Roland Barthes was of the opinion that narrative "is simply there like life itself . . . international, transhistorical, transcultural" (1977, 77). Hayden White, to whom we owe some of the most profound studies on the subject (1973, 1978), viewed narrative as "a panglobal fact of culture" (1980, 5). One may well claim, therefore, that "narrative and narration are less problems than simply data" (White 1980, 5). It is, however, precisely that which we take most for granted and without which we seem least able to exist that tends to elude our full attention. The very ubiquity of narrative subtly distracts us from according critical recognition to our narrative impulses and performances. We need reminding that narrative, although there like life itself, is not itself life. "No one and nothing *lives* as story" (White 1978, 111). For life, after all, does not narrate, and narrative is always artificial. Perhaps the impulse to narrate is not quite as "natural" as it seems.

In the context of ancient literary history, the canonical Gospels can hardly claim uniqueness as far as narrativity is concerned. The golden age of Hebrew narrative extended roughly from the tenth to the seventh century B.C.E. Prose narratives, especially in the form of biographies, were a standard feature of Hellenistic culture. In part, at least, they owed their existence to the desire to keep alive the memory of extraordinary deeds and powers that were associated with famous poets, philosophers, and rulers. It is entirely reasonable, therefore, to examine the Gospels by analogy with Greco-Roman forms of narrative. But it remains questionable whether the Gospels are fully assimilable to, and explicable by, Hellenistic narrative models, if only because the narration of a crucified Son of God was a moral, aesthetic, and literary monstrosity, contradicting Jewish, Hellenistic, Roman, and barbarian sensibilities. Appeal to Hellenistic biographies will not entirely explain the impulse to narrate the gospel stories. One may also remember that narrative was far from being a uniform mode of expression in the early Christian tradition. Substantial parts of the canon suggest that a faithful commitment to the Christ did not perforce require narrativity. Moreover, a segment of noncanonical Christianity, as will be shown, appears to have been less than friendly toward narrative syntax. It would follow, on this view, that the nonnarrative and the antinarrative tradition in early Christianity itself does not allow us to take the narrative gospel for granted.

Literary critics have been far from generous in recording the Gospels' contribution to Western culture. The monumental research compiled by H. Munro and N. Kershaw Chadwick on nearly 2,400 pages of *The Growth of Literature* (1932–40), for example, makes only incidental reference to the gospel stories. In what has justly been called a classic, Robert Scholes's and Robert Kellogg's *The Nature of Narrative* (1966), the history of narrative is traced from its oral beginnings to the heights of the nineteenth- and twentieth-century realistic novel without according the Gospels a place in it. Nor are the Gospels mentioned in a recent study of the postclassical, Hellenistic birth of the novel, Thomas Hägg's *The Novel in Antiquity* (1983), which examines inter alia Philostratus's *Life of Apollonius,* the Alexander Romances, the apocryphal Acts of the Apostles, the Pseudo-Clementines, and various hagiographical materials. The critics' reluctance to assess the Gospels' significance in literary history is all the more puzzling in that these ancient Christian stories continue to occupy a commanding position in Western culture. With the exception of the ancient Hebrew narratives, the Gospels are to this day read and recited more than any other single story composed in antiquity. Does overfamiliarity prevent us from regarding them with fresh attention? Or does their character as sacred texts forbid an assessment in the general context of literature? Or do the Gospels seem unpleasantly doctrinaire—tyrannical even? Perhaps the literary critics considered the Gospels the exclusive domain of biblical scholars. Whatever the reasons for the neglect, the breakthrough toward a literary appreciation of the Gospels, it is often said, came with Erich Auerbach's sensitive reading of Peter's denial in Mark (1953, 40–49). In the wake of Auerbach, literary critics of the stature of Robert Alter (1981), Frank Kermode (1979), and Herbert N. Schneidau (1976) have recently turned to aspects of biblical narrative to show how these perplexing and often disturbing texts have informed Western literature and our sense of reality.

If until recently literary critics have left the Gospels to the biblical specialists, they were by and large left in the lurch. For although biblical scholarship has for over two centuries subjected the Gospels to exquisite scrutiny, it has failed to grasp what matters most about them, their narrative nature. Few theses proved as influential in setting hermeneutical standards as Papias's report concerning Mark's transcription of Petrine teachings. It was widely understood to mean that the narrative gospel resulted from preservation of unassimilated, uninterpreted information. Preservation from forgetfulness was assumed to be a prime motive for the composition of the Gospels, a concept prone to encourage historical criticism more than narrative criticism. In the West, the rise of idealistic philosophy and historical consciousness brought the interpretation of the Gospels to a head. For the most part biblical interpreters sought to distill from the Gospels an ideational, preachable core or a residue of verifiable fact. Hans Frei (1974) has documented the inability of eighteenth- and nineteenth-century biblical hermeneutics to come to terms with the Gospels as realistic narratives. His report can and should be extended into the twentieth century, for it was only in the past two decades that biblical critics, mostly North Americans, began to appreciate the literary and rhetorical dimension of the Gospels. At this point we have taken only a very tentative step toward understanding the narrative impulse in the early Christian tradition, the nature of the narrative Gospels, and our ways of interpreting them.

The impulse to narrate in the Christian tradition is frequently taken as a matter of course. The Gospels' life-to-death pattern, one of the most common of all plot constructions, appears quintessentially like life itself in moving toward death. What more natural beginning than birth, and what more realistic ending than death! But no matter how natural or realistic the narrative, artifice is unmistakably present, raising the issue not of the represented world out there, but of how it is represented. When it was recognized—rudimentarily by Papias, and also in Luke's prologue—that the Gospels originated out of tradition, pertinent questions as to the relationship between gospel and tradition tended to be answered by the eyewitness theory. The

death of the first generation of witnesses was assumed to have
prompted the writing of the Gospel narratives. Accordingly, a
principal function of the Gospels was to preserve continuity of and
with tradition. This theory lies at the root of the popular (and to some
extent still professional) paradigm of a single, directional course of the
tradition leading from the historical Jesus into the written Gospel.
Form criticism, for all its methodological inadequacies, succeeded in
alerting us to the significance of the tradition. If nothing else, the
discipline sensitized us to the variability and complexity of the
pre-Gospel history of the tradition. Yet form criticism still operated
under the presupposition of relatively uncomplicated Gospel beginnings. Bultmann assumed that the Gospels narrated "nothing in
principle new" that had not already been said by oral tradition (1963,
321). For many scholars the narrative impulse appears self-evident
owing to the facts or forces of tradition.

In seeking to account for the narrative gospel by appeal to
tradition, one tends to disregard the diversity of traditions and the
divergence of transmissional processes. Ricoeur is right in pointing to
parable for the purpose of stressing the "requirement of narration
internal to the proclamation itself" (1984, 511). Indeed, the parable
joins proclamation to a story which, it has been suggested, became
instrumental in the formation of the narrative gospel (Crossan 1975,
10, 124; 1984, 15; Kelber 1983, 117–31). Yet parable is only one
element in the tradition, and commitment to narrative is only one trait
of the tradition. The aphorisms of Jesus, for example, constitute
nonnarrative units, and the processes governing their transmission
cannot be shown to generate the narrative gospel. In his book *In
Fragments* (1983), John D. Crossan traced the conduct of synoptic
aphorisms as they coalesce into compounds and clusters, become
attached to stories, and develop into dialogues and series of
dialogues. As Crossan rightly saw, the aphoristic tendency toward
clustering, dialogue, and discourse, although well recognized in the
orthodox tradition, became a generically fateful influence in what he
calls the Gnostic tradition (1983, 237, 268). What comes to mind are
such documents as the Gospel of Thomas, the Dialogue of the Savior,
the Apocryphon of James, and many others, and also Q, the sayings
source, whose genre was, however, dispersed and displaced by
Matthew and Luke. Is it permissible to discern in the aphoristic
clustering a movement toward an alternate, a nonnarrative gospel?

Few noncanonical documents have as great a potential for
implementing a revision of our view of tradition as the Gospel of

Thomas. This is all the more true if, as mounting evidence suggests, the bulk of Thomas is not only independent of the canonical Gospels, but antecedent to them. The document consists of single aphorisms, aphoristic and dialectical dialogues, and parables, all spoken by the living Jesus. Strictly speaking it is not a consistently composed dialogue or discourse genre, and it "lacks" a unifying narrative setting. Whether the term *logoi* in the incipit (Oxy P654) was the authentic designation of Thomas's genre, with *gospel* being second-arily appended as subscription so as to make Thomas competitive with the canonical Gospels, or whether *gospel* was the authentic term for nonnarrative Thomas has yet to be decided. The fact remains that Thomas was perceived quite early as a distinct genre, a sayings collection, and already in its Greek version understood to be a gospel, a sayings gospel. What we observe in this case is the principle of aphoristic clustering being carried to the point of generic consumma-tion. When viewed from the standpoint of the Gospel of Thomas, therefore, the aphoristic behavior to cluster among its own kind appears in a fresh light. Now one may discern in it the potential for the production of a gospel sui generis. It is clear from this example that the needs for narrativization do not account for all the elements of the tradition. The aphoristic proclamation may well have a momentum of its own toward a nonnarrative genre, the sayings gospel.

The Nag Hammadi documents—a collection of fifty-two writ-ings of predominantly Christian origin, discovered in 1945 in Upper Egypt (Cf. Pagels 1979)—have brought into sharper focus the nature of the aphoristic processes vis-à-vis the narrative performance in emergent orthodoxy. When viewed from the canonical standpoint, it strikes one as remarkable how ill at ease these documents are with narrative syntax. In fact, none of these texts comes even close to the genre of the orthodox Gospel. Whereas the canonical Gospels commence with birth or baptism and end with resurrection, an-nounced or fully narrated, or with ascension, the predominant generic proclivity of the Nag Hammadi documents is toward the sayings discourse that stakes its authority on the teachings of the living or risen Jesus. This quite extraordinary phenomenon deserves close scrutiny not only from those interested in linguistic aspects, but from those who explore the social world of early Christianity. What kind of communities are we to imagine that showed such conspicu-ous partiality toward the aphoristic genre?

Based on these observations, I have recently suggested that the time has come to draw a conclusion of considerable import for our understanding of the early Christian tradition (Kelber 1985). Henceforth we must reckon with two gospel genres in early Christianity, the sayings or cluster gospel, and the narrative gospel. The sayings or cluster gospel elevated the *logoi* proclamation to generic significance, promoting a Jesus who taught and redeemed through words of wisdom. The narrative gospel shaped a heterogeneous repertoire into biographical synthesis, favoring a Jesus who redeemed through the conduct of his life and death, followed by resurrection. Crossan (1984), on the other hand, proposed the existence of three gospel genres: the cluster gospel, the dialogue gospel, and the narrative gospel. As aphoristic clustering furnished the condition for the sayings or cluster gospel, so did the aphoristic arrangement by way of comment/response or question/answer format prepare for the dialogue gospel (Dialogue of the Savior, Sophia of Jesus Christ, etc.) Recognition of a duality, and perhaps even a plurality, of gospel genres compels us to contemplate the narrative gospel with renewed curiosity.

Perhaps agreement can be reached on the following four points. First, we may discern at least two, and possibly three, gospel genres, provided it is understood that both the cluster and the dialogue gospel arise out of the aphoristic processes and that they are for this reason closely related, whereas the narrative gospel is generically unrelated to the aphoristic tradition. Second, the narrative gospel, the one genre accepted by orthodox Christianity for canonical inclusion, appears to be the formal heir not of the aphoristic processes, but of parable. Both in its narrative form and in its disorienting, metaphorical proclivity, canonical Mark operates according to the hermeneutics of Jesus' parables. Third, it is tempting to speculate that each of the two basic speech forms attributable to the historical Jesus, the aphorism and the parable, were consummated in a gospel of its own: the aphorism in the sayings (and dialogue) gospel, and the parable in the narrative gospel. Fourth, while the sayings (and dialogue) gospel and the narrative gospel may each invoke continuity with Jesus, they grew out of different compositional needs and transmissional processes. Such are the differences in form, choice of materials, and christology that it is difficult, if not impossible, to assume direct, evolutionary connections between the aphoristic genre and the narrative genre. They will have developed separately, and they could well have existed in tension with each other.

If narrativity cannot be taken for granted in the early Christian tradition, neither can the strident tone in which it asserted itself in the canon. This point was reiterated by Elaine Pagels, who after years of work on the Nag Hammadi texts continues to be astounded by the polemics of the canonical gospels: "The gospels which came to be accepted as orthodox generally interpret Jesus traditions in confrontational terms" (1981, 62). Her statement suggests that the Gospels' polemics are occasioned by the manner in which these narratives relate to tradition. Preservation of traditions is not the sole purpose of the narrative gospels. I have recently sought to enlarge our understanding of the connections between Mark's deeply polemical narrative dynamics and antecedent traditions. I proposed that the canonical gospel form had arisen out of a conflict with the genre of the sayings gospel (Kelber 1983, 90–139, 184–220). Mark's reserved attitude toward sayings (as compared with Matthew, Luke, and John), the displacement of the vital oral authorities, the banishment of the Twelve to the outside, the extensive narrative explication of Jesus' earthly life, the narrative focus on his death, and a withholding of the living Lord are all features hostile to the genre built on sayings spoken by the living or risen Jesus. In the sayings gospel the living Jesus alone utters the words of life, whereas in Mark death puts an end to his speech. In terms of narrative form and focus, of christology, of principal features of dramatization, and of the rhetorical impact on hearers/readers, the corrective function of the polemical narrative seems to be plausible. Methodologically, I wished to demonstrate that a gospel can (and should) be read both as a coherent narrative and in relation to tradition, whereby tradition is understood not only as a process of continuity, but in terms of discontinuity as well.

In Robinson's view (1970, 99–129 [1982a, 11–39]; 1982b, 40–53; 1982c, 5–37), Mark's narrative genre must be understood in the context of "the bifurcating orthodox and gnostic positions" (1970, 114 [1982a, 27]). In what he calls the gnosticizing trajectory, the risen Christ, freed from bodily encumbrance and authorized by heavenly experiences, initiates "the time of a new hermeneutic as the time of the Spirit" (1982c, 26). In placing ultimacy upon the risen Christ, one tends to relegate to insignificance his earthly life "as just a lower and hence irrelevant prelude" (1970, 113 [1982a, 26]). Easter has thereby become the "time differential" (1982b, 48), that is, the hermeneutical turning point separating a period of concealment from the time of revelation. Or, as gnosticizing texts tended to put it, before Easter Jesus spoke in riddling parables, but at Easter the risen Christ spoke "openly" (*parrhēsia*). Speaking "in parables" and speaking "openly" thereby became "the technical contrasting terms for designating the literal and spiritual levels of meaning . . . used to distinguish the sayings of Jesus before and after Easter" (1982c, 30). Parabolic speech, moreover, can itself be typical of Christ's post-Easter instruction imparted to a group of understanding disciples (1982c, 49). Insofar as the Christ of higher, esoteric revelation became the focal point for sayings and parables revealed to a select group of initiates, the gnosticizing trajectory was on its way toward the genre of the sayings and discourse gospel.

From the perspective of these gnosticizing proclivities, Robinson finds sufficient clues in Mark to assume shifts from a post-Easter to a pre-Easter level of interpretation that are deeply connected with the genesis of the orthodox Gospels. In Mark the period of higher revelation begins when Jesus announces his first passion-resurrection prediction by speaking "openly" Mark 8:32: *parrhēsia*). In this case the gnosticizing " 'Easter' shift" (1970, 111 [1982a, 29]) has been retrojected into the pre-Easter period. Consequently, the higher revelation is refocused from the parables and sayings spoken by the living Jesus to the earthly Jesus and the proclamation of his death and also resurrection. It is this orthodox emphasis on death followed by resurrection that accounts for Mark's focused narrative engagement in the passion. One might add that it also clarifies the absence and silence of the risen Christ. If death is the point of higher revelation, then the earthly Jesus has already said and accomplished all that matters. Robinson, confirming the thesis, draws attention to the analogous gnosticizing type of apparition story (1970, 116–18 [1982a, 29–31]). Many Gnostic gospels are cast in the form of a luminous epiphany of the risen Lord on a mountain. Based on this analogy, the transfiguration has all the appearance of an apparition story relocated in close proximity to the new hermeneutical turning point, the first passion-resurrection prediction. Jesus' esoteric instruction in parables (Mark 4:1–34) likewise shows traces of a pre-Markan functioning. It resembles precisely the kind of higher revelation that in the gnosticizing genre is reserved for the post-Easter disciples. In Mark, however, the esoteric instruction is purposely undermined "in that the disciples, in spite of the interpretation, remain as much in the dark as do the outsiders" (1970, 112 [1982a, 25]). These and other observations suggest to Robinson that in Mark "Easter material is embedded back into the public ministry" (1982b, 52) with the intent to refocus or correct the gnosticizing trajectory by placing the highest revelatory premium on the earthly Jesus and his death. According to Robinson's well-known formula, "Gnosticism's Gospel *Gattung* begins just as regularly after the resurrection as the orthodox *Gattung* ends there" (1970, 114 [1982a, 27]). When thus examined in the light of bifurcating traditions, the narrative gospel presents itself as an attempt on the part of emergent orthodoxy to block the gnosticizing sayings genre and to assert itself "as a replacement for the all too ambivalent Q" (1982c, 37).

Yet another approach that arrived at a similar assessment of Mark's gospel was undertaken by Eugene Boring (1982). He proceeded from early Christian prophecy and its modes of discourse. A distinctive feature of early Christian prophets, according to Boring, was their role as inspired spokespersons of the risen Lord. Conscious of being commissioned by the Lord, they spoke his sayings in his name and on his authority. The hermeneutical rationale for prophetic speech was not, therefore, to preserve the teachings of the Jesus of the past, but to keep his voice and authority alive in the community. This study of the prophetic function of the synoptic sayings brings Boring finally to posit his thesis concerning the genesis of the narrative gospel. Mark carries only a little more than half as many sayings as either Matthew or Luke. Apart from the eschatological discourse, Boring can identify only five of Mark's sayings as prophetic speech (1982, 183–203). In addition, Boring sees Mark as withholding all sayings from the risen Lord. The latter "is not only absent, he is silent" (1977, 377 [1982, 203]). When viewed against the prophetic mode of representing Jesus' sayings as an address of the living Lord, the purpose and achievement of the narrative gospel appears in a new light. Both the gospel's paucity of sayings and its scarcity of specifically prophetic sayings, and also its ending at 16:8, which confines traditions to a strictly pre-Easter framework, find an explanation in Mark's intention to compose an alternative form to the prophetically functioning sayings tradition. Mark's achievement was to curb the prophetic use of sayings as post-Easter revelation of the living or risen Jesus by creating the pre-Easter form that endorses the earthly Jesus.

That Robinson, Boring, and my own recent work regard the narrative gospel as a corrective to the type of sayings genre weighs all the more heavily in that we proceeded largely independently and with the aid of different methods. Robinson took his cue from William Wrede (1981), critically advancing his epochal work *(The Messianic Secret (Das Messiasgeheimnis in den Evangelien)* with fresh insights derived from the Nag Hammadi documents. Boring undertook a study of early Christian prophecy from its beginnings up to the formation of the narrative gospels. My own more theoretically conceived work developed the early Christian hermeneutics of orality versus textuality. Whether one understands the narrative gospel as a corrective to the gnosticizing trajectory or as an attempt to control prophetic speech and revelations or as a rigorous application of textuality versus an oral ontology of language, all three of us view the narrative gospel as a reaction to, or reinterpretation of, an antecedent stage in the tradition.

If we now include in our reflections the vital aspect of speech in the tradition, a model of three orders of operation suggests itself: orality, the sayings genre, and the narrative gospel. This model is not intended to impute a sense of evolutionary ascendancy to tradition, as if it were propelled by inexorable regularity to move from speech to the sayings gospel, only to peak in narrativity. Orality, sayings gospel, and narrative gospel are meant to be viewed as characteristic components in the tradition, not as sequential stages in an orderly process. After all, the issue of narrativity was already entrusted to tradition with parabolic speech; the sayings gospel flourished before, concurrently with, and after the canonical gospels, and speech remained a fertile ground all along. Indeed, the most difficult part of the tradition to understand may be the interactions that existed not only between texts and texts, but the recycling of texts into speech, the transformation of speech into writing, and an oral remembering and dismembering of texts, all processes little or not at all understood in biblical scholarship. As a possible step toward clarifying the role of gospel narrativity in the tradition, however, the model of the three orders may prove helpful.

The tradition commenced with aphorisms and parables, the two units attributable to the historical Jesus. It seems inescapably obvious that they are primary phenomena of speech. As such they inhabit a world quite different from words that are fixed on papyrus to be seen. In the oral world, aphorisms and parables operate largely on acoustic principles. They constitute speech acts, consisting of pitches and pauses, stresses and silence. "In oral speech, the sound is the sign of the meaning" (Havelock 1978, 231). Put differently, meaning is a kind of rhythmic envelope. As long as aphorism and parable function orally, one may speak of a *first order of operation*. Although it is true that written words "are on the whole far more likely to be misunderstood than spoken words are" (Ong 1967, 115), hermeneutical complications were an inalienable part of oral tradition. Parables in particular created the need for interpretation in the tradition from its inception. Their metaphorical and withholding proclivities encouraged notions of secrecy, or insider versus outsider, and of revealing versus concealing. "Their kinship with the enigma cannot be too strongly emphasized" (Ricoeur 1975, 133). "He who has ears to hear, let him hear." But how does one hear parabolic story, and what did the parabolist intend to convey? Questions of this kind launch the process of interpretation. But in the first order of operation interpretation is not linked to fixed parable texts in the manner of Mark, who attached interpretive discourse to the parable of the sower. The oral transaction of aphorisms and parables consists in multiple recitals, tailored to specific circumstances, without the auditors' ever hearing them as departures from binding texts. In the absence of aphoristic and parabolic texts, one does not trade in originals and variants thereof. One knows no way of testing speech against fixed models. But the condition of interpretation exists from the outset, forcing hearers to wonder and ponder and the parabolist to adapt and restate.

With clustering, a *second order of operation* gets under way. Aphorisms and parables were collected and placed one next to the other in cluster arrangements or in dialogues set in slim narrative frames. Pheme Perkins, virtually the only New Testament scholar to use the categories developed by Walter Ong, has suggested that the genre of the revelation dialogue still operates within the conventions of oral tradition. Indeed, many of the Gnostic writings that have come to light at Nag Hammadi attracted predominantly speech material, much of which reflects "the liturgy, teaching, preaching and polemic of their respective communities" (1980, 201). In the case of the sayings and dialogue genres, Jesus' oral proclamations, his very spoken words, had fashioned for themselves gospels in their own right. Their primary interest was neither philosophical nor cosmological, but soteriological. To this end they sought to retain the living voice of Jesus and to extend it into the communal present. Yet all of this was accomplished through writing, and writing is deconstructive to the vital concerns of orality. While aphorisms and parables generally retained their oral form, a specific stage of the tradition was frozen, inviting comparison and disclosing thereby the interpretive nature of its materials. Wisdom showed itself to be the focal point of the Gospel of Thomas and the Son of Man apocalypticism of Q. The principle of clustering itself is not in the best interests of orality. As far as is known, oral conventions do not favor speaking in clusters of like materials. The compilation of sayings and parables, a textually contrived arrangement, invites reflection and analysis, further heightening the sense of interpretation. In this second order of operation interpretation becomes a self-conscious activity. This is evident from the first saying of the Gospel of Thomas, which summons hearers to the task of interpretation: "Whoever finds the explanation of these words will not taste death." The 114 sayings of Thomas require interpretation (*hermeneia*), and finding the right interpretation is perceived to be a matter of life and death. Despite the textual aspects of the sayings and dialogue genres, one must be mindful of the oral context of their functioning. The communities in which they originated did not look upon texts as the normative source of revelation and interpretation. While these gospels contained true tradition and continued the voice of Jesus, "truth is not [understood to be] definitively embodied in an inspired text. Gnostic interpretation is still the hermeneutic of an oral tradition" (Perkins 1980, 202). In different words, what mattered most was the experience of the Christ, of the Kingdom, or of Wisdom.

While the second order was (inter alia) committed to the two authentic speech acts, the narrative gospel in turn deprived aphorisms and parables of their oral status by subordinating them, together with a good deal of additional material, to the literary ordering of narrative. When reflecting, therefore, on the synoptic tradition from the perspective of its vital oral inception, something in the nature of a mutation suggests itself in the shifting from the second to the third order. Orality, the voice of the living Jesus, the ground and life of the tradition, and the very gospels of Jesus' proclamation were overruled by the more complex ordering of narrative textuality. It is, on this view, not entirely surprising that the third order of operation, the narrative configuration, asserted itself canonically in tension with the second order. Interpretation further intensified on this level. Insofar as Mark enacted an alternative to the sayings gospel, his narrative accomplished the interpretation of an interpretation. Ironically, Mark redescribed the second-order genre via the dynamics of parabolic reversal (Kelber 1983, 117–29). The narrative gospel reversed the inside view so as to subvert conventional expectations and placed an additional burden on its hearers/readers by forestalling closure. It was precisely this parabolic posture of the Markan narrative that solicited further interpretation. Here we can see how a narrative that had already come into existence by virtue of reinterpretation was itself destined to engender more interpretation. When viewed from the perspective of tradition history, therefore, Matthew and Luke are interpretations of the interpretation (= Mark) of an interpretation (= sayings gospel). Both Matthew and Luke domesticated the Markan narrative, blunting its parabolic edges and furnishing closure. No longer faced with Mark's task of correcting the sayings genre, they could open their gospels more readily to aphorisms and parables. The latter, however, had to comply with the rules of their respective narrative houses. In the end, orthodoxy would disallow the sayings gospel as a genre in its own right and would admit the second and first order of operation into the canon only through mediation of the third order. Narrative, the most thoroughly textualized piece, emerged as the victor in the canonical ratification of the synoptic tradition.

The time has come to include in my reflections a controversial item that, if proved authentic, further complicates our thinking about the tradition and the role of narrative within it. My reference is to the Secret Gospel of Mark. Space compels me to confine the review of this intricate case to its barest essentials. The discovery of Secret Mark dates back to 1958, when Morton Smith came across an incomplete copy of a letter of Clement of Alexandria at the Greek orthodox monastery of Mar Saba in the Judean desert (1973a, 1973b, 1982, 449–61). In this letter, written to an otherwise unknown Theodore, Clement cites a portion of Secret Mark. It is the story of a rich young man whom Jesus raises from the dead. Having been brought back to life, he loves Jesus and beseeches him that he might be with him. "After six days" the youth, "wearing a linen cloth over his naked body," spends a night with Jesus to be initiated into "the mystery of the Kingdom of God." Clement himself proposed that Secret Mark was a revision of canonical Mark, a view to some extent shared by Smith (1973a, 142; 1973b, 145, 163, 194). More recently, however, first Helmut Koester (1983, 35–37) and then Crossan (1985, 91–121) have advocated a reversal of the compositional sequence: canonical Mark has revised Secret Mark. Canonical Mark's revision is assumed to have been motivated by the Carpocratians, who gave the resurrection-baptismal story in Secret Mark a homosexual slant in the fashion of Gnostic libertinism. Faced with an exceedingly delicate situation, Mark proceeded to eliminate the explosive story by dismemberment and redistribution. In other words, canonical Mark is assumed to have scattered its textual debris across his own text. The naked young man now appears at the arrest (Mark 14:51–52), the motif of love is transferred to the story of the rich man and rephrased in the sense that Jesus loved him and not the reverse (Mark 10:17–22; cf. 10:21), the six days are connected with the transfiguration (Mark 9:2), the mystery of the kingdom is relocated after the public parable (4:11), and so forth. Having thus decomposed the controversial text, canonical Mark appears to have successfully met the Carpocratian scandal, for their erotic version would henceforth give the impression of having been secondarily produced out of bits and pieces from canonical Mark.

Bearing in mind that Secret Mark poses uncommonly labyrinthine problems that await a good deal more philological and historical work, we may at this stage draw four preliminary conclusions. First, there may well have been more narrative in the tradition before canonical Mark. Texts are never simply created out of lived experience, least of all perhaps biblical texts, which are multifariously enmeshed in tradition. It appears likely that there existed something of a Markan school tradition not unlike the one we have long recognized with respect to the Johannine materials. If Secret Mark indeed has priority over canonical Mark, we can only speculate as to the narrative impulse of the former. Our knowledge of the history of the synoptic tradition should caution us against assuming that in Secret Mark we have arrived at "pure" narrative equivalent to the bedrock of history. As Clement himself seems to indicate, the setting of Secret Mark was the Alexandrian baptismal ritual. Second, although we have known of the Gospels' involvement in tradition, canonical Mark may be more deeply and actively engaged than we ever thought possible. It can never be sufficiently stressed that fidelity to the *history* of its subject matter cannot account for the canonical narrative. I suspect we will increasingly find dependencies and displacement features in canonical Mark that testify to his wrestling with traditions. Crossan has reason to assert that canonical Mark was not only decomposing the resurrection-baptismal story of Secret Mark, but was also redacting Egerton Papyrus 2 (1985, 65–87) and revising the passion narrative of the Gospel of Peter (1985, 125–35). In all this, Crossan sees intertextuality triumphing in the tradition. Yet the principle of intertextuality, far from being simply a matter of hard evidence, is also a presupposition of our method. Trained to interpret texts, impressed by the ubiquity of texts, and working single-mindedly with texts, we are bound to discover intertextuality. But how is one to imagine—

technically, psychologically, religiously—Mark's skillful juggling of a number of texts, using them, revising them, deconstructing them, while all along composing an impressively coherent narrative? Are we not asking canonical Mark to juggle too many balls at once? At any rate, the larger the number of traditions we find canonical Mark coping with, the less persuasive or imaginable the principle of intertextuality becomes. Third, if canonical Mark does interact with multiple traditions, oral apperception seems to be the most plausible procedure. How could he have laboriously picked first from one text, then from another, revised one scrap of papyrus and scattered another? He is more likely to have operated from a memory that was in possession of a plurality of traditions. What to us textually bound scholars appears to be tight intertextuality may in hermeneutical actuality have been free composition, "especially in antiquity, when most writers, even in citing explicitly, cited from memory" (Smith 1973b, 143). Of all the traditions canonical Mark may have displaced, the genre of a sayings gospel still is my favorite candidate. Its deconstruction best explains the genre of the canonical narrative. Fourth, is Clement's view of the priority of canonical Mark over Secret Mark beyond all redemption? What if the naked young man at the arrest, owing to his enigmatic presence in the narrative, gave rise to the resurrection-baptismal story in Secret Mark on the one hand and to the Lazarus story in John on the other? If, in different words, Mark 14:51–52 was experienced as a narrative secret, an "indeterminacy gap," one proven way of coping with it is more narrative.

A reading of gospel narrativity from the angle of tradition history is currently not much in favor with many biblical critics who have embarked upon a literary examination of narrative. The study of the interior narrative world is now widely held to be incompatible with reflection on its possible involvement in tradition. What cannot in any circumstances be questioned is the significance of our growing sensitivity to the narrative quality of the gospels. To read narrative texts both as "mirrors" reflecting self-contained worlds and as "windows" opening upon the prenarrative history seems to be almost a violation of proper hermeneutical conduct. It is not entirely clear, however, whether biblical hermeneutics is categorically divisible into the literary versus the historical mode of interpretation, one having precedence over the other. Murray Krieger, from whom I borrow the metaphors of "mirror" and "window," sought to maintain their simultaneous functioning so that meaning arises "not just *through* the work and not just *in* the work but at once *through* and *in* the work as body" (1964, 28). Following Krieger's critical theory, perhaps we can arrive at a more judicious, less apodictic assessment of literary criticism if we locate the latter in the broader context of cultural, linguistic developments. If, for example, one traces the cultural history in terms of orality, scribality, and typography, then literary criticism in the exclusivist, "mirror" sense described above is most closely allied with typography, the phase dominated by printing. This deserves some explication.

The existence of speech appears odd when viewed from a literary perspective, because it "lacks" a visual, objectifiable presence. Oral words cannot be locked into space. They are uncontainable in formal, visual models. Bound to the authority of the speaker and inseparable from auditors, they are inevitably enmeshed in the human lifeworld. To regard spoken words as knowable in terms strictly of themselves and as operable apart from historical contextuality is a notion that has no conceivable reality in oral culture. Oral utterance cannot exist in transauthorial objectivity. Speech, we observed above, is rhythmically structured sound, and it acquires meaning as a contextual phenomenon. I must add here a caveat against understanding orality strictly in terms of sound, rhythm, acoustics, and human contextuality. Both ancient and medieval oral culture exhibited a visual element as well, not of course in the sense of external visualization of speech through writing, but as an inner visualization (Yates 1966). Mnemotechnics did not facilitate instant recall simply based on sound tracks drilled into the mind. They also involved the formation of memory images— that is, heroic figures, dramatic scenes, striking places, and so on. The ideal was to express everything one wanted hearers to retain in a way that encouraged imaging. A flourishing of imagination and visions, a rich inner visualized world, was an essential part of ancient oral operations.

With scribality the shift from sound to sight—external visualization—gets under way. Words written down enjoy a stable existence denied to spoken words. Demands on the *vis vivendi*, the most discriminating of the senses, intensify in scribal culture. "The eye lends distance to things, it makes them into objects" (Snell 1960, 33). Detachment, objectivity, abstraction, and introspection, all virtuous contributions to the civilizing process, benefit from the shift to scribality. The art of memory, however, the life of visions and imagination (the making of inner images), declines.[1] And yet the notion that texts, laboriously manufactured (handmade), relate interiorly back unto themselves, and only to themselves, is foreign to scribal hermeneutics. Contemporary scholars living in a typographically dominant civilization have rarely been trained to appreciate the ancient and medieval manuscript culture except through a consciousness shaped by the invention of printing. In her monumental work *The Printing Press as an Agent of Change* (1979), Elizabeth Eisenstein made the point that it is easier for us print-oriented people to understand orality than to grasp medieval, let alone ancient, scribality:

> The gulf that separates our experience from that of literate élites who relied exclusively on hand-copied texts is much more difficult to fathom. There is nothing analogous in our experience or in that of any living creature within the Western world at present. The conditions of scribal culture thus have to be artificially reconstructed by recourse to history books and reference guides. Yet for the most part, these works are more likely to conceal than to reveal the object of such a search. Scribal themes are carried forward, postprint trends are traced backward in a manner that makes it difficult to envisage the existence of a distinctive literary culture based on hand-copying. (1979, 1:9)

Manuscripts in scribal culture were not under the spell of the objectifying standards set by printing or high technology. Rarely, if ever, were ancient texts thought to be fully closed, and rarely, if ever, was a narrative text viewed as a hall of mirrors, reflecting nothing but internal relations. Both manufacture and use of manuscripts readily interacted with orality, be it through dictation or recitation. That most ancient manuscripts were meant to reach out toward readers, or more likely hearers, so as to influence their views and play on their emotions is something reception theorists have discovered only

---

1. Frances A. Yates (1966, passim) offers a brilliant explanation of the decline of the interiorly imaged world in the sixteenth century and the corresponding iconoclasm, that is, the destruction of external images. With the Reformation, memory was omitted from the discipline of rhetoric. The omission was, of course, closely linked with the invention of printing and an increased availability of pamphlets and books. What happened in Calvinism, and to some extent in Lutheranism, was a projection of the interior erasure toward the outside, resulting in the demolition of pictures that were often the artistic outcome of inner imaging: "There can be no doubt that an art of memory based on imageless dialectical order as the true natural order of the mind goes well with Calvinist theology" (1966, 237).

recently. Yet what today we call reader-response criticism was part of scribal hermeneutics, which by and large was still committed to the art of persuasion and unfriendly toward fully closed systems. This relative hermeneutical openness applies with special force to biblical manuscripts. Whether prose or poetry, epistle or narrative, wisdom or apocalypse, biblical texts aim at being heard, read, and actualized. More often than not they are the products of rewriting themselves, and in turn they can be subject to revision. And revising in biblical hermeneutics is not bound by modern standards of literalness but inspired by a passion for vivification through inspiration.

With printing, technical control over words reached a state of perfection unimaginable in chirographic culture. More than ever words took on the appearance of autosemantic objectivity. "Print encouraged the mind to sense that its possessions were held in some sort of inert mental space" (Ong 1982, 132). Centuries of interiorization of typographical consciousness gave birth to the Saussurian principle of integrity of language whereby meaning is figured as relations within language and not as reference to something outside it. Both the Russian formalism and the so-called New Criticism, though originating independently, epitomized typography in advocating the transauthorial autonomy of texts. In the light of these critical disciplines, narrative was understood as a system of interrelations rather than as a product of causes. Structuralism penetrated the interior world of texts ever more deeply. With respect to narrative, the hidden structure was given priority at the expense of the plotted story line. Genetic considerations were held to be irrelevant at worst and secondary at best as far as a proper understanding of narrative was concerned. Here we have come full circle back to our earlier observation about the hermetic, "mirror" type of literary criticism being a favorite child of typography. When placed in the broader context of cultural, linguistic processes, literary criticism of the formalist type appears to be flourishing at a stage in intellectual history when the technologizing, objectifying impact of printing has culminated in the apotheosis of the text as a closed system. Many biblical critics who have lately adopted literary criticism accepted it in this formalist mode. We turned to it enthusiastically, though somewhat unreflectively, out of disillusionment with centuries of grossly referential hermeneutics. In this situation, biblical narrative and even parable were appreciated as self-referential entities, standing on their own as aesthetic objects.

What bears repeating is the significance of the literary assessment of the Gospels. The analysis of their narrative nature not only is justifiable, it is imperative. In view of the long dominance of the historical paradigm in Gospel studies, literary criticism truly marks a Copernican revolution. Our task now is to move beyond formalism in literary theory and practice, although not in the sense of retreating to the older historical, philological model of interpretation. "A crucial test of the viability of contemporary criticism is whether it can formulate a program of literary history that uses the strengths of formalism and yet avoids its current impasse" (Hoy 1978, 9). To this end literary critics of the Gospels should become more circumspect about the degree to which not only narrative, the object of their study, but all our ways of approaching narrative and literature are inescapably bound up with language and its technological developments. Once we learn to see distinctions between a chirographically and a typographically informed hermeneutic and grasp a sense of the hermeneutics of revisionism and vivification typical of ancient biblical manuscripts, might we not grow more tolerant methodologically, acknowledging the Gospels both as integral narratives and as narrative participants in tradition, as documents of both synchronic integrity and diachronic depth? Or to put it more provocatively, are not the Gospels both "windows" and "mirrors," giving us worlds that interact with other worlds? In any case, fear of the "referential fallacy" should not cause us to disclaim the manifold ties the Gospels have with tradition, for no text is composed in complete referential neutrality—not in antiquity, and least of all in the biblical tradition.

To say that the Gospels work out of and respond to tradition is to suggest the possibility of undertaking the study of narrativity and tradition-historical analysis as mutually enriching and corrective enterprises. On the one hand, comprehension of a Gospel's linguistic and narrative world could well serve to revise our view of its relation to tradition. If, for example, a stylistically and literarily sensitive examination of the fourth Gospel were to show that the so-called aporias—ideological, stylistic, and contextual discrepancies—are integral to John's narrative rhetoric, a vital argument for the existence of the Gospel of Signs (Fortna 1970) would be called into question. Whatever the eventual outcome of the assumed Gospel of Signs, repetition of catchwords and phrases, a notable feature of Fortna's reconstruction, is dubious evidence for editorial activity. For redundancy, which in various degrees is common to all canonical Gospels, is first and foremost an index of the rhetorical style of ancient narrative prose. What to our modern perception of the flow of realistic narrative appears to be "repetition" was to the ancients a conventional, hearer-friendly mode of composition. Hence an analysis of the interior Gospel world may aid us in shaping, or even challenging, a view of tradition.

On the other hand, familiarity with a feature of tradition may illuminate Gospel narrativity. Discipleship in Mark, for example, is intelligible up to a point as a particular narrative enactment. Dan Via chose to interpret it as a pattern of contrast whereby the disciples act out the role of alazoon-opponents vis-à-vis the agonist-hero. It is a role primarily conditioned by the dramatic structure of comedy and only secondarily, if at all, by pressures outside narrative (1975, 45, 117). Joanna Dewey has carried the hermetic hermeneutics of narrative to its radical conclusion in suggesting that the key to discipleship in Mark was to be found nowhere but "in the needs of the narrative itself" (1984, 13). Since story thrives on conflict and the disciples do their very best to produce conflict, their role is intelligible as "the result of telling the gospel in the form of a story" (1984, 13). If, however, we rest content with the assumption that the disciples' conflict is narrated merely for the purpose of fulfilling narrative requirements, we deprive ourselves of raising deeper questions—or rather protect ourselves from them. To be sure, inasmuch as discipleship can be shown to fulfill a particular narrative emplotment, such as role reversal from insiders to outsiders, its function in the Gospel is understood. But the very logic of that emplotment, far from settling all our questions, prompts further inquiries. Whence this boldness to narrate the disciples' dysfunctional role? Why cast the very ones to the outside who are known to the narrator as the appointed insiders? Although we may know the mechanics of the discipleship plot, we still lack an answer concerning its motive. These are questions intrinsic to the narrative, yet not susceptible of explanation in terms of the narrative itself. If answers are not forthcoming from the interiority of the narrative, are we not entitled to turn to the larger frame of reference and to take note of narrative and tradition as intersecting worlds?

There is one component in the discipleship narration that Mark appears to have retrieved from tradition: the disciples' role as privileged insiders. The spotlight inevitably falls on Mark 4:1–34, the first of two major sayings collections in the Gospel. The pre-Markan formation of the core of this collection is almost universally acknowledged, though details of the reconstruction remain controversial. Here we encounter Jesus as speaker of parables and aphorisms, and the Twelve as privileged insiders. If one replaces the earthly Jesus with the living Lord, we have in fact arrived at a miniature model of the sayings gospel or, in Robinson's words, at the "immediate precursor of the Gospel of Thomas," where "much of this material recurs" (1982b, 47). Once we become sensitive to Mark's involvement in tradition, or rather to the traces tradition has left in Mark, it will no longer do to attribute the discipleship plot simply to the pleasure of telling a good story. For now we can read Mark's reversal of the disciples' fate as a subversion of the scenario of a sayings gospel. Given Mark's singular narrative focus on Jesus' earthly life culminating in death, the withholding of the risen Lord, and a reservation toward sayings, the reversal of the role of the disciples must not entirely surprise us, for all these features converge in revising the posture of a sayings gospel. In different words, Mark's narrative emplotment of discipleship is part and parcel of a revisionist text. We have arrived at an understanding of the mechanism of and the motivation for the discipleship plot in Mark. This goes to show that tradition history may indeed play a part in illuminating our understanding of Gospel narrativity.

As literary criticism of the Gospels commences in earnest, we do well not to lose sight of the interdependence that exists between the canonical narratives and the wider orbit of tradition. Exclusive attention to internal, synchronic relations is less than faithful to scribal hermeneutics. It may also, unwittingly perhaps, introduce a false sense of foundationalism. When viewed from the diachronic perspective, the Gospels reveal their interpretive status. They came into being under the pressures of interpretation. Whatever authority they exude, and however foundational an impression they may create, each Gospel is bound up with a process of interpretive traditioning. Given this state of affairs, anything resembling a foundational level is likely to elude us, whether it be that of history or of uninterpreted narrative. The first time we encounter narrative in the full light of canonicity, we encounter it not as the ground of tradition, but as a pattern of elementary tensions. It represents a revisionist text, intent on displacing the genre of the sayings gospel, and perhaps of other gospels. When Robinson referred to the transfiguration story as belonging to a tradition "suppressed in orthodox Christianity, and surviving in the New Testament canon only indirectly, at mislocated positions" (1970, 117 – 18 [1982a, 30]), he was employing, quite appropriately, the language of revisionist hermeneutics; suppression, indirect survival, and mislocation. In the Gospel of Thomas a strong precursor has literally returned, challenging conventional views of the traditioning process and of the rise of the narrative gospel. Strong precursors have a way of coming back, disclosing the present as displacement of the past.

Narrative as interpretation is a notion that readily crosses boundaries we have come to take for granted. If the canonical narrative was itself born in the act of interpretation, then readers faced with interpreting this narrative persist in an activity that is observable not only in Mark, but as far back as tradition will take us. Whether in our time we interpret by reading or preaching, through books or commentary, by augmentation or radical revision of anteriority, we are in the process of perpetuating interpretation. Both narrator as interpreter and interpreters of narrative jointly partake in the embracing activity of hermeneutical translations. This hermeneutical condition has been elevated by Gadamer to the level of an epistemological principle (1980). It does not seem feasible, from this perspective, to draw a firm line between the literary study of the Gospels and the analysis of their tradition history. For what distinguishes the canonical gospels from what preceded them is not primarily a matter of literature versus history, but rather one of interpretation turning canonical. Canonicity, far from terminating the interpretive impulse, ensured survival of the narrative gospel in a prestigious position, thus rendering it normative for the continuing history of interpretation. Nor can a categorical distinction be drawn between the Gospels as mirrors and as windows. Precisely because they participate in the ongoing discourse of tradition, narrative gospels contain traces of absent others that, though integrated into their respective gospel worlds, may serve as windows for those who know the scope of the tradition. When viewed from these perspectives, therefore, opposites such as narrative versus interpretation, literary versus historical readings, and mirror versus window views of language dissolve into the single overriding reality of interpretation. And interpretation is more than a matter of method and more than a manifestation of madness. It is our essential mode of living.

References

Alter, Robert. 1981. *The art of biblical narrative.* New York: Basic Books.
Auerbach, Erich. 1953. *Mimesis: The representation of reality in Western literature.* Princeton: Princeton University Press.
Barthes, Roland. 1977. *Image—music—text.* New York: Hill and Wang.
Boring, M. Eugene. 1977. The paucity of sayings in Mark: A hypothesis. In SBL *Seminar papers,* 371–77. Missoula, Mont.: Scholars Press.
———. 1982. *Sayings of the risen Jesus: Christian prophecy in the synoptic tradition.* SNTS MS. 46. Cambridge: Cambridge University Press.

Bultmann, Rudolf. 1963. *The history of the synoptic tradition.* New York: Harper and Row.

Crossan, John Dominic. 1975. *The dark interval: Towards a theology of story.* Niles, Ill.: Argus Communications.

———. 1983. *In fragments: The aphorisms of Jesus.* San Francisco: Harper and Row.

———. 1984. Language and creativity: Jesus as aphorist and parabler. Presentation at SBL/AAR/ASOR annual meeting in Chicago.

———. 1985. *Four other gospels: Shadows on the contours of canon.* Minneapolis: Winston Press.

Dewey, Joanna. 1984. Literary criticism and the Gospels: Meaning in narrative. Unpublished manuscript.

Eisenstein, Elizabeth L. 1979. *The printing press as an agent of change: Communications and cultural transformations in early-modern Europe.* 2 vols. Cambridge: Cambridge University Press.

Fortna, Robert T. 1970. *The Gospel of Signs: A reconstruction of the narrative source underlying the fourth Gospel.* SNTS MS. 11. Cambridge: Cambridge University Press.

Frei, Hans W. 1974. *The eclipse of biblical narrative: A study in eighteenth and nineteenth century hermeneutics.* New Haven: Yale University Press.

Gadamer, Hans-Georg. 1960. *Wahrheit und Methode: Grundzüge einer philosophischen Hermeneutik.* Tübingen: Mohr.

Hägg, Thomas. 1983. *The novel in antiquity.* Berkeley: University of California Press.

Havelock, Eric A. 1978. *The green concept of justice: From its shadow in Homer to its substance in Plato.* Cambridge: Harvard University Press.

Hoy, David Couzens. 1978. *The critical circle: Literature and history in contemporary hermeneutics.* Berkeley: University of California Press.

Kelber, Werner H. 1983. *The oral and the written gospel: The hermeneutics of speaking and writing in the synoptic tradition, Mark, Paul, and Q.* Philadelphia: Fortress Press.

———. 1985. From aphorism to sayings gospel, and from parable to narrative gospel. *Facets and Foundation Forum* 1:1–8.

Kermode, Frank. 1979. *The genesis of secrecy: On the interpretation of narrative.* Cambridge: Harvard University Press.

Koester, Helmut. 1983. History and development of Mark's Gospel (from Mark to Secret Mark and "canonical" Mark). In *Colloquy on New Testament studies: A time for reappraisal and fresh approaches,* 35–57. Macon, Ga: Mercer University Press.

Krieger, Murray. 1964. *A window to criticism: Shakespeare's sonnets and modern poetics.* Princeton: Princeton University Press.

Ong, Walter J. 1967. *The presence of the word: Some prolegomena for cultural and religious history.* New Haven: Yale University Press. (Reprinted, Minneapolis: University of Minnesota Press, 1981.)

————. 1982. *Orality and literacy: The technologizing of the word.* New York: Methuen.

Pagels, Elaine. 1979. *The Gnostic Gospels.* New York: Random House.

————. 1981. The orthodox against the Gnostics: Confrontation and interiority in early Christianity. In *The other side of God: A polarity in world religion,* ed. Peter L. Berger. Garden City, N.Y.: Anchor Doubleday.

Perkins, Pheme. 1980. *The Gnostic dialogue: The early church and the crisis of Gnosticism.* New York: Paulist Press.

Ricoeur, Paul. 1975. Biblical hermeneutics. *Semeia* 4:27–148.

————. 1984. From proclamation to narrative. *Journal of Religion* 64:501–12.

Robinson, James M. 1970. On the *Gattung* of Mark (and John). In *Jesus and man's hope,* 1:99–129. Pittsburgh: Pittsburgh Theological Seminary.

————. 1982a. On the *Gattung* of Mark (and John). In *The problem of history in Mark and other Marcan studies,* 11–39. Philadelphia: Fortress Press.

————. 1982b. Gnosticism and the New Testament. In *The problem of history in Mark and other Marcan studies,* 40–53. Philadelphia: Fortress Press.

————. 1982c. Jesus: From Easter to Valentinus (or to the Apostles' Creed). *Journal of Biblical Literature* 101:5–37.

Schneidau, Herbert N. 1976. *Sacred discontent: The Bible and Western tradition.* Baton Rouge: Louisiana State University Press.

Scholes, Robert, and Robert Kellogg. 1966. *The nature of narrative.* New York: Oxford University Press.

Smith, Morton. 1973a. *The Secret Gospel: The discovery and interpretation of the Secret Gospel according to Mark.* New York: Harper and Row.

————. 1973b. *Clement of Alexandria and a Secret Gospel of Mark.* Cambridge: Harvard University Press.

————. 1982. Clement of Alexandria and Secret Mark: The score at the end of the first decade. *Harvard Theological Review* 75:449–61.

Snell, Bruno. 1960. *The discovery of the mind: The Greek origins of European thought.* New York: Harper and Row.

Via, Dan O. 1975. *Kerygma and comedy in the New Testament: A structuralist approach to hermeneutic.* Philadelphia: Fortress Press.

White, Hayden. 1973. *Metahistory: The historical imagination in nineteenth-century Europe.* Baltimore: Johns Hopkins University Press.

————. 1978. *Tropics of discourse: Essays in cultural criticism.* Baltimore: Johns Hopkins University Press.

————. 1980. The value of narrativity in the representation of reality. *Critical Inquiry* 7:5–27.

Wrede, William. 1981. *The messianic secret.* Cambridge: T. and T. Clark. Originally published 1901.

Yates, Frances A. 1966. *The art of memory.* Chicago: University of Chicago Press.

4

Ceremonial Dialogues in South America

Greg Urban

In native South America there is a widely distributed ritualized form of linguistic interaction known as the ceremonial dialogue (Fock 1963, 219–30). This chapter explores this dialogic form from the point of view of a specific hypothesis about its semiotic functioning, namely, that ritualized dialogue is a sign vehicle constructed from characteristics of everyday conversational dialogue and is therefore an icon or "model of" that dialogue. At the same time, because ceremonial dialogues select only certain features, they are also "models for" ordinary conversation and, indeed, social interaction more generally. In particular, they convey a message about solidary linguistic and social interaction.

If ceremonial dialogues are models for solidary interaction throughout native South America, the dialogues within a given culture convey as well as culture-specific message about solidarity, that is, a message about how cohesion is and should be achieved in that society. This culture-specific message is communicated by means of an indexical connection between the ceremonial dialogic form, as sign vehicle, and the type of linguistic interaction for which it is employed—negotiation, myth telling, greeting, and so forth—as meaning, as well as by a culture-specific iconicity. Ceremonial dialogue, as highly salient linguistic behavior, draws attention to itself and to the linguistic interaction for which it is employed. Simultaneously, because it embodies a cross-linguistic ideal of sociability, it suggests that that linguistic interaction is itself an instance of social solidarity.

From an analytical point of view, a distinction can be made between "semantic" and "pragmatic" dialogues. The concept of a semantic dialogue corresponds with ordinary notions of dialogue, wherein there are "turns" at speaking. A "turn" implies a semantic contribution on the part of a speaker and specifically excludes what are sometimes called "back channel responses," that is, hearer responses that punctuate the main speaker's "turn," such as "uh-huh" in English, keeping the linguistic interaction going but not contributing to the overall semantic meaning. Not all native South American ceremonial dialogues are semantic dialogues of this sort. However, they are all "pragmatic dialogues"; they are dialogic in the special sense of counting "back channel response" as a turn at speaking. By virtue of a palpable rhythm of alternation, all South American ceremonial dialogues foreground such pragmatic turn taking.

In what follows, I demonstrate the utility of this hypothesis by investigating the formal characteristics of ceremonial dialogues, showing what image of ordinary conversation they embody and how, as sign vehicles, they achieve salience. I then show that the dialogues in fact occur in social situations where solidarity is at issue, namely, interactions involving maximum social distance between participants and consequently an ever-present possibility of conflict.[1] Finally, I examine the type of linguistic interaction for which ceremonial dialogue is employed, together with the social context in which it is used, to show that dialogues are in fact drawing attention to culturally specific mechanisms for the production and maintenance of solidarity, thereby suggesting how social cohesion can be achieved.

The Ethnographic Cases

This chapter considers five ethnographic cases: (1) the classic Carib style of ceremonial dialogue as found among the Walwai of Guiana and the Trio of the Brazil-Suriname border; (2) ceremonial dialogues of the Yanomamö Indians of the Brazil-Venezuela border region; (3) ritualized dialogic "greetings" of the Jivaroan Shuar and Achuar of eastern Ecuador; (4) dialogic gathering house chanting of the Kuna Indians of the San Blas islands in Panama; and (5) dyadic origin-myth telling style of the Gê-speaking Shokleng Indians of southern Brazil.

Fock reports the possible occurrence of ceremonial dialogue in forty-two South American Indian societies (1963, 219ff.). These are

1. The germ of this hypothesis is contained in Rivière (1971), which demonstrates a correlation between social distance and the ceremonial dialogue for the Trio. Before Rivière Fock (1963, 219) had suggested the connection between the dialogues and situations of potential social conflict. The present analysis builds upon these earlier correlational hypotheses.

concentrated primarily to the north of the Amazon basin. However, for many of these societies data are simply too fragmentary to allow determination of whether the phenomena at all resemble those discussed here. I prefer to focus on cases where good ethnographic description is available, with transcribed texts or tape recordings of actual dialogues (or both).

The classic Carib pattern was known originally through the descriptions of Fock (1963, 216–30, 303–16), who himself observed the phenomenon known as *oho-karï* ("yes saying") among the Waiwai. The materials available include detailed descriptions of the formal linguistic and contextual features, as well as of social purposes, and translations of two actual dialogues. Waiwai ceremonial dialogues involve two typically elder men, who sit on stools opposite one another. One man takes the lead, speaking in short sentences, which among the Waiwai are uttered in a "special chant-tone . . . with rising pitch at the end" (1963, 216). After each sentence or sentence fragment, the respondent utters *oho* ("yes").

A variant of the Carib pattern has been described for the Trio by Rivière (1971, 235–38, passim; 1971, 293–311), who distinguishes three types of dialogue, all showing certain common characteristics. In the most formal type *(nokato)*, two men sit on stools, as among the Waiwai. The lead man speaks in short sentences, each containing at the end a rhyming word *(kara* or *t me)*. The second man responds with a "low murmuring grunt" (Rivière 1971, 299). In the least formal type, known as *tes miken,* no rhyming word is used, and the respondent utters the word *ir r* ("that's it"). In addition, the speakers need not sit on stools, and indeed women sometimes participate in this kind of dialogue. The intermediate type of dialogue, known as *sip sip man,* is also formally intermediate, lacking the rhyming word but using either the grunt or *ir r* in responses.

Regarding Yanomamö ceremonial dialogues, we have a reasonably extended account by Cocco (1972, 326–30) and one by Migliazza (1978), a description by Shapiro (1972, 149–51), and numerous brief references in other ethnographic accounts. In addition, one such dialogue can be observed in the Chagnon and Asch film *The Feast.* There we see two men facing in the same direction, one squatting in front of the other, engaging in a rapid back-and-forth dialogue, in which the speaker behind leads with a one- to three-syllable utterance and the speaker in front responds at regular intervals with another one to three syllables. Shapiro (1972, 150) mentions a more "intense form of ritualized conversation" (*yaimu*) in which partners are "seated together on the ground locked in a tight embrace, sometimes even groin to groin and with legs intertwined." The speech alternation is "so rapid that the two are often exchanging monosyllabic utterances."

The Jivaroan Shuar and Achuar ceremonial dialogues have recently been described in detail by Gnerre (1984), although they were reported earlier by various observers, notably Karsten (1935), and indeed Harner's (1972b) recording of Shuar music includes an example of the ceremonial greeting. Janet Hendricks, who has recently returned from two years among the Shuar, has also made available a tape of Shuar war dialogues. At least two types of ceremonial dialogue must be distinguished for Shuar and Achuar: a "greeting" used in visits between settlements and a "war dialogue" used when warriors arrive in the house of a leader who takes them into battle. Both types occur inside the house. In greetings, the interlocutors are seated across from one another. The lead speaker utters a short sentence to which the respondent replies with a monosyllabic word like "yes," "wow," "true." War dialogues take place from a standing position, with each speaker moving back and forth in time with his speech.

For Kuna, Sherzer (1983) supplies detailed descriptions of "gathering house chanting" performed by chiefs, although there are also older accounts of this *onmakket* ("gathering house") style (e.g., Wassén 1949, 46–54; Holmer 1951, 16–21). Sherzer has also made available tapes and transcriptions of actual instances of this ceremonial dialogue. In Kuna ceremonial dialogues, two interlocutors—the chief and his respondent—lie in hammocks slung next to one another in the communal gathering house. The chief chants a line characterized by a distinctive, generally falling intonation contour (Sherzer 1983, 52–53). As he protracts the final vowel of this line, the respondent enters in with a harmonized *teki* ("indeed"), the final vowel here in turn being protracted, at which point the lead speaker begins another line. The entire Kuna performance is distinctly musical.

For data on the Shokleng dyadic origin-myth telling style, known as *wãñeklèn*, I drew upon my own field research (see Urban 1984, 1985 for analyses of this style), which involved the tape recording and transcription of actual instances of origin-myth telling. A brief description had been given earlier by Jules Henry (1941, 126). In the *wãñeklèn*, two men sit opposite one another in the middle of the plaza, their legs entwined in a manner reminiscent of the Yanomamö. One interlocutor leads, utterring the first syllable of the origin myth. The respondent repeats that syllable, after which the first speaker utters the second syllable, and so forth, in rapid-fire succession. Speakers move their heads and upper torsos rhythmically in time with the syllables, which are shouted with extreme laryngeal and pharyngeal constriction.

Formal Characteristics of the Ceremonial Dialogues

Cycles and Pragmatic Turns

All ceremonial dialogues analyzed here involve taking "pragmatic turns." One speaker utters a stretch of speech—a syllable, word, line, or sentence—and this constitutes his pragmatic turn at speaking. The respondent replies with another stretch of speech—a syllable, word, line, or sentence—that constitutes his turn. Initial turn and response taken as a unit I call a "cycle." Within a given type of ceremonial dialogue, the cycle is organized in a characteristic way. However, in each case the cycle achieves an acoustic prominence through its temporal regularity, making a veritable "best" discernible.

The extreme cases in this regard are the Shokleng and the Kuna. Among the Kuna, cycles are so long that it becomes difficult to speak of a cycle "beat," although, because of the musical character of these dialogues, an actual beat can be tapped out during a given pragmatic turn. Measurements of two instances show that Kuna cycles are in fact remarkably regular. The cycle may be represented graphically as follows:

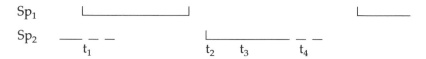

Sp_1 represents the lead speaker and Sp_2 the respondent. The cycle begins at time t_1. Typically, the voice of the respondent can be detected at the outset, as he completes a response to the previous utterance. However, his voice trails off with declining pitch and intensity, making it difficult to determine precisely where his response ends. The onset of the lead speaker, however, is unmistakable. He proceeds to chant a line of narrative, consisting on average of twenty-five syllables. At t_2 the respondent begins to utter the word *teki* ("indeed"), the onset of this word overlapping the drawing out of the final vowel by the lead speaker. At t_3 the lead speaker completes his line, while the respondent protracts the final vowel of *taki* until beyond t_4, when the lead speaker begins the next line. One complete cycle lasts from t_1 until t_4.

Measurements of elapsed times involved in Kuna cycles reveal a regularity. A study of one text, containing eleven lines, yielded the following results:

	Average	Standard Deviation	Maximum Range
t_1-t_2	11.08	1.03	10.2–13.5
t_2-t_3	0.59	0.40	0.2–1.4
t_3-t_4	4.82	0.40	4.4–5.4

An entire cycle typically lasts about 16.5 seconds.

Further study shows that there is variation between different occurrences of this style as regards the average times but that the differences are not great. Moreover, within a given telling there is consistency despite the divergence between tellings. For example, in the results from a second instance of Kuna chanting, the length of lead speaker–respondent overlap is systematically greater than in the first instance.

	Average	Standard Deviation	Maximum Range
t_1-t_2	11.54	0.61	10.7–12.2
t_2-t_3	2.68	0.43	2.2–3.1
t_3-t_4	6.64	0.67	6.1–7.4

It is important to recognize that overlaps between turns form an integral part of Kuna ceremonial dialogues. Because the two speakers are actually chanting, their voices may be described in terms of "musical," as opposed to "speech," pitch. At the t_2-t_3 overlap especially, the two voices harmonize, giving hearers the impression of a totality of discourse created by cooperation. This harmonizing contrasts markedly with the aggressive-sounding overlap between speakers found in Shuar war dialogues.

If the Kuna provide a limiting case in the direction of extremely long cycles, the Shokleng provide a limit in the direction of short cycles. Here a "turn" consists in uttering only a single syllable. Normally there is no overlap between turns. One can imitate the *wãñeklèn* style by oneself doubling each syllable one utters, while maintaining a fluid, uninterrupted flow of sound, stressing each syllable and articulating it with a constricted pharynx and larynx. Measurements show an average cycle length of some 0.58 seconds, as contrasted with 16–21-second cycles among the Kuna. The rhythm of cyclicity in Shokleng is simultaneously signaled by head and body movements.

The other cases of South American ceremonial dialogue range between these extremes. In the absence of tapes, I have been unable to do measurements on the Waiwai and Trio ceremonial dialogues. Nevertheless, the existence of a palpable rhythm of cyclicity is borne out by Rivière (1971, 298), who refers to even the least formal variety of Trio ceremonial dialogue as "readily distinguishable from everyday speech both by the speed at which it is carried on and by the continual and formalized response of *ir r*, which gives the conversation a slightly staccato effect." He adds (Rivière 1971, 309 n. 10): "After I had been among the Trio a few days only and while busy writing in my hammock, my attention was drawn to it by the change in rhythm of the conversation going on around me." Some idea of cyclicity can be had from the brief transcription he supplies (Rivière 1971, 309 n. 14). The lead speaker's turns involve uttering between five and ten syllables, as contrasted with an average of twenty-five syllables among the Kuna and one syllable among the Shokleng.

Among Shuar-Achuar, in samples measured, the lead speaker's turn lasts typically only 1.37 seconds, during which time he utters on average 7.4 syllables. Average syllable length here is thus 0.19 seconds, and the overall average including response is just 0.21. This contrasts with the Shokleng case, where syllables take nearly 0.29 seconds to produce, and the Kuna, where the average syllable length is 0.64 seconds.

In Shuar-Achuar cycles there is generally no overlap between lead and response turns. Indeed, there may be a slight (0.20–0.30 second) pause. However, there is often overlap at the other end. The lead speaker frequently begins his utterance as the respondent's trails off. This does not produce a musical effect, as among the Kuna. Rather, one senses an aggressive penetration of the respondent's speaking time by the lead speaker.

Judging from the descriptions, Yanomamö dialogues seem to vary in cycle length. Analysis of the Chagnon and Asch filmed example suggests that lead speaker and respondent utter between one and three syllables per pragmatic turn, the average cycle length being equal to that of the Shokleng *wãñeklèn* (5.8 seconds). Cocco (1972, 330, passim) refers to repeated occurrence of *trisílabos*, and Shapiro (1972, 150) mentions an especially rapid form in which the pragmatic turn is reduced to a monosyllable, as among the Shokleng. The rhythmical nature of the Yanomamö cycle can be sensed in any case. Acoustically, this dialogue is most reminiscent of Shuar-Achuar ceremonial greetings, though it sounds not unlike the Shokleng *wãñeklèn*.

For each tribe considered here, there is a distinctive cycle associated with the ceremonial dialogues. The Kuna cycle is long, syllables are uttered slowly and in a chanted voice, and there is an emphasis on harmonic overlap between turns. Among the Shokleng the cycle is short, syllables are uttered rapidly in a shouted voice, and there is no overlap between turns. The other types of ceremonial dialogue seem to range between these extremes. However, Shuar-Achuar dialogues are noteworthy as well for their aggressive character, manifested in the penetration of the respondent's speaking time by the lead speaker.

Despite the diversity, an important similarity underlies all of these dialogues. In each case, alternation between speakers is regularized. Simultaneously, the alternating character itself is foregrounded. This regularization draws attention to the entire linguistic interaction, suggesting that the interaction is something of note, something distinct from the ordinary run of events.

At the same time, a regularized pragmatic cycle is a way of making a metapragmatic comment on the linguistic interaction in which it occurs. It labels the interaction as "dialogic," as involving the coordinated efforts of two speakers. Performing these dialogues requires skill and practice on the part of performers, who must pay attention to the other person and coordinate their own behavior with his behavior in mind. In this sense ceremonial dialogues become a model of and for coordination more generally, this coordination in turn representing a fundamental building block of social solidarity.

Finally, by regularizing the pragmatic cycle, ceremonial dialogues remove timing of response from the sphere of possible actor manipulation. In ordinary conversation, interlocutors can manipulate this timing, as in American English, by increasing the rate of pragmatic response signals that one is about to take over the semantic turn. In ceremonial dialogues such manipulation is not possible, and there is consequently introduced a norm of "politeness," in the sense of hearing the other speaker out without interfering. This is another component of the cross- linguistic model of solidarity built into ceremonial dialogic process.

The Pragmatic Response

A striking characteristic of South American dialogues concerns the limitations placed upon possible pragmatic responses. These are positive or affirmative responses designed to keep the dialogue going, in keeping with their "back channel" nature. They are not semantic responses to the lead speaker's statement.

The classic case is the Waiwai ceremonial dialogue, which is literally called "yes saying" *(oho-karï)*. According to Fock (1963, 216), "After each sentence the opponent answers with a hardly audible 'oho,' that is, 'yes.' " Judging from two dialogues (Fock 1963, 303–16), this "yes" is never a semantic response to a previously formulated yes/no question. Instead, the response indicates that the interlocutor is comprehending what the lead speaker has to say. It is a form of acknowledgment, as in the following excerpt (Fock 1963, 217):

I want your hair-tube	oho
so I came	oho
you live here	oho
have lots of beads	oho
you can make another one	oho

A similar pattern is found among the Trio. Rivière (1971, 298–99) reports that for the least formal type of dialogue, the response is *ir r* ("that's it"), and for the most formal "a low murmuring grunt," which we must presume indicates acknowledgment or comprehension. Judging from the one excerpt of a marriage negotiation dialogue (Rivière 1971, 309, n. 14), the lead speaker again merely states his case:

I have come
I am good
things I am wanting
your daughter I want
my wife, I want
my woman, her being, I want

The desire is formulated in declarative terms, with the respondent replying affirmatively. The affirmative reply, however, only acknowledges that the lead speaker has that desire. It does not indicate that the respondent will in fact help to fulfill it by making his daughter available to the speaker.

Waiwai and Trio ceremonial dialogues suggest a delicacy in language use, in which the speaker is allowed to state a desire but does not press for an immediate yes/no response. The respondent in turn acknowledges the desire but does not thereby agree to do anything about it. Positive initiative is still left with him. Simultaneously, however, interlocutors are kept in the dialogue by the foregrounded pragmatic turn taking, which constitutes one overt social purpose of the interaction, and which both interlocutors strive to maintain.

Among the Kuna, response is again systematically affirmative, the lead utterance being followed by a *teki* ("indeed") or occasionally, apparently, an affirmative realized phonetically as [*ayie*]. Since Kuna dialogue is used for narration, the lead speaker's semantic turn is typically an actual monologue. Here the respondent's affirmation acknowledges the lead statement and simultaneously makes the semantic monologue appear as a pragmatic dialogue. This is of importance in connection with the culture-specific notion of solidarity embodied, to be discussed subsequently.

The Shokleng *wãñeklèn* seems anomalous in this context, since the respondent utters exactly the same syllable he has just heard from the lead speaker. However, the Shokleng repetition response is actually a signal of comprehension as well. The model for the *wãñeklèn* style is the "teaching" style (Urban 1984). The Shokleng method of teaching is to have a learner repeat verbatim, syllable by syllable, what he has just heard. If the imitation is judged incorrect, the teacher repeats the syllable until the learner has pronounced it correctly. This is the method, indeed, used in teaching the origin myth itself to initiates. Repetition is an affirmation and, in particular, a sign of comprehension, just as *teki* indicates affirmation and comprehension among the Kuna.

In Shuar-Achuar dialogues, the respondent has available various possible responses. In one text (Gnerre 1984), seven distinct response types occur, including *chua* ("wow"), *nekása* ("true"), and even *tsaa* ("no"), which occurs in two out of fifty turns, although here it is probably used in an affirmative sense vis-à-vis a negative statement. There are also cases where the respondent actually repeats the line uttered by the lead speaker, something that is an echo of the Shokleng pattern. Finally, at certain points, typically at changeovers of semantic turn, the two interlocutors are both uttering sentences. Although the Shuar-Achuar pattern is distinctive, it fits squarely into the general pattern of pragmatic acknowledgment found in other South American ceremonial dialogues.

For the Yanomamö, Cocco indicates that the respondent repeats what the speaker says or requests (1972, 326). Response is again an expression of comprehension, functioning to keep the two interlocutors interacting. Moreover, the respondent can make alternative but pragmatically equivalent responses, and these include repetition of the last syllable of what has just been uttered (Migliazza 1978, 574), once again echoing the Shokleng pattern.

From translated texts, it appears that the Yanomamö are more overt than the Waiwai and Trio in pressing their demands through dialogue, as in the following excerpt (Cocco 1972, 326), for which, unfortunately, the pragmatic responses are not indicated: "Give me, give me, nephew. Give me, give me an axe. They have have told me that you have axes." However, despite the pressing character of the statements, participation in the ceremonial dialogue keeps interlocutors interacting for some time, each making his case, until the entire issue has been thoroughly talked out. In this regard, Yanomamö dialogues are analogous to those discussed previously. They estabish a norm of linguistic interaction in which each side is heard out at length.

In all cases, ceremonial dialogues foreground pragmatic dialogicality, with the pragmatic response signaling comprehension simultaneously as it cues the lead speaker to continue. It does not commit the respondent in any way to what has been semantically said. Because of its saliency, the pragmatic response cycle itself becomes a sign vehicle. While it imitates ordinary conversation, in which back channel responses play a constant part, it also becomes a "model for" how conversation—and in particular the conversation at hand—ought to proceed.

If solidarity consists of coordinating one's actions with actions of another, as imaged in the pragmatic cycle, it also consists of a positive acknowledgment of the other, a due sign that one has taken cognizance of the actions of the other and has comprehended their "meaning." Through regularization of pragmatic response, ceremonial dialogues embody an icon of the general semiotic character of a solidary relationship. Simultaneously, these dialogues suggest indexically that solidarity is present in the specific linguistic interaction in which it is employed; that is, they are also "models for" solidarity.

Because pragmatic response is formally constrained—it must be a signal of comprehension—what is again a variable in ordinary conversation is fixed in ceremonial dialogue. The pragmatic response may not be used to convey an opinion about the lead speaker's utterance or to take over the semantic turn, as is common in everyday conversation. The respondent may only signal his acknowledgment, and this aids in the establishment of a norm of hearing the other out.

Contexts of Use

During ceremonial dialogues, the resources are removed from individual control and made part of a culturally imposed regime, to which participants in the dialogue are subject. The purposes of linguistic interaction must be accomplished, therefore, using highly restricted means, once again constraining interlocutors to hear the other out. Simultaneously, insofar as ceremonial dialogues are also models for linguistic and social interaction more generally, these limitations contribute to the modeling of solidary interaction.

However, to establish the "natural" or cross-cultural function of ceremonial dialogues as models of and for solidary interaction, it is not sufficient to demonstrate that we can interpret the formal regularities, isolated by comparative means, in this way. It is necessary to show as well that the dialogues are actually employed in contexts where solidarity is an issue. In this regard there is a range of possible contexts in which solidarity may be called into question, and these can vary from culture to culture. From a comparative point of view, however, solidarity is always called into question when the relationship between actors is in social terms maximally distant. I wish to demonstrate that in each of the societies discussed, ceremonial dialogues are in fact employed in the maximally distant relationships. The proposition is an implicational one. The dialogues may be employed in other, less distant relationships, but if they are, they are also employed in the more distant ones.

Rivière sums this up for the Trio by saying that the "ceremonial dialogue is used between strangers or kin and acquaintances between whom the relationship has temporarily lapsed" (1971, 301). Trio society is organized into villages, which are in turn arranged in "agglomerations," which are in turn ordered in terms of "groups." According to Rivière, the "ceremonial dialogue is not used within the boundaries of the agglomeration" (1971, 304). It is used when individuals visit between villages of different agglomerations or groups—that is, when the relationship is maximally distant.

It is difficult to obtain a clear picture of Waiwai society in this regard. *Oho-kari* can be used within the village, for example, in the chief's appeal to communal work or in connection with a death (Fock 1963, 217–18). However, it is also used between villages in negotiating trade and marriage and in issuing invitations to feasts. Fock (1963, 219) argues that in general it occurs in social situations where conflicts might otherwise erupt. His ethnographic generalization is in keeping with the proposition put forth here.

Among the Yanomamö, ceremonial dialogue is exclusively associated with "the feast," which occurs during visits between two villages (Chagnon 1977, 146–69). Yanomamö society is organized into villages that are largely autonomous and that are in frequent conflict with one another. Feasts are the principal mechanism for establishing intervillage alliances, which in turn ensure peace, allow for trade and marriage exchange, and furnish military allies. However, according to Chagnon's descriptions, intervillage alliances are always fragile, and feasts frequently erupt in violent intervillage confrontations. Migliazza also notes that ceremonial dialogic style is "most practiced" and idiomatic usages are most common in "areas where warfare is more intense" (1978, 573). It is safe to infer that ceremonial dialogues in fact occur in contexts where conflict is close to the surface.

Kuna social structure is of a different, more hierarchical, nature. Ceremonial dialogues take place within the "gathering house" in each village and may be performed by "chiefs" exclusively for members of the village (Sherzer 1983, 73–76). However, chanting also occurs during chiefly visits between villages of a given island and on the occasion of the more formal interisland visits (1983, 91–98). While ceremonial dialogues operate within the village, therefore, perhaps even there helping to create solidarity—indeed, Sherzer himself has remarked that the purpose of Kuna gatherings is to maintain "social control and social cohension" (1983, 89)—they also function in more distant relationships where social solidarity is definitely at issue.

The same may be said for the Shuar-Achuar, though here the fundamental residential unit was traditionally the "household" (Harner 1972a, 41, 77–80), there having been no multihousehold villages analogous to those found in the other tribes under consideration. Ceremonial dialogues took place on the occasion of interhousehold visiting (Gnerre 1984), which, as with intervillage feasting among the Yanomamö, was a situation fraught with danger owing to the general condition of feuding that prevailed. A variant form of dialogue also took place when men assembled for a war party. In addition to establishing solidarity within the war party, these dialogues, with their aggressive-sounding display, probably functioned to key up the participants for battle.

Among the Shokleng, the *wãneklèn* is performed during the communal ceremonies associated with death. Significantly, the Shokleng have no peaceful intervillage relations, villages being traditionally the highest level of social integration. Moreover, death ceremonies typically took place during reunions of different trekking groups, in the days before the Shokleng were permanently settled. The relationships involved were of maximum social distance within the limits established by this tribe. Moreover, when village fissioning did occur, it typically did so along trekking-group lines. The Shokleng pattern thus conforms to the general proposition.

Ceremonial dialogues are everywhere used in interactions where the participants are maximally distant in social terms. In four of the six groups sampled here—Shokleng, Shuar-Achuar, Trio, and Yanomamö—ceremonial dialogues occur only in contexts of maximum social distance. In the other two, they occur in the maximally distant relationships but also in closer ones. Evidently a "natural" linkage exists between these contexts of potential conflict and the ceremonial dialogue itself. The semiotic arguments put forth above make sense of this linkage. Ceremonial dialogue, as a cross-culturally definable form of linguistic interaction, is a model of and for social solidarity.

Types of Linguistic Interaction and Solidarity

Thus far no attention has been given to the overt communicative purposes of the linguistic interaction involved in South American ceremonial dialogues. In fact, this is the one aspect of the phenomenon that varies most widely. I propose that the purpose or type of linguistic interaction correlates with the culture-specific model of solidarity operating in the given society. Here three typological poles may be distinguished: (1) societies wherein the basis of solidarity is seen as exchange of material items or women or both; (2) societies wherein solidarity is seen to emerge from the sharing of a common culture and common traditions; (3) societies wherein solidarity is portrayed as the result of a "balance of power." The Yanomamö, Waiwai, and Trio—tribes clustered in the northern South American area—fall closer to the first type. The Kuna and Shokleng, very distant from one another geographically—the Kuna being in Panama and the Shokleng in southern Brazil—can nevertheless be typologically grouped under the second. Finally, the Shuar-Achuar, of the western Amazonian region, conform more closely to the third.

The Kuna and Shokleng are tribes wherein the overt communicative purpose of the dialogues is semantically monologic. Among the Shokleng, ceremonial dialogic form is used exclusively in connection with narration of the origin myth, which can also be told in narrative style by a single narrator. Among the Kuna, dialogic form is used by chiefs for narrating myths, histories, reports of personal experience, "metacommunicative descriptions" of the gathering itself, and counseling (Sherzer 1983, 76–89).

From the point of view of the present hypothesis, ceremonial dialogic form functions to define these communicative situations as "dialogic," despite the underlying semantic monologicality of the discourse. Ceremonial dialogicality suggests that, for monologic communication to be successful, it is necessary that there be present a listener who is actually comprehending what has been said. Of course, in the Shokleng and Kuna cases, the pragmatic respondent is only one among many listeners. His pragmatic response signals comprehension to the narrator, but it simultaneously communicates to the audience the importance of comprehension. The audience hears the lead speaker, but it also hears the respondent, and the interaction between speaker and pragmatic respondent comes to the fore as a model of (and for) the communicative process itself, suggesting the necessity that the audience play an active role in listening if communication is to be successful.

This suggests that among the Kuna and Shokleng the basis of solidarity is the sharing of a common culture and, especially, of common linguistically transmitted traditions. The transmission process, which is at the heart of sharing, comes to the fore as the principal type of linguistic interaction for which ceremonial dialogic form is employed. What makes two individuals cohere in these societies is their shared knowledge of the world. In effect, like is seen as attracting like.

Among the Waiwai, there is a different conception operating, one reflected in the semantically dialogic nature of ceremonial discourse. In some cases considerable stretches of semantic monologue appear within this overarching semantic dialogue. In one dialogue translated by Fock, the longest single semantic turn is 468 lines, the line here being defined by the *oho* response (1963, 303–12). This is comparable in length to an entire myth narrative. However, among the Waiwai, there is always a semantic response. In the dialogue mentioned above, the first turn lasts two lines and is followed by the 468-line turn mentioned. This is followed by a 219-line response. The other dialogue reported by Fock consists of two semantic turns, the first consisting of 255 lines and the second of 52 lines (1963, 312–16).

The Waiwai ceremonial dialogue is apparently used exclusively for semantic dialogues. Fock reports that there is actually a pragmatic cue for indicating change of semantic turn; the lead speaker "terminates the first phase of the *oho* by a sentence falling in pitch or by a humming sound" (1963, 216). Semantic turn taking is built into the very structure of the Waiwai *oho*.

Implicitly, semantic dialogue means that each participant makes a distinctive contribution to the single totality of ongoing discourse. Neither individual alone could produce the desired effect. This stands in sharp contrast to the Kuna and Shokleng system, in which only one individual is necessary for production of the semantic content and in which, if two individuals do produce semantic content, that content is the same. Among the Waiwai, the contribution of each individual must be distinct. If there is a culture-specific model of solidarity built into the Waiwai ceremonial dialogue, it is one in which solidarity is produced through the distinctive contributions of two individuals to a single whole. In effect, different attracts different.

The Waiwai dialogues are associated with situations of actual exchange of material goods and with marriage (Fock 1963, 217). Underlying the model of solidarity embodied in the notion of semantic dialogue, therefore, is a material counterpart.

A similar pattern is found among the Trio and Yanomamö. Rivière does not describe the semantically dialogic character of Trio ceremonial dialogues, but his discussion leaves no doubt that they are of this nature, each participant making a distinctive contribution. He describes the dialogue as a form of "verbal duel which is won by the man who can go on arguing the longest" (1971, 299), and also as resembling the "institutionalized haggling of the marketplace" (1971, 302). Simultaneously, as among the Waiwai, dialogues are used in situations of actual exchange. Indeed, in contrast to the Waiwai, ceremonial dialogues function virtually exclusively in this connection. Rivière remarks that they have "three main purposes: to receive visitors or announce one's arrival in a village, to trade, and to obtain a wife" (1971, 301). The overall pattern conforms to that found among the Waiwai and reflects a model of solidarity grounded in exchange.

The Yanomamö dialogues translated by Cocco are all semantically dialogic in character, with semantic turns being comparatively short, the equivalent of at most a few Waiwai lines. Again, the dialogues are used primarily in connection with exchange transactions. Cocco confirms Shapiro's observations in this regard, claiming that the dialogues are used to perform economic exchanges, to make invitations, to plan marriages, or to make general announcements (1972, 326). Evidently, as among the Waiwai, these dialogues embody a model in which solidarity is produced through the distinctive contributions of two individuals rather than through the sharing of common traditions.

Trio, Waiwai, and Yanomamö ceremonial dialogues are never used in the narration of myths and legends; Kuna and Shokleng dialogues are never used in negotiations surrounding trade and marriage. This does not mean, however, that a perfectly sharp distinction exists between these groups as regards the dialogic versus monologic character of discourse on the semantic plane. In fact, as Sherzer describes, when Kuna chiefs visit between villages, they take turns addressing the gathering: "First the visiting 'chief' chants and his host serves as responder . . . ; then they switch; and finally they switch once again" (1983, 91). Moreover, the extended monologic passages in Waiwai dialogues have already been mentioned, and some of the overt purposes of these dialogues, for example, the "appeals to communal work" (Fock 1963, 217), could presumably be accomplished through an actual monologue. Nevertheless, there is an obvious distinction to be made here. The Trio, Waiwai, and Yanomamö clearly tend toward semantic dialogicality and toward a model of solidarity based upon differential contribution. The Kuna and Shokleng tend toward semantic monologicality and toward a model of solidarity based upon the sharing of common traditions.

In relation to these patterns, the Shuar-Achuar dialogues appear as divergent. There is a reference to their use in connection with trade (Karsten 1935, 249), but it is clear that their primary use is in connection with "greetings" in the context of interhousehold visiting (Gnerre 1984). The dialogues involve semantic turn taking—in the dialogue presented by Gnerre, there are three turns of eighteen, thirty-eight, and nineteen lines—but the "semantic turn" contains largely formulaic content, as one would expect for a greeting.

This may be contrasted with the classic semantic dialogue of northern Amazonia. There the turn appears as much more of a contribution to a semantic totality, with unification arising out of the different but complementary contributions of two individuals—a kind of jigsaw puzzle approach to solidarity. Among the Shuar-Achuar, considerably more emphasis is placed on individual display, on "manifestation of supernatural powers," as Gnerre (1984) has suggested, and also on skill and aggressivity. It is as if the mutual display of power and aggressivity is what maintains solidarity, in a kind of intracultural "balance of power" theory of social relations.

However, the general limits, as in the other cases, are laid down by ceremonial dialogue as a model for cohesion. There is a delicate balance between aggressive display, through penetration of speaking time, and maintenance of coordination. Ever present is the possibility that too much aggressive penetration will throw off the pragmatic cycle and hence destroy the coordination that ceremonial dialogues model. The trick among the Shuar-Achuar is to appear as aggressive as possible while simultaneously paying attention to how this display is affecting the other, endeavoring to achieve a balance that results in coordination.

The model for social integration embodied in the Shuar-Achuar dialogues is one that differs in important ways from the shared culture and exchange models. There is the same underlying notion of mutual coordination and recognition. However, the shared culture model posits that there should be in addition a commonality—the tradition—while the exchange model posits that there should be complementarity—giving and getting what one needs or wants from a different other. In the balance of power model, solidarity is created through a kind of mutual respect—through the manifestation of a capability to coerce the other and through the recognition, simultaneously, of the capability of the other to coerce oneself.

It should be emphasized that these three models are ideal types, and that the ceremonial dialogue complex in a given society is really a unique blend of the three. The balance of power model is clearly also present, in some measure, among the Waiwai and Trio, where there is frequent reference to ceremonial dialogue as "verbal dueling." The participants there are also expressing their individual skills and capabilities. Nevertheless, a decided tendency exists for the ceremonial dialogues in a society to cluster around one of the three poles. The differing models of solidarity embodied in these dialogues seem to correlate with the broader social mechanisms by means of which cohesion is produced in each case.

Conclusion

In much of the foregoing analysis, little emphasis has been placed, in establishing the semiotic functioning of native South American ceremonial dialogues, on the "semantic content" of the discourse for which they are used. Instead, ceremonial dialogue is seen as a form of linguistic interaction, and that form itself functions as a sign vehicle. That is, the ceremonial dialogue is a meaningful form of linguistic interaction quite apart from whatever meaning derives from "what has been said." If we are to understand the role that ceremonial dialogues play in native South America—their significance for ongoing social action—we need to examine the former type of meaningfulness in minute detail.

I have suggested that the general function of ceremonial dialogues everywhere throughout native South America is to direct attention to the process of social coordination and to the solidarity that is consequently achieved. This coordination is something that is present in the dialogue itself. Each dialogic performance is an instance of solidarity achieved through the mutual paying of attention to another and through the overt acknowledgment or signaling of comprehension of the other. Simultaneously, each dialogic performance suggests how that solidarity can be achieved in other social interactions. In this sense, ceremonial dialogue is capable of acting as a "model for" conduct, as a blueprint for how solidarity is to be achieved.

If all South American ceremonial dialogues are models for a general kind of solidarity, based upon coordination, each tribe discussed here has developed its own unique model of solidarity, which is reflected in the specific formal characteristics of the dialogic interaction. I have been concerned especially with two formal parameters in this regard: the extent to which the discourse in the dialogue is semantically monologic or dialogic, and the extent to which it is formulaic or substantive. These two parameters give rise to three ideal types of solidarity, which I have distinguished accordingly as they are based upon "shared tradition" (semantically monologic), "exchange" (semantically dialogic), and "balance of power" (formulaic).

The analysis proposed here is not merely interpretive. It is grounded in correlational hypotheses that grow out of a limited comparative study and that can be tested by further comparative research. Specifically, first, I have tried to show—supporting the interpretation that all native South American ceremonial dialogues model general solidarity—that the ceremonial dialogues of the societies studied here are actually used in situations where social cohesion is at issue, namely, in interactions involving participants who are maximally distant in social terms. Second, I have tried to show that the distinct types of ceremonial dialogue in fact occur in social situations that are appropriate to them. Semantically dialogic ceremonial dialogues in fact occur in situations of negotiation, for example, trade and marriage, and the actual topics of discourse in these dialogues have to do with exchange. Semantically monologic ceremonial dialogues in fact occur in situations where the transmission of culture is at issue, and indeed the topics of discourse in these dialogues tend to revolve around myth and tradition. Finally, the largely formulaic dialogues tend to occur where we know from other ethnographic information that mutual sizing up as regards power is constantly at work. These are testable hypotheses and serve to ground an otherwise interpretive semiotic analysis.

The broader issue raised by this research concerns the role of metacommunicative devices in social action generally. It may be proposed that, for individuals to regulate their own conduct, they must be able to apprehend that conduct through signs. This does not mean they must necessarily bring the conduct into consciousness through encoding in the semantic portion of language. I have suggested that the formal characteristics of a sign vehicle, which has itself achieved some kind of perceptual salience or foregrounding, may be adequate in this regard, directing attention at some level to the "regulated" aspects of reality. Native South American ceremonial dialogues appear to be "metacommunicative" in this sense. They model the communicative situation in which they are actually being employed. They allow one to form an image of what the process is simultaneously as it is occurring. However, they are also a kind of distorting lens (a "model for") shaping perception after their own image and suggesting, consequently, the way that process ought to continue.

If the present interpretation is correct, the core ritualized communicative, and especially linguistic, events ought to assume a special significance relative to culture as a whole. They are the generative core of regulation, being themselves self-regulating, through their metacommunicative character, and also regulative relative to other nonritualized behavior by virtue of their status as sign vehicles. If this is so, we should be able to demonstrate their semiotic functioning through interpretive analyses, coupled with correlational hypotheses, such as those discussed above, that can be tested by comparative research. This chapter represents an initial contribution to this broader research effort.

References

Chagnon, Napoleon A. 1977. *Yãnomamö: The fierce people*. Case Studies in Cultural Anthropology. New York: Holt, Rinehart and Winston.

Cocco, P. Luis. 1972. Iyëwei-teri: Quince años entre los Yanomamos. Caracas: Edicíon de la Escuela Técnica Popular Don Bosco Boleíta.

Fock, Niels. 1963. Waiwai: Religion and society of an Amazonian tribe. Ethnographic Series 8. Copenhagen: Danish National Museum.

Gnerre, Maurizio. 1984. Ceremonial speech and mythological narrative in Jivaroan-Shuar and Achuar. Paper presented at the Native South American Discourse Conference, University of Texas at Austin.

Harner, Michael. 1972a. *The Jivaro: People of the sacred waterfalls*. Garden City, N. Y.: Doubleday.

———. 1972b. *Music of the Jivaro of Ecuador*. Ethnic Folkways Album FE 4386. New York: Folkways Record and Service Corporation.

Henry, Jules. 1941. *Jungle people: A Kaingáng tribe of the highlands of Brazil*. New York: Vintage.

Holmer, Nils M. 1951. *Cuna chrestomathy*. Etnologiska Studier 18. Göteborg: Göteborgs Etnografiska Museum.

Karsten, R. 1935. The head hunters of the western Amazon. Commentationes Humanarum Litterarum, Societas Scientiearum Fennica, 7, 1. Helsingfors.

Migliazza, Ernst C. 1978. Yanomama diglossia. In *Approaches to language*, ed. William C. McCormack and Stephen A. Wurm, 561–80. The Hague: Mouton.

Rivière, Peter. 1971. The political structure of the Trio Indians as manifested in a system of ceremonial dialogue. In *The translation of culture*, ed. T. O. Beidelman, 292–311. London: Tavistock.

Shapiro, Judith. 1972. *Sex roles and social structure among the Yanomama Indians of northern Brazil*. Ann Arbor, Mich.: University Microfilms.

Sherzer, Joel. 1983. *Kuna ways of speaking: An ethnographic perspective*. Austin: University of Texas Press.

Urban, Greg. 1984. Macro-parallelism in the Shokleng origin myth. Paper presented at the Native South American Discourse Conference, University of Texas at Austin.

———. 1985. The semiotics of two speech styles in Shokleng. In *Semiotic medication*, ed. B. Mertz and R. Parmentier, 311–29. New York: Academic Press.

Wassén, Henry S. 1949. *Contributions to Cuna ethnography*. Etnologiska Studier 16. Göteborg: Göteborgs Etnografiska Museum.

5

Qur'anic Dialogics:
Islamic Poetics and Politics
for Muslims and for Us

Michael M. J. Fischer
and Mehdi Abedi

Con-texts to Dialogue

In the buginning is the woid, in the muddle is the sounddance and there-
inafter you're in the unbewised again.

James Joyce, *Finnegans Wake*

The trace left by the Infinite is not the residue of a presence; its very glow
is ambiguous.

Emmanuel Levinas, *Otherwise Than Being*

[A wake: a town mollah read the Qur'an] as a sermon . . . in plainsong
. . . *showing* the Koran's beauty, *urging* devotion to it. . . . [Next, a
villager read with] such a muted, mellow expression that one could not
understand any words, but the listener sensed a oneness, a pouring out
of sorrow and faith. . . .[Then the literacy corpsman] took the holy book
in hand[as if] . . . a vast piazza lay before him . . . his chant reviewed
the troops . . . the Arabic poetry now barked out in perfectly measured
military cadences.

Grace Goodell, *The Elementary Structures of Political Life*

Three sorts of dialogue are central to the reading of the Qur'an:
dialogue in the colloquial sense of oral communication between two
face-to-face persons; dia-logue in the Greek etymological sense of
cross-play between arguments; and dialogue in the sense of juxtaposition of points of view in a political struggle for hegemonic control of
interpretation of how the world should be seen (be it, today, between
fundamentalist Islam and liberal Islam or between Islamic national-
isms and cosmopolitan secularism).

These translate into three ethical registers: the ethnographic
effort to understand other people(s) in their own terms, the political
effort to establish a public world where the rights and interests of all
can be protected and negotiated, and the self-evaluative or self-
reflective effort to break out of ethnocentrism and to place one's own

perspectives in historical and dialogical relation to others. This chapter is written in all three registers:[1] (1) It sketches how Muslims historically have read the Qur'an: how there has been a constant tension between the sound of sense and the sense of sound; between the vocal melodic, emotional pragmatics of presence and the textual, debatable graphics of absence; between the sounddance and the woid; thus, how the Qur'an is recognized to be poetic and enigmatic, composed of dialogues and other genres, requiring both an ear and interpretive skills, both for reciting and for reading. (2) It argues that only by knowing at least the structure of this hermeneutic and debate tradition can we effectively deal with or understand the powerful contemporary political movements in the Islamic world, both Shi'ite and Sunni (cf. Fischer 1980, 1982, 1983). (3) It argues that reviving this tradition can provide an ethical poetics and a tool of critical self-awareness, a mirror into our own half-forgotten ethical dialogic and scriptural traditions.

The Qur'an is a profoundly enigmatic text. For Muslims it is the word of God, divine in both its meanings and its language, infinite, beyond human capacity for definitive exegesis. To teach its exegesis (*tafsīr*) is inevitably to tread on dangerous theological ground, to court the hubris and heresy of claiming to know God's intent. Thus exegesis is not a required course in the traditional theological colleges (Fischer 1980, 247–51). It is taught on the side, and every Muslim must engage in it. The moral struggle is similar, though the emphasis is quite different, to Jewish relationships to the Torah.[2] But the Qur'an is more profoundly enigmatic than just on mythic or dogmatic grounds. Though a text generative of a

1. This is an abbreviated version of a fuller chapter in *Debating Muslims* (Fischer and Abedi 1990). Italicized English words refer to Islamic technical terms and are used both for the convenience of English readers and for comparative play with other essays and themes in this volume: for example, *sayings* for *ḥadīth* (cf. Kelber), *transcript* for *mus-haf* (compare text, script, scripture), *recitation* for *qira'at'*, *verse* for *ayah*, pl. *ayāt*. Some of these terms have important other meanings: for example, *ayāt* are also "signs"; *ḥadīth* are not only sayings of God, Muhammad, or the Imams, but also "traditions" by others about their words and deeds.

2. Contrast the famous, frequently cited, midrash (B. Metzia 59a, 59b) in which God is asked for a sign of agreement with one of the debaters about a point of law. He gives the sign, but it is disqualified on the grounds that "You gave the Torah at Mt. Sinai, in it Thou hast written: after the majority must one incline." Elijah is asked God's reaction: "He laughed in approval, saying, 'My sons have defeated Me, my sons have defeated Me.' " Here and elsewhere the Talmud asserts that the Oral Torah, given to Moses on Sinai, includes all the interpretations the rabbis will ever make; for example, Yer Peah 6:2.

scholastic tradition, the Qur'an insists on its own orality and musicality and warns against writing: It is a *qur'an* (oral recitation), not merely a *muṣ-ḥaf* (written text). Memorization/preservation (*hifz* is the word for both) are obligatory for each Muslim community (*waǧib al-kifā'i*) and may not be left to pen and ink. Muslims pride themselves that their "book" resides not on paper but in their breasts. The Qur'an, after all, is enigmatically allusive, constantly calling upon knowledge that must be brought to the text. It is allusive to stories from the Torah (and secondarily from the New Testament and pre-Islamic Arab lore). It is also allusive to the historical circumstances of its own production. This allusiveness generates a discourse about references and meanings, a generativeness that produced increasingly analytic disciplines of grammar, history, phonetics, poetics, law, theology, and hermeneutics— disciplines that variously interacted with, or were distinguished from, both Greek-influenced philosophy and logic and the talmudic discourses of Mesopotamia.

Early Muslims seem to have been as ambivalent about writing as was Plato (especially in the *Phaedrus*), and Islamic tradition has always emphasized the oral over the written. In the *Phaedrus*, Plato warns that the technology of writing can destroy the arts of memory and the disciplines of educating the soul; texts all too often are dead, not open to cross-examination or further question. Only the world of dialogue—argument and counterargument and (perhaps) the actual presence of the debaters so as to monitor the communicative pragmatics as well as the referential sense of the arguments—provides the space for ethical communication. In *The Republic* Plato attempts to find a way of writing that calls attention to its own devices, that constantly subverts any one reading, that sustains a critical attitude of dia-logue ("across arguments") between text and reader, so as to undermine that uncritical attitude of simple mimesis or repetition into which the modes of Homeric epic, the tragedians, and the comedians can slide. Plato relies upon a layered or polyphonic structure of irony (not only the irony of Socrates, the arch *eiron*, but also his own authorial irony in his presentations of Socrates' dialogues) to make his text provocatively enigmatic or poetic in the profoundest sense (Berger 1987; Griswold 1986; Rosen 1987; Seery 1985).

If Plato relies upon irony to keep his texts dialogically supple, the Qur'an relies upon midrashic narrations generated by key words, letters, incidents, sayings, parabolic stories, and dialogues. The *ḥadīth* ("sayings" of God, of the Prophet, his companions, and the Imams), *sunnah* ("precedents" of the Prophet), and *asbāb al-nuzūl* ("occasions or reasons of revelation") that serve to provide the con-texts and elaborations for Qur'anic fragments, themselves require authentication and interpretation. The entire structure of Qur'an and *ḥadīth* is a fun house of mirrors playing upon appearances and resemblances (*mutashābih*) that may or may not be grounded (*muḥkam*) depending upon the perspective and knowledge of the interpreter. It is a structure necessitating a critical sense, but one ambivalently also permissive of uncritical belief and false leads.

It is thus a profoundly ethical structure insistent upon debate (Persian, *baḥth*; Arabic, *mubāḥatha*) and dialectic (*jadal*), adjustable to the level of knowledge of each person and open to the educative process of those more knowledgeable. Irony too exists in the Qur'an: for example, when Umma Salama complained to Muhammad that the Qur'an seemed to be only about men and their rewards in heaven, Muhammad had the revelation (just listen to the irritation): *al-muslimīn wa al-muslimāt, wa al-mu'minīn wa al-mu'mināt* ("male Muslims and female Muslims, male believers and female believers") (33:35)—which, as any feminist can tell, only accents the complaint. Ironic readings, like ethics, depend upon the reader/interlocutor, as do dogmatic ones, be they dogmas about the uniqueness of Greek/Western ethical consciousness or dogmas about the meaning of the Qur'an.

Juxtaposing cultural traditions, each taken seriously in its own right, thus can serve as an educative ethics, another form of dialogue. Khomeini, for instance, part of whose authority derives from the regulative ideal of the Platonic philosopher-ruler,[3] serves to remind us of the play in Plato's *Republic* upon *paideia,* justice, individual soul, and collective governance, terms that have also become slogans in the Islamic revolution. *The Republic* flirts with moral transcendence (utopia/totalitarianism) but returns to debate, dialogue, dialectics, and politics as defenses against totalitarianism, against monologic

3. It also is derived within Islamic reasoning from the verse, "Obey God, obey His messenger, and obey the issuer of orders" (4:62); Shi'ites have taken the last to mean the Imams, and perhaps after them those who know the law, the clerics. Khomeini elaborated this into a doctrine of political governance, *wilāyat-i faqīh* ("guardianship by the *faqīh*/jurisconsult"), against the opposition of other *faqīh* or *mujtahids* (like Plato's philosophers, those who exercise independent, disciplined reasoning), who pointed out that traditionally the term *wilāyat-i faqīh* applied only to the estates of orphans and widows (see Fischer 1980, 151–55, 221, 237).

fixity, against authoritative textualism. Similarly, key contemporary texts of "Islamic fundamentalism," such as Khomeini's effort to argue for a political activist role for the clergy (Khomeini 1981), are internally hampered by a tradition of dialectical debate that restrains utopian enthusiasms.

This essay is divided into three parts for the three forms of dialogue. First, we discuss the performative, oral Qur'an: the dialogue of the I-Thou relation with God, of the historical God-Mohammad relation, and the staged narrative dialogues between God and Satan, God and Moses, Moses and Khidr, Abraham and Nimrod, and so forth. Second, we discuss the exegesis of the textual Qur'an: the dia-logue of hermeneutical understanding that grows with engagement of the text through dialectical disputation. Third, we discuss how this latter inhibits Khomeini's arguments for the involvement of clerics in governance. We conclude—and frame throughout with epigraphs—with the contemporary dialogic context of Rabbinic-Islamic-Catholic mirroring; of nationalist versus global shadowboxing ("East versus West," as the perverse cliché puts it); and of scholastic roots versus postscholastic ethics.

Dialogue and Presence: Iqra! ("Recite!"): The Sounddance, the Oral, Performative Qur'an

> Recite: In the Name of thy Lord who created; created Man of a blood clot.
> Recite: And thy Lord is the Most Generous, who taught by the Pen;
> taught Man, that he knew not.   96:1–5 (the first revelation)

> The divine utterance is silenced as soon as it is pronounced. But we cling
> to its resonant ring, our inspired words.   Jabès, *Book of Questions*, 85

Listen to a recitation of *surah* 96, considered the earliest revelation in the Qur'an: it is clear that it is made up of different fragments. The rhythm or music changes, and the content indicates differences between the times the fragments could have occurred. "Recite!" occurred while Muhammad was in the cave, withdrawn from society. In the second fragment reference is made (albeit without naming him) to Abu Lahab's refusal to submit to Islam, which happened after Muhammad returned to Mecca from the cave.

In these two fragments, we already have several distinctive features of the Qur'an: (1) a dual order: the first revelation chronologically does not come first sequentially (the *surah* or "chapters of verses" are ordered roughly by length, the shortest coming last); (2) the narrative unit is the fragment, not the *surah*; (3) meaning is conveyed by the sound and would be much more difficult to establish by the text alone ("taught by the Pen . . . taught man that he knew not"); (4) meaning is further established by a knowledge of the occasions or allusions of the fragments, without which the text is inscrutable: legible, but unintelligible; (5) the fragments are of various genres, including dialogues (*a*) with staged voices (e.g., between God and Abraham, or Moses and Khidr, or God and Satan, or Moses and Pharaoh), requiring dramatic recitation; (*b*) implicit dialogues where Muhammad has been asked a question by Jews or by unbelievers and must ask God for the answer, and the Qur'an provides the answer, "Say to them (*qul!*) . . ."; (*c*) the address of God to both Muhammad and through him to Muslims: "Recite (*Iqra* !) . . .; (6) only by recapturing the divine sound, as best one can, is one able to approach the presence of God and apprehend his divine word: as human speech is inadequate to the divine, so is the written text a poor transcription of the divine tablet (*lawḥ maḥfūz; Umm al-Kitāb*) of the Seventh Heaven.

More generally, the stress on the oral, performative, dialogic Qur'an is encoded in (1) the dogmas of Muhammad's illiteracy (protecting the Qur'an's divinity: it is not the product of a crafty man; the Prophet could not write), and the Qur'an's inimitability (resting in part on its onomatopoetic aptness of word choice: no poet could have created such resonance); (2) the story of its dual revelation, with interpretation dependent upon the sequence not recorded in the written text; (3) the debates about the desirability of writing down the Qur'an, and about the way an official transcript was produced, including the Hadith of Seven Recitations or Dialects (Ḥadīth Sab'at Aḥruf), which provides a charter myth for cantillation variability, with consequent variants in understanding; (4) the technical demands (*a*) of a *scriptio defectiva* (as long as the Arabic script lacked diacritical marks for vowelization, punctuation, intonation, and pitch, an authoriative reciter, rather than the written text, was the *ḥāfiz*— preserver, memorizer, guardian— of the text),[4] and (*b*) of interpretive skills to keep the text supple and poetically densely layered with meanings; (5) the centrality of the dialogues in the Qur'an about

4. These began to be introduced in the first century of Islam but took a number of centuries to be accepted.

uncertain knowledge and the fallibility of unguided reason; (6) the pedagogy of never studying alone or with a text alone.

The story of revelation is that the primal Qur'an, the Umm al-Kitāb ("Mother Book"), which resides in the seventh heaven, descended to the heavenly sphere on the twenty-seventh, nineteenth, twenty-first, or twenty-third[5] of Ramadan, and thence via Gabriel into the heart of the Prophet. Muhammad first heard the sound of bells and was set the task of reproducing the heavenly voice of Gabriel reciting from the Umm al-Kitāb. Muhammad instructed his followers to reproduce this sound: "Embellish the Qur'an with your voice"; "He who does not recite the Qur'an melodiously is not one of us." The art of cantillation *tajwīd* is aimed at preserving the original celestial music of the Qur'an, that sound that encodes senses beyond human language. Etymologically, *tajwīd* is said to be an Arabicization of Avestan "gatha" (Taleqani, n.d., 1), the form of inspired/inspirational poetry chanted by the prophet Zoroaster, a form whose efficacy is said by some to reside as much in the cosmic vibrations of the sound as in the poetic vision. Cantillation styles range from the more "ornamental" (*mujawwad*, from the same root as *tajwīd*) to the "plainer" (*murattal*, from the same root as *tartīl* in *verse* 73:4: "recite in measured clear chant," *wa rattil al qur'ana tartīlan*). Qur'an, *qirā'at* ("recitation"), *iqra* ("recite") all come from the same root and (like the Persian word *khondan*) mean both singing and reading, in contrast to words for pure texts such as *ḥadīth* (the *sayings* of the Prophet), which are never sung, or *muṣ-ḥaf* (the *transcript* of the Qur'an).

The Qur'an was twice revealed to Muhammad (just as, he said, were the two sets of tablets to Moses):[6] first complete, in the order of the present text; and a second time in fragments during the course of his twenty-three-year prophetic career (610–32 C.E.). The latter is the object of interest for historical, literary, and jurisprudential purposes, but it is the former that is the divine order of the Umm al-Kitab, and suggestions to publish a Qur'an in the best possible reconstruction of the latter historical sequence have been resisted, although Shi'ites

---

5. Perhaps to encourage prayer, the exact date is unknown: prayers on the night of revelation are worth a thousand prayers any other time. For differences in Shi'ite and Sunni valuation and meaning of Ramadan, see Fischer (1980, 24–25).

6. The breaking of the tablets, like the breaking of the vessels, is the making human: " 'Is not My word like a hammer that breaks the rock in pieces?' [Jer. 23:29] — as the hammer causes numerous sparks to flash forth, so is a scriptural verse capable of many interpretations" (Sanh. 34a). And Jabès: "It was necessary for Moses to break the book [tablets] in order for the book to become human" (Gould 1985, 23, 66).

believe that the *transcript* compiled by 'Ali was arranged in the chronological order of revelation. 'Ali's *transcript*, no longer extant, is said to have been preserved by the Imams and will be made public upon the return of the Mahdi at the end of time—a neat charter myth for the efforts of Muslims to reconstruct the Qur'an's plenitude of contexts and meanings.

The debates about the compilation of the *transcript* provide rich material for contemporary discussions of the continuum between oral and literate cultures and for the rationales for the primacy of the oral over the written in judicial matters that continues to the present. Traditional Islamic accounts credit only "seventeen" persons (like "forty," a stereotypic number) in Mecca with literacy—more in Medina, a center of Jewish literacy—and speak of Islam as a vehicle for the spread of literacy. The metaphoricity of the Qur'anic vocabulary referring to literacy is itself interesting both in marking intercultural relations and in hints about attitudes toward the technology of literacy. *Qirṭās*, "paper," is from Greek *chartes; surah* 68, "the Pen" begins with the letter *nūn*, meaning "fish" in Hebrew, explained by Muslim exegetes as referring to a fish whose flesh was used in making ink; Muhammad in the story attached to Luqman's rival scripture asks that it be read out, perhaps reflecting, if not his own illiteracy, an era of unstandardized shorthand notations, or simply unvoweled and unpunctuated scripts, giving texts a private, aide-mémoire character, so one might not easily have been able to read another's notes. Companions of the Prophet, who had private transcripts of the Qur'an, are thus said to have destroyed their notes before they died, lest the notes mislead others. Similarly, after the Caliph Uthman had an official *transcript* compiled, he destroyed all other variants (whence his title Ḥarrāq al-Masāḥif, "Burner of Mus-hafs"), and he sent a reciter with each copy of the official *transcript* to the provinces. Still today, reciters of the Qur'an learn their *recitation* from oral masters, not from the written text; scribes write down the text from *recitations*, not from other texts; and students study with a teacher, never alone with a text. The oral remains authoritative for the written, not the other way around.

The effort to protect the oral Qur'an from deformation due to tampering with the written text only begins with the *scriptio defectiva* and the ambiguities that remain even after diacriticals were introduced (vowels, punctuation, cantillation marks): they involved vigilance, as well, against perennial efforts to "improve" the transcript, including "straightening out" the grammar, replacing words with better ones (*shādhdh*, "odd" changes), or making the text conform to reason. As late as 1958 two shaykhs were tried, forced to recant, and expelled from Cairo's al-Azhar University for issuing a decree allowing *shādhdh* recitations. The grammarian al-Mubarrad, in the third century of Islam, opined that were he a reciter he would say *barr* (charitable) in 2:177 rather than *birr* (charity) to make it grammatical. Mu'tazilite *kalām* philosophers argued that God could not have recommended suicide (2:54), perhaps not recognizing the passage as a citation of Exod. 32:27, or accepting the argument that the Torah, corrupted by the Jews, cannot mean what it says. Zamakhshari, in the sixth century of Islam, notorious for his efforts to correct the Qur'an, suggested 5:112 should read "ask your God to send" rather than "can your God send," on the grounds that Jesus' disciples would not ask about God's nature or his capacities. Orthodoxy refused all such corrections: oral *recitation (naql)*, not reason *('aql)*, is authoritative.

Disputes over such matters illuminate and mark the history not only of literacy, or of theology, poetics, grammar, logic, and hermeneutics, but also of resistance to authority being taken out of the dialogic face-to-face context. There is considerable lore on the misreadings caused by different ways the script alone could be interpreted, and hence the stress on always studying with a teacher. Imam 'Ali is credited with the well-known lines, "He who obtains knowledge orally from a master, he is safe from being misled and from misreadings. But he who obtains knowledge from books, his knowledge is nil according to those who know." Perfection in teaching for Shi'ites lies with the Imams, who are in fact called "the speaking Qur'an." At the Battle of Siffrayn (657 C.E.), when his men hesitated to fight because the enemy had placed Qur'ans on their lances, 'Ali cried: "What you see on the lances is but paper and ink; I am the living Qur'an, the speaking Qur'an." Distrust of the text is not limited to Shi'ites: Imam al-Shafi'i also admonished that it is a mistake to take the written page as your mentor, that he who learns jurisprudence from the book alone loses sight of the law (as-Said 1975, 54).

The decision to preserve the Qur'an by collecting a definitive *transcript* is said to have been taken after hundreds of reciters were killed in the Battle of Yamāmah (12/633). A question arose about a certain verse, and it was feared that all who knew that verse had been killed. Still the Caliph Abu Bakr hesitated, saying that if Muhammad did not collect the Qur'an, perhaps it should not be done. Abdullah ibn Abbas, the father of Qur'anic exegesis, later would report a *saying* of the Prophet that the cause of the ancients' downfall was partly due to writing. The Qur'an itself says: "If we had sent you writings on paper so that they could teach it, the unbelievers would surely say, it is nothing but magic" (6:7), and "Who then sent down the book that Moses brought? A light and a guidance to man. But you make it into paper for show, while you conceal much" (6:91).

Zayd ibn Thabit was asked to oversee the compilation of the definitive *transcript*, completing it under Uthman, the third caliph, and using the dialect of the Quraish tribe (that of Muhammad, but also, like thespian Hannoverian German, said to be the clearest, most enunciated of the dialects). When Uthman saw/heard the final version, traditions relate that he commented, "I notice some *lahn*] inconsistences in 'dialect' or 'melody', but the Arabs will straighten it out with their tongues." A variant says: "Had the men of Hudhayl [best in elocution] dictated it and men of Thaqif [best in transcription] written it down, such *lahn* would not have occurred."

Establishing a single *transcript*, of course, was no guarantee of uniform *recitations*. Muhammad, in a *saying* universally recognized to be a fabricated mythic charter (the Hadith Sabatu Ahruf), says that the Qur'an was revealed in seven permissible dialects or styles of *recitation* (cf. also Qur'an 43:3: "Verily we have made it an Arabic Qur'an," i.e., not just a Quraishi one). So collectors of recitations gradually categorized all variants into seven. These collectors, as opposed to collectors of the *transcript*, were teachers of cantillation, knowing where to pause, how to place emphasis, what tonalities to use to bring out emotions, and so on. The first such collector is said to have been the Jewish convert Harun ibn Musa or the Shi'ite Aban ibn Taghlib.

The differences among *recitations* are not just stylistic, but involve different articulations that can lead to quite different meanings: for example, *salāmun 'alā iliyasīn* ("blessings upon the followers of Elias/Elijah") versus a slight pause amid the last syllables, *salāmun 'alā āli yasīn* ("blessings upon the children of Yasin"), Yasin being an epithet of Muhammad. The latter is the preferred reading by Shi'ites, for whom the children of Muhammad are the Imams. Clearly, then, an effort must be made to limit the ways the Qur'an can be articulated. One guards against modes of recitation that lack reliable chains of teachers, that contain inventions by scholars, or that add parenthetical exegeses. Ten ways are recognized as legitimate: the seven *mutāwatir* ones that have more than one independent and fully trustworthy chain of teachers back to the early days of Islam, plus three *mash-hūr* ones, famous variants based on a particular reciter. They are distinctive even to the uneducated listener: for example, Warsh has long durations of syllables, dropping of glottal stops (*muminun*, instead of *mu'minun*), and *imalah* (shifts from /a/ to /e/); Hamzah, by contrast, accents glottal stops with pauses before them. Different recitations became fashionable by region and era: for example, in Egypt since Ottoman times, the style of Hafs replaced that of Warsh.

In the 1950s the Egyptian Labib as-Said began to tape all "eighty" ways of recitation, to document them, to preserve them from modern musical contamination, because he feared the art of recitation was in danger of dying. If it died, the Qur'an itself would no longer be *mutawātir* (certified by multiple chains of trustworthy reciters). There proved to be considerable opposition to the project: many Egyptian Muslims preferred to promote the recitation of Hafs as the only acceptable one, lest scoffers at Islam be able to claim that Muslims could not even agree on the words of what they claim to be divine revelation.

What finally is important about the oral recitations of the Qur'an is the way they articulate, transmit, and evoke the Mother Book in the seventh heaven, the Preserved Table (*lawḥ maḥfūz*). Cantillation manuals include explanations of phonology: the points of articulation in the vocal tract, allophones, rules of assimilation, nasality, duration.[7] They include rules of sectioning of the text, of rhythms, and of recognizing repetitive phrases (*mutashābih*) in the text that act as refrains and echoes throughout. Just as a single narrative may be scattered through the text in different fragments, so too in the performance structure, melodic patterns can be used to refer to other parts of the text, other *recitations*, and other reciters. The beauty and inimitability of the Qur'an reside primarily in the use of the sound of the language, in its frequent onomatopoetics, in the way melodic modes are correlated with emotional moods to picture and color meaning.

Surah 105, "The Elephant," for instance, tells of the Abyssinian invasion to destroy the Ka'ba of Mecca in the year of Muhammad's birth, and how God sent flocks of birds with stones that so bombarded the elephants and men of the invading army that they were like masticated leaves. The words for leaves (*'asf*) is both ugly

7. See Nelson (1985) for expansion.

and impossible to say quickly: it sounds like a violent clearing of the throat. It is in onomatopoetic ways like this that the Qur'an is said to be inimitable and precise. The phonetic structure of the Qur'an—the alternating rhyme and parallel rhythms; the use of rhyme to unify long verse lines; the use of short lines for special emphasis; the use of longer and longer lines in a verse to delay and intensify final resolution—is distinctive. So too is the way a reciter may repeat a word, or first present short, clear phrases and then repeat them in single long units. Thus the first word in 24:55, Allah, meaning "God," but also an exclamation of wonder and delight, may be isolated, before being put together with the line "God is the light of heaven and earth." Using such repetitions with different intonations, the reciter can bring out different meanings. Two voices in dialogue can be set off musically. Verses about hell are colored in full, heavy voice, while those about heaven sparkle with bright, light voice. When the infant Jesus stands up to speak in the *surah* "Maryam," the reciter moves from a low voice register to a higher pitch and volume. While various emotions—joy, awe, yearning, grief—are invoked, the master tones are those of *khushu'* (humility, awe, submission), *huzn* (sorrow, grief), and *shaha* (choked-up emotion). Ibn Khaldun says, the Qur'an is a place of *khushu'* as it is a reminder of death and what comes after it; it is not an occasion to give pleasure in the perception of beautiful sounds" (Nelson 1985, 97). Al-Ghazali agrees: "The reciter contemplates what is in it of threat and intimidation and covenant and contract, then he considers his own shortcomings . . . so that without a doubt it affects him with *huzn* and he weeps" (p. 98).

Among the most dramatic, and theologically central, passages of the Qur'an are the dialogues between God and the angels (2:30–33), God and Iblis (15:32–41; 7:21 ff.; 38:75–84), God and Abraham (2:260), God and Moses (7:143), and Moses and Khidr (18:66–78). They all turn on uncertain knowledge and the fallibility of reason. In the first, the angels question why God should want to create men and women who will corrupt the earth and shed blood. God retorts: If you are so wise, reveal the "names of things." They cannot, but Adam, his new creation, can. Involved in this "naming" are not just words and things (knowledge, language) but hidden qualities, inner feelings, essences as opposed to appearances. Adam of course is not as adept as God; only God truly knows what is concealed, but angels, being pure reason without animal passion, do not have even the capacity for moral struggle, for ap-

proaching God through interiority, love, or faith, modalities of intention hidden beneath the surface. Iblis refuses to bow to Adam,
perhaps out of a kind of pride: he was made of fire, Adam merely
of mud. God reminds, it was "dry, sounding clay" (resonant,
speech) and into it he breathed his spirit. Mud, wet (animate life)
contrasts with fire, scorching winds from which Iblis and the jinn
were made. Muslims often comment that Satan's sin was not just
pride, but monomaniacal insistence on reason, a warning to fanat-
ics, self-righteous egoists, and rigid legalists: God commanded one
bow to no one but God, and so Iblis insists he is being true to this
command and monotheism. Again, it is through misuse of reason
that Satan deceives Adam and Eve: they have been told not to
touch the tree; if Iblis hands the fruit to them, so Iblis argues, they
technically would not have touched the tree.

Abraham's dialogue also turns on the problems of reason and
appearances. Abraham asks God to show him how he revives the
dead. God remonstrates, Do you not believe? (After all, this is the
man who is willing to sacrifice his son.) Abraham says: Of course, but
I want a demonstration so that my heart may reach certitude. God
complies, telling him to cut up four birds, putting them on four
mountains, and call to them; they will come flying. In a variation,
Moses (whose epithet is "he who talks directly with God," Kalimul-
lah) asks God to show himself, and God replies: You cannot see me
directly, but look at the mountain. The mountain disintegrates into
bits, and Moses faints. When he recovers his senses, God says: I
chose you, gave you a mission and words; take the revelation. The
story of the tablets and the golden calf follows. (Muhammad rejects
such miracles as signs of his mission, saying that previous prophets
had used them, but to little lasting effect.)

Moses' famous dialogue with Khidr, the saint who moves
between this world and the heavenly realms (retold in various
folktales with other characters, also in a midrash of Joshua and
Elijah), also turns on these same themes of the limitations of reason
in a world of appearances. Moses asks if any man is wiser than he (a
riddle form also used in stories about others, such as 'Ali), and is told
to follow Khidr. Khidr agrees on condition that Moses not question
his actions. Moses cannot resist, and they part, but Khidr explains the
riddles of why he scuttled the boat in which they were traveling, why
he killed a young man, why he took no recompense for setting
upright a wall that was falling down in an inhospitable town. The
boat would have been conscripted by an evil king downriver, and the

boatmen would have lost their livelihood; this way they would recover their boat when danger had passed; the boy would have become a parricide; the fallen wall would have exposed a treasure intended to support orphans, which would have been looted by the evil townspeople.

The richness of these dialogues is elaborated through the repetitions, modifications, parallels, and cross-references that reverberate through the Qur'an. The richness of the dialogues is also heightened through dramatic recitation, staging the different voices, and invoking conventional emotional musical modes (*maqām*).[8]

One can, of course, recite the Qur'an in a low, inaudible voice to oneself, as well as with full voice to an audience, and each manner has *sayings* to support its virtues. Thus Abu-Bakr, asked why he was reciting so inaudibly, replied, "Verily, He in whom I confide hears me"; Umar, asked why he recited so loudly, replied, "I awaken the sleepy and drive away Satan." The point is to recite with sincere desire to draw near to God. For this reason, al-Ghazali says that reciting from a *transcript* is better than reciting only from memory, for it is an additional action of viewing and thinking about the Qur'an and thus is an additional act of devotion (Abul-Qasem 1982, 56). In fact, there are textual conventions that add not only beauty of calligraphy but also other reminders. In chapter 2, "The Cow," for example, the first five *verses* are usually on a page by themselves, so that they are separated from the unbelievers mentioned beginning in *verse* 6.

These five *verses* are interesting, for they imply that the Qur'an is not self-explanatory—one cannot just read it and be guided. Nor is it a guide for everyone; it can mislead those who are not pious and who do not have six additional characteristics. One needs guidance not to be misled. Such guidance comes in various dialogic forms: in the teacher-student, Iman-follower, or student-student debating of dialectical argument–counterargument so as to clarify the basis for decision making. One may not study alone, with the text alone. The *sic et non* disputational method of Peter Abelard, and the dialogue forms of Renaissance philosophy, historically, are borrowings from Muslim Spain of this Islamic (and Jewish) style of unveiling the arenas of truth.

---

8. Egyptian reciters use the term *maqām;* Iranians do not because it is associated with music, but they talk about the idea.

The Graphics of Absence

Guides through the Woid: Plain Meaning, Prolepsis, the
Knowledgeable, the *Ḥadīth* Game

> Every person, place and thing in the chaosmos of Alle anyway connected
> with the gobblydumped turkery was moving and changing every part of
> the time.   James Joyce, *Finnegans Wake*

> The heart of dialogue beats with questions.   Jabès, *The Book of Dialogue*

Consider *verse* 3:7, which serves as a kind of litmus test among
exegetes:

> He it is who sent down to thee the Book, wherein are verses/signs [*ayāt*]
> of plain, firm, basic or established meaning [*muḥkamat*] that are the
> essence/foundation of the Book; and others that are ambiguous or
> allegorical [*mutashābihāt*]. Those whose hearts are perverse [*zaygh*,
> "inclining toward falsity"] and desiring its interpretation or hidden
> meanings [*ibtighā' al-fitnah*], and desiring its interpretation or hidden
> meanings [*ibtighā' tawīlihi*], but no one knows its hidden meanings or
> interpretation EXCEPT GOD. AND those firmly grounded in knowledge
> [*al-rasikhūn fi al-'ilm*] say, "we believe in it; all is from our Lord"; and
> none grasps the message except men of understanding.

It is deceptively simple, indeed the labyrinth gateway, warning
against losing oneself in the funeral maze of resemblances, appearances, metaphors, allegories, resonances, interpretations, representations, and symbolizations, yet all the while using these very
a-maze-ments and a-muse-ments to praise plain sense. God is "He,"
Muhammad is "thee," and "sent down the Book" is (already)
figurative: Muhammad did not receive a book, but a series of
revelations over twenty-three years, which were memorized, or
jotted down by the "scribes of revelation," and were subsequently
recollected into a book after the death of the Prophet. The first real
"sign" of trouble is *āyah* (pl. *āyāt*): "sign," "miracle," "fragment of the
Qur'an," "verse." "Wherein are the signs of established meaning" is
quite different from the possible gloss "the verses of plain meaning":
divine signs may signify more than they say. For Shi'ites, for
instance, it is quite established that "the Qur'an is a *khaṭṭ* [inscription]
occulted between two covers; it does not speak with a tongue; it must
have an interpreter [*tarjumān*]; it is men who speak on its behalf"
(*Nahj.* 182); the speaking Qur'an (*al-Qur'an al-nāṭiq*) is the twelve
Imams. "This Qur'an, make it speak! It shall not speak, but I inform

you of it" (*Nahj*. 223). "Beware! The Qur'an, its *zāhir* [exoteric sense] is elegant, its *batin* [esoteric meaning] is deep, its wonders never end, and the darkness is not broken except through it" (*Nahj*. 18).

But exegesis requires controls on interpretation, and the first major methodological puzzle comes with the terms *muḥkam* (plain meaning) and *mutashābih* (allegorical meaning). Philologically, *muḥkam* is a cognate of *ḥukm* (judgment, verdict) and *ḥikmat* (wisdom); its root (*h-k-m*) connotes "restraint." *Muḥkam* seems to be a *verse* with limited and unquestioned meaning. In contrast, *mutashābih* is a cognate of *shibh* (likeness) and *shubhah* ("obscurity," "vagueness," "uncertainty," "doubt," "specious argument," "sophism," "judicial error"), and of *ishtibah* ("to mistake one thing for another due to an apparent similarity"). *Mutashabih* contrasts with *mushabih* ("similar"): the latter refers to "real" similarity; the former to "apparent" similarity. *Muḥkam verses* thus might be expected to contain a *ḥukm* or *ḥikmat*, while *mutashabih verses* might be figurative or allegorical, if not chimeras of similarity, mis-takes, and misinterpretations.

In fact the definitions of *muḥkam* versus *mutashābih* in the exegetical literature contain a fan of meanings:[9]

Muḥkam	Mutashabih
Regulations, prescriptions, rules	Objects of faith, opinion, meditation, insight
Apparent, clear, one interpretation, plain meaning	Figurative, allegorical, multiple interpretations, requiring *ta'wīl* (interpretation)
Independent to itself: direct understanding, rationally comprehensible	Must be referred to something else (a similar *āyah*, relevant *sunnah* or *ḥadīth*); interpretable through research
Words not repeated in other parts of the Qur'an	
Abrogating verses (*nāsikhāt*)	Abrogated verses (*mansūkh*)
Present in all scriptures, and thus in the Mother Book	Esoteric signs such as the *sigla* (letters that stand independently before some verses)
Knowable	Unknowable: things no one can know (e.g., the time of resurrection); things knowable only by the *rāsikhūn;* things knowable to scholars
Human language	Sublime language

9. Citations for each of these in the exegetical literature are supplied in the fuller essay (Fischer and Abedi 1990). See Wansborough (1977) for a full account.

All the ambiguities opened up by *verse* 3:7, interestingly, do not make Muslim exegetes classify it as *mutashābih*. It is classified as *muḥkam*. The Qur'an describes itself in 11:1 as "a book whose *verses* are made *muḥkam* and further explained in details"; but in 39:23 it admits, "God has revealed a book that is *mutashābih*." A classical solution to this apparent contradiction is to say that *muḥkam* and *mutashābih* refer to the form of the *verses* rather than their content: the Qur'an is well founded (*muḥkam*) throughout, as the various techniques of exegesis elucidate, with each of its words and phrases aptly selected. Since some *verses* resemble others, it is *mutashābih*. Obviously also what is *muḥkam* to a more learned exegete may seem *mutashābih* to a less learned one. But there are other answers as well.

Al-Raghib al-Isfahani, a twelfth-century exegete, provides a typology of *mutashābihāt* by human capacity for understanding: some *mutashābihāt verses*, he says, are about things no one can actually know (e.g., the time of resurrection, and other metaphysical matters); some are things that can be known only by those the Qur'an calls "the well grounded in knowledge"; and some *verses* can be known by ordinary scholars of the Qur'an. A similar formulation is given by contemporary Shi'ite theologians: man's language is made for daily life, not for sublime meanings; sublime meanings require figurative language, especially when attempting to communicate with common folk. The Qur'an intends to provoke thought, not lay everything out for passive reception, and (a particularly Shi'ite insistence) the *mutashābihāt* are a way of indicating that the book cannot be read without guides, the infallible Imams.

Where this leads, of course, is to (*a*) the ultimate unknowability of much of the Qur'an, and thus to (*b*) an openness of interpretation that requires (*c*) moral struggle as well as (*d*) access to the disciplines and traditions of interpreting the Qur'an. Four important guides are available: the disciplines for laying bare the plain meaning of the Qur'an (including most importantly the identification of which *verses* abrogate other ones, the historical circumstances of revelation, and grammatical analysis); interpretive means of *tafsīr* and *ta'wīl* (exegesis, prolepsis) and dialectical disputation (*bahth*); the "well grounded in knowledge"; and the politics of the *sayings* game also played through dialectical disputation with *ta'wīl* and grammatical analysis.

Abrogation is a cause of some *verses* being considered *mutashābih*. If a *verse* commands something, but that command is no longer in force, an unskilled exegete might be misled. Theoretically, there are three types of abrogated *verses*: outdated commands (*ḥukm*) that at some point in the life of the Prophet were replaced by other *ḥukm,* yet the *verses* continue as part of the Qur'an; *verses* whose wording has been abrogated but whose *ḥukm* remains in force (e.g., the alleged *verse* about stoning for adultery); *verses* whose wording and *ḥukm* have both been abrogated. Only the first of these is accepted by most Muslim scholars. The other two are most often rejected on the grounds that they imply imperfection in the "perfect word of God" and open the sensitive debate about the incompleteness of the Qur'an. An example of the first type of abrogation is the three *verses* about drinking: 4:46 says, "O believers, do not pray when you are drunk until you know what you are saying." The story is that some drunks attempted to recite *surah* 109, a *verse* of negations, but forgot the negations. A stricter rule came next: "There is both good and evil in alcohol, but the evil outweighs the good" (2:219). Finally, the absolute prohibition was revealed: "Alcohol is of Satan" (5:90).

Obviously, one needs to know the historical contexts of revelation to know which abrogates which. These are recorded in books of *ḥadīth, sirat* (biographies of the Prophet), and *maghāzi* ("raids," esp. those Muhammad took part in). Two occasions of revelation are given for *verse* 3:7, each tagged to a phrase. First, tagged to the warning against hidden meanings (*ibtigha' ta'wīlihi*) is the story of Christians who asked whether Jesus was not God's spirit (*rūḥ*) and logos (*kalimah*), as is said in 4:171. Muhammad had to agree but denied the implication that this confirms the trinity of God, for 3:59 explicitly says, "Jesus is to God as is Adam: he created him from dust, then said, 'Be!' and he was." Again, 43:59: "Jesus was no more than a servant [of God]: we granted our favor to him, and we made him an example to the children of Israel."

The other, tagged to the warning against interpretations made with the intent of seeking dissension or testing (*ibtighā' al-fitnah*), is a story about the *sigla* (the letters) with which a number of chapters of the Qur'an begin: Hayy ibn Ykhtab, his brother, and some other Jews tell Muhammad that numerology provides the interpretation of these mysterious letters. Those of *surah* 3 add up to seventy-one, the number of years Islam will last. This is but one of the Qur'an's examples of Jewish illegitimate and mischievous play, which Muhammad rejects, noting that other chapters begin with other letters that add up to larger totals.

Grammatical analysts of the *wāw* ("and") in *verse* 3:7 is perhaps the most controversial part of the exegesis: Is the *wāw* a connective or a disjunctive? Does one pause before it ("no one knows its hidden meanings except God"), or does one not pause ("except God and those firmly grounded in knowledge")? Two other ambiguities: To what does "its" refer—the Qur'an in its entirety, or only its *mutashābihat?* And who are the "well founded in knowledge"? For most Shi'ites, the latter are the Imams, and in this case the *wāw* would serve as a connective, not a disjunctive. However, the Shi'ite philosopher and exegete Allameh Sayyid Muhammad Husayn Tabataba'i is among those who stop at "Allah": God alone knows.

On the side of those who take the letter *wāw* ("and") to mean inclusion are *verse* 3:18 ("There is no God but He: that is the witness of God, his angels, and those endowed with knowledge") and the arguments that the companions of the Prophet and the exegetes have discussed the *mutashabihāt,* so there is nothing in the Qur'an known only to God; or more cogently: God commanded the believers to meditate on the Qur'an and to try to understand it. How could he ask his servants to do the impossible? *Ḥadīth* in Sunni collections, not only Shi'ite ones, are read by Shi'ites to support the idea that the Imams are the "well founded in knowledge" who know the *ta'wīl* ("interpretation," but see below) of the Qur'an. The prayer of the Prophet for Ibn Abbas says, "God, make him knowledgeable in religion and teach him *ta'wīl* ." Q. 10:38 and 27:82 condemn those who are not knowledgeable about the Qur'an and its interpretation. The Prophet had a mission to clarify the revelation. How could he be ignorant of parts of it? Imam al-Sadiq bitterly condemned those who regarded any portion of the Qur'an as ambiguous, since the Imams know God's meaning.

On the other side, with those who read the *wāw* as meaning exclusion, are the traditional *recitations.* The nontraditional *recitations* of Abdullah ibn Abbas and Ubyy ibn Ka'b (first century A.H.) even change the word order, putting the verb before the subject, making the exclusion yet clearer: *wa yaqūl al-rāsikhūn.* Those who stop at "Allah," God alone knows the interpretation, range from those who refuse any but the most minimal figurative interpretation of any *verse* of the Qur'an to those, like Tabataba'i, who think of *ta'wīl* and *tafsīr,* two words for "interpretation," as essentially different.

Ta'wīl, understood to mean prolepsis, prefiguration of events that come to pass, is an extremely interesting control on interpretive freedom. The word occurs twice in *verse* 3:7 and seventeen times in the Qur'an. It is a key term. The story of Joseph, where it occurs seven times, uses it in the context of dreams; the story of Moses and Khidr applies it to the humanly unknowable; 4:58 and 17:35 use it to mean a decision in a dispute; 7:53 and 17:35 use it to indicate a kind of fulfillment.

There are four dreams requiring interpretation in the Joseph story of the Qur'an. First there is the dream of the eleven stars, sun, and moon bowing to him. Jacob provides an interpretation, suggesting that God has chosen him as a prophet, like Abraham and Isaac, and will teach him the *ta'wīl* of *aḥādith* (dreams, stories, events). Here the sun and the moon appear as Abraham and Isaac. But later events reveal the real interpretation of the dream, with Joseph ensconced like a king, with his father and mother (sun and moon) bowing to him as well as his eleven brothers. "O my father, this is the *ta'wīl* of my dream of old; God has made it come true" (12:100). In prison, Joseph is told two dreams by fellow inmates. The first, of pressing wine, Joseph interprets literally: the dreamer will become a presser and server of wine to the king. The second, of birds eating bread off the dreamer's head, Joseph interprets with only slightly less literalism: the man will be crucified and the birds will eat off his head. Perhaps bread and flesh are symbolic substitutions here. According to some *ḥadīth*, this second dream was a fabrication to test Joseph, both to find an interpretation and to see how far from plain meaning he might stray into dangerous, unconfirmable *ra'y* ("personal opinions"): events substantiate Joseph's interpretations as literal meaning. There is a further literal meaning and moral lesson: folklore has it that one who fabricates dreams will die. Finally there is Pharaoh's dream of seven fat cows and seven lean ones, seven full ears of grain and seven withered ones. Pharaoh calls for an interpretation of his *ru'yā* (visions), but his sages find them to be merely *adghathu aḥlām* (meaningless dreams), the same words used by the unbelievers to describe Muhammad's revelations in 21:5. Joseph finds mildly symbolic keys: there will be seven years of plentiful food (meat and grain) and seven years of poverty. The proof of the *ta'wīl* in all these cases comes through subsequent events. (Prescience of events that would actually occur is the restricted definition of the miraculousness of the Qur'an according to Ibrahim al-Nazzan and his Mutazillite defenders; al-Nazzam was condemned by Abd al-Baghdadi [d. 429/1037] for contradicting a broader definition of the Qur'an's miraculousness, suggested in 17:90, that it is forever inimitable.) Note that even in dream interpretation, symbolism is used with great restraint. This is characteristic of orthodox *ta'wīl* and is used to distinguish the orthodox from the mystics and sufis (the *"bāṭini"*); Shi'ites are systematically relatively more *bāṭini* than Sunnis, but they too recognize a gradation between orthodox plain meaning, or interpretations provided by the Imams, and dangerous mystical or personal flights of fancy.

The story of Moses and Khidr (18:66–78; related above) poses the problem of *ta'wīl* as one of knowledge of the unseen. When they part, Khidr reveals the *ta'wīl* of his riddlelike actions. Q. 7:53 and 10:39 use *ta'wīl* for the final fulfillment, the end of the world; and those who seek *ta'wīl* are sarcastically asked to await that time when it is too late. This sense of the final interpretation is posed slightly differently in 4:58, where disputes are referred to God and his messenger for *ta'wīlan*. Also in 17:35 *ta'wīl* means "decision" or "settlement of a dispute."

There is thus a sense in which *ta'wīl* is something that ultimately will be settled only by God or by the course of events. And so it is *tafsīr* that Muslims use instead to refer to exegesis. Interpretation (*ta'wīl*) can lead astray, but *tafsīr* is rather a disciplined explication (including pointing out the sources of ambiguity). Thus, for instance, while Utabari (d. 310/923) seems to use *ta'wīl* and *tafsīr* interchangeably, Tha'alabi (d. 428/1038) distinguishes *ta'wīl* as *ḥaqīqat al murād* ("the truth of the meaning"), from *tafsīr* as the means of reaching *ta'wīl*.

To return then to our *verse* 3:7 in its usual Shi'ite recitation, "But none knows its *ta'wīl* except God and the well grounded in knowledge," who are the well grounded in knowledge? At issue here is a larger difference between Shi'ite and Sunni exegesis than merely the Shi'ite identification of the well grounded as including at least the Imams. Sunnis rely upon the *sunnah*, the precedents of the Prophet and his companions, for interpreting the Qur'an. Shi'ites rely on these and on the interpretations of their Imams. Two variants of the Ḥadīth al-Thiqlayn codify the difference: according to Sunnis the Prophet said, "I leave among you two weighty ones, the book of God and my *sunnah*." The Shi'ite version is: "I leave among you two weighty ones, the book of God and my family; the two shall not be separated." So while for Sunnis, the *sunnah* act as the standard of meanings in the Qur'an, for Shi'ites it is the Imams who provide the standard. Thus, for instance, the Qur'an mandates fasting, and how one is to fast is determined by the practice of the Prophet. Here the *sunnah* are the standard of interpretation: deeds interpret words.

But, *verse* 62:9 mandates Friday communal prayer. For Sunnis this is an obligatory practice mandated in the Qur'an and practiced by the Prophet. But the Shi'ite Imams forbade it because control of the communal prayers and sermons had fallen into the hands of usurpers, and these occasions were tools of propaganda and mobilization. For Shi'ites what an Imam does is a *ḥujjat* (authoritative precedent). Through the ages Shi'ite jurists have taken differing stands on the obligation of Friday communal prayer: a minority regarded it always as obligatory, on the grounds that the reason for the ban by the Imams was historically limited and no longer in force. Another minority regarded it as forbidden, either because since there is still a living Imam (albeit occulted) it would have to be he who removed the ban, or more usually on the grounds that unjust government still ruled and so the reason for the original ban still existed. Many of those who took this position abandoned it with the establishment of the Islamic Republic of Iran: now at last there was a true Islamic government, and not only was the Friday noon communal prayer again obligatory, but the sermons were also an obligatory organizational device for the polity. And so we have the now familiar picture of the leaders of the Friday prayer holding the sword or gun of authority in one hand as they deliver their sermons. The majority through the years took a politically flexible stance, regarding Friday communal prayer, even led by state-appointed *imam jumua'hs*, as either allowable or recommended for the general solidarity of the community. The point here is that the word of the Imam acts for Shi'ites as an abrogator of the Qur'an: the Imam is the standard of meaning.

Or again, take *verse* 9:36: "the number of months, with God, is twelve in the book of God, the day that he created the heavens and the earth; four of them are sacred. That is the right religion. So wrong not each other during them. And fight the unbelievers totally." What could be clearer, say the Sunnis; no *verse* is as *muḥkam* as this. But, says Imam al-Ṣādiq, God would not be so simpleminded as to merely tell us that there are twelve months in a year. Rather, here is a reference to the twelve Imams, four of whom are sacred, that is, four of whom have the name of God, 'Ali (the first, fourth, eighth, and tenth Imams). "Religion" refers to the imamate, and the day that God created the heaven and the earth refers to the *nūr* doctrine, the doctrine that at the beginning the prophets and the Imams were created from a ray of divine light (*nūr*), and that these divine sparks were breathed into human form at appropriate points in the unfolding of history, often making for a miraculous birth (see Fischer 1980, 26).

There is, however, a difficulty for Shi'ites regarding the Imams: they failed to provide their followers with the kind of *ta'wil* that would clarify all the ambiguities of the Qur'an. Those said to be "the well grounded in knowledge," aside from the Imams, must be persons who know the discipline of *tafsīr* and who are pious in the sense of not allowing their personal opinions to distort the application of the methodology of *tafsīr*. Little wonder, then, that when an exegete ends his comments he humbly says, "God knows best" (*wa Allahu a'lam*). One may well wonder how many legitimate ways of interpreting *verse* 3:7 and the Qur'an there are. Abdullah bin Abbas, the founder of Qur'anic exegesis, recognized four: one no one is excused from knowing; one is known primarily to the Arabs (the cultural linguistics of the Arabic of the Qur'an); one is known to the learned; and one is known to no one except Allah.

The existence of esoteric meanings known to the Imams and transmitted orally to their disciples opens up a continuing possibility of conflict between the scholars who are merely literate (however good their critical skills) and those who claim to have access to this protected *chain* of interpretive understanding. We will see a hint of this conflict in the next section, when we turn to a key political text of the present day.

The Politics of Interpretation

Exposing the Unbewised: The *Ḥadīth* Game, (Blind) Followership, Rule by Faqih/Amir

The Qur'an calls itself *aḥsan al-ḥadīth* ("the best of the *ḥadīth*," 39:23). Most *ḥadīth* are *sayings* of the Prophet: some are explicitly, like the Qur'an, regarded as divine *sayings*, and the rest are inspired. *Verses* 53:3–4 say that the Prophet speaks not of his own account, but via revelation. Shafi'i, founder of the Shafi'i legal school, used this verse to justify the *ḥadīth* (sayings) and *sunnah* (practices) of the Prophet as bases for Muslim law (while still attempting as far as possible to use the Qur'an alone; hence the insistence that the stoning *verse* once existed.) In the second/eighth century there were three competing schools of *ḥadīth* collections: in Damascus at the Umayyid court of Mu'awiyya *ḥadīth* were collected supportive of that dynasty; in Medina the bias was toward collecting *ḥadīth* of Muhammad and his four caliphal successors as patterns for a just Islamic government; Kufah was suspected by the other two schools as having Shi'ite leanings.

What is of compelling interest to those who play the game of invoking *ḥadīth* are the challenges of the ideological, legal, or political outcomes, of gaining a consensus and thereby formulating history among those skilled enough to point out weaknesses in *chains* of narration, contradictions or anachronisms in the texts of the alleged narrations, and so on. If experts agree that all links in the *chains* are reliable, the *ḥadīth* is graded ṣaḥīḥ ("correct"); several independent reliable *chains* make it *mutawātir* ("confirmed"), the highest grade. Below these two grades, *ḥadīth* may be evaluated as *maqbūl* ("accepted"), *ḥasan* ("good," but not fully reliable), *mursal* ("lacking connected *chains*"), *ḍaʿīf* ("weak"), or *majʿūl* ("fabricated"). The culling of fabrications reflects the development both of critical judgments and also of sectarian canons. Two central political issues will illustrate: followership and rule by the cleric or amir.[10]

Taqlīd, the duty of ordinary Shiʿites to follow the *fatwā* ("opinion" reasoned through the disciplines of exegesis) of the leading jurist of the day, became a key political issue during the past century as various *mujtahids* were called upon to rally Muslims against imperialism. Until the late nineteenth century Shiʿites followed regional *marjaʿ taqlīd* ("sources of imitation"), but from the time of Shaikh Mortaḍa Ansari (d. 1864), single supreme *marjaʿ* were periodically recognized: Mirza Hasan Shirazi in 1891–92 when he rallied Iranians with a *ḥukm* ("judgment," not merely an opinion) against giving a tobacco monopoly to the British; Mirza Muhammad Taqi Shirazi in 1919–20 when he rallied Shiʿites in Iraq in a *jihād* against the British manipulation of Iraqi politics; Shaikh Abdul-Karim Haeri-Yazdi from 1920 to 1935 when he revitalized the theological colleges of Qum; and Ayatullah Hossain Borujerdi from 1944 to 1961. (On the history of the debate over the role of the *marjaʿ taqlid* and its projection backward into history, see Fischer 1980, 86 ff., 252–53, 275 n. 11).

The debate over *taqlīd* divides the two "schools" of Shiʿite jurisprudence—the Akhbaris and the currently ascendant' Usulis—and lays the groundwork for Khomeini's argument that the supreme *marjaʿ taqlīd* should exercise political rule. The Usulis initially advocated *taqlīd* as a means of rebuilding the institutional structure and activism of the clergy after the fall of the Safavid dynasty in 1732. To do *taqlīd* meant in part to give to the *marjaʿ taqlīd* that half of the *khums* tax called *sahm-i iman* ("share of the Imam"), which helped provide the Shiʿite clergy an independent financial base. The Akhbaris rejected *taqlīd*, placing a heavier duty of religious caution and responsibility on individual Muslims. Mortaḍa Motahhari, an Usuli and a leading figure in the Iranian revolution, points out that the Akhbaris are also thus more tolerant than the Usulis, since reliance on

---

10. *Amir* in Sunni fundamentalist political theory, *faqīh* in Khomeini's Shiʿite version.

weighing the evidence of one position versus another for oneself tends to teach one humility (1962, 46).

The debate over *taqlīd* illustrates the tactics of argumentation that Khomeini later also used, which place on the defensive not only common folk, but also the merely literate who depend upon texts (such as the authors and readers of this chapter), asserting special privilege for jurists with superior oral chains of authority and permission. Both Shaikh Morteza Ansari in the nineteenth century and Khomeini in the twentieth century admit that the key *hadīth* supporting *taqlīd* and Khomeini's idea of *wilayat-i faqih* (guidance by the jurists) are very weak. Yet, they say, these *hadīth* have the "scent of truth." In effect, they claim access to the truth independent of the *hadīth* text. Khomeini might challenge our analysis of his use of *hadīth* by saying: Where do you get your information? And when we reply "from al-Kāfi, from *Wasā'il al-Shiʿah*," he could reply in the manner of Plato's *Phaedrus* and in the manner of the early Muslims, "Ah, only from books; but you have no *permission* or access to the interpretive intent as I do through the oral chains of *hadīth* narration, being both a master narrator and a *faqih* [one who can evaluate and distinguish among *hadīth*]."

One of the fascinating contemporary sociological dramas is to watch to what extent this kind of argument can continue to carry any weight: Dr. ʿAli Shariati prematurely thought its time was finished, telling young Iranians that, being literate, they no longer needed the clerics. One can, after all, respond to such invocations of special privilege with the traditional retort: "I suspect you of fabrication; are you the only one to have heard what you say? Either others can be cited to support your position or you are, at best, on weak, non-*mutawatir* grounds." Hence the importance of multiple narrators. But fabrication is not always deceitful falsification: it often is done relatively openly to provide mythic charters for contemporary events, much as an advertiser creates a jingle to lodge a product in one's mind. For instance, when Khomeini returned to Iran, a calendar was published, ornamented with several newly minted *hadith* saying a leader would come from Qum and would be beset by the world powers, but they would be unable to defeat him.

Although several *hadīth* may be invoked in support of *taqlīd*, the key one is narrated by Ahmad ibn Abi-Talib al-Tabarsi from the eleventh Imam, in which in the midst of a passage condemning *taqlīd* in favor of each Muslim's assuming full responsibility for his own actions, the following occurs. "But among the jurisprudents, whoever is pious, keeper of his faith, pursues reason independent of his own desire, and is obedient to God—it is the duty of common folk to follow him." Defenders of *taqlīd* to enforce unified political action cite only this part of the *ḥadīth*. Moreover, this *ḥadīth* is not found in any of the four basic Shi'ite collections. It comes instead from Shaykh Hurr al-Amil's *Wasā'il al-Shi'ah*. Amili unequivocally rejects *taqlid*, challenging both the chains and the interpretation of the text by advocates of *taqlīd*. He cites thirty-four other *ḥadīth* that also condemn *taqlīd*. The story behind the *ḥadīth* is said to be Imam al-Ṣādiq's reply to queries about the Qur'anic *verse* condemning Jews and Christians who took their rabbis and monks as lords (19:31): It meant not that rabbis or priests asked people to worship them, but that blind obedience is wrong. Because people indulged in uncritical obedience, unscrupulous rabbis and priests were able to falsify the law, making what is proscribed permitted and vice versa. All that is permitted by the full *ḥadīth*, Amili points out, is clarification of technical matters by a *faqīh*, for example, the validity of a narration or a judgment about the technicalities of law. It excludes personal opinion and decisions having to do either with basic principles of jurisprudence (*'uṣūl*) or with religious duties (*furū'*); and it has nothing to do with politics. One problem (or strength, from a political institutional point of view) with the doctrine of *taqlīd* as it has evolved is that it is not divisible: one cannot decide that one will follow a particular *marja'* in all matters except a few where one feels oneself better informed than he. One must follow in all things; however, one can switch *marja'*. Among the thirty-four *ḥadīth* condemning *taqlid* cited by Hurr al-Amili is this: "Beware of leaders who seek leadership. No sandals followed a man, save that he perished and made others perish."

Hurr al-Amili is not alone in his rejection of *taqlīd*. This was the common position before the reassertion of a vigorous Usuli point of view by Wahid Behbehani. Opponents of *taqlīd* invariably invoke the couplet from rumi's *Mathnawi*.

Khalq rā taqlīdishān bar bād dād.
Ay dosad la'anat bar īn taqlīd bād.

It was the *taqlīd* of the people that made them bend with the wind.
Two hundred curses upon this *taqlīd*.

More orthodox, perhaps, is the riddle attributed to Mulla Sadra on the impossibility of *taqlīd*: you must be a *mujtahid* (be educated enough to exercise the disciplines of knowledge and interpretation) to have the ability to pick someone to follow, and *mujtaheds* are not allowed to follow others. Another frequent hostile saying is that the *marja' taqlīd* not only are *muqallad* (one who is imitated), but are also *muqallid* (one who imitates), because they are swayed by the financial support they get from bazaar merchants. Most recently, Dr.' Ali Shariati, asked if he practiced *taqlīd*, is said to have curtly replied: "I am not a monkey." Shariati did attempt to reinterpret the notion of *taqlīd*, claiming that the original application was for an underground resistance organization against tyranny, built on four principles: leadership (imamate), secrecy or dissimulation (*taqiyya*), readiness to die (martyrdom), and unquestioning obedience (*taqlīd*). In a free society, however, he argued, there is no place for *taqlīd*. Shariati's argument is implicitly reflected in the popular punning response to the question," Do you practice *taqlīd*?" "Do I want a [dog] collar [*qallādah*] around my neck?"

From debate over *taqlīd* in the last century, and over a supreme *marja' taqlīd* in this century, Khomeini shifted debate in the 1970s and 1980s to political leadership and rule by the jurist.

There is a key text, which is not a text but a faulty textual record of a "Socratic" dialogue, that serves not only as the legitimating argument behind the constitution of the Islamic Republic of Iran, but also as a model of the dialogic method of the *faqīh* or jurist in interpreting the Qur'an and Islamic revelation. This is Khomeini's *Hokūmat-i Islāmi: Wilāyat-i Faqīh* (Islamic Government: Guardianship by the Clerical Jurisconsult), in which he attempts to show with the help of a series of *hadīth* that the highest rank of the clergy are the successors to the Prophet and the Imams, and that they were intended to provide governmental leadership: that they and not merely the Imams are the referent of the Qur'anic *verse*, "O you who believe, obey God, his messenger, and the issuers of orders among you [*wali al-amr*]" (4:59). Eventually these lectures served as support for the new constitution, for elevating Khomeini in his role as supreme *faqīh* to head of state, and for justifying a majority of the parliament being composed of clerics.

Hokūmat-i Islāmi originated in 1970 as a series of oral lectures to clerical students in Najaf. Some students previously had asked Ayatullah Abu'l Qassem Musavi Khoi if the clergy were entitled by Islamic law or the *hadīth* to take active government posts such as head of state, legislator, or governor. Khoi took a traditional quietist position and said no. Khomeini, in response to this opinion of a leading *mujtahid* and *marja' taqlīd*, attempted to stake out the activist position that Islamic jurists were to "exercise all the worldly functions of the Prophet" (p. 124). The lectures were circulated on cassette tapes and in mimeographed form from student notes, then later edited, added to at the beginning and the end, and published both in Persian and in Arabic translation. The first edition was a third the size of the third edition used by Hamid Algar for his English translation. One can recognize in places where the textual discontinuity seems to imply objections and questions by listeners.

In reading the text, one must exercise one's imagination to listen to an oral dialogue, much as Hans-Georg Gadamer has recently taught us to listen again to Plato, asking always: What questions are the recorded comments answering? The Persian text marks breaks in continuity with spacing, headings, and graphic separators between oral segments. Algar's translation suppresses these (as well as several of Khomeini's parenthetical asides) and often does not provide the full *chains* or texts of the *ḥadīth* that introduce oral segments, skipping to Khomeini's glosses, losing thereby some of the interplay between the text and the reinterpretation. The Persian text, interestingly, provides the *ḥadīth* in their Arabic original and then a Persian translation, a fingerprint of the fact that the printed text is amended for laymen: the clerical students to whom Khomeini was speaking would not have needed translations.

Imagine, then, that we sit with Khomeini's students in Najaf as he delivers these lectures. Khomeini's style is not to answer questions or objections that are tossed out during the flow of his talk. Rather, he receives these oral interruptions silently and begins with them at the start of the following day's session or works them in at breaks in the flow of his thought. A dramatic dialectic form guides his lectures, as it does for other teachers in the seminary system. This form is called *ishkāl* ("criticism," "question") and is triggered in three ways. The lecturer uses traditional or common opinions as foils, or he anticipates questions and objections from his audience, or his audience actually interjects questions and objections.

Khomeini is quite clear that he is testing the limits of an argument, and that the game of *ḥadīth* on which as a *faqīh* he must base himself provides shaky grounds: "If the only proof I had were one of the traditions I've been citing, I would be unable to substantiate my claim" (1981, 99). Four sources of authority are in fact invoked: reason, the practices of the Prophet and of 'Ali, the Qur'an, and the *ḥadīth* of the Prophet and the Imams. Although a score of Qur'anic *verses* are cited at various points—some to illustrate governmental functions of an Islamic government such as taxation (8:41, 9:03) or implementing the penal code (24:2), some to illustrate the command to rise up against tyranny of kings and pharaohs, against idolators (*ṭāghūt*) and corrupters of the earth (28:4), some to illustrate the condemnation of religious leaders who fail to guide their followers (5:63, 5:75–78, 9:71)—one *verse* in particular and the one preceding it are central: "O you who believe, obey God and obey the Messenger and the holders of authority [*wali al-amr*] from among you" (4:59). For Shi'ites, the holders of authority are the Imams, the twelfth and last of whom remains alive, albeit in occultation.

Khomeini wants to show that "holders of authority" must also refer to the highest rank of the clergy—the *fuqaha* or *mujtahidīn*—those who have attained the level of knowledge in which they are not only permitted, but enjoined, to wield the interpretive rules for coming to independent decisions on novel questions (*ijtihād*). The preceding *verse* is: "God commands you to return trusts to their owners, and to act with justice when you rule/judge among men." Khomeini wants to show that the "trusts" are not merely, as traditional interpretations have it, worldly property to be returned to rightful owners and divine trusts or Islamic law, which to Shi'ites means the return of political and religious leadership to the Imams, usurped by the first three Sunni caliphs, the Umayyids, and subsequent monarchies. In addition he wants to show that the "trustees" here are the *fuqaha*; the word for "rule/judge" means "rule," not just "judging."

Khomeini marshals sixteen *hadīth*—three major ones and thirteen lesser ones—of varying reliability and applicability. What he accomplishes is not a proof, but only a plausibility that an Islamic society should be guided or ruled by jurisconsults (of Islamic law). Whether this is to be through a single *faqīh* or a college of *fuqahā* (the debate over a supreme *marja' taqlīd*), or even through a combination of *fuqahā* and laymen is not explored (although it is raised, 1981, 64); indeed, the principle that one *faqīh* cannot override another is affirmed (1981, 54). The constitution of the Islamic Republic enshrines all three possibilities: Khomeini as head of state represents a singular guardian; this is to be continued if possible after him, but provision is also made for a collegial leadership, and a Council of Guardians composed of both *fuqahā* and secular members was instituted to veto parliamentary legislation contravening Islamic law.

What, finally, is most interesting here is the degree to which this structure reflects Islamic restraint about knowing what God really wants: it is remarkable, given Khomeini's iron will and drive against compromise with the shah or with *fuqahā* who provided cover for oppositional factions to Khomeini's role as supreme *faqīh* (especially

Ayatullah Muhammad-Kazem Shariatmadari and Sayyid Mahmud Taleqani), that Khomeini's style of leadership over government and policy formation has systematically been one of arbitration among factions rather than either dictating policy or backing one faction against another. Nowhere is this clearer than in the remarkable history of factional stalemate about economic policy represented most symbolically by land reform. Hashemi-Rafsinjani, the speaker of the Parliament, repeatedly, in 1981, 1983, and 1984, asked Khomeini to intervene and direct Parliament, the Council of Guardians, or the executive branch to follow what he designated as correct policy: Khomeini refused. One grounding of this restraint lies in the degree to which there is an Islamic economics encoded in the Qur'an and *ḥadīth*. Contrary to the strident apologetics of lay Muslims, professional *fuqahā* move very carefully in this territory, because to fulfill the program of a political economy such as is envisioned in Khomeini's *Hokūmat-i Islāmi* considerable *ta'wīl* is required. It is an interesting exercise, and it is astounding how little patience for it have even such *fuqaha* as the late Ayatullah Muhammad-Baqir Sadr, who wrote the fullest contemporary Shiʿite statement on the subject but whose *Iqtiṣāduna* (Our Economics) is amazingly poor in locating proof texts in the Qur'an, *ḥadīth*, historical *fatwas*, or *ḥukms*.

The point here is not that the *ḥadīth* literature is such a mass of contradictions and fabrications as to make it unusable for serious history, but on the contrary that the *use* of *ḥadīth* can provide access to ideological, sectarian, social, and political history. This is a history that must be approached dialectically (aware of the range of counterarguments in a given historical period), hermeneutically (aware of the allusions and contexts, nuances and changes in word usage), and dialogically (aware of the political others against whom assertions are made). It is an ethical discourse in the sense that it is always conducted in a communicative environment that assumes persuasive dialogue with others, that attempts to persuade those others to join one's own moral and political community.

Conclusion: Dialogue, Ethics, Politics

A wake! Come a wake! . . . Every old skin in the leather world, infect the whole stock company of the old house of the Leaking Barrel, was thomistically drunk. . . . But twill cling hellish like engels opened to noneuropeans, if you've sensed, whole the sum. So be vigil.

James Joyce, *Finnegans Wake*

Western audiences, out of ignorance, yield too easily to fundamentalist Muslim claims that Islam is prescriptive in a simple way. To argue otherwise requires knowledge of Islamic hermeneutics, dialectics, and dialogics. This knowledge is difficult to attain for those who have lost contact with their own Christian and Jewish traditions of hermeneutics, dialectics, and dialogics or with those of ancient Greece, which too often are nostalgically idealized and hypostasized into paragons of virtue no longer viable.

We have argued not only that such dialogic traditions are neither obscure nor distant, but that they are fundamental to ethical discourse, whether written or oral. They constitute a family of resemblances with overlapping origins and many commonalities, but it is only through the play of their differences and their acknowledgment of cultural interreferences that the fullness of the dialogic emerges from its parochial veiling and monologic chauvinism. Consider only the metaphoric differentials of stress in Greek "biblos" (from the Phoenician city that exported papyrus); Christian "scripture"; the Jewish oral and written "torah" (from *ohr*, "light"); and the Islamic "qur'an." Christian tradition seems to privilege the archetype relation: the world as realization of the *logos*, language as representation, the New Testament as realization of the Old, writing as secondary to an originary word. Jewish tradition privileges the "trace," "divine sparks," or play of meaning (Israel, "he who wrestles with God"), claiming that both written and oral forms require disputational, hermeneutic explorations to pursue the plenitude that through language creates the human, moral world. (In the language of Levinas and Derrida, there is no presence "behind," only a creative absence: Luria's *tsimtsum*,[11] the universe contained in the dot of the b of *bismillah*.[12]) It is this play that seems to draw the frustrated wrath of the Qur'an upon the Jews,[13] this embrace of the ambiguities of the text with which Muslims also struggle. Muslim tradition privileges the oral, the Qur'an, viewing the written book as

11. Isaac Luria Ashkenazi (1534–72), the foremost of the Sofed Kabbalists, formulated the doctrine of *tsimtsum*, that God created the world by contracting to an infintesimal point.

12. There is a Muslim saying that the whole of the Qur'an exists in the *bismillah* ("in the name of God," the first word of the invocation), and the whole of the *bismillah* exists in the first letter, *bā*, and the whole of the *bā* exists in its dot (which distinguishes it from other similarly shaped letters).

13. For the renewed fundamentalist stress on this wrath, see Sayyid Qutb's influential "Our Struggle with the Jews" (Nettler 1987).

but an imperfect *transcript*,[14] seeing the Torah and Gospels as corrupted texts that illustrate the dangers of writing. It plays up context, intent, face-to-face event, and distrusts both archetype *ta'wīl* (Christians mistook the crucifixion) and hermeneutic play, although adept at both: the search is for plain meaning in a world of appearances.

It is perhaps James Joyce who most fully provides a cosmopolitan text that explicitly acknowledges the interplay of these traditions and places them in the postmodern context of centers and peripheries (Europe-Ireland, America-Iran) that generate "Third World" political moral dilemmas. And it is perhaps Edmond Jabès who is the poet of the contemporary world where dialogue and its discontents are the (w)hole condition of meaning. Can the tradition of disputation (*mubāhatha*, Gadamer's hermeneutics, Habermas's communicative ethics) provide an image of a democratic public ethos, particularly given the role of *taqiyya* (dissimulation) as a concrete element symbolizing both the necessity to incorporate the realities of power/interests into the model of communicative ethics and strategies of feigning temporary communicative agreement for long-term advantage? Can one protect against the old Platonic and modern Hegelian tendencies of statism (Khomeini's *wilāyat-i faqīh*)? In the contemporary Muslim world, can the tradition of disputation overcome the unitarian ideologies (*tawḥīd* that deny and suppress all conflict, be it class conflict or other principled divisions within the *umma* (community of believers)? Can the polysemic and nomadic meanings of a text such as the Qur'an overcome the unbewised efforts to reduce it to monologic decree? At issue methodologically is the distinction between a dialectics that assimilates some arguments, refuting others that cannot be digested, and a dialectics that provides synoptic visions of the entire range of argumentation (cf. McKeon, this volume). Given the unknowability of the Qur'an (there is no single correct interpretation, either because of the infinity of God's writing and speech or because of the limitations of human hermeneutics in the absence of an infallible interpreter or Imam), and given the labyrinths of *ḥadīth* and other interpretive con-texts, is it possible for such an enigmatic text as the Qur'an to function as a poetic touchstone for a universalistic ethic?

The political dialogues of the contemporary Islamic world,

---

14. Compare the suggestion that Muhammad attempted in his later career to transform the Qur'an into a book but abandoned the effort (Bell and Watt 1970, 143).

grounded in traditional scriptural-based dialectical disputation and in dialogically performative experience, provide an interesting mirror (*a*) to our Western roots (e.g., the *sic et non* Catholic disputational methods borrowed from Muslim Spain; the shimmering similarities of Muslim and Jewish hermeneutics); (*b*) to our global present in which Islam presents a paradigmatic dialectic of a Third World constructed against and within a world system; and (*c*) to the effort to construct a democratic pluralism that protects cultural differences without yielding to cultural positions that claim unique access to the truth.

References

Abul-Qasem, Muhammad. 1982. *The recitation and interpretation of the Qur'an: Al-Ghazali's theory*. London: Kegan Paul International.

Bell, Richard, and Montgomery Watt. 1970. *Introduction to the Qur'an*. Edinburgh: Edinburgh University Press.

Berger, Harry, Jr. 1987. Levels of discourse in Plato's dialogues. In *Literature and the question of philosophy*, ed. A. Cascardi. Baltimore: Johns Hopkins University Press.

Duri, A. A. 1983. *The rise of historical writing among the Arabs*. Princeton: Princeton University Press.

Fischer, M. M. J. 1980. *Iran: From religious dispute to revolution*. Cambridge: Harvard University Press.

———. 1982. Islam and the revolt of the petit bourgeoisie. *Daedalus* 111 (1): 10–26.

———. 1983. Imam Khomeini: Four ways of understanding. In *Voices of a resurgent Islam*, ed. J. Esposito. New York: Oxford University Press.

Fischer, M. M. J., and M. Abedi. 1984. Foreword to R. Khomeini, *A clarification of questions*. Boulder, Colo.: Westview Press.

———. 1990. *Debating Muslims: Cultural dialogues in tradition and postmodernity*. Madison: University of Wisconsin Press.

Gould, Eric. 1985. *The sin of the Book: Edmond Jabès*. Lincoln: University of Nebraska Press.

Griswold, Charles. 1986. *Self-knowledge in Plato's "Phaedrus."* New Haven: Yale University Press.

Khomeini, Ruhullah. 1981. Hokūmat-i Islami: Wilayat-i faqih. In *Islam and revolution: Writings and declarations of Imam Khomeini*, ed. H. Algar. Berkeley: Mizan Press.

Motahhari, Mortada. 1962. Ijtihad dar Islam. In *Bahthi darbareye Marjaiyat va Ruhaniyat*, ed. S. M. H. Tabataba'i et al. Tehran: Enteshar.

Nelson, Kristina. 1985. *The art of reciting the Qur'an*. Austin: University of Texas Press.

Nettler, Ronald L. 1987. *Past trials and present tribulations: A Muslim fundamentalist's view of the Jews*. Oxford: Pergamon Press.

al-Radi, al-Sharif, Muhammad ibn al-Husayn. 1967. *Nahjul al-Balagha*. Beirut: Dār al-Turāth al-'Arab.

Rosen, Stanley. 1987. *Hermeneutics as politics*. New York: Oxford University Press.

as-Said, Labib. 1975. *The recited Koran*. Princeton: Darwin Press.

Seery, John E. 1985. Political returns. Ph.D. diss., University of California at Berkeley.

Taleqani, S. Mahmud. n.d. *Partovi Az Qur'an*. Tehran: Enteshar.

Wansborough, John. 1977. *Qur'anic studies*. London: Oxford University Press.

Literary Experiments
with Dialogue

6

The Other in Question: Dialogical Experiments in Montaigne, Kafka, and Cortázar

R. Lane Kauffmann

> To hold a dialogue is to suppose a third man and to seek to exclude him.
> Michel Serres

Invoking the Other

Characters and *Setting:* Maria and Jack, graduate students (in anthropology and comparative literature, respectively), converse while strolling on the campus of a university somewhere in the southwestern United States.

Jack: Thank you for recommending Todorov's *Conquest of America: The Question of the Other* — I've just finished reading it. Shall we discuss it as we walk along? But you must promise to walk slowly, so I can develop my thoughts.

Maria: I take it you plan to do most of the talking! I promise to keep an appropriate pace.

Jack: The question of the Other is very fashionable these days. Critics invoke it talismanically, as if to ward off the evils of centric discourse (I refer to anthropo-, ego-, ethno-, Euro-, logo-, phallo-, and other proliferating "centrisms"). But it's easier to invoke the Other than to communicate with it, or her, or him. Todorov's study on the conquest of Meso-America shows that even sympathetic constructions of alterity tend to deny "the existence of a human substance truly other, something capable of being not merely an imperfect state of ourselves."

In deference to its dialogue form, I have decided not to encumber this text with footnotes. Interested readers will find in the References the sources mentioned or alluded to by Jack and Maria.

Maria: Must we settle for this gloomy solipsism? I'd rather submit to a dialogical imperative, to some version of what Todorov calls "non-violent communication," both as an ethical and as a methodological principle. Todorov's sympathetic study seems proof enough of what is to be gained by such a dialogical approach.

Jack: His study offers many insights. But I find his invocation of the "Other," and your defense of it, a bit *too* sympathetic.

Maria: Too sympathetic! To whom or to what, pray tell?

Jack: Curiously enough, that's precisely the question: to *whom,* or to *what?* Does the author's vision of the Other correspond to a human referent—the conquered indigenous tribes of the Americas—or to a lifeless abstraction? Empathy is the study's founding gesture: you recall that the book is dedicated to the young Indian woman prisoner who—according to an anecdote repeated by the author—was thrown to the dogs by the conquistadores after she committed suicide to avoid betraying her spouse by having sexual relations with her Spanish captors. But after reading the study, I have an uneasy feeling that the Other invoked by Todorov is based on empathy of a feckless and sentimental kind. It's a sophisticated version of the old "noble savage" myth forged by European intellectuals, a myth whose function here is to extend colonization by hermeneutic means.

Maria: Goodness, I'd forgotten what a cynic you can be! Are you suggesting that Todorov deliberately mystifies in order to prolong colonialism? Surely he's aware of the ideological uses of the noble savage myth.

Jack: I'm not saying that the mystification is conscious or deliberate. If it were, it would be too obvious to be interesting. No, I'm simply suggesting that behind the fashionable liberal impulse of emphathizing or identifying with the Other stands an urge to co-opt and appropriate—either by appointing oneself spokesperson for the Other or by defining the speech context in such a way that the Other's freedom is preempted, her response virtually predetermined. Often the impulse is motivated by a guilty conscience—or perhaps I should say a guilty *unconscious.* In any case, it pretends to atone discursively for the nondiscursive sins committed by the European conquerors and colonizers. And I know what you're about to say, with your stubborn sense of fairness: that not all colonizers were horrid or mistreated the natives. But examples such as the good Padre Bartolomé de las Casas only confirm that the discourse of atonement began almost simultaneously with the process of conquest and colonization. Todorov's is just an updated version.

Maria: I find your argument provocative, but a bit far-fetched. By accusing Todorov's *critique* of colonialism of being a more insidious form of colonialist ideology, aren't you succumbing to a conspiracy theory of ideology-critique?

Jack: Not at all. I'm speaking of a long-standing literary tradition, perhaps even the mainstream, of European ethnography, of writing about other cultures. Try to conceive of this tradition, whether in its scientific or its fictional guise, as consisting of fables of communication between European and indigenous cultures—fables of dialogue, with diverse scenarios of confrontation, atonement, reconciliation, and revenge. Mind you, I'm not claiming that this tradition, or Todorov's book in particular, is obscurantist or "unenlightened." Todorov shares with his predecessors—Las Casas, Montaigne, and Rousseau—the virtue of lucid self-criticism, an admirable capacity to relativize European values and achievements. Particularly suggestive is his thesis that the European conquest of America was in large part a hermeneutic conquest, as exemplified by Cortés's ability to defeat the Aztecs by assimilating and manipulating their linguistic and cultural sign systems. But I wonder whether the critic and the reader aren't in a similar relation of semiotic seduction; whether we readers aren't in danger of being persuaded that the critic speaks from an Archimedean point beyond relations of interest and power. Because the critic's argument is compelling, we forget to apply it to his own discourse, thus failing to see that it's only a subtler version of the old logocentric appropriation of alterity.

Maria: How can you equate Todorov's empathy with Cortés's tactical maneuvers? One seeks to understand, the other to subdue. Doesn't the ethical intent make a difference?

Jack: If we're to begin thinking dialogically, we must first be suspicious of discourse that universalizes, idealizes, or prematurely identifies with the Other. Instead of ignoring or underestimating the distance between Self and Other, one should stress the incommensurability between subjects and cultures—while being wary of those who would ontologize cultural differences to ground racist doctrines. In such a beginning, one should not forget the difficulties involved in achieving what Todorov calls "difference in equality" and what Adorno called the utopia of "distinctness without domination." It's significant, by the way, that Adorno's version of the dialogical imperative takes the form of a critique of traditional identitarian epistemologies that base knowledge (whether of human beings or their creations) on a presumptive identity between the knowing subject and the known object. Adorno insists on the irreducible difference or nonidentity between the order of phenomena and that of our conceptual constructions.

Maria: But Adorno's negative dialectics remains shackled to idealist epistemology, in that it conceives of the Other as an object of knowledge, not as a subject of discourse. The hermeneutic-dialogical turn taken by experimental ethnography in recent years moves away from the monological model of ethnography as a scientific description of the savage (the savage as an object to be known and analyzed—or, in some versions, rescued) and moves toward dialogical interaction, conceiving the native as an equal who generates utterances and perspectives to which we must attend—letting the Other speak for herself, as it were. This inverts the old hierarchy of knowledge over discourse, cognition over communication. The idea now is not to represent the Other, but to understand and communicate with her.

Jack: Fine. But can the hierarchy of cognition over communication simply be reversed—or stood on its head, as the Marxists say—without thereby committing the opposite error and enshrining another hierarchy, that of discourse over concept? Isn't epistemology still relevant to the extent that dialogical intercourse is always framed by and grounded in our cultural knowledge, or ignorance, of the Other—conditions that can lead our attempted dialogues to succeed or to fail?

Maria: I suppose so. But allow me to observe that the opposition you keep making between Self and Other, subject and object, can also be questioned. After all, the category of the Self is as suspect as its privative, the Other; neither is to be taken as a fixed entity or an autonomous monad. Dialogical and dialectical traditions show that the Self is a social being, constituted through the language and social pressure of others, just as the Other is partly a projection of ourselves.

Jack: My point was that empathy and commitment to dialogue, however noble in themselves, do not make one immune to ethnocentrism. For methodological reasons, it seems advisable to start with the pessimistic assumption that constructions of the Other are usually self-projections that need to be deconstructed. The critical task would be to give the soberest possible account of texts claiming to interpret the Other or represent her in dialogue, by analyzing the mechanisms of projection and appropriation as they function in those texts.

Maria: Please go on; you're beginning to make sense. Perhaps that should worry me!

Jack: Indeed it should. If you listen properly, you'll probably be obliged to surrender a few cherished illusions before I'm through.

Maria: You're insufferably conceited, as usual. But I'll forgive you for that as long as what you say continues to interest me. Anyway, I was only pretending to be worried: I have no fear that in the end my innate good sense will be quite sufficient to resist your brilliant sophistries. Continue, please, and let's have some examples, if you know any, of those "dialogical fables" you mentioned.

Jack (smiling): Very well. I have several examples in mind, three to be precise, each from a distinct national tradition and historical period. These differences of language and cultural tradition will of course make precise comparisons difficult. But I'll attempt to satisfy you that each of these European invocations of otherness—in which some form of radical alterity is imagined and presented in ostensible dialogue—turns out to be a case of co-optation or, figuratively speaking, of colonization.

Maria: I'm eager to hear your demonstrations. But first, let's withdraw to my study, so we can refer to the original sources as necessary. We might also have a cup of tea there in the coolness of my library.

Jack: Dear Maria, that's an excellent idea. I'm parched.

Conjuring the Other

(In Maria's book-lined study: a small but comfortable room, looking out on a desert landscape.)

Maria: Now that we're refreshed, shall we resume our conversation where we left off?

Jack: By all means. First, let's consider an early example of the European myth of the noble savage. Do you know Michel de Montaigne's "Of Cannibals"?

Maria: Yes, I'm familiar with it. But where's the dialogue there? Isn't that text a straightforward essay?

Jack: There are no straightforward essays.

Maria: You know what I mean. It's a monologue, the author speaking in his own voice, reporting an experience. It was clever of you to choose it as an early example of ethnography, but in what sense is it a *dialogue?* I don't recall that the Brazilian Indians Montaigne describes actually *talk back.* Is there some generic confusion here?

Jack: If so, it's not mine. You'll excuse me if I occasionally take a didactic tone, but if we're to get anywhere, we really must leave generic essentialism by the wayside. By that I mean . . .

Maria: You mean one should not reify genres and then proceed to classify texts as though they were governed by a single and constant form of presentation. Genres are not frozen set-pieces but complex formal models for interweaving multiple speech acts. Isn't that how the lecture goes?

Jack: Precisely. One shouldn't be misled by surface textual appearances, such as whether interlocutors are shown taking turns *in persona,* and so on. The true boundaries of discourse may be less clearly marked. If we understand dialogue in the sense of the Russian theorist Bakhtin—that is, in terms of the speaker's orientation to the addressee's discourse—then the modes and manifestations of this commerce with alterity are precisely what need to be explored and delineated, rather than being read off from the surface features of a text. Do you see what I mean?

Maria: The point is apparently that one may have a formal dialogue without having its substance; that what looks like a dialogue may in fact be covert monologue; and conversely, that what looks like a monologue or essay—or any other genre—may be quite dialogical in function, *n'est-ce pas?*

Jack: Lesson well recited; now let's try to apply it. I daresay we will find Montaigne's venture to be dialogical, precisely insofar as we never encounter the Other speaking for himself in this essay. Let me explain the paradox. You'll recall that Montaigne wants exact knowledge of other cultures. If direct contact is not possible, let's have firsthand testimony by reliable witnesses who'll report without embellishment or interpretation, says Montaigne. Questioning the reliability of classical speculations about the New World, Montaigne prefers the unvarnished testimony of a simple, dull-witted fellow who had spent some time in what would later become Brazil. "For clever people observe more things and more curiously, but they interpret them. . . . We need a man either very honest, or so simple that he has not the stuff to build up false inventions and give them plausibility; and wedded to no theory." But the expected testimony, the promised encounter, is constantly postponed in the essay, and the reader is left wondering why.

Maria: Instead, as I recall, we are treated to Montaigne's own interpretation of the Brazilian cannibals.

Jack: Yes, the irony is strong. The essayist is the epitome of the interpretative dilettante, the nonspecialist whose only license is curiosity, who in effect thumbs his nose at the knowledge of specialists. So one already begins to suspect that Montaigne is giving the reader reasons to be skeptical of his own ruminations. In the same passage, he has recourse to the perspectivism that became the favorite trope of enlightened ethnographic discourse in Montesquieu and others: "Each man calls barbarism whatever is not his own practice." Thus we're led to question not only the author's perspective, but our own as well. (By "we," I mean of course the European or Eurocentric perspective, which is that of the implied reader of Montaigne's essays.) We're reminded that "we have no other test of truth and reason than the opinions and customs of the country we live in." Accordingly, we're duped by our own language: we call anything foreign "wild," with a pejorative sense, "whereas really, it is those that we have changed artificially and led astray . . . that we should rather call wild."

Maria: Yes, I'm familiar with the passage. There follows Montaigne's rhapsodic celebration of the natural: the presumed "savage" exists in a state of pure nature, uncorrupted by European civilization. I see the irony of invoking experience, then engaging in a rhapsody. The inversion of a commonplace is still a commonplace. The only dialogue he engages in here is with Plato, whom he quotes to authorize and embellish his hymn to nature, and whom he then invokes as an imaginary interlocutor. He contrasts early poets' and philosophers' conceptions of the ideal state or golden age with "what we actually see . . . by experience," when it is plainly *not* his own experience but an interpretation or gloss that he presents here. We're promised an encounter with the savage Other, but that Other never materializes; we have only reports of encounters. The Other's speech is always quoted in the indirect discourse of Montaigne's interlocutors: ancient authors, his simple traveler, the king, and bystanders when three Indians were displayed in Rouen. And when Montaigne goes to question the natives himself, in the essay's final passage, communication is impeded by a bad translator. The closest thing to direct discourse quoted in the essay are native songs that have been transcribed and translated before coming into Montaigne's possession: discourse, in other words, that's been converted into textual, aesthetic artifacts.

Jack: Yes, and still more ironically, he praises these songs not for their naturalness or simplicity, but for their resemblance to Anacreontic poetry—an eminently European poetic mode, a refined imitation of the natural. "Their language, moreover, is a soft language, with an agreeable sound, somewhat like Greek in its endings." These Euro-sympathies, perhaps innocent in themselves, nonetheless reveal a pattern. Montaigne prides himself on being able to describe unflinchingly the cannibals' most "barbaric" qualities. He even manages to mitigate his horror at their cannibalistic practices by arguing that they compare favorably with torture methods practiced by his own countrymen during the religious wars; at least the cannibals kill their victims first. But Montaigne's apology for the cannibals normally proceeds by discovering likeness rather than difference. His highest praise for them is reserved for qualities dear to a European humanist: bravery, loyalty, the capacity for reason and aesthetic appreciation. Lest the reader assume that the natives' behavior is based on the authority of mere custom, "without reasoning or judgment," Montaigne cites a native love song to prove the natives' ratiocinative powers. "You see," he seems to be suggesting, "their barbarism is only skin-deep. These savages are actually quite civilized; they even write good poetry." Underlying surface differences, in other words, is a shared human identity: they are really like us—only more natural, more noble, less corrupt than we are. This he underscores by falling back, in mock resignation, on a superficial if graphic difference between the two cultures: "But what's the use? They don't wear breeches." Hasn't it always been a subtle way of domesticating the Other to confer upon him the honor of being like oneself?

Maria: To take an illustrious example, when Lévi-Strauss says that all thought is *pensée sauvage* (which he elsewhere reduces to an algorithm), what he is really saying is that the "savage mind" is rational too; only, like Montaigne's bottomless cannibals, it doesn't *appear* to be so. This allows the subject of ethnocentric discourse to have it both ways: on the one hand, to universalize his own presuppositions—in this case, reason as the highest value—and on the other hand, to get credit for being magnanimous enough to recognize these traits in the Other as well.

Jack: Exactly. One might say that Montaigne is least "dialogical" when he is most sympathetic.

Maria: And, conversely, I suppose you'd say he's most dialogical when he seems most monological?

Jack: In a sense, yes. We've noted that Montaigne's project falls short of genuine dialogue. But this failure is relative and can work dialectically in the service of dialogue. While calling for unmediated knowledge of the Other, direct experience without interpretation, what he shows instead is the difficulty of attaining such knowledge or experience. What we're shown again and again is the inaccessibility of the Other: he's never quite where we expect him to be (nor, for that matter, is the knowing subject—Montaigne, we ourselves). By revealing the linguistic and cultural opacity of interpretations, the trickiness of translation, Montaigne shows that the Other can *only* be interpreted, never captured, and then only by examining one's own modes of knowledge and communication. This is the groundbreaking moment of ideology critique. With its devices of irony and perspectivism, Montaigne's essay qualifies the happy positivity of Enlightenment thought. Calling for knowledge without interpretation but giving us only the latter, Montaigne "deauthorizes" his own testimony, giving the reader a skeptical tool with which to deconstruct his own and, by implication, all Eurocentric representations of the Other.

Maria: Aren't you perhaps making too much out of this admittedly suggestive essay on cannibals? Perhaps the whole problem stems from the contingent fact that very few Europeans of Montaigne's time could speak the language of the Brazilian Indians, and hence visitors had to rely on unreliable translators. Their only recourse was to interpret, to speculate on the nature of the Other. As Todorov points out, ignorance of another's language makes each of us "the other's barbarian"—thus the Greeks called other peoples barbarous because of their improper pronunciation of the Greek language.

Jack: You're underestimating the hermeneutic problem, for which translation is only a metaphor here. Do you recall the passage in Wittgenstein's *Philosophical Investigations* where he observes that "if a lion could speak, we could not understand him"? This is an extreme case of otherness, an interspecies communication barrier, which serves to remind us that language barriers are not the only, or even the most impenetrable, form of otherness. The language problem between Montaigne and the cannibal pales beside their cultural differences—such as their diets!

Maria: An interesting point, but what about the hermeneutic barrier between two people of the same language *and* the same culture? For example, there are more than enough differences between a man and a woman to make an interesting hermeneutic problem, without worrying about interlinguistic or intercultural, much less interspecies, modes of otherness. Indeed, Woman as colonized Other seems to me a rich subject of analysis, involving all the problems of power, control, and domination that arise in colonial discourse. Surely women of both northern and southern latitudes are victims of many of the same modes of colonization as the cannibals who were captured and paraded around Europe in Montaigne's time. But perhaps *that* Other is too familiar, the setting not exotic enough, the colonization scenario a little too close to home for some?

Jack: Maria, you always want to translate epistemological and hermeneutical questions into political or ethical ones. But there is no need for hostility. You know full well that I neither deny nor condone the existence of sexism in any form. Nor do I dispute the validity of feminist critique. But your question begs its own answer: in the case of the exploitation of women within our own culture, the hermeneutic problem tends to disappear behind the more obvious facts of power and exploitation. The gender matter is already too politicized for a calm consideration of its more subtle hermeneutic dimension. But to address the feminist position more directly: here as well one encounters the problem that the "Other" is never quite where one thought, or where she pretends to be. Even the female feminist (the case of the male feminist is more obvious) cannot simply equate herself with "Woman" or "the female gender," which would be to mistake the instance for the category and to suggest that one occupies a privileged locus *beyond* centric discourse, free from particular motives and interests. Insofar as the feminist also stands within Western "phallogocentric" discourse, her critique can claim no privileged access to pristine otherness, nor adequate representation of this Other. Like Montaigne vis-à-vis the cannibal, the feminist is condemned to the role of presumptuous spokesperson or unreliable interpreter. Like Montaigne, she discovers that the Other is never fully accessible but appears only through mediating stand-ins, interpreting screens.

Maria: There's more to be said, particularly regarding your caricature of feminism, but for the sake of argument, let's tentatively grant your first example. Before moving on to the next, allow me to refill your cup. You must be thirsty after such a lengthy diatribe—excuse me, I mean dialogue.

Aping the Other

Jack (puts down his cup): Now then, where were we?

Maria: You were defending your example of Montaigne's cannibals against my suggestion that we consider intracultural forms of otherness instead.

Jack: Ah, yes. There's of course no reason we can't consider both. And yet, as I was saying, I believe there are advantages in highlighting the communication gaps between subjects. It allows one to focus more precisely on the semiotic processes by which the Other is constituted and appropriated in each case. Therefore I propose to return to the problem of interspecies dialogue by comparing two animal tales that are, I know, familiar to you: Kafka's "Report to an Academy" and Cortázar's "Axolotl." If we contrast their narrative strategies . . .

Maria: Pardon the interruption, but why choose animal tales for an investigation of the hermeneutic problem? Isn't this a reductio ad absurdum of the communication barrier between Self and Other? Remember Wittgenstein's dictum that if a lion could speak, we couldn't understand him. Even if animals could manipulate a verbal code, the gap between their lifeworld and ours would still be unbridgeable. So why consider our dealings with animals to be in any way paradigmatic of dialogue?

Jack: The choice of talking animals as Others is anything but fortuitous. It is motivated by the ambivalent ideological relationship humans have with other creatures. Do they represent inferior, once rival, species, to be used as needed for our food, experiments, and pleasure? Or are they our own ancestors, primitive versions of ourselves? We harbor feelings both of fear and of sympathy. Heidegger speaks of the "abyss" separating us from other animals, of our "appalling and scarcely conceivable bodily kinship with the beast." Besides, why allow the thought experiment to die so quickly? Wittgenstein is being a wet blanket here—denying the premise of his own experiment, refusing to play his own language game. For if the lion *could* use human language, couldn't his speech in principle be understood? Western literature is in fact full of texts that push the counterfactual premise further and ask: What if animals could speak and we *could* understand them?

Maria: So you see the animal tale as a thought experiment in which one imagines oneself eavesdropping on the otherness of the Other.

Jack: Precisely.

Maria: Fine. But—and please excuse me if I seem overly empirical— is this the way animal tales really work? Think of Aesop's fables:

Don't they simply anthropomorphize, making animals the mouth-pieces of human desires and emotions? As fiction, such tales are obviously not bound by the constraints of real dialogue. Don't they reveal more about the author's fantasies and projections than they do about the nature of the Other?

Jack: I agree that fantasy and projection are the mainsprings of the animal tale, but then I think they are the mainsprings of constructions of the Other in general. The apparent impossibility of interspecies dialogue in the beast fable is just what makes it appropriate as a symbolic limit case of the hermeneutical aporias we encounter in human interaction. The very speechlessness of animals enables them to function as metaphorical substitutes for various mute or dispos-sessed others in human experience—slaves versus masters, "primi-tive" versus "civilized," oral versus text-literate cultures, and so on; the allegorical possibilities multiply. Freed from the scientific and empirical constraints of official ethnography—or so one imagines—and freed, by their license to fantasize, from realistic codes of verisimilitude, animal tales are an ideal test case for imagining otherness. This relative freedom from generic constraint does not mean that animal tales are innocent of ideological projection. Quite the contrary, it may be that such projection appears there in a less inhibited form. Anthropocentrism in the animal tale becomes a trope for centric discourse in general. By looking more closely at how the Other is constituted discursively in these tales, one might hope to clarify the pitfalls of, and discover possible escapes from, the pessimistic solipsism you accuse me of.

Maria: I applaud the aim of inquiry, as you state it. Proceed. On what basis do you propose to compare the two stories?

Jack: Both stories depict the surrender or accommodation of a subject to an alien species and lifeworld. Insofar as both claim to depict interspecies communication, they may be regarded as experiments in dialogue that attempt to go beyond anthropocentrism—thus antici-pating the recent dialogical experiments in ethnography you mentioned earlier. Both are tales of conversion, or metamorphosis, narrated retrospectively. From the outset of each, we are the addressees of a message whose sender is alleged to be to some degree nonhuman and explains to us how he came to acquire consciousness and the power of speech.

Maria: Shall we now let Kafka and Cortázar, or rather their animal narrators, speak for themselves, as it were?

Jack: Agreed. This time I'll ask you to set the course of analysis, seeing that you're eager to do so, and having total confidence in your analytical powers . . .

Maria: You are too kind, Herr Doktor Professor. As you were saying, from the first line of Kafka's story, we find ourselves in the implied audience—an academy to whom an ape makes a report. We're told how he came to be wounded and captured by hunters, why he took the trouble to acquire human language, and how he evolved to attain the "cultural level of an average European." The premise of the story is that of Darwinian evolution at fast forward, of phylogeny telescoped into ontogeny—the premise that in a single lifetime an ape has become humanized. Once we've suspended disbelief and accepted that premise, the narrative is almost conventional in its development. If one wanted to describe it generically, it's a lecture that has the narrative structure of a *Bildungsroman*—or better yet, a *Bildungsmärchen*, or fable of acculturation.

Jack: A brave beginning. But you won't deny that the truly "Other" here is not the educated ape, but the savage one, prior to speech; nor that *this* Other, which is the most interesting to his audience, is precisely inaccessible and declared to be so by Rotpeter himself (we might as well use the ape's given name). He begins with the caveat that he cannot comply exactly with the academy's request to give an account of his former life as an ape. The price he has had to pay for his transformation has been the forgetting of his origins. "In revenge, . . . my memory has closed the door against me more and more." The past has become inaccessible; the "opening" through which Rotpeter might once have returned has narrowed irretrievably. He can only "indicate the line an erstwhile ape has had to follow in entering and establishing himself in the world of men." He returns to this topos of limited expressibility, noting that "what I felt then as an ape I can represent now only in human terms, and therefore I misrepresent it, but although I cannot reach back to the truth of the old ape life, there is no doubt that it lies somewhere in the direction I have indicated." But you see my point: Kafka cannily insists that there is no unmediated access to the ape's past; this otherness is mediated by the ape's fallible memory and by the opacity of an alien medium—human language.

Maria: Granted. But let's not overlook the satirical and allegorical dimensions of the tale. One may say that Kafka has at least two targets in mind. First, by parodying Darwin's theory of evolution, he mocks the rhetoric of contemporary science and the linear models derived from it. Second, as is well known, Kafka takes aim at the phenomenon of Jewish assimilation into the mainstream of European bourgeois society. The ape's abandoning of his origins and early remembrances, his adaptation through abject mimicry of the coarse sailors, and his refusal of sentimentality add up to a bitter and poignant critique of this phenomenon—one that lets neither the assimilating Jews nor the imitated Gentiles off the hook.

Jack: Yes, Kafka, an alienated Jew writing literature in German while living in Prague, was extremely sensitive to the desire for and the price of assimilation. But without forgetting either of these satirical targets, may we not posit a third way of interpreting the tale— namely, as a critique of anthropocentrism? After all, Rotpeter's testimony is full of potential embarrassments for the members of the academy. The behavior of their human confreres is lamentable. Rotpeter is first wounded by a hunter's "wanton shot," then mistreated by his captors. Particularly striking is the humans' automatic assumption of their superiority. This hubris is evident even in those who do not openly mistreat the ape but befriend him, instructing him in human ways. Rather than accommodate in any way to the ape, they oblige and assist the animal to become more like them, more "civilized." They are delighted by the ape's mimetic talent, and there is something quite narcissistic in the enthusiasm with which they encourage his assimilation, as though the ape's humanization somehow did them credit.

Maria: Their vaunted civilization is deflated as we survey its highest values and examples from the animal's point of view. The ape loses no time in clarifying that his accommodation to human culture and values is not voluntary but compulsory. He denies that his decision was motivated by desire for "freedom" as humans define it. Indeed, he scorns their sublime conception of freedom, which he believes is exemplified in the "self-controlled movement" of trapeze artists. ("What a mockery of holy Mother Nature! Were the apes to see such a spectacle, no theater walls could stand the shock of their laughter.") The ape's quest is not for freedom, but for something more urgent; he seeks "only a way out; right or left, or in any direction, . . . To get out somewhere, to get out! Only not to stay motionless with raised arms, crushed against a wooden wall." His motive can only diminish the ape's acculturation in the eyes of his audience, since it shows that he has chosen this path only as a desperate expedient.

Jack: The surest deflation of human pretensions is achieved through the ape's account of the acculturation process itself. You recall that it is only through "inner calm," great discipline, and heroic sacrifice that the ape can overcome his revulsion for things human. His method of self-transcendence is one of disciplined observation and mimicry of human habits and gestures. Consider for a moment the semiotics of this process of becoming human. His tutelage begins with the imitation of gestures and manual tasks and ends with the aping of speech. His apprenticeship, abetted by the cynical sailors, involves—to use the suggestive terms of Deleuze and Guattari—a progressive "deterritorialization" of the oral region, away from its standard simian functions, and its "reterritorialization" to the "human" ones of spitting, smoking, drinking, and, finally, speaking. Throughout, the human creatures he imitates come off worse than the ape by comparison. "It was so easy to imitate these people. I learned to spit in the very first days. We used to spit in each other's faces; the only difference was that I licked my face clean afterward and they did not." The culmination of his education— his initiation into the human community by yelling "Hallo!"— comes immediately after he has downed a pint of despised schnapps. The breakthrough to language is accompanied by the senseless gluttony learned from his teachers. Thus the ape learns the "discontents" of civilization the hard way. True, he is exhilarated by the learning process, but he is careful not to overestimate his attainment of the "cultural level of an average European. In itself that might be nothing to speak of," he notes—and here one imagines the squirming of his audience!—"but it is something insofar as it has helped me out of my cage."

Maria: Rotpeter's revenge is to turn the tables on humans, make them squirm, using the very tools he has learned from them—language, irony, and objectivity. Through the testimonial function of speech, he holds up a mirror to his human tormentors, revealing their true natures to them with merciless accuracy. It is, after all, this studied tone of pitiless objectivity, and the ape's effective mimicry of the very rhetoric and genres of science—especially his final appeal, "I am only imparting knowledge, I am only making a report"—that make the tale's critique of anthropocentrism so devastating.

Jack: I would only add that these tools of civilization are, even at the end, not only his means of liberation and of revenge, but also a kind of open-air cage, a permanent exile from his original animal state. While the story may be seen as an ironic variant of the "noble savage" myth, the ape is no longer entirely savage, nor is he entirely noble; though he is as dignified as one could expect in the circumstances, and apparently more noble than his captors, on whom he even takes pity. ("They were good creatures, in spite of everything.") He is something in between—a lucid but resentful savage. He has exchanged a literal cage at the beginning of the tale for the metaphorical, cultural one at the end; but he is no less "trapped" at the end than at the beginning.

Maria: I'm not surpised to see you emphasizing the symbolic distance between the ape and his human interlocutors.

Jack: Just so—because the lesson of the tale and its effectiveness depend on this distance. Rotpeter stresses his complete transformation to humanity, but the process, as Saki's Reginald once said about human ascent from the apes, is far from complete. The melancholy ending of the tale makes this point clear. The tragedy is that Rotpeter sacrifices his ape nature without ever becoming fully human. He remains stuck in a hybrid, in-between state, neither ape nor human. "With my hands in my trousers pockets, my bottle of wine on the table, I half lie and half sit in my rocking chair and gaze out of the window." This alienated, in-between state is further indicated by the nature of his only intimate relationship: "When I come home late at night from banquets, from scientific receptions, from social gatherings, there sits waiting for me a half-trained little chimpanzee, and I take comfort from her as apes do. By day I cannot bear to see her, for she has the bewildered look of the half-broken animal in her eye; no one else sees it, but I do, and I cannot bear it." Such is the price of his assimilation. It is his chosen way out, and he refuses to be pitied or told that it was not worth the trouble. But neither can he be complacent, for he senses that he can never be fully accepted by humans, nor can he himself identify fully with the products of human culture, to which he stands mainly in instrumental relation (for him they are only professional tools, actor's props for his performances). His lucidity and his alienation are inseparable. Kafka's allegorical critique of anthropocentrism suggests the dark side of assimilation under duress. But it also underscores the hubris of pretending that such transformations could ever be complete or entirely successful.

Maria: I catch the drift of your argument, and I'm eager to hear your comparison of this story with "Axolotl" by Cortázar. May I suggest a brief pause before moving to your final example?

Jack: By all means. The conversation has left me a bit winded.

Rescuing the Other

> Objects in mirror are closer than they appear.

Maria: To let you catch your breath, allow me to begin by recalling the main narrated events of Cortázar's "Axolotl." An anonymous individual who frequents the zoo in Paris one day visits the aquarium instead, where he becomes obsessed with the axolotls—the Nahuatl term for "water monster," applied to the larval form of a Mexican species of salamander. Returning almost daily, he begins to see the axolotls as avatars of the precolonial Aztec kingdom. At this point there occurs a metamorphosis—or perhaps a metempsychosis, a transmigration of the soul. The formerly human consciousness now finds itself inside the aquarium, trapped in the salamander body, condemned to silence and to futile awareness. Like "Report," then, "Axolotl" is a conversion tale narrated retrospectively by a nonhuman narrator. But whereas in the Kafka story an ape accommodates to human nature under duress, here a human voluntarily assimilates to the animal's lifeworld. Will this do as a preliminary characterization of the story?

Jack: As a point of departure, yes. But the situation of the narrator is more problematic in "Axolotl" than in "Report." Cortázar's tale is told by an "unreliable" narrator who announces from the outset that "there was a time when I thought a great deal about the axolotls. . . . Now I am an axolotl." While most of the story is told as a "flashback" from the "human" point of view, this central part of the tale is actually framed or quoted by the axolotl's (postmetamorphic) discourse. Since the metamorphosis here goes from the human to the nonhuman, the reader naturally wants to know how the axolotl gains access to the consciousness and language necessary to tell the story. The narrative premise that the *axolotl* controls narrative voice is difficult to accept. Even if we grant the fact of transmigration, there is no explanation of how the act of narration itself is accomplished, until the end of the story; and the explanation offered there is a bit far-fetched for my taste. It raises the question whether it's really an "Other" who accedes to language here, whether the narrative voice isn't projected onto the axolotl by human consciousness in a kind of narrative ventriloquism.

Maria: Perhaps you're going to give a reprise of Wittgenstein's wet blanket, demanding a rational explanation for everything, and refusing to play this language game of the fantastic mode?

Jack: My dear, I've hardly begun to play. Let's take the full measure of Cortázar's experiment. Discussing the function of the "fantastic" in his stories, Cortázar once observed that it allowed him to "cross over certain limits" and to "install myself in the territory of the Other." He compared his stories to a voyage of discovery into a Conrad-like "heart of darkness," giving him access to "archetypal regions"; to a primitive or archaic Other that seemed threatening to Western civilization. In his stories, this otherness appears as a sudden disruption of our everyday modes of perception. It is a temporary escape from Western reason and logic, enabling one to adopt an unfamiliar perspective that he referred to as "the latent possibility of a third frontier, of a third eye" (as found in some Oriental texts).

Maria: Literature, for Cortázar, has the function of "taking us for a moment out of our habitual boxes and showing us, if only ironically, that perhaps things do not end at the point where our mental habits fix them." Cortázar's experiment is rich in intergeneric associations: there are parallels not only with the fantastic journey and the animal tale, but also with the ethnographic account. One may read the story as an ethnographic fable, a parable of an attempt to penetrate the mystery of another cultural lifeworld, to overcome through empathy the obstacles of distance, fear, and lack of communication. By portraying a subject who carries this quest so far as to actually *become* the Other—one can hardly get more empathic than that—the story holds out the imaginative possibility of transcending the stultifying lifeworld of postmodern industrial societies.

Jack: The tale can indeed be read as an ethnographic fable; only I would take the fable as a parody, as an ironic allegory demonstrating the *futility* of empathy. It is a reductio ad absurdum of the attempt to solve the enigma of the Other through empathy and intuition. The Other adduced here is a pseudo-Other, an archetypal cliché. But let's proceed as we have with our previous examples, by inquiring first into the identity and provenance of the Other who is supposed to be narrating the Cortázar story.

Maria: From the first encounter, the narrator senses, behind the "Aztec faces" of the axolotls, a nonanimal presence to which he feels a strong affinity: "I knew that we were linked, that something infinitely lost and distant kept pulling us together." The Other posited here is even more remote than in the Kafka tale. At the risk of committing a biographical fallacy, allow me to suggest that the exotic aspect of the Other, and its ambivalent appeal to the human subject in the story, is motivated by personal and ideological factors that, when taken into consideration, give the story an existential resonance and allow for a more sympathetic "political" reading of it.

Jack: I'm all ears.

Maria: I must say, for someone who's all ears, your speech output is remarkable. Now let me rephrase the question: How is one to understand the nature of the affinity or "link" between the human narrator and this tiny larval form? I'll give only the bare outline of an answer. While one must avoid drawing facile parallels between the author and the narrator, one can scarcely ignore that the author is a European-born Argentine who emigrates back to Paris as an adult and who, precisely in the period when he writes the story, begins to develop a political consciousness and to affirm his solidarity with the oppressed peoples of Latin America. In this biographical constellation, many details seem charged with political and ideological tension. It becomes significant that the axolotl, of Mexican origin and "Aztec" appearance, has the traits of adaptability (it is amphibious), of nomadism or dispersion (specimens have been found in Africa), of being edible (they were previously used, like cod-liver oil, for alleged therapeutic value), of perpetual underdevelopment (it is the larval form of the salamander), and finally, as concerns these specimens, of being found captive, in involuntary exile in a Parisian aquarium, exploited objects of curiosity for humans in their leisure time. With this text, Cortázar participates vicariously in a European guilt complex with regard to the conquered and oppressed peoples of Latin America. This complex—which is not without historical justification—must have been felt in a acute and intricate way by Cortázar, given his problematic identity, at once double (Argentine and European roots) and divided (he identified culturally with Europe and politically with Latin America). If one wonders why this identity problem figures here as an ambivalent relationship between man and axolotl, it may be that the axolotl represents, in the story's unconscious logic, not Latin America as a political entity, nor the author's biographical and emotional roots in that continent, but rather its precolonial, autochthonous element—the indigenous tribes conquered and assimilated by Europeans. This archetype, as important symbolically as it was empirically inaccessible, was apparently available to the author's Europeanized imagination only in the guise of this small, totemic animal.

Jack: You apparently read the story as an Argentine emigré's version of *Roots!*

Maria: And why not? I believe the hypothesis of such a guilt complex best accounts for the narrator's paranoid construction of the axolotl. Detailed psychoanalytical interpretation of the story would reveal the interacting mechanisms of projection, transference, idealization, and identification operating in the narrator's discourse; here we must be content with a few suggestions. You'll recall that, as he recounts the conversion process, the human narrator is obsessed above all with the eyes of the axolotls: "They spoke to me of the presence of a different way of life, of another way of seeing." As the narrator's empathy grows, he denies that they are animals and begins to see them as the result of "a metamorphosis which did not succeed in revoking a mysterious humanity." The paranoid basis of this empathy, and its historical-allegorical associations, become evident in passages such as the following: "The axolotls were like witnesses of something, and at times like horrible judges. I felt ignoble in front of them; there was a terrifying purity in those transparent eyes. Behind those Aztec faces, without expression but of an implacable cruelty, what semblance was awaiting its hour? . . . They were lying in wait for something, a remote dominion destroyed, an age of liberty when the world had been that of the axolotls." The axolotls are interpreted as metamorphosed avatars of the ancient Aztec kingdom, whose current suffering (*tortura rígida*, "rigid torture") recalls their historical oppression at the hands of the narrator's European ancestors.

Jack: Though denying that he is anthropomorphizing, the narrator states, in a passage foreshadowing his own fate, that he "imagined them aware, slaves of their bodies, condemned infinitely to the silence of the abyss, to a hopeless meditation." He even begins to perceive in their "blind gaze" the supplication, "Save us, save us." Could there be a clearer case of anthropomorphic projection? The ethnocentric prototype of such projection is the redemptive gaze of Bartolomé de las Casas and other missionaries who, doubtless with absolute sincerity, perceived in the Indians a "wild" Christianity and a latent desire to be saved by conversion. And "save" them they did. God knows what happened to the ones who didn't want saving.

Maria: The projection is clearly shown, I agree. But in a story, as in psychoanalysis, projection is far from arbitrary; what matter are the patterns and motives it reveals to the interpreter. The most interesting example of paranoid interpretation is the "cannibalism of gold" the narrator detects in those closely watched eyes. Admitting that he is afraid of them, he tells the anecdote of the guard who remarked jokingly: "You eat them alive with your eyes, hey? . . . he likely thought I was a little cracked. What he didn't notice was that it was they devouring me slowly with their eyes, in a cannibalism of gold." It is as though the axolotls were avenging themselves for the historical crime committed by the Europeans against the Aztecs, whose riches they "devoured" and whose kingdom they destroyed. And now it is gold, the main motive for that crime, that appears inscribed, with strange but appropriate metonymy, in the implacable gaze that both accuses and "devours" the human narrator. The symmetry of this symbolic retribution could not be more exact. His fear, it must be noted, does not keep the narrator from sympathizing with the axolotls, even idealizing them. Paranoia is not incompatible with idealization of a feared Other. While feeling himself judged and about to be consumed by the axolotls, the narrator also perceives in them an overwhelming purity and regrets their idyllic past, the lost kingdom stolen from them.

Jack: Here we have a phantasmagoric variant of two related European myths of the New World: that of the noble savage and that of the precolonial past as a lost paradise. But even if one grants your main point—that the human protagonist's imaginary transmigration into an axolotl has the psychological function of expiating or mitigating a vicarious guilt complex, of assuaging the bad conscience of postcolonial European man—that hardly bolsters the authenticity of the encounter with the other in this story, whose status remains that of a paranoid delusion.

Maria: Who's to say that the narrator's recognition of and sympathy for the Other are inauthentic? Listen to passages such as the following: "Leaning over in front of the tank each morning, the recognition was greater. They were suffering, every fiber of my body reached toward that stifled pain, that rigid torment at the bottom of the tank. . . . Not possible that such a terrible expression . . . on their stone faces should carry any message other than one of pain, proof of that eternal sentence, of that liquid hell that they were undergoing." Isn't this a rather convincing case of empathy, an intuition based on shared suffering and recollection of an epochal historical injustice? This reading shows that the Other is no mere archetype; it stands for a submerged aspect of the author's own historical consciousness that needed to be recuperated. In that sense the story captures a dialectical process of rediscovering oneself in the Other, and the Other in oneself.

Jack: I fear your own sympathy for the Cortázar story, and for the underdog axolotls, is clouding your judgment, preventing you from seeing that the axolotl remains an archetypal cliché, however ingeniously developed by the author. The problem with sympathy, to put it crudely, is that it's essentially monological; it either looks down, confirming one's superiority over the pitied one; or else it sentimentally eliminates all distance, denying the differences between Self and Other—a denial that turns out to be equally nondialogical. The elimination of emotional distance dispels cognitive distance, and with it the possibility of rational communication, dialogical or otherwise. Perhaps that's why most proponents of dialogical thinking advocate some kind of disengagement as a necessary precondition for the dialogical engagement. For Buber, "genuine conversation" begins only with the acceptance of what he calls "the elemental otherness of the Other." Bakhtin calls this enabling function of distance "exotopy" or "extralocality." And don't forget Adorno's call for the preservation of nonidentity.

Maria: Read a page or two further in Buber and you'll see that this "distancing" is only a necessary first step, and by no means a sufficient one, in the dialogical encounter. The realization of genuine dialogue is made possible by what Buber calls the almost universal human capacity of "making present" or "imagining the real," which he defines as something very close to what we know as empathy: "This making present increases until it is a paradox in the soul when I and the other are embraced by a common living situation, and (let us say) the pain which I inflict upon him surges up in myself, revealing the abyss of the contradictoriness between man and man." I believe you can see how one could apply this, mutatis mutandis, to the Cortázar story. But enough said.

Jack (drily): Enough has been said on that score, surely, but not enough on the parodistic, ironic aspects of the story, which run counter to your idealizing interpretation. Let me try to convince you of the satirical and critical functions of the tale. Comparing the semiotic constitution of the Other in this tale with that in Kafka's "Report," it is striking that vision, the gaze, is the only medium of interaction between the human and the axolotl. In "Report," the ape can tell us what he is thinking; in "Axolotl" the narrator can only project meanings onto the axolotl's blank stare. I need hardly remind you that, from Plato forward, vision has provided the metaphorical basis for most Western ontology; it's in visual terms that we construct the reality of the world and of our fellow beings. In the story we're examining, the narrator visually objectifies the axolotl before identifying with it. He observes, studies, and catalogs the specimens, describing minutely their delicate anatomy and lethargic movements. He even goes to the library to "look them up" in the dictionary before deciding against specialized research in favor of direct experience.

Maria: Following the ethnographic analogy, this corresponds to the "fieldwork" phase, when the investigator immerses himself in the empirical details of the culture studied. For in traditional ethnography, the eyewitness account guarantees the unmediated perception

of the Other and thus warrants the truth of ethnographic representation.

Jack: But for all the references to the axolotl's gaze, the visual
encounter is completely unilateral. The axolotl doesn't even register
the presence, apparently, of the one who importunes him: "It was
useless to tap with one finger on the glass directly in front of their
faces; they never gave the least reaction." But this lack of feedback
does not dampen our narrator's enthusiasm; it is precisely what
attracts him. He perceives in the motionless apathy of the axolotls a
philosophical intention—that of the stoic *ataraxia:* "Obscurely I
seemed to understand their secret will, to abolish space and time with
an indifferent immobility."

Maria: That philosopheme has its oriental counterpart in the Buddhist
nirvana. At least the narrator is cosmopolitan.

Jack: But his philosophical slant is distinctly Western. Witness his next
strategem: he employs Descartes's methodical doubt to confirm the
veracity of his perceptions and to convince himself (and the reader)
that the Other he intuits is not an anthropomorphic illusion:
"Hopelessly, I wanted to prove to myself that my own sensibility was
projecting a nonexistent consciousness onto the axolotls. They and I
knew." Even the suffering he imputes to them—that of remaining
"aware, slaves of their bodies, condemned infinitely to the silence of
the abyss, to a hopeless meditation [*reflexión desesperada*]"—is a
recurrent nightmare of Western literature and, as such, yet another
indication of anthropomorphic projection. This "rationalist" nightmare, presupposing the Cartesian distinction between *res cogitans* and
res extensa, not only is the basis of the narrator's empathic identification with the axolotls, it is the generating premise of the story itself.

Maria: I see how ironic it is, under your interpretation, that the
construction of the Other as narrated is primarily visual in character.
Not only do appearances deceive, but our trusted sight is itself an
instrument of deception, the vehicle of self-hypnosis. The "blind
gaze" of the Other, which seemed to beckon us into its "diaphanous
interior mystery," is actually a mirror that reflects back the observer's
own pallid face, his stereotyping gaze. And the aquarium glass,
which we thought transparent, is the cage that literally encloses the
Other.

Jack: I couldn't have said it better myself. The clincher is of course the moment after the metamorphosis, when the narrator discovers that the ghost behind the Aztec mask, the Aztec spirit or soul he has posited, is nowhere to be found; there's no one home but us humans. There ensues the horror of finding himself "prisoner in the body of an axolotl, metamorphosed into him with my human mind intact, buried alive in an axolotl, condemned to move lucidly among unconscious creatures." So much for empathy as a way of "getting into" the Other! It was one thing to admire them from outside, but to be trapped inside one, groveling in the muck on the bottom of the aquarium, is quite another, thank you. Instead of linking up or communicating with the Other, the human consciousness is left stranded, trapped in an alien body. The narrator's consciousness is left unmodified; only his address has changed—from outside to inside the aquarium. The anthropomorphizing of the axolotls is complete when the narrator declares paradoxically, "I am an axolotl for good now, and if I think like a man it's only because every axolotl thinks like a man inside his rosy stone semblance." Thus the otherness of the Other is reduced to the spatial coordinates of its body, while its mind is presumed to be identical to that of the perceiving human subject. (Remember that, according to Rotpeter, there's a difference: apes think with their bellies.) Nothing reveals more clearly the limits of the anthropocentric imagination, its incapacity to imagine or conceive a form of subjectivity different from its own. The success of the Cortázar story lies in the lucidity and black humor with which it shows the absurdity of the Western hermeneutic project of rescuing the Other through empathy. We can't hope to comprehend the Other without leaving the security of our own ontological schemes and categories.

Maria: Your exposition is cogent. But I wonder if an alternative interpretation of metamorphosis in the story isn't possible. Metamorphosis would stand for the possibility of (metaphorically) overcoming rigid oppositions as applied to problems of identity—in this case, the subject-object distinction between European and indigenous cultures. It embodies the possibility of performing culturally and politically the kind of crossing or exchange that was already accomplished in the crude genetic sense in the colonial period, with *mestizaje*—intermarriage between the two broad ethnic groups. If the story is taken not simply as a fable of intercultural dialogue as *exchange,* but also as a metaphor for the desirable form of dialogical praxis by individuals—native or European, but especially the latter—

a different lesson emerges. It suggests that any productive change in relations with others has to occur not primarily as a result of the Other's reforming her*self* (e.g., being baptized, getting civilized, or following the prescriptions of the International Monetary Fund), nor of the Self reforming the Other. Rather, the observing subject must himself undergo a metamorphosis; he must *change himself*, or be changed. "Man" must become "woman," as the feminists would say; the "North" must see itself in the "South." Maybe empathy, putting yourself in the Other's place, is not the final solution—I grant that the story effectively satirizes the literalization of such empathy—but it may be a precondition of self-transformation in the sphere of praxis. So it is not empathy, much less metamorphosis per se, that is called into question by the story, but only naive exoticism—schoolboy fantasies of lost kingdoms and vengeful avatars, things of that ilk.

Jack: What a sharp tongue you have sometimes. I fear my worst sarcastic tendencies are rubbing off on you.

Maria: You flatter yourself, as usual. But you also change the subject, and not quite in the way I had in mind. May I take it you agree with my interpretation?

Jack: Not entirely. Oh, I concede that your analysis of metamorphosis as an overcoming of dualism is suggestive. But it doesn't alter the fact that here the "metamorphosis" is a trick done with pronouns. Nor does it contradict the story's own implicit parody of the peek-a-boo methods and rhetoric of Western thought.

Maria: Again, your criticism amounts to a refusal to suspend disbelief, to accept the story as fiction instead of reportage. All fantastic fiction is based on "tricks done with pronouns" and similar devices; by rejecting them out of hand, you refuse to play the game. But what if this narrative zigzagging is actually the key to Cortázar's experiment? We agreed that the "fantastic" mode uses language to question received modalities—the commonsense separation of the real from the nonreal, the sharp boundaries between the actual, the possible, and the impossible. This brings us back to the question of "who" or "what" is speaking in the tale. Your interpretation presupposes all the rationalist modalities: it cannot be the axolotl speaking; that's impossible. It cannot be that the narrator's identity is divided between a human and a nonhuman voice; this doesn't happen in the real world. It would be more exact to say that this dispersion of the narrator's identity doesn't *usually* happen in first-person narrative genres. This is why Marta Sánchez classifies the tale as belonging to a "modernist" variety of fantastic rather than a nineteenth-century "realist" one. Whereas the earlier mode featured an uncanny effect at the level of plot or reported event, causing the reader to wonder *what* in the devil had happened and how, the Cortázar story creates an uncanny effect at the level of the narration itself—the act of telling the tale—causing the reader to wonder just *who* is doing the narrating. This effect is strongest at the end of the story, when the referent of the narrative "I" shifts back to the axolotl. "And in this final solitude . . . I console myself by thinking that perhaps he is going to write a story about us, that, believing he's making up a story, he's going to write all this about axolotls." This ending constitutes a *mise-en-abîme* that makes it formally undecidable who is speaking at the end. The axolotl's implicit claim to be telepathically dictating to the human author makes plausible Sánchez's reading of the story, according to which the speechless or colonized Other appropriates the colonizer's language to denounce him or assert his own autonomy, just as Shakespeare's Caliban—or Kafka's Rotpeter—uses the language learned from the master to reproach that master. Recall Caliban's defiant speech to Miranda: "You taught me language, and my profit on't / Is, I know how to curse. The red plague rid you / For learning me your language!" Lulled by the central "human" part of the narration, and presumably forgetting that this part is a flashback framed within the axolotl's account, the reader initially assumes "that man 'speaks' the axolotl: they are his subject matter and objects. The real case, however, is that the axolotl 'speaks' man. Our traditional notion of 'man as narrator' is undermined." The European, human master is upstaged, his role as controlling narrator usurped by a Third World salamander. Even if you reject this last implication, you can't deny that the enigma of the narrator's identity works to undermine the cherished logocentric notion of an autonomous author with sovereign intentions and full control over his expressions.

Jack: Ah, but I can and do deny it. Even if one suspends disbelief and entertains the idea that a metamorphosis of some sort has occurred, it's still the same human consciousness that controls both narrative voices. The mind-body hierarchy is not challenged; the human consciousness has simply emigrated to a less developed body.

Maria: You forgot to say "QED."

Jack: I'm not finished. The echo of the master-slave dialectic you hear in the story's final sentence might well be called the Caliban effect, to mark the moment when the colonized Other confronts the colonizer and asserts his autonomy. But Caliban, like Rotpeter, was taught to speak; the axolotl was not. That is why the axolotl's autonomy is illusory; the human consciousness goes right on speaking for the axolotl. If the axolotl "speaks man"—that is, makes him speak—with the final sentence, he does so only in the sense that the man first, and constitutively, makes the axolotl speak by putting words in his mouth. Incidentally, the constitution of the Other by projection and visual empathy in "Axolotl" follows rather precisely the construction of the Other in traditional Western ontology. However inadvertently, the narrator of "Axolotl" fulfills the basic axiom of transcendental intersubjectivity as paraphrased by Theunissen, namely "that 'I,' the absolute unique ego, constitutes the Other, and everything else as well." The constitution of the Other takes place in external perception, as "sensible seeing," rather than in hearing or the sphere of language, as it does in Buber's dialogical model. For Husserl, the Other is always an "intentional modification" of the transcendental ego, a noematic object that remains dependent upon that founding intentionality. In view of this parallel, it is small comfort indeed to suppose that European man, who holds the pen and "thinks he is imagining a story," instead writes a report on the Third World axolotls—whose only self-determination would be the dubious honor of smuggling themselves in as the thematic subject of the report!

Maria: Is your point in drawing this analogy to show that neither the author nor the narrator does justice to a particular Other—that he falsifies its "true nature"? That would be a strangely essentialist argument in view of your claim that the Other in question is already a fabrication, an archetypal cliché.

Jack: No, my point is rather that the way of constructing the Other exemplified in this story is not, as your reading would have it, a way out of the Western ontological cage, but a revolving door that leads only back inside, as it were. Perhaps I can clarify this by reference to the ethnographic analogy. The anthropocentrism of the narrator in "Axolotl" has its counterpart in the ethnocentrism of ethnographic discourse, characterized by Stephen Tyler as "an intertextual practice which, by means of an allegorizing identity, anaesthetizes us to the other's difference." Just as the narrator speaks ventriloquistically for the axolotl, so the traditional ethnographer claims to speak for the native, translating her secrets into a neutral descriptive language—which of course presupposes the universality and transparency of the experience translated. This bureaucratic-instrumental mediation precludes the mutuality of dialogue in Buber's sense—the authentic, reciprocal meeting of "I" and "Thou," the creation of an "in-between" transcending both egos—and means that for the ethnographer, the Other is always spoken *of* instead of *to*; as a third person, or what Buber calls an "It." The Other is an object, not a subject, of discourse. In Tyler's words, "The basso of the ethnographer still speaks for the falsetto of the native. There is not yet in ethnography a real effacement of an enunciating subject, of an authorial presence."

Maria: Not yet, maybe. But don't we find a literary anticipation of this self-erasure of the enunciating subject in the last sentence of "Axolotl," which makes the referent of the narrative "I" formally undecidable? If Montaigne's essay on cannibals was dialogical precisely in its demonstration of the difficulty of dialogue, doesn't the same argument apply in spades to the Cortázar story? The incommensurability between the human narrator and the axolotl is precisely what potentiates the allegorical dimension of the story, whose satirical thrust you've explicated. With its open ending and its touch of black humor, the story seems to invite its own deconstruction.

Jack: You've mastered my argument and made it your own. I have nothing more to add at this point. Shall we take a break for dinner? Then perhaps we may finish our conversation with an evening stroll.

Maria: Now there's an idea I can endorse.

Shifting Others (a Metadialogue)

Jack: I noticed your pensive mood during dinner, and I've been expecting your counterattack.

Maria: I hope I won't disappoint you. Despite your characteristically insolent final comment that I had "mastered" your argument, we seem to have distinct readings of the Cortázar story. In mine, the reader is to a degree "taken in" by the *mise-en-abîme* ending, feeling the eeriness of the narrator's shifting identity, the possibility that the axolotl is indeed calling the narrative shots. You'll probably want to call this the Twilight Zone effect. The other way of reading, namely yours, is to interpret the story as yet another ironic variant of the "noble savage" myth, a dark parody of the European, anthropocentric imagination. But are these interpretations necessarily incompatible? They might function for some as successive moments in the reading process—the second reading being stimulated by the first, then subsuming it as the initial estrangement gives way to critical analysis. For to insist that one must choose either surprise or irony, when it may be the function of the tale to lead us from one to the other, is perhaps to reify the story and its potential meanings and to ignore the conceivably multiple intentions of the author. It is to foreclose that mode of "dialogical criticism" envisioned by Todorov, a criticism that "speaks not *of* works but *to* works, or rather *with* works. It refuses to eliminate either of the two voices present. The criticized text is not an object to be taken over by a 'metalanguage,' but a discourse which encounters the critic's discourse; the author is a 'thou,' not a 'he,' an interlocutor with whom one discusses and even debates human values."

Jack: There's inevitably a degree of assimilation, a neutralization of strangeness, in every act of interpretation. To that extent it behooves the critic not to effect an absolute closure by pretending he commands the full or "correct" meaning of a text, but rather to acknowledge the residues of strangeness or nonidentity between text and interpretation. But one should also guard against romanticizing the hermeneutical act by pretending it is one of transparency, openness, and dialogue toward every conceivable Other. Gadamer defines dialogue as a discourse grounded in the concern of two parties for a third thing that always eludes full comprehension. In Todorov's example, the third thing or *tertium quid* would be the "human values" at issue in the conversation between the text (and through it, of course, the author), on the one hand, and the critic on the other. But do you suppose it's possible for the critic to maintain this dialogue with the text without hypostatizing or reifying in some way those human values at issue? Consider what Michel Serres says of dialogue, that *"to hold a dialogue is to suppose a third man and to seek to exclude him;* a successful communication is the exclusion of the third man. The most profound dialectical problem is not the problem of the Other, who is only a variety—or a variation—of the Same, it is the problem of the third man. We might call this third man the *demon*, the prosopopoeia of noise."

Maria: In that regard, one can analyze the narrative speech acts in the stories we've read as dialogical moves addressed to the reader. In Montaigne's text, the cannibals are obviously the "third man," whom the author represents sympathetically to his fellow Europeans. The talking ape in Kakfa's story speaks to the academy about his former wild self. His ape nature is thus the "third party" here, even though he uses the first person for both his former and his present self. Insisting on the distance he has traveled, he tries to convince us that his ape nature is entirely behind him, but his comments reveal that part of it remains, refusing to be suppressed. But the story's full satirical effect is felt only when we realize as readers that we members of the "academy" who receive the report are in a sense *both* the addressee *and* the "third man" of the discourse—when we recognize something of ourselves in the humans whose barbarous acts are recounted in the ape's report. In the Cortázar story, the identity of the excluded third is also ambiguous: it is in one sense the narrator's former human incarnation, now a "zombie" figure who returns only occasionally and with dwindling recognition. But it is also the Aztec spirit or archetype that remains trapped in mythical silence and that is never able to speak for itself but is instead spoken for, like Montaigne's cannibals. But who, according to Serres's notion, is the "third man" for us here and now? Whom or what are *we* seeking to exclude in our own conversation about these stories—perhaps other readers?

Jack: Perhaps the authors. Isn't all criticism, *pace* Todorov, an attempt to hold a conversation not with but *about* a text, thereby turning the text into an absent "third person" at the moment when the critic proposes an interpretation, whether he does so in conversation or in writing?

Maria: But by quoting these authors, aren't we, to the contrary, making them *present* in a sense—activating their words and stories in the present critical context?

Jack: Only by abolishing the original speech context; the authors' words become a dead letter that we plunder for our own purposes, reintroducing them montagewise into a new context where, laundered, they conform to our interpretations. We turn the author into a third-person authority or "expert witness" who can give only the testimony we allow him to give. We quote him (or her) just as the narrator quotes the primitive Other in the tales we have discussed, or as the ethnographer quotes his native informants—that is, selectively, elliptically, and preemptively.

Maria: You do have a taste for the melodramatic; but surely you exaggerate the inevitable violence of the act of quoting, as well as the quoter's ability to make excerpts say exactly what he wants them to say and no more. Can anyone predetermine the way such quotations will be received and interpreted? Don't you underestimate the potential for what we might call *discours sauvage*—the possibility that quoted discourse may erupt unpredictably in new texts and contexts, that the voice or meaning of the quoted Other may escape the colonizing intentions of the quoter?

Jack: And you said I was the melodramatic one. This unintended eruption of *discours sauvage* sounds to me like a variant of the dogma of stable authorial meaning—the notion that the original text has a definite intended meaning that survives even in paraphrase or quotation—a "spirit" that haunts the "letter" of a text, even in a new context. This subversive spirit or meaning is nothing but the imputed intention of a projected Other. So your *discours sauvage* is an updated, textualist variant of the "noble savage" theme we saw at work in the stories. Your reading combines the aestheticist habit of treating the text as an isolated spectacle—a contest, in this case, between two archetypes—with the good liberal gesture of declaring the colonized "underdog" the winner. This politicization of the text is misplaced.

Maria: Is it really? You're very fond of invoking Wittgenstein on language games and of quoting poststructuralists who argue that there is no discourse without a power struggle. And as we've seen, there are strong conflicting forces at play in the stories we're discussing, such as the "struggle" for control of the narrative voice and identity in "Axolotl."

Jack: Yes, but it's naive to treat these conflicting forces as though they were bounded and enclosed *within* the tale or story; the text is a dialogical move in a contest in which the reader is also engaged. Your well-intentioned adjudications overlook the hidden co-optative mechanism at work generally in European discourse about the Other—whether the Other in question be oriental or occidental. (What Said has said about "orientalism" in this regard applies just as well to European discourse about the "New World.") This language game—European solicitations of the Other—is rigged in advance in favor of the European, logocentric mode of thought. The Other, in turn, has a built-in handicap: like Caliban, she can learn the rules of the game of language and can play, turning language against those who taught it to her. But she doesn't *make* the rules of the game. For example, the rules that say that there are two unequal antagonists, one historically indentured to the other; that whereas the inequality was originally imposed by force, the Other in subsequent dealings must renounce force and employ only reason and language to communicate and resolve disputes. The handicapped Other never makes these rules; she can only *accept* them and play the game or refuse to play altogether, thus condemning herself either to silence or to inarticulate violence. This is why the "European" role in these tales, whether it is filled at any particular moment by author, character, or reader, occupies always, like the ethnographer vis-à-vis his native informant, the position of Miranda, who says to Caliban: "I pitied thee, / Took pains to make thee speak, taught thee each hour / One thing or other. When thou didst not, savage, / Know thine own meaning, but wouldst gabble like / A thing most brutish, I endow'd thy purposes / With words that made them known." In all three of the tales we have discussed—if you will pardon the recapitulation—the Other is quoted and encapsulated in Eurocentric representations. It is the *producer* of the discourse who endows the Other's purposes, words, and actions with meaning. Miranda has the first *and* last word, because what she says has ontological priority over what Caliban says in response. Which is to say, the Other is always a projection of the European-Caucasian-Cartesian subject. And this time I will say it: *Quod erat demonstrandum!*

Maria: Your argument isn't entirely incoherent. But insofar as we, as readers, both participate in that Cartesian subjectivity and remain outside it—and we do, to the degree that we recognize it and criticize it—we can refuse to play that language game and choose to play other games instead.

Jack: In which we will inevitably create new myths and dream up new Others to reify.

Maria: What bothers me is that your own discourse pretends to take a position above the rhetorical fray. Montaigne's essay on cannibals, and Todorov's study of the conquest of the Americas, already implied some ironic distance from the noble savage myth, as do the animal tales we have read; but you claim to take irony a step further—or one rung higher up the ladder—from which you can look down and show all others to remain within a pathetic naïveté, or a misplaced empathy. Isn't this a case of what the Germans call *Besserwissenschaft*, or "knowing it all"? Your critique of rigged language games is itself a rigged game. It is enlightenment with a vengeance—a kind of hypercriticism that claims to outflank and debunk all myths of enlightenment by exposing their blind spots, or at least exposing how they do this themselves. Doesn't your own position have its blind spots too?

Jack: It seems you've used an outflanking maneuver against me. *Chapeau!* To your echo of Wittgenstein's ladder analogy, I answer that I don't let go of the ladder. That is, I don't simply dismiss the texts I choose to comment on, but defend and espouse their critical and experimental aspects, using them against ideological or uncritical positions, whether in the same or in other texts. For example, I concede the innovation of Cortázar's narrative experiment while refusing to be entirely duped by it.

Maria: Even so, I'm not at all sure that the last laugh isn't on your skepticism. For all your talk of the animal narrators' being "trapped" in Cartesian cages at the end of the tales, doesn't your own critique of dialogical reason leave the interpreter trapped in his own solipsistic, monological cage? In your skeptical critique, we can never know or hear the Other, because the Other is defined as a chimera, produced by our hermeneutic schemes and ontological categories and projected onto our fantasy screens. Defined as the privative of the Self, that which we are not, that which is concealed by our blind spots, your Other is like the Kantian *Ding-an-Sich*, something that remains forever and a priori out of reach. We have no more hope of representing or communing with it than we have of catching our own shadow. Your hypercritical hermeneutic in effect plugs its ears while issuing an injunction against all forms of otherness, reducing the Other's expressions and will to communicate to an echo of the critic's own voice. Your skepticism is dogmatic: it claims to know in advance that no textual expression of otherness is possible and insists that, even if it were, we couldn't tell the difference. This might be a good test of an interpretation that pretends to be dialogical: Is it still listening to the text at the end, or has it turned off its hearing aid, listening only to itself? That your corrosive deconstructions have their merits and exhilarating moments, I am far from denying. But taken to excess, they lead to paralysis of the will. To accept your position would collapse the ethical impulse of dialogical thinking, the dialogical imperative we spoke of at the beginning. If one is constantly questioning one's own terms and categories of understanding, one never gets around to understanding anything. And your critique of rationalist thinking recalls Kafka's reminder to those who put down everyday life: after all, it's the only one we have. The same can be said of your antihumanism. What choice is there, ethically, but to use our cognitive and aesthetic tools to pursue our human values, as we define them? The chronic lament that we can never have perfect knowledge or unmediated dialogue with the Other becomes an excuse for not undertaking any sort of dialogue. One falls into the pathos of solipsism; the idea that we are condemned to monologue becomes a self-fulfilling prophecy.

Jack: To prove to you that I'm less dogmatic than you think, I'll admit that, for once, your moralistic bent has risen to inspired heights. I'm moved. And I'll even try to practice your dialogical imperative—without, of course, ceasing to be skeptical. If I may invoke Nietzsche: give me any skepticism to which we can say, "Let's try it out." Let's experiment—but dialogically, as have Montaigne, Kafka, and Cortázar. For it's only through such experiments that the possibility of true dialogue can be disclosed in texts.

Maria: If this change of tone signals a humane shift in your thinking, I approve. On those terms, I'm prepared to embrace your dialogical experimentalism—skepticism and all. Only, for my part, give me an experiment that causes one to listen to the voice of the Other.

Jack: Speaking of listening to voices, have I ever told you how lovely yours is? Now that it's dark, and I can no longer gaze into those big, brown eyes of yours . . .

Maria: All the better to objectify you with, my dear.

Jack: . . . you are all voice, and I can only listen, until we touch . . .

Maria: Here we go again.

The End

References

Adorno, Theodor W. 1973. *Negative dialectics*. Trans. E. B. Ashton. New York: Seabury.

Bakhtin, M. M. 1986. *Speech genres and other late essays*. Ed. C. Emerson and M. Holquist. Trans. V. McGee. Austin: University of Texas Press.

Buber, Martin. 1965. *The knowledge of man*. Trans. M. Friedman and R. G. Smith. New York: Harper and Row.

Clifford, James. 1983. On ethnographic authority. *Representations* 2:132–41.

Cortázar, Julio. 1967. *"End of the game" and other stories*. Trans. P. Blackburn. New York: Harper and Row.

———. 1976. The present state of fiction in Latin America. In *The final island: The fiction of Julio Cortázar*, ed. J. Alazraki and I. Ivask. Norman: University of Oklahoma Press.

De Certeau, Michel. 1986. *Heterologies: Discourse on the Other*. Minneapolis: University of Minnesota Press.

Deleuze, Gilles, and Félix Guattari. 1986. *Kafka: Toward a minor literature*. Trans. D. Polan. Minneapolis: University of Minnesota Press.

Gadamer, Hans-Georg. 1975. *Truth and method*. Trans. and ed. G. Barden and J. Cumming. New York: Seabury.

Heidegger, Martin. 1977. *Basic writings*. New York: Harper and Row.

Kafka, Franz. 1952. *Selected short stories*. Trans. W. Muir and E. Muir. New York: Modern Library.

Kauffmann, R. Lane. 1986. Julio Cortázar y la narración del otro. *INTI: Revista de Literatura Hispánica* 22–23:317–26.

Kaufmann, Walter. 1968. *Nietzsche: Philosopher, psychologist, Antichrist*. New York: Vintage.

Lévi-Strauss, Claude. 1966. *The savage mind*. Chicago: University of Chicago Press.

Marcus, George E., and Michael M. J. Fischer. 1986. *Anthropology as cultural critique: An experimental moment in the human sciences*. Chicago: University of Chicago Press.

Montaigne, Michel. 1981. *The complete essays of Montaigne*. Trans. D. Frame. Stanford: Stanford University Press.

Palmer, Richard. 1984. Expostulations on the postmodern turn. *Krisis* 2:140–49.

Robertson, Ritchie. 1987. *Kafka: Judaism, politics, and literature.* Oxford: Oxford University Press.

Said, Edward W. 1979. *Orientalism.* New York: Vintage.

Sánchez, Marta. 1976. Caliban: The new Latin American protagonist of the *Tempest. Diacritics* 6(1): 54–61.

———. 1982. A view from inside the fishbowl: Julio Cortázar's "Axolotl." In *Bridges to fantasy,* ed. G. E. Slusser et al., 38–50. Carbondale: Southern Illinois University Press.

Serres, Michel. 1982. *Hermes: Literature, science, philosophy.* Ed. J. V. Harari and D. F. Bell. Baltimore: Johns Hopkins University Press.

Theunissen, Michael. 1986. *The Other: Studies in the social ontology of Husserl, Heidegger, Sartre and Buber.* Trans. C. Macann. Cambridge: MIT Press.

Todorov, Tzvetan. 1984a. A dialogic criticism? *Raritan* 4(1): 64–76.

———. 1984b. *Mikhail Bakhtin: The dialogical principle.* Trans. W. Godzich. Minneapolis: University of Minnesota Press.

———. 1985. *The conquest of America: The question of the Other.* Trans. R. Howard. New York: Harper and Row.

Tyler, Stephen A. 1985. Ethnography, intertextuality and the end of description. *American Journal of Semiotics* 3(4): 83–98.

Wittgenstein, Ludwig. 1980. *Philosophical investigations.* Trans. G. E. M. Anscombe. New York: Macmillan. Originally published 1953.

closely linked in a wide range of relations. The purpose of this chapter is to analyze several dimensions of their interrelation. The first section examines the virtually dialogic quality of narrative; in the second section I discuss the narrative structure of dialogue; the third section outlines some changes in the discourse on narration and dialogue that have taken place recently.

The Dialogic Structure of Narration

Dialogue through Narration

It is perhaps worth asking whether the reader is really condemned to the passive role sketched out above. In reality he has the opportunity to intervene in literary communication in various ways. He may communicate his opinion of the work to the author and influence the latter's writing by means of this critique. If we consider the economic dimension of the literary institution as a part of its communicative situation, that is, as a dimension of the semiotic system within which it functions, then the success or failure of one book might influence the composition of the next. Furthermore, the reader's control does not apply only to the communicative space between one novel and the ensuing one, but can also influence the actual composition of a book. Prepublication of various chapters in newspapers or literary reviews, which happens so often in the era of mass media, give the reader occasion to modify the composition of a novel and thus to assume the role of an active counterpart. Finally, the possibilities of feedback that are at the disposal of the users of new media (e.g., the electronic novels) level most of the differences in the degree of active participation of author and reader; these possibilities will probably deeply transform, if not definitely dissolve, our notions of the author/reader roles more effectively than all Foucauldian criticism ever could do (cf. Foucault 1974, 17 ff.) We can also resort to literary history to find examples of dialogical narration: the most famous case of an author's including his readers directly in the writing process is probably Charles Dickens, whose novels were prepublished by installments in the feuilletons of important newspapers. This gave occasion for Dickens to invert roles and to become in the pubs of London the attentive listener of his readers; they explained to him how they imagined the continuation of the story and what they thought about its characters and composition. These "great expectations" of the public made it possible to continue the dialogue thus begun within the novel itself. The readers took part in the composition of the work, and the author conceived his actual writing partly as an answer to their requests and anticipations. By such a procedure readers' reactions are systematically incorporated into the signifying process itself, and the author can use them as a basis for further development. He may fulfill readers' hopes or disappoint them ironically and thus initiate a pleasant, stimulating game with them.

In his theory of hermeneutics Gadamer shows that this dialogical element of literary communication is not accidental to understanding. Since the meaning and sense contained in a work exceed the intentions of the author (Gadamer 1960, 354)—an assumption shared by both deconstruction and hermeneutics—and since no reconstruction of the question to which the work is an answer coincides with later reconstructions, since the two are separated by the necessary prejudice given by their respective horizons of sense (1960, 282), understanding means more than mere realization of the author's intentions. Reading operates in a never-ending dialogue between past and present, the actual understanding consisting of a fusion between the horizon of our own historical sense and the one in which the work is placed (1960, 289).

However, one is inclined to object, all these examples are not valid illustrations for the dialogical nature of narration itself, since they only elucidate the fact that narration might be included in a dialogue between past author and present reader. They are far removed from showing the dialogic fundamentals of narration itself. In other words, the examples given confirm that narration can engender a dialogue external to itself, but not at all that narration itself functions as a dialogue. The remarks made above deal only with the work as an object of a dialogue between author and reader, but not with the novel itself as a semiotic system realizing dialogue within its boundaries. Until now nothing has been advanced to suspend the strict opposition between dialogue and narration within the work itself. So far I have shown only an alternation of the roles between author and reader, which occurs not within the confines of the text but outside them, on a level of communication that transcends the work in question.

Narration as Dialogue

Mukarovsky's Definition of Dialogue

It was the Russian semiotician Mikhail Bakhtin and the structuralist Jan Mukarovsky who furnished the basis for an analysis of the dialogic character of narration itself. Trying to perceive the entire range of such a polymorphic phenomenon as dialogue, Mukarovsky stakes out the fundamental characteristics of dialogic communication:

1. Every participant must have the opportunity to realize the roles of both the active and the passive partner of communication. Consequently the roles of speaker and hearer alternate (Mukarovsky 1977, 86).

2. Speaker and listener must be able to incorporate the situation surrounding them into their exchange by making elements of it the theme of their conversation or by designating them by means of gestures or deictic words ("there," "here," etc.) (1977, 87).

3. There must be a characteristic specific to dialogue, which defines its semantic structure: "Unlike monologic discourse, which has a single and continuous contexture, several or at least two contextures interpenetrate or alternate in dialogic discourse" (1977, 87). Of course there must be a frame of reference within which the differences between the two contextures can operate. This unity, however, is granted not by the subject but by the object, that is, by the theme of the conversation.

Since as a functionalist Mukarovsky conceives of language as a means appropriate to the realization of certain goals of expression (1940, 82), he presupposes that dialogue functions as an instrument already at hand; dialogue evolves within the framework of a preexisting language. Although the participants can determine the choice among different functional languages (emotional, literary, or intellectual), language preconceived as a whole circumscribes the actual communication. Indeed, if we translate Mukarovsky's aspects into the terms of Jakobson's model of communication, it appears that Mukarovsky takes into account only the emotive (speaker), conative (hearer), phatic (channel), referential (context), and semantic functions of linguistic signs; he completely neglects the metalinguistic function, which deals with the relation between utterances and the code they are derived from. There is no reason the code should not also become the object or theme of dialogue. Moreover, metacommunication as an extreme case of conversational practice can be realized only in a dialogic way, and perhaps this is one of the most interesting cases of dialogic practice. Thus we can complete Mukarovsky's list of features by adding the elaboration of new common codes, of new languages (cf. Kloepfer 1982, 88 ff.). Here, as in all other dimensions of dialogical communication, a certain unity and interpenetration is a condition for dialogue, as well as the tension that breaks up virtual monologic unity.

Having thus established the basis for his theory of dialogue, Mukarovsky uses the classical differentiation between the concrete psychophysical individual and the subject to distinguish between superficial dialogic features and a deeper "dialogic quality." The essential conditions for dialogue are provided chiefly by the third aspect mentioned above, that is, by the interpenetration of several contextures. The indispensable condition of the "interpenetration of two semantic contextures" is not necessarily bound to the existence of two individuals but can also be fulfilled by a single psychophysical individual's becoming the vehicle for two well-differentiated subjects of an utterance. Thus, in the so-called soliloquy, one individual assumes the roles of two subjects and alternately takes the roles of speaker and hearer. Mukarovsky partly anticipates what Roman Jakobson would reformulate twenty years later in linguistic terms: it is the possibility of splitting and thereby doubling all the constituents of literary communication that permits a single author to divide into two well-distinguished subjects or "voices" who actually engage in a dialogue. In the light of Jakobson's terminology, Mukarovsky's claim brings to the fore how narration may be dialogic. The concrete individual author is capable of entering into a true dialogue with his real counterparts; such a dialogue takes place on the first level of literary communication, which is the principal object of traditional hermeneutics. Yet the problem of dialogue really asserts itself on the second level, that of the literary work. On this level, the participants of the internal dialogue of the novel (narrator and narratee, implicit author and implicit reader) result from the doubling of the concrete author into two different subjects. Thus the real author can address the receiver in quite a direct way, as Sterne does with predilection in *Tristram Shandy* , begging his reader, for instance, to close the door or advising him to skip over the next chapter because it might not please him (Sterne 1967, 38). Narration, however, need not espouse such an explicit form of dialogue. Even when not embodied as a figure of narration, the reader may exist as a kind of implicit counterpart to the narrator. Actually, the anecdote above about Dickens listening to his readers illustrates very well what happens between the narrator and the implicit reader. The narrator knows very well the readers' "horizon of expectation" (Jauss 1975, 131) and can consequently satisfy, frustrate, or just play with those expectancies to the extent that the narratee finally becomes an autonomous "voice," incarnating a certain conception of the world altogether different from that of the narrator. Though concrete real readers is absent, their narrative voice is present in the dialogue of writing. If the distinctive mark of dialogic conversation is above all the interpenetration of different conceptions of the world, then the tension between two contextures will suffice for the realization of dialogue. Instead of a strict separation between monologue and dialogue, we have a scale of several degrees of dialogue according to the relative dominance of the two contextures.

Bakhtin's Concept of Dialogism in the Novel

In disagreement with what seems to be the commonsense opinion, Bakhtin claims that the novel is the dialogic genre par excellence and that novelization subverts all kinds of monologic speech. Since literature consists of a discourse that represents another discourse, it offers a genuine occasion for dialogue. In the novel even the smallest entity of discourse, the single word, is not as homogeneous as it seems. In the searchlight of Bakhtin's theory of dialogism it becomes disseminated.

The reason for this virtual dissemination belongs to the very structure of language and communication: the identity of an utterance (its being present to itself) already has the structure of differentiation, because the constitution of linguistic utterances presupposes their iterability, which gives place to deviations of sense. Hence the semiotic mark grounds in the remark (Derrida 1977, 186). The sameness of an utterance consequently is guaranteed not by the permanence of a sense but by a "nonpresent remainder" *(restance non présente)* that subverts all absolute presence (p. 191). Since the reiteration presumes by virtue of a genuine temporal gap the possibility of the absence of initial intentions and meanings, alternation of sense is already inherent in language as the necessary condition for its functioning. Every mark is divided and deported in advance, by its iterability, toward other words, removed in advance from itself. This remove makes its movement possible. This remove is its condition of possibility; it is not an eventuality, something that befalls it here and there, by accident (Derrida 1977, 194). The dialogic principle as it is exposed by Bakhtin is only the systematic application of this basically differential structure of communication to the discourse of the novel. In his essay *Discourse in the Novel*, Bakhtin extends the dialogic dissemination to the single word:

> What we are calling a hybrid construction is an utterance that belongs, by its grammatical (syntactic) and compositional markers, to a single speaker, but that actually contains mixed within it two utterances, two speech manners, two styles, two "languages," two semantic and axiological belief systems. . . . It frequently happens that even one and the same word will belong simultaneously to two languages, two belief systems that intersect in a hybrid construction—and, consequently, the word has two contradictory meanings, two accents. (Bakhtin 1981, 304 ff.)

By the same word, which belongs simultaneously to two languages or two belief systems, the author can represent in his own speech the worldview of one of his heroes and thereby make him converse not only in the dialogues with other characters on the level of the *story* (direct speech), but also on the level of narrative *discourse* (cf. Genette 1972, 74). The characters as well as the readers can change the level of fictionality by a narrative metalepse (pp. 234 ff.) and become autonomous voices conversing with the author within the boundaries of the work. Since there is no "transcendental word" closing the dialogic structure of language, and since no word can be closed to other usages, every word has already served for other subjects and is deeply marked by this previous usage. By virtue of its openness, every word necessarily establishes a relation not only with the objects but also with other individuals who used it before and will use it later.

Bakhtin's concept of dialogism brings to the fore that dialogue contains a temporal kernel, which unfolds under appropriate conditions. Of course every word, simply by virtue of its diacritic nature, by drawing its meaning from its relation to other words (Saussure 1979, 166), already carries the marks of these others. Narration, however, owing to its temporal dimension, is especially appropriate for the development of this dialogicality. Particularly the novel, with its syntagmatic dimension, is able to unfold the story of the different uses of utterances made by different subjects and thereby to set off a tension between different conceptions of the world. In the course of a novel words acquire their own history and assume the marks of different users, with whom they maintain a close relation.

One is immediately inclined to object that the polyphonic structure of the novelistic word, which allows the hero and the implicit reader to become autonomous entities of narrative discourse, is only superficial, because it will always be basically hierarchic and therefore monologic. Actually, it is to the author that the words belong: he pronounces them with the voices of the others; he is the one who controls and manipulates them in conformity to his own intentions. In parody and irony, for instance, the narrator uses the utterances of others for the purpose of unmasking and ridiculing them, thus manifesting his superiority. Bakhtin introduces another modality of polyphony, one in which the voice of the Other represented by the discourse of the Self is active and dominates the author's discourse. In the modalities mentioned above the author uses the discourse of the Other to express his own orientations. In the fourth type, which Bakhtin christens "polemic," the Other's discourse remains outside that of the author and is thus promoted to the latter's independent autonomous counterpart, acting upon it and determining it (Todorov 1984, 71). The degree of the presence and dominance of one of the voices is variable: the hero's or the reader's voice, ideological system, conception of the world, may obtain such a predominance that the narrator's voice vanishes and loses control over the making of the novel. This happens, for instance, in *The Life and Opinions of Tristram Shandy* and in *Jacques le fataliste et son maître*, in which the heroes, by their strange and eccentric behavior, compel the authors to modify their programs. The modification of the narrator's attitude by his own creations may also affect the real author: for example, Louis-Ferdinand Céline (Destouches), who adopted not only the name but also the character of his principal picaresque hero, progressively identifying himself with his creation. Thus the literary dialogue may (quite similarly to the so-called inner monologue, which is in fact a polylogue) induce the person to obey the voice of the fictive Other; the paranoiac execution of the orders given by a stranger's voice is only an extreme case of this.

If, on the one hand, a true dialogue may take place within a single person, on the other hand, the existence of several participants in communication does not guarantee its dialogic character. As the example of so-called discussions in totalitarian systems illustrates, one voice or subject may be disseminated through different individuals having the same opinions, sharing the same value system and the same language. Even though all external premises for dialogue are fulfilled, the internal condition, the tension between two or more semantic contextures, is completely missing. The case of the novel illustrates very well the opposite phenomenon, that of a dialogue taking place within a single individual. If one accepts Mukarovsky's explicit replacement of the concrete individual by the subject of dialogue, a presupposition that also underlies Bakhtin's definition of dialogism, then the objection that the dialogue between narrator and hero is not real because one of the partners controls the other is no longer pertinent. Of course, authors can manipulate their characters for their own purposes (Ehre 1984, 176). But the "manipulations" of the individual and concrete author are a result of a dialogue between two or more voices that has already taken place within himself; this is so irrespective of whether it was the narrator's voice, the implicit reader's, or the hero's that got the upper hand. Here the Latin etymology of the word "concrete" (from *concrescere,* "to merge") reveals its full sense: the concrete author is a result of the polylogue between different voices merging with different degrees of predominance. On this basis we can show that it must not be that the more-or-less implicit narrator dominates the dialogue in the novel, but that the actual writing and final position of the concrete author can also be due to a predominance of the reader's voice. If we admit, on the basis of Mukarovsky's distinction between subject and individual, that the main premise of dialogue is not the existence of two individuals exchanging messages but the tension of two subjects penetrating each other, then the dialogue is real, even though this might not be the case for the individuals taking part in it.

The commonsense objection to Bakhtin's thesis in fact has its roots elsewhere. It is an objection not so much to the fictionality of the participants of dialogue as to the hidden narrative base that sustains dialogic communication. The argument that the concrete author manipulates his heroes as a marionette player his puppets is not primarily concerned with the fact that there is only one individual supporting the conversation. In particular it is based on the presupposition of an author completely unmodified by the concrete and material process of writing, which is carried out in time and in the course of which the author may himself change. The objection excludes from dialogue the very element within which it evolves: it presumes that the concrete author is an already and forever finished subject and thus eliminates time. In fact the concrete author of a work does not exist before the act of writing, but only after the dialogue with his persons has come to an end. The author is author only after writing the book, not before. As author he is the result of the process of writing, which progresses in the form of a conversation with his characters and with the implicit reader.

The gist of the argument against the virtually dialogic nature of narration consists in the reversal of the actual perspective. It looks back on the narrative process from the point of view reached by the author at its end, explaining the whole as a realization of his initial intention. The voices of his characters are thus considered to be objects of his manipulation, and thereby writing is seen as a monologue, or at best as a dialogue in which one subject masters the others. If the author manipulates his creations, we must not forget that the "objects" of this manipulation were once counterparts in dialogue with the author. The same argument is valid with respect to the author himself. Is it pertinent to say that the author at the end of the narration manipulates the author at the beginning only because the first has attained the final point of narrative? Surely in a closed system of narration the final voice of the narrator has the last word, but this is not the case during the act of reading and writing. Thus the monologic character of literature appears only when one inverts the perspective of writing and reading and looks back on the work; to do this, one must take away the temporal element essential to it—the aesthetic process by which it was constituted. This kind of backward prophecy provides a distorted vision of narration. The circularity of the argument is obvious. The concrete author is supposed to manipulate the dialogue with his heroes and readers: however, this is impossible insofar as he himself is bound to the final temporal state of his writing.

The assumption that literature is monological discourse arises only on the grounds of the idealistic premise that the author exists as an entity that remains unchanged by the dialogical and material process of writing. In reality, narration supports Gadamer's claim of the "conversation that we are" in a special way for the concrete author: he is the conversation realized by his work, as it appears in its final state. He is—so to speak—the harmony or disharmony of the voices of the narrator, of the implicit reader, and of the hero. The same is also valid for the reader, who, in dialogic narration, becomes a true coauthor.

In summary, I have argued that narration has a virtually dialogic structure that is essential to it, and that this stems from the fact that both narration and dialogue are grounded in a specific structure of time.

The Temporal Dimension of Narration and Dialogue

The Ontological and Anthropological Foundation
of the Dialogic Relation in Temporality

The similarity between narration and dialogue is founded upon their common temporal character, a feature that distinguishes them from the epistemic attitude. According to Emmanuel Levinas, the dialogic relation excludes representation and presence of the Other. In contrast to knowledge that regards the Other as an object, which is "present" and "at hand," the dialogic relation does not reduce the partner to presence or copresence. The Other transcends the representation of the subject-object-relation and cannot be made present. Time corresponds to a relation that does not exclude the otherness of the Other, that guarantees the nonindifference of this relation to the thinking mind (Levinas 1979, 9). Between "You" and "I" there is no coincidence in synchrony but only the diachrony of a fundamental difference; hence time means the everlasting relation of noncorrespondence to the Other (1979, 10).

However Levinas's ontological foundation of the dialogic relation in time confronts the philosophy of dialogue with two problems: first, as merely negative definitions, nonpresence and the negation of representation are perhaps not sufficient conditions for the constitution of time; second (and this is closely linked to the first), the ontological analysis has to clarify why we need the dimension of time at all, because heteroglossia alone might already serve as the ontological foundation of dialogue.

The necessity of a negative definition of time by nonpresence stems from the ontological status of time itself, because it resists a metaphysics of presence that is firmly anchored in Western culture and language. The only positive statement that can be made about time is that it "temporalizes," that it engenders its own forms in contact with Western metaphysical presuppositions and reduces them to substance and essence. The pure negativity of time with regard to these logocentric assumptions compels it to hypostatize itself: time is already and at once its difference, its substantified Other. The basic negativity of temporality expresses itself by different positive figurations or forms of time. Thus the impossibility of a positive definition of time on the ontological level is intrinsic to temporality. For the sake of terminological transparency a distinction can be made between the general principle of *temporality* and the different specific forms of *time* it produces.

If there were only the noncorrespondence between the I and the Other (mere heteroglossia), a basic condition of dialogue would not be fulfilled: an element would be lacking in which this difference could be articulated. However, since every identity that serves as a basis for the articulation of the ontological difference would reduce otherness to sameness, there remains only an element whose identity consists precisely by, in, and through difference itself. As temporality encompasses mere ontological difference without reducing it to a final identity but unfolds the difference between the I and the Other, time constitutes the dimension in which the dialogic relation can evolve.

The ontological foundation of dialogue in time is confirmed by the anthropological analysis of the constitution of identity. Identity cannot be realized in a kind of Munchausen act in which one extricates oneself from the morass by pulling on one's own hair. The process of self-identification can be closed only in relation to others: Being, abstracted from the relation binding it to the Other, is inconceivable. According to Bakhtin, we can neither conceive nor perceive ourselves as a unity without referring to something that transcends and encompasses us. "I achieve self-consciousness, I become myself only by revealing myself to another, through another and with another's help. The most important acts, constitutive of self-consciousness, are determined by their relation to another consciousness. . . . I must find myself in the other, finding the other in me" (Todorov 1984, 96). Just as the body is initially formed in the womb of the mother, so human consciousness awakens surrounded by the consciousness of others (p. 96). Moreover, the I hides in the Other and in others: it wants to be but another for others, to fully penetrate the world of others as another.

Despite this congruence between narration and dialogue, consisting of their common foundation in time, there seems to be a fundamental difference: the dialogic mode of time is contingent, while the time of the story is teleological, because it is founded on our preconception of action. Although both are rooted in time, dialogue and narration seem to be incompatible, especially because of the different modes that time espouses in them. Perhaps the analysis of dialogue in the light of Buber's philosophy of time may help to make clear the real structure of dialogic time. Buber differentiates two fundamental attitudes of man toward the world. The relation from the I to It as a relation of subject to object is only one human possibility, which exists in addition to the encounter of the I and the You. In contrast to the It, the You cannot be fixed by notions or serve as means to our ends (Buber 1984, 16 ff.). The encounter with the You transcends the subject-object relation. Nevertheless, the You must become an It when dialogic communication is not actually realized or finished. This is, for instance, the case in memory, where the You is perceived as an object and thereby transformed into an It (Buber 1984, 37). One might object that this reification of the Other at the end of a dialogic relation must not at all confer a narrative structure on dialogic temporality, because the end itself might occur as a mere contingency. Dialogic time thus would still lack any of the organic developments characteristic of traditional narration. To resolve the apparent incompatibility between the specific times of narration and of the dialogic relation, we have to examine how the fundamental contingency resulting from the relation between the I and the Other is transformed into the narrative time of concrete dialogue.

From Dialogic Relation to Dialogue: Narrativization of Dialogic Temporality by the Pragmatic Rules of Dialogic Speech

The narrative transformation of the contingency of the relation between the You and the I is due to the pragmatic rules of dialogue taken as a specific form of speech, as established by Plato. In the *Gorgias*, Socrates reminds Polos that the dialogic genre and its rules are quite different from the rules of the agonistics of sentences composed for validity before a tribunal and in dialectics (*Gorgias* 471e–472c). In dialogue, only the opinions of the two participants are relevant, and the aim of their conversation is their assent alone (475d). In contrast to the participants of the *agon*, those of dialogue are witnesses and judges at once (*Republic* 348b). The simultaneous accomplishment of the two roles naturally requires a higher communicative competence, a condition that some participants do not fulfill (cf. *Sophist* 346c; *Laws* 893a–b). Its specific pragmatic rules confer a teleological structure on dialogue, which places it in opposition to other communicative genres. The participants in dialogue are forced to arrive at a consensus by themselves, since no judges are available to propose a solution to their conflict. A final consensus thus constitutes the aim toward which the dialogue is directed. Therefore it is necessarily progressive; the participants solve one problem after another, establishing agreement first on the premises and rules and then on the content of their confrontation. By contrast, progression is not obligatory for the agonistic genre, since the final sentence of the judge is not necessarily the natural and organic result of a maturing process, but rather puts an external and in some sense artificial end to speech. The partners can maintain their position from beginning to end because the judgment is the duty of a third party. Since they are not provided with this higher third party, the participants in dialogue (pleading and judging at the same time) are obliged to constitute a judgment of themselves by finding a consensus that functions as this higher instance. Actually, the consensus is credible only if the partners can be sure it was arrived at by a dialogue free of coercion.

Thus dialogue presupposes, as Habermas declares in his theory of communicative competence, an ideal speech situation with the following features: (1) systematic and equal distribution of the opportunity to select and perform speech acts; (2) exchange of the dialogic roles of speaker and hearer; (3) equal distribution of choosing communicative, regulative, representative, and stative speech acts; (4) The possibility of putting in question all possible norms and opinions; (5) presupposition of good faith of the partners (Habermas 1971a, 136–39).

These conditions are never fully realized, but nevertheless the possibility of their realization is the a priori condition the participants must anticipate if they want the dialogue to take place. Like Plato, dialogue for Habermas is necessarily directed to consensus, evolving in an appropriate realm created by the regularization of the moves permitted by dialogue. The legitimacy of each move and each speech act is given by its contribution to this aim (Lyotard 1979, 106). Concrete dialogues are determined by special rules of the genre that confer a unity on them. They evolve in the sphere of a common metalanguage, the universality of which guarantees that the consensus obtained will be a just one.

This consensus-oriented teleologic premise of dialogue shared by dialogic theory and practice from Plato to Habermas confers a narrative scheme on dialogue. Indeed, all dialogues ending with a consensus can be recounted as narrations; the final agreement has the same function as the voice of the narrator in the novel. If we take this into consideration, it becomes a matter of less importance whether narration is dramatized—that is, whether only one narrator is speaking or also the persons whose story he is telling.

However, the narrative structure of dialogue is grounded not only in its essential orientation to consensus, but also in an even more fundamental condition of communication. As the speaker presupposes the full understanding of his utterances, which never can be realized by his concrete counterpart, he conceives his speech as directed not only to the real addressee but also to a kind of superior receiver living in a far-removed future. In this way, every dialogue is also included in a narration tending to a full understanding:

> Every utterance always has a receiver . . . whose responsive understanding is sought and anticipated by the author of the verbal work. He is a "second" (in a nonarithmetical sense). But in addition to this receiver the author imagines, more or less consciously, a higher

super-receiver (a third) whose absolutely appropriate responsive understanding is projected either into a metaphysical distance or into a distant historical time. In different periods and in different conceptions of the world, such super-receivers and their . . . responsive understanding receive various concrete ideological expressions (God, the absolute truth, the fragment, impartial human conscience, the people, the judgment of history, science, etc.). (Todorov 1984, 110)

In order for true dialogue to take place, the full understanding of a superaddressee is to be presupposed and becomes an a priori condition of communication. The possibility of being completely understood must be guaranteed to the speaker, even though it is never completely realized. Installing this superaddressee as a kind of transcendental a priori of dialogic discourse, Bakhtin founds the contingent dialogic time on a continuous flow of history. Narration is relegated to the frame in which dialogue takes place. As history is elevated to a transcendental category, the initial contingency is transformed into continuity. The superreceiver's full understanding functions as a sort of Kantian regulative idea of dialogue motivating all speech.

It is important to underline here that implicitly Bakhtin's claim presupposes not real history (*res gestae*) but narration (*narratio rerum gestarum*). The speaker in a concrete dialogue, by presupposing an absolute addressee, requires not a history of his dialogue, but rather the possibility of arranging the events in a story directed to a perfect understanding. It is for this reason that dialogue is rooted in narration and not in history. In summary, narration can be dialogic because dialogue is anchored in time by its pragmatic rules and its communicative a priori.

Grand Narratives and the Historical a Priori of Dialogue

Lyotard (1979) asserts that the narrative structure of communication is not accidental but is a structure that is essential to communicative pragmatics. Distinguishing between traditional and modern narratives, Lyotard claims that the traditional stories confer a cultural identity on their speakers, hearers, and objects, separating them from other communities by referring them to a common origin (Lyotard 1979, 40 ff., 45 ff.; 1986, 84). In contrast to this, the modern metanarrations (which also constitute a kind of a priori for the communicative community) already encounter a fundamental separation of the subjects; they even presuppose the dispersal of the members of a community (1986, 78), creating their unity by relating them not to a common origin but to a common future or end of history. For example, the narrative script of enlightenment is that of a continuous progression toward the emancipation of the subject from ignorance by cognition; the Marxist script is that which progresses toward a liberation from alienation and exploitation by the socialization of work; and the capitalist script narrates the emancipation from poverty by technoscientific development. Yet according to the pragmatics of narration, these scripts legitimate the subject to speak in the name of the liberty toward which history is striving and to assume the role of the universal subject who encompasses and absorbs all particularity. The differences between the individuals in dialogue are transcended by a collective singular, a process that creates the universal subject of history. Analogous to the double position of the narrator of the novel (who, on the one hand, is himself included in the time of narration as one subject among others but, on the other hand, transcends narrative time, anticipating the final point of the story and thus authorizing himself to speak in the name of all his characters), the particular individual derives his legitimation to speak in the name of others through the anticipation of the aim of history that will bring about a unitarian subject. In both cases dialogue takes place within the limits of a virtually collective monologue, and the individuals become the inner voices of a universal subject to be realized in the future. This universal subject will also encompass the persons who as yet are admitted only as objects of the dialogue and who later will acquire the competence necessary to participate as autonomous subjects in the course of the formation of universal history. This does not at all mean that dialogue is *in reality* monologic and that it consists only of the monologue of reason excluding its Other; it simply relativizes the notions of dialogue and monologue with regard to the level and to the temporal dimension of communication. However, the metanarrative a priori of dialogue, which confers a narrative structure on dialogic communication, is not transcendental in the Kantian sense but historical in the sense of Foucault's notion of discourse (Foucault 1966, 13 ff.).

The End of the Era of Metanarratives: Dialogue beyond Narration?

Since metanarratives of emancipation refer not to the past but to the future, they are virtually subject to falsification. And according to

Lyotard, falsification by history has taken place. For him all metanarratives are rejected without exception. Like Adorno, he states that the speculative narration was refuted by Auschwitz, the capitalist one by the economic crises of 1917, 1929, and 1974–79, the Marxist discourse by the bloody crushing of the revolts in Hungary (1956), the German Democratic Republic (1958), Czechoslovakia (1968), and Poland (1982) (Lyotard 1986, 53). One could add the refutation of the technoscientific discourse by the increase of pollution and the accident of Chernobyl (1986). The progress of scientific and technical knowledge has not liberated human beings, but rather has subjugated them to the necessities of technical and economical reason, thus producing a further alienation instead of liberating mankind. In this situation the universal metanarratives of emancipation lose their credibility, a loss that fundamentally transforms the pragmatic conditions of the grand narratives. The subjects of the narration are no longer universal but are dispersed among many particular individuals. The fundamental ontological structure of dialogue that was bound to the narrative a priori breaks down. The You and the I of dialogue become particular instances, no longer authorized to speak in the name of the emancipation of mankind.

Yet the delegitimation of the grand narrations destroys the atmosphere surrounding and protecting dialogue. Since there is no more authority to legitimize the sender and receiver, the presupposed metalanguage disseminates into a multiplicity of particular autonomous languages. This has the consequence that an utterance belonging to one language will be a victim of injustice through its exposition to another. The sequence of speech acts is no longer regulated: the initial contingency of the dialogic relation breaks through and also determines the concrete dialogic speech. The subjects of communication lose their universal character and are cut down to particular voices among a multiplicity of others. Since dialogue is no longer synthesized by a consensus or a common metalanguage, no universal pragmatics can close the gaps opening between the utterances. Dialogue no longer follows narrative scripts conforming to certain rules: rather, the latter are incorporated into and made the objects of conversation itself. Thus they emphasize one element of narration, the *event* that transforms the structure of dialogue itself, changing the rules of communication and allowing for the development of new codes and thus new ideas. In dialogue within the framework of the grand narratives, the rules preceded communication: now they are included in it. This is exactly the case Wittgenstein refers to: "And is there not also the case where we play and make up the rules as we go along? And there is even one where we alter them as we go along" (1958, 39). In this case narration is not the a priori framework of dialogue; it does not encompass it as a progression toward a never-fulfilled ideal but rather is included in dialogue itself. The relation between dialogue and narration characteristic of modernity seems to be reversed: dialogue is not legitimated by narration; rather, narration takes place in a fundamental metadialogue or metapolylogue of different languages that motivate it. Literature has very often tried to establish dialogue by creating new codes and new languages. The new languages could compensate for the wrong done to an individual by the rule of a single, monologic discourse because they produce new moves, create new languages that could express elements repressed by the monologic coercion. Perhaps the surrealistic conception of dialogue constitutes an extreme case of the new form of the dialogic relation. In the first *Surrealistic Manifesto* Breton asserts that surrealism is able to reestablish dialogue in its absolute truth, leaving behind all obligation of politeness. Thus liberated from pragmatic rules, every individual follows his own soliloquy without drawing any dialectic pleasure from it. In his definition of true dialogue Breton explicitly violates the fundamental premise established by Mukarovsky: there is no common theme; the words of the Other just serve as a stepping-stone for new appropriations and creative misunderstandings. The surrealistic dialogue does not care about the self-love of the partners; it permits all manner of responses and thereby the creation of new language games. Thus surrealistic dialogue installs a metadialogic relation to the language game of rule-governed and consensus-oriented dialogue. It makes transparent the norms and presuppositions of universal pragmatics it calls into question. By breaking up the universal pretensions of so-called neutral metalanguage, it makes the latter become one language among others, introducing it as a mere partner in a dialogue no longer rooted in a positive grand narration but grounded in a general polylogue of languages.

This kind of dialogue no longer counts on the possibility of full representation of one of the partners by the other. By a common neutral metalanguage it draws the conclusion of the incommensurability of language games and languages. However, the absence of a neutral metalanguage does not prevent dialogue, as Lyotard believes, from presupposing a grand narration. Naturally, refutation of the grand narrations and the lack of a common metalanguage lead to a proliferation of language games. Dialogue becomes a kind of semiotic "performance," or signifying practice, that develops its own codes through and by means of the communicative acts themselves. Also, the succession of different speech acts is no longer regulated by a priori rules; the rules are developed throughout the unfolding of the dialogue itself in time. Since there is no common metalanguage regulating their succession, the choice of speech acts is completely arbitrary. Since one speech act that is chosen necessarily does injustice to another, Lyotard concludes that the only guarantee for justice lies in the dissemination of the principle of continual recreation of languages and language games. This principle, he claims, will compensate for the injustice that the choice of one language game does to another, because it supplies a guarantee for the realization of a maximum of possible utterances. But does the postmodern condition really put an end to narration as the structure and a priori of dialogue? Two comments can be made concerning this relation under the new circumstances Lyotard describes.

My first point concerns narration as the structure of dialogic communication: every language game creating its own rules in the way mentioned above can be considered *post festum* as a genre following certain rules. However, these rules are to be constructed at the end, and they do not structure communication in a way the participants are aware of. Thus, postmodern signifying practice being contingent *in actu* can be interpreted by some rules constructed a posteriori. Hence a narrative structure can be conferred on dialogic communication when the latter has ceased. The only difference in the narrative structure of dialogue within the discourse of modernism resides in the possibility of constructing several rules and multiple narratives in co-occurrence with one another. This is the case for such a strange example as surrealistic dialogue, which also functions according to certain rules such as echolalies, differential repetition, dissemination of the theme, or the possibility of choosing speech acts independent of any known rules.

My second comment concerns narration as a historical a priori or regulative idea of dialogue. Indeed, the loss of legitimacy on the part of the grand narrative and the incommensurability and co-occurrence of several languages do not prevent Lyotard's alternative discurse ethics based on the principle of dissemination from being legitimated by a kind of metanarrative. To have this new metanarrative serve as legitimation for the postmodern amplification of genres is no longer sustained by the realization of a potential aim of history but rests on a prevention of it. The conclusion Lyotard draws from the fundamental tension between language games and the dissemination principle is grounded upon a negative history. The end of this history would be a universal language, some Orwellian Newspeak that has become real, quite independent of whether it was achieved by consensus or by coercion. Thus, Lyotard's concept of dialogue as constantly transgressing and modifying its own rules does not presuppose the abolition of all narrative, but rather assumes their negative transformation. The negativity of the *telos* changes the temporal form of dialogic time by emphasizing the contingency of linguistic events. But still narrative remains what it has always been to dialogue in the modern epoch: its temporal structure and historical a priori.

References

Bakhtin, M. 1981. *The dialogic imagination: Four essays by M. M. Bakhtin*, Ed. M. Holquist, trans. C. Emerson and M. Holquist. Austin: University of Texas Press.

Benjamin, W. 1977. *Illuminationen: Ausgewahlte Schriften.* Frankfurt: Suhrkamp.

Buber, M. 1984. *Das dialogische Prinzip.* Darmstadt: Wissenschaftliche Buchgemeinschaft.

Derrida, J. 1967. *De la grammatologie.* Collection Critique. Paris: Minuit.

———. 1972. *La dissémination.* Collection Tel Quel. Paris: Seuil.

———. 1977. Limited, Inc. In *Glyph*, 2:162–254. Baltimore: Johns Hopkins University Press.

Diderot, D. 1972. *Jacques le fataliste et son maître.* Paris: Librairie Générale Française.

Eagleton, T. 1983. *Literary theory: An introduction.* Oxford: Blackwell.

Ehre, M. 1984. M. M. Bakhtin: The dialogic imagination. *Poetics Today* 5:1:172–77.

Foucault, M. 1966. *Les mots et les choses.* Paris: Gallimard.

———. 1974. *Schriften zur Literatur.* Munich: Nymphenburger Verlagshandlung.

Gadamer, H. 1960. *Wahrheit und Methode: Gründzuge einer philosophischen Hermeneutik.* 4th ed. Tübingen: Mohr.

Genette, G. 1972. *Figures III.* Paris: Seuil.

Habermas, J. 1971. Vorbereitende Bemerkungen zu einer Theorie der kommunikativen Kompetenz. In *Theorie der Gesellschaft oder Sozialtechnologie—Was leistet die Systemforschung*, ed. J. Habermas and N. Luhman. Frankfurt: Suhrkamp.

Jakobson, R. 1979. Linguistik und Poetik. In *Poetik: Ausgewählte Aufsätze, 1921–1971*, ed. E. Holenstein and T. Schelbert, 82–121. Frankfurt: Suhrkamp. Originally published 1960.

Jauss, H. 1975. Literaturgeschichte als Provokation der Literaturwissenschaft. In *Rezeptionsasthetik*, ed. R. Warning. Munich: Fink.

Kloepfer, R. 1980. Dynamic structures in narrative literature: The dialogic principle. *Poetics Today* 1:115–34.

———. 1982. Grundlagen des dialogischen Prinzips in der Literatur. In *Dialogizität*, ed. R. Lachmann. 85–106.

Levinas, E. 1979. *Le temps et l'autre*. Paris: Quadrige.

Lyotard, J. 1979. *La condition postmoderne: Rapport sur le savoir*. Paris: Minuit.

———. 1986. *Le postmoderne expliqué aux enfants: Correspondance, 1982–1985*. Paris: Galilée.

Mukarovsky, J. 1977. Two studies of dialogue. In *The word and verbal art: Selected Essays*, trans. and ed. J. Burbank and P. Steiner. 65–80. New Haven: Yale University Press. Originally published 1940.

Plato. 1961. *Werke*. Heidelberg: Lambert Schneider.

Ricoeur, P. 1983. *Temps et récit*. Vol. 1. Paris: Seuil.

Saussure, F. de. 1979. *Cours de linguistique générale*. Ed. Tuillio de Mauro. Paris: Payot.

Sterne, L. 1967. *The life and opinions of Tristram Shandy, gentleman*. Middlesex: Penguin. Originally published 1760.

Todorov, T. 1984. *Mikhail Bakhtin: The dialogical principle*. Trans. Wlad Godzich. Minneapolis: University of Minnesota Press.

Wittgenstein, L. 1958. *Philosophical investigations*. Trans. G. E. M. Anscombe. New York: Macmillan.

part IV

Therapeutic Dialogue

8

Psychoanalytic Dialogue and the Dialogical Principle

Sven Daelemans and Tullio Maranhão

The book on Freud produced by Bakhtin's circle has a disputed autography. *Freudianism: A Marxist Critique,* written in 1926–27, was published under the name of V. N. Voloshinov, Bakhtin's friend and a member of his intellectual circle. In the 1960s, a time of revival of interest in Bakhtin's work in Russia, it was revealed that Bakhtin himself was the author of *Freudianism.* Although still alive then, Bakhtin is reported to have acknowledged the authorship of the book to friends but never to have done so publicly. His life as a thinker and author was surrounded by secrecy owing to the need to survive as a religious believer and innovative revolutionary intellectual in the Stalinist regime. Interestingly, one of the objects of his challenges was the notion of autonomous authorship. He argued that the author did not create his discourse but "appeared as its creator." However, he never went as far as to deny the individuality of speakers and writers, and the question of their identity looms centrally in his philosophical anthropology.

Voloshinov/Bakhtin's criticism of Freud's work can be summarized in the points that follow. (1) Freud's reliance on sex to explain human conduct reflected a bourgeois ideology of despair at a historical moment (the turn of the century in Vienna) when the values of the bourgeois family were vanishing. (2) Freud avoided the variables of history by reducing human conduct to biological motivation. (3) Interpretation in psychoanalysis makes sense only in terms of Freud's metanarrative (the Oedipus story, the mechanics of narcissism, the growth and development of ego structures, etc.), but this metanarrative does not have better grounds to explain human conduct than any other. (4) Psychoanalysis depends entirely on introspection, but introspection is the work of consciousness, and since consciousness is always the consciousness of ideological motives, psychoanalysis deals in ideology, not in the deep psychological causes of action. (5) The concept of the unconscious is untenable; the unconscious is that which is not readily present in consciousness for myriad reasons, most of which are sociological, not psychological. (6) Freud made psychoanalytic treatment dependent on language, a medium ideologically charged, overlooking the fact that the word is always the word of another speaker and thus can never be completely revealing of the motives of the person speaking in the here and now. (7) Freud ignored the overriding sociological nature of human conduct, thereby dehistoricizing man.

We will not review every point of Bakhtin's criticism of Freud but will focus instead on those aspects of greater relevance for the status of dialogue in psychoanalysis.

Voloshinov/Bakhtin divides *The Critique of Psychoanalysis*, the Freudian concept of the unconscious, into three stages. In the earliest conception, the unconscious is the repository of forgotten experiences; it is not founded on an organismic base; and its products are retrieved only by means of the language of consciousness. The conflict between conscious and unconscious is sporadic (Voloshinov 1976, 34–35). In the second phase of definition, the conflict between conscious and unconscious becomes permanent, as the unconscious acquires a dynamic nature. In this phase the unconscious is not "the forgotten" but, more emphatically, "the repressed," that is, those meaning contents that have not yet found their way into utterances (p. 37). Finally, in the third phase of Freud's concepts, the unconscious becomes associated with changes introduced in the theory of drives or instincts. The sexual and self-preservation instincts are combined, and the death instinct is added to the theory. Life is characterized by the constant unconscious struggle between Eros and Death; this is the content of the id (pp. 45–46).

The unconscious is, then, the catching net for all those things the organism wanted under the pleasure principle, if it could only be free from reality and culture. But those wanted things are not organismic; they are "ideological through and through" (p. 24). Indeed, we can learn about the unconscious only through consciousness. The impulses emanating from the unconscious keep trying to break through the censorship, eventually succeeding and lodging their contents in consciousness. But such impulses can accomplish the breakthrough only "with the help of *compromises and distortions*" (p. 49) that allow them to deceive the surveillance of the ego's censorship. In their new conscious abode the impulses are unrecognizable and constitute the subject matter of analysis. In order to reconstitute their original meaning, Freud proposes the method of free association. The patient resists the full clarification in consciousness of the repressed materials. Whenever these topics come to his mind, he thinks that they are irrelevant, that they have already met with a satisfactory explanation, or he suppresses them from consciousness altogether. This is the work of what Voloshinov/Bakhtin calls the "legal or official conscious" (p. 51). The unconscious is the "unofficial conscious," and the psychic struggle is nothing but a replica of the social struggle lived through language in discourse.

What Freud does is to propose a reason for forgetting, thereby transforming it into suppression of memory. There are hierarchies of relevance operating in the mind, and many explanations of their logic have been forwarded, Freud's being a very ingenious and popular one. He could have gone along with prepsychoanalytic psychology in regarding the gaps of memory as unproblematic facts of life. Or he could have cast psychoanalysis on the unproductive line of self-recursion in which every smattering of meaning is explored in its endless ramifications. But he chose instead to suspect the hierarchies of relevance operating in the mind and to treat them as smokescreens hiding what is truly relevant. This effect is accomplished by a theory of the mind based on the functioning of conscious and unconscious, of the relations between id, ego, and superego, and by the metanarrative of the history of the human psyche told in terms of the tales of Oedipus and Narcissus, of the instinctual drive toward sex, pleasure, and aggression, of the fear of death, and of the self-preserving efforts, resulting in defense, culture, and repression. Voloshinov/Bakhtin discards the metanarrative as totally unwarranted.

Once in consciousness, the repressed materials are represented or replaced by symbols that exercise a placebo effect over the psyche, making it feel as if its wishes had been fulfilled. These symbols are as polyvalent as any other signifier in language. What allows the psychoanalyst to narrow down the interpretation of meaning is the metanarrative of psychoanalysis. Furthermore, the polyvalence of these symbols, unlike the other signifiers of discourse, is not poetic but neurotic; that is, it works not to explore new avenues of meaning, but precisely to suppress the unbearable meaning of desire.

The contents of the unconscious smuggled into the conscious under distortion can be tapped only by introspection, and introspection falls within the limits of consciousness (Voloshinov 1976, 69). This is not something for any Freudian to disagree with, for Freud himself always thought that consciousness was the only locus for dealing with the unconscious. The bone of contention here is the nature of consciousness: it is ideological for Bakhtin and reality based for Freud.

Consciousness cannot encompass in a single context and in a particular moment the entire gamut of meaning available to the mind; no one has immediate access to all potential or possible meanings. Freud chooses to call "unconscious" meanings that are left outside in a given act of retrieval. However, *concealed* meanings are indeed more obviously the result of the refraction obtaining in the contrast between the Self's use of a word and the Other's use of the same word. This characterization of accessible meaning and unavailable meaning inspired by the dialogical principle of discourse can be recast in translinguistic terms—language as an encounter of many languages. One might say that the record of such refracted meanings constitutes language or, still better, in Bakhtinian parlance, that it constitutes translanguage. Since it is impossible (and useless) to recollect all those meanings in a natural history of signification, the dialogical metaphor for talking about the production of meaning is more riveting than the linguistic metaphor. In this sense dialogue is a negotiation about which meanings should be part of the conversation and which should be left out.

Voloshinov/Bakhtin does not find any evidence for a concrete existence of the unconscious. Psychoanalysis, he concludes, is merely "verbal utterances" and the "interpretation of utterances" (Voloshinov 1976, 76). Since utterances flow in the domain of consciousness, the "dynamics of psychical forces" is nothing but "a dynamics of various motives of consciousness" (p. 77).

The conflict studied by psychoanalysis is not that between the unconscious and the conscious; rather, it is the clash of discursive interests between doctor and patient. The patient insists on a certain biographic narrative, while the analyst "endeavors to wrest confessions from the patient and to compel him to take the 'correct' point of view on his illness and its symptoms" (p. 78). Such is Voloshinov/Bakhtin's characterization of the therapeutic encounter. The conflicting interests of analyst and analysand are ideology laden by the institutional establishment of the social relationship. The patient has his story and believes in it; the doctor has been trained to doubt firsthand stories and prods his interlocutor to yield the concealed surplus of meaning. As a consequence, psychoanalysis is not about the patient's psyche, but about the relationship between analyst and analysand—once that relationship became historically established with the institutional triumph of the psychoanalytic project. But even such a seemingly negative assessment of psychoanalytic therapy does not call for a rebuttal by those analysts who regard the analysis of transference as the most important part of the therapy. Nevertheless, analysts would contend that what leads the patient to transfer feelings and reactions to the analyst is triggered by unconscious forces.

In the final chapter of the book on Freudianism, Voloshinov/ Bakhtin turns to propounding his own theory of ideology as the content of consciousness. He begins by pointing out Freud's "distrust of the unconscious" (p. 85)—Ricoeur's hermeneutics of suspicion— and joining him in that stance, since the Russian writer too professes such a distrust, although for different reasons. A person's conscious explanation of his conduct must not "be taken as a scientific explanation" (p. 85). The content explanation is just another form of ideological and conscious account, and it is as distorted as the person's conscious and candid explanation. The unconscious is thus called the "unofficial conscious" as opposed to the "ordinary 'official conscious' " (p. 85). The content of the utterances stems not from the "unconscious," but from the fabric of social, political, and historical collective life. No matter how seemingly representative of the person's innermost character, every utterance bears the ideological stamp of its social interest.

At times Voloshinov/Bakhtin reads like an orthodox Marxist who reduces all meaning to the mode of production of the society under study. The author writes: "The content of our consciousness . . . in its entirety and . . . individual utterances with . . . which that content and that psyche manifest themselves outwardly *are in every respect determined by socioeconomic factors*" (p. 86; emphasis added). Statements like this fly in the face of Bakhtin's ideas about word, language, symbol, and meaning and invite us to read them as concessions made in order to appease Stalinist censorship. But there is a difference between arguing socioeconomic determinism and indicating the social interest present in every utterance. We speak inside contexts of conversation that are always generated in social situations and—adding Habermas's (1982) discourse to Bakhtin's —that reflect the history of power relations and the concern with labor. Treading on very similar territory, Bakhtin calls the emancipatory criticism of socially constituted discourse "inner speech." Inner speech accumulates doubts about the official or outer speech and swims against the tide of "official ideology." However, inner speech is not counterideological; it opposes a particular official ideology but draws inspiration for its language from the same sources as does its adversary (Voloshinov 1976, 88). Voloshinov/Bakhtin tries to show that the thematic of the discourse of Freud's patients—unconscious, unofficial conscious or inner speech—is conditioned by social context by arguing, for example, that while in Freud's polity homosexual inclinations are regarded as symptomatic, in ancient Greece they were part of the outward speech (p. 89). In an effort to explain the distortion or incompleteness of unconscious symbols, he argues that as long as inner speech remains barred from the domain of outer speech, it begins "to lose [its] verbal countenance, and little by little, really does turn into a 'foreign body' in the psyche" (p. 89).

According to Voloshinov/Bakhtin, Freud thwarted the natural dialogism of discourse in psychoanalysis by proceeding like the linguists and entrusting the work of interpretation to a monological language that neither overcomes ideology nor lets the free ideological interplay of discourse unfold unhindered. Psychoanalysis in his opinion is totalitarian, dogmatic, and transideological in the sense that it avoids the critique of ideology as well as ideological controversy by claiming to have the only key to open the door to understanding human conduct. This is obviously a devastating criticism of psychoanalysis. It is constructed with many imprecisions and with an unfavorably slanted reading of Freud. Nevertheless, it is not our purpose to rebuke Voloshinov/Bakhtin's argument and come out in defense of Freud. We wish instead to show some deep similarities betwen Bakhtin's dialogical principle and the psychoanalytic dialogue. To do that, we must review a few important concepts in Bakhtin's thought.

The Ethics of Answerability

In spite of the wide range of topics of interest in Bakhtin's work, there is one underlying "theme" that undergirds all his attempts at describing the dialogical workings of discourse. This is the (metaphysical) project of reconciling epistemology, ethics, and aesthetics (Kant's three Critiques) into a comprehensive system of pragmatic and ethical action. For Bakhtin this connection can be established only through the architectonic operations of the mind (cf. Clark and Holquist 1984, chap. 3).

The Bakhtinian theory starts out with the commonsense observation that two people cannot occupy the same (physical) place simultaneously. This implies that "my" spatiotemporal, or chronotopic, location not only is constantly shifting, but exclusively and uniquely belongs to "me" and to "my" architectonic construction of reality. Thus, Bakhtin's "Law of Placement" very simply states that each of "us" observes the given world from a temporally and spatially different perspective. Of course this also means that the "same" event is always different for Self and Other. As a result, "otherness" is not necessarily a metaphysical deduction but is a physical inevitability, while the Self is not a Kantian transcendental essence but a unique "locus of apperception" bound by specific chronotopic contingencies. Bakhtin refers to the Self/Other distinction as "alterity." Moreover, the basic architectonic operator in the Self's construction of reality and of itself is the "surplus of seeing," that particular perceptual slice of the world "I" alone can see from "my" chronotopic platform. In this sense, Bakhtin maintains, "we" are all unique, since "we" all share a potential for chronotopic differentiation.

The "noncoincidence" of Self and Other is further supplemented by Bakhtin's architectonic construction of the relation between mind and world, which is an effort to "detranscendentalize" the Kantian solution to that problem. Indeed, philosophical systems before Kant emphasized the interaction between mind and world in the construction of knowledge and reality but became stranded either on the idealist (Locke) or the realist (Leibniz) shores. Kant's revolutionary solution consisted of installing a dialogical interaction between mind and world, through which a synthesis between sensibility and intelligibility was achieved. For Kant the moment of (rational) judgment was made possible only through a "transcendental synthesis," facilitated by the a priori concepts of the mind. Bakhtin basically agrees with the Kantian concept of dialectic but does not see the necessity for a "transcendental synthesis"; instead he posits that the architectonic activities of the mind partake in a dialogue that is influenced by the *hic et nunc* characteristics of the most immediate reality.

Bakhtin's two dialectics—Self/Other and mind/world—are extended to the dialectical processes that undergird "my" self-expression (the I-for-myself), that is, the chronotopic and concomitant axiological values that give "this" time and "this" space their specific contextual pigmentation. This dialectic of the Self with "the markers of Self" leads Bakhtin to the deconstruction of the pronoun "I" ("an empty term"), but also to a repeated emphasis on the necessity of the Other for one's own completion, a completion that can never reach totality. Much in a Levinasian sense, the Self becomes a project for whose "completion" the Other is always needed: as "I" cannot see the Self that is "my" own (owing to the "Law of Placement"), "I" must try to capture it in the "eye" of the Other (Bakhtin 1984, 311–12).

Clearly, Bakhtin posits the primacy of heterology by virtue of the fact that "otherness" constitutes the life breath of all existence, while "dialogue" emerges as the primary process for the successful completion of "my" project. From an ethical standpoint, however, the Self/Other distinction forms the basic material for an architectonics of action. This brings us to Bakhtin's emphasis on "answerability."

Bakhtin's interest in Darwin provides him with a starting point for exploring the interactions of organisms with their environments in their quest for survival. All life-forms seem to have what Bakhtin calls a certain "addressivity" toward their immediate environment; this addressivity is highly preprogrammed for lower life-forms, but for human life it is characterized by a great variety of choices. However, organisms cannot avoid "answering" the call of their environments if they want to remain alive. In other words, one has to answer or one cannot exist. Therefore, Bakhtin maintains, there is "no alibi for being."

The combination of this inevitable "answerability" and the necessary "architectonics" in building the bridge between Self and Other—conditions necessary for being "in existence"—leads to an ethic of response-ability, in which "we" are accountable for "our" unique placement in existence. Furthermore, as dialogism and alterity constitute the foundation of all existence, the ethical project consists in a respons-ible calibration of "my" chronotopic needs and deeds to those of the Other. However, in Bakhtin's philosophy of action, the world is an "axiological desert" devoid of preexisting meaning and values. Therefore the ethical project not only entails a calibration of the Self's deeds to those of the Other, but also the construction of an "axiological coexistence," that is, the creation of (communal) values.

In the dialogical distance between mind and world we still encounter Bakhtin's strong Kantian influence: the world, recognized only through the activity of a dialogue, is a "given" and without meaning. Consequently, only through an act of consciousness is a worldly meaning created. Since consciousness never completely coincides with the world, its chronotopic operations fundamentally transform the "already there," investing it with temporal and spatial categories and creating meaning. This creation of meaning always involves a value judgment if "I" am to act in the world I have (co)created. These values can reflect hegemonic or counterhegemonic ideologies or can be refractions of an official or an unofficial conscious, but they cannot not occur: one cannot be a conscious human being and live a value-free life. Consequently, answerability is found not at the level of meaning, but at the level of value: we have a (response-able) choice whether to act according to the values of our reigning place and time (hegemonic "passivity"), or according to our own values (counterhegemonic "activity"). As a result, response-ability corresponds to a Heideggerian "call of Being" as the activity of answering the world's demands for new meanings. For Bakhtin, ethics resides not on a semantic but on an axiological level.

However, as Bakhtin equates Self with consciousness and consciousness with (co)consciousness of the Other, all acts of answerability share existential community. The question thus arises: How can we keep dialogue going if all elements in the dialogue are indiscriminately flowing into each other? Indeed, a dialectical synthesis of the contradictory elements in dialogue would ultimately undermine its fundamental premise—the endurance of the struggle of difference. Bakhtin's answer to this dilemma, admittedly a Kantian one, goes somewhat as follows. Making the Self/Other distinction requires the appreciation of the inadequacy of the perceptual operators "I" employed in "my" construction of the Other and of my reality. There is always a perceptual discrepancy between the architetonic operations and (e)valuations that are mine and the spatiotemporal qualifications derived by the Other. At this point in his argument, anticipating Gadamer, Bakhtin develops his conception of dialectical exchange, that is, the excursion into otherness followed by a return to the familiar. Only through the "eyes of the Other," from the Other's surplus of seeing/being, only from a platform of chronotopic extralocality, can I come to recognize and enhance my Self. Like Gadamer, Bakhtin considers this double movement to be the essence of aesthetic activity.

Bakhtin's mechanism of architectonics in which the Self and the Other are coconstructed amalgamates ethics and aesthetics into a new version of "pragmatics" (in contrast to Kantian transcendentalism). Moreover, not only does Bakhtin see this principle as guiding the everyday practice of life, but he also sees it as the main principle at work when authors construct novelistic characters: the author is actually inside and outside the characters he creates. The correspondence with Gadamer's notion of *Bildung* ("the historical conformation within language and culture") is uncanny, although Gadamer does not explicitly make the leap to ethics (1975, 15). *Bildung* (that is, "cultural and linguistic conformation"), the hermeneutic procedure par excellence, is characterized by a similar structure of alienation and return, excursion and reunion or, in Bakhtinian terms, of identification and exotopy. As for Gadamer, in the homecoming of Bakhtin's prodigal Self, the Self becomes "more" than it was before: after returning home from its long journey, the Self is more itself, more fully itself. There is, in ontological terms, an "access of being," or from the storehouse of "my" "surplus of seeing," "I" can now, upon return in my own unique "placement" in existence, complete the Other, since I have the Other's vantage point and some extra features to which only I have access.

In summary, Bakhtin's description of "architectonics" not only welds together ethics and aesthetics but also establishes the dialogical principle as the primary process for the architectonic confluences.

Chronotopic Instantiation

A chronotope (literally, time-space) refers to a particular perceptual organization of the dimensions of space and time in the construction of our sense of reality. Consequently, the chronotope is a concept for engaging reality, for creating a worldview, for building a bridge between the two worlds of meaningless matter and conscious mind. But the chronotope is not a (Kantian) transcendental a priori, since it is (co)constructed in the immediacy of the moment. Bakhtin is primarily interested in the use of the chronotope as a distinctive measure of the features of time and space within different literary genres. The chronotopes "provide the basis for distinguishing generic types; they lie at the heart of specific varieties of the novel genre" (Bakhtin 1981, 251). Moreover, "Language, as a treasure-house of images, is fundamentally chronotopic" (p. 251). As a result, different historical times and different cultural valuations will result in different chronotopes, which can be studied only through the literary genres of those same epochs. Every genre, then, constitutes not only a particular way of looking at the world, but also a particular image of man. The development of worldviews and anthropological images culminates in the works on Dostoevsky (dialogism) and on Rabelais (carnival), in which Bakhtin includes in his analysis insights deriving from the cultural and ideological backgrounds of these literary works. As a result of this extended analysis, the notion of genre becomes identified with that of discourse of everyday life. These are the basic building blocks of Bakhtin's architectonics of response-ability. They also constitute the foundation of an elaborate philosophical anthropology, which the Kantian tradition pursues as an answer to the question What is man? The aesthetic dimension resides in a preliminary question of the Kantian quest, namely, What can I know? The ethical dimension is introduced by the following two questions: What should I do? and What can I hope for? The answers to the aesthetic and ethical questions provide us with glimpses of what man is upon every return after *Bildung*.

Translinguistics

Bakhtin's emphasis on "transgredience" in the process of completing the Other (as well as Self) regards language not as a linguistic system of signs, but as living discourse, as language in its concrete living totality. The focus on the interaction of language with the context of the utterance (a context that is always historical) is first called *metalinguistics* and later *translinguistics*. In contrast to the sentence as the unit of language and main focus of linguistics, translinguistics analyses the utterance as the *unit of communication*. As a result, the "replacement" of linguistics by translinguistics has a pragmatic flavor as it situates itself on the level of the concrete and singular (thus contextual) utterance, or "everyday discourse." Indeed, the utterance is not simply what is said, as it is not the reflection of an extraverbal "object." Rather, discourse, as dialogical energy, is active and productive; it makes something happen. As such, discourse does not represent a particular situation but, conversely, is an architectonic singular event of communication and dialogical connection between two or more people. This joining or communication is another example of how Bakhtin explains the constitution of Self through dialogical interaction. Two combined elements are important in his theory of utterances: the confluence of the said (the speech of the speaker) and the unsaid (the context of the situation), through intonation, that is, the acoustical adjustment of the message to a particular Other (cf. Todorov 1984, 46).

Consequently, in the social scripts and scenarios of everyday speech we breathe life into the architectonic categories with which we construct our lifeworld, while intonation, as "social evaluation," transforms the chronotopic valuations into specific and contextually "appropriate" interpretations of reality. Bakhtin's emphasis on "social dramaturgy" and "translinguistic heroism" testifies to his contention that every utterance punctuates the struggle of the utterance as a social "event" toward self-identification. In the utterance the dialectic of Self/Other is transposed into the dialogic symbiosis between the said and the unsaid and bridged by intonation. As a result, "meaning" (which means "life" for Bakhtin) can be understood only in the discursive conjunctions of the reiterative and the nonreiterative, in the perpetual dialogue between the said and the unsaid.

Monoglossia and Heteroglossia/Monologism and Dialogism

Given his philosophical anthropology, which emphasizes a plurality of (co)consciousnesses, and given the translinguistic concentration on the utterance as the foundation of dialogic communication, Bakhtin suggests that human life—everything that has meaning and significance—is permeated by dialogue as a universal (and constitutive) principle. Contrary to the linguistic spirit of Saussure, which involves the individualization or monologization of the general (*unitary language*), Bakhtin posits the study of the heteroglot, multivoiced, multistyled, and often multilanguaged elements of (novelistic and quotidian) discourse (cf. 1981, 275).

Bakhtin's highly distinctive conception of language is characterized by an internal struggle or dialogization; a savage battle occurs between the *centrifugal* forces of heterology and the *centripetal* forces of unification and totalization. Ultimately, internal dialogization grounds the whole texture of translinguistic existence and finds its best expression in the polyphonic dialogues between novelistic characters, particularly those of Dostoevsky and Rabelais. However, these two disparate tendencies are not of equal force, and each corresponds to a different kind of reality construction: centrifugal forces, on the one hand, are most powerful; they are always *in praesentia*, since they determine the way we actually experience language as we use it—and are used by it—in the contextual particularity of everyday life. The unifying centripetal forces, on the other hand, are less powerful and require a purposeful and rhetorical action of totalization and systematization. The dialectic between centripetal and centrifugal forces pulsating behind what we usually call "language" embodies a series of other more fundamental tensions, such as those between form and process, stability and change, hegemony and revolution, or totality and infinity. Without centrifugal forces change would be impossible, since communication would be dominated by a hegemonical ideology of unification and totalization; however, some kind of "unification" or perhaps "sensus communis" (to pursue our analogy between Bakhtin and Gadamer) is necessary if we are to achieve communication in order to proceed with the architectonic completion of Self and Other.

The notion of heteroglossia, or internal dialogization, provides Bakhtin with a first avenue to explore the fallacies of mimetic theories of language. Indeed, in contrast to representationist theories of signification, Bakhtin counterposes the internal dialogization of the signifier before it meets the signified. In monological and representationist theories of meaning, "the word acknowledges only itself (that is, only its own context), its own object, its own direct expression and its own unitary and singular language" (Bakhtin 1981, 276). Any other word is merely a "potential for speech," not a potential for influencing the first word. In this conception of language, words are found in isolation from one another. Their only sign of life resides in the object they purport to speak, but they can do that only partially. However, between the word and its object there are other words claiming the same object, jamming the iridescent environment of signification that is so "difficult to penetrate" (p. 276). It is only in such an environment that the word can be individualized. This artificial individualization of the word was the choice of linguistics, and it became in Voloshinov/Bakhtin's argument the condition sine qua non of Freudian psychoanalysis.

Bakhtin emphasizes the double working in the concrete utterance of the speaking subject: not only is there a moment of mimesis (necessary for mutual understanding), but there is always an inevitable moment of newness that ensures the continuous becoming of the Self. As such, "the processes of centralization and decentralization, of unification and disunification, intersect in the utterance; the utterance not only answers the requirements of its own language as an individualized embodiment of a speech act, but it answers the requirements of heteroglossia as well; it is in fact an active participant is such speech diversity." Consequently, "every utterance participates in the 'unitary language' (in its centripetal forces and tendencies) and at the same time partakes of social and historical heteroglossia (the centrifugal, stratifying forces)" (Bakhtin 1981, 272).

Bakhtin's ideas crush two traditional conceptions of language. The first refers to the notion that any given language is the single, complete, "real" language (e.g., English as the only language and not coconstituted by, among others, Latin, Greek, and Germanic roots).

This mistaken view coincides with a deafness to polyglossia, or interlanguage difference. "Where languages and cultures interanimated each other, language became something entirely different, its very nature changed: in place of a single, unitary sealed-off Ptolemaic world of language, there appeared the open Galilean world of many languages, mutually animating each other" (Bakhtin 1981, 65). The second mistaken conception about language branches off from the first and assumes that the utterance reflects the structure of a unified and homogeneous language system, not the kaleidoscopic stretch of the communicative situation.

Intertextuality

In Bakhtin's discourse there are at least three unequivocal levels of dialogism: the dialectic between Self and Other, the relations between the exchanges of a dialogue, and the relations binding every utterance to another. We discussed above how the Self needs the Other in order to constitute itself. The turn taking of dialogue carries the Self's need of the Other further into the ethics of answerability. Finally, every utterance finds a kindred utterance in the history of the speech community. The dialogism of utterances that Todorov calls "intertextuality" (1984, 60) is represented not by the repetition of a sentence in a language, but by the ideological affinity every statement must perforce have with another (in order to escape the metaphysics of originality).

Any given language is a congeries of languages. Every utterance is an additional decentering of something already said. The utterance in a dialogic turn taking receives an author who becomes identified as "the creator of the utterance" (quoted by Todorov 1984, 61); in the speech situation the utterance is the "face" of the speaker. Nevertheless, the utterance is far from exhausting the uniqueness and individuality of its author. In a way, every utterance ideologically creates its author, but in Bakhtin's philosophical anthropology, man cannot be reduced to the statements he utters. The utterance only identifies its author ideologically in the absence of a correlative utterance expressing an alternative worldview. Consequently, to speak means to enter the realm of controversy about the world.

The three levels we have been discussing (Self/Other, dialogue, and utterance) cannot be readily equated with one another. But the overlaps that do take place are not random. They can be approached, on the one hand, by the relation between word and object, and on the other hand, by the pragmatics of speaker and utterance. Bakhtin's use of the metaphor of prose and poetry is clarifying in this regard. A poem is an utterance and as such brings to the foreground the relationship between the word and the world. The ideological slant of the author disappears behind the tearing complexity presiding over the relationship of words and objects. In prose there are several degrees of distanciation between author and discourse. The purest manifestation of prose is the novel. In it the author creates characters and juxtaposes divergent opinions, breathing life into a text that thus looks like vicarious reality. The novel writer is capable of stylizing the whole universe of discourse in everyday life, thereby opening a gulf between his act of creation and the discourse whose strings he pulls. The code of the novel-writing game resides in the concealment of the author, which is simultaneous with an emphasis on the autonomy of the discourse. The poet, on the contrary, "is utterly immersed" in the poem (Bakhtin 1981, 285). He fully expresses his intention through his words: "There must be no distance between the poet and his word" (p. 297). In poetry we should not find any ossified genres or other intermediations of discourse. *"Everything* [every utterance] *that enters the* [poetical] *work must immerse itself in Lethe, and forget its previous life in any other contexts"* (p. 297). Like Heidegger, Bakhtin regards poetry as refractory against representation. Both thinkers wish to capture a certain essence of orality hidden away in writing that poetry would somehow preserve (cf. Heidegger 1971, especially "The Nature of Language"). Bakhtin eventually recants his position, pondering that an "authentic voice can only be a second voice" (Todorov 1984, 68), and consequently even poetry cannot help but serve as a vehicle for the representation of poetical discourse. The poetical utterance itself is not free from intertextuality.

Psychoanalytic Dialogue

Is the psychoanalytic transaction an effort to produce a text? The metaphor of text composition to explain analytic interpretation is a very powerful one (cf. Schafer 1980; Spence 1982; Derrida 1978; Maranhão 1986). The patient comes to therapy with a version of his life problems, a story, a biography, a narrative, through which he tells who he thinks he is, what has happened to him, how he feels and reacts to others, and so on. This is, naturally, a biographic text.

Initially he may complain about other people's attitude toward him, exempting himself from being the cause of their disturbing conduct, but even if he takes full responsibility for what happened to him and for how he feels, the analyst will listen to him with suspicion.

The psychoanalyst is trained to place his listening above the level of the story. He focuses on the "intonation" of the patient's discourse—in the Bakhtinian sense of the expression—that is, he listens to the adaptation of the utterance to the particular context of addressivity. The analytical working hypothesis is that the patient tells his tale as a vehicle to communicate to the analyst, by means of transference, something that is not present in the semantic content of his words. The "true" story that attempts to burst forth through the cracks of the patient's speech is generally about love and hate, dependence and independence, acceptance and rejection, self-aggrandizement and self-denigration, and it is fastened into the patient's biography. The analyst also has his textual agenda. He listens to what the analysand does in saying what he says, links it to what is actually said in the guise of biography reconstruction, and performs these operations oriented by the psychoanalytic metanarrative of his theoretical persuasion.

In this sense the psychoanalytic encounter is like a meeting between author and editor, resulting in a polished and mutually acceptable text. Even the circle of readers for whom the text is prepared is not absent from this comparison, as the patient finds himself tested by his relations in the world in the changes he experiences himself as undergoing.

If this is the case, we will be justified in assuming that psychoanalysis is the art of producing the right biographic texts. The corollary to such an assumption is that neurosis consists of inadequate biographic texts. Thus psychoanalysis can be regarded as dogmatic and as imposing its principles of text adequacy on the patient's semiliterate skills. This is clearly the view espoused by Voloshinov/Bakhtin in *Freudianism*, while one of the mainstays of the criticism he levels at psychoanalysis resides in the fact that hegemonic textualization is not necessarily more right than counterhegemonic textualization. The illiterate text referred to above, which consciousness will perfect, is represented by the unconscious manifestations surfacing in dreams, slips of the tongue, and free associations. Voloshinov/Bakhtin does not think the two texts can be compared under the value judgment of quality and completeness. He argues that the unconscious's rough text is an "unofficial conscious," while the "official conscious" is merely the established discourse, or the discourse of power superordination.[1] Texts are by nature contradictory among themselves, and their hierarchy tells us only about their use for domination. As Voloshinov/Bakhtin would put it, the text or word is ideological par excellence, and the psychoanalytic privileging of its own tales denounces its totalitarian inspiration. Psychoanalysis would cure by subjugation or by indoctrination.

However, neither Freud nor his followers ever insisted that the patient should learn the words of the story that best describes his illness. Indeed, the psychoanalytic treatment is the domain of heteroglossia. It is the contextual features of the patient's discourse that assign meaning to his words, not the relation between signifier and signified. The role of the analyst consists in calling the analysand's attention to the meaning that sprouts from his free association, or from linking contexts he least suspected could be related to one another. Now we might feel tempted to conclude that although it does not impose its metanarrative plot on the patient, psychoanalysis cures by taking away from him, however temporarily, his right to autography. Neurosis would be a question of authorial overconfidence or uncertainty; the psychoanalytic metanarrative would be the transitional instrument that breaks the symbiotic attachment between the analysand and his story and restores his ability to read the texts of life transparently, thereby heeding the principle of reality, always kaleidoscopic and shifting, demanding flexibility from the interpreter. Neurosis would be a fixation on a particular text or a fall into total disbelief about the meaning of texts in general. Obviously, most analysts would not agree with this assessment, except perhaps a few—among them Lacan, to whose ideas we shall turn briefly in the following section. Yet there seems to be an element of truth in this portrayal of psychoanalytic treatment since the days of Freud.

Lacan's Conception of the Unconscious as Language

Lacan extrapolates the Saussurean formula of signification to the Freudian insights by suggesting that Signified:Signifier::Conscious-

---

1. The critique of the psychoanalytic characterization of the discourses of doctor and patient has been very common in France, where the argument has been repeatedly made that the discourse favored in analysis as healthy is identified with the discourse of power and domination, while the discourse of illness is subversive and exists only as a reaction against the official discourse (cf. Deleuze and Guattari 1977). Although a neo-Kantian and an avowed anti-Nietzschean, Bakhtin did read the nihilist philosopher and had a Nietzschean infatuation in his youth (cf. Clark and Holquist 1984, 26), and he may have conserved some strands of "irrationalist" criticism in his thought.

ness: Unconscious. "The Unconscious is the whole structure of language" (1977, 147), he writes, and "the dreamwork follows the law of the signifier" (p. 161). Lacan's notion of a floating or internally dialogic signifier offers a first point of contact with Bakhtin: the battle between consciousness and the unconscious is not a binary opposition of clear-cut entities, but a multilevel and polyvoice struggle between heteroglot languages and signifiers. As such, both Bakhtin and Lacan emphasize the discursive nature of the psyche whose rhetorical tropes (or "ideological" motives of power) need to be explicated or psychoanalyzed. Lacan introduces the dialogical interplay of the discursive formations of consciousness and the unconscious, whereby the "outer speech" of the official conscious (Bakhtin) or consciousness (Lacan) constitutes only the visible and the speakable evocations and condensations of the unconscious subtext (Bakhtin's "inner speech"), which itself remains unspoken and inaudible. In short: consciousness is only a psychorhetorical evocation of the internally dialogical interanimation of the floating signifiers, whose "defiles" sporadically submerge in the language of dreams, slips, and free association and whose political economy of rhetorical devices is amenable to interpretation.

An important consequence of delineating the psyche as an irreferential locus of a psychorhetorical struggle lies in the conceptions Lacan and Bakhtin offer for the intrapsychic process of repression, in contrast to Freud. The latter insists on distortive and repressive operations, on a presumably undistorted signifier, while Lacan and Bakhtin emphasize the a priori condition of "distortion" (or internal dialogization) that characterizes the floating textuality of the dreamwork. In a truly postreferential sense, both Lacan and Bakhtin question the validity of an *original* locus of psychic "purity" (a centered subject) or of a secret stratum of untainted self- identical meanings (a "true" object). The immediate result of this position is that psychoanalysis is no longer an operation of "psychological purification" or the removal of "unconscious distortions" that hamper "healthy self-fulfillment" but becomes, in a Gadamerian sense, a process of becoming, an access of being.

Lacan emphasizes the dialogicality and the bifocality of the therapeutic stage as the "therapeutic reading" engulfs analyst and analysand. In contrast to the analyst's monologic and homophonic interpretations of the analysand's unconscious rhetoric, Lacan posits the dialogical reflexivity of the unconscious languages of both analyst and analysand. Indeed, interpretation of the subtexts of the unsaid and the partially evoked unconscious is a dialogical activity of both analyst and analysand in which they recursively inform each other of what remains unsaid and unknown. The reason for this primordial dialogicality undergirding the therapeutic process is that the unconscious is not merely the object of the analytic dialogue but is also its subject: "The unconscious . . . is not simply *that which must be read* but also, and perhaps primarily, *that which reads*. The unconscious is a reader" (Felman 1987, 22–23). As such, Lacan maintains that "the psychoanalytic act has but to falter slightly, and it is the analyst who becomes the analysand" (1977, 47).

Therapeutic discourse is primordially dialogic, and that dialogicality is not merely a "formal requirement" of the therapeutic "talking cure": the therapeutic dialogue constitutes the evocative meeting place where the unconscious speaks both in and between the analyst and the analysand, but only when they meet; that is, only when there is an Other. Consequently Lacan can contend, "It is therefore in the position of a third term that the Freudian discovery of the Unconscious becomes clear as to its true grounding. This discovery may simply be formulated in the following terms: The Unconscious is that part of concrete discourse in so far as it is transindividual, that is, not at the disposal of the subject in reestablishing the continuity of his conscious discourse" (1977, 49). Only in "the inmixture of the subjects" of the psychoanalytic dialogue can the truth of the unconscious enter the sphere of reality.

Provided with the redefinition of therapeutic process as the dialogical play of the evocative dialects of the unconscious, Lacan introduces his heterology by suggesting that the unconscious is the discourse of the Other. "The Other is, therefore, the locus in which is constituted the I who speaks together with the one who hears, that which is said by the one being already the reply. . . . But in *return* this locus also extends as far into the subject as the laws of speech, that is to say, well beyond the discourse that takes its catchwords from the ego" (1977, 141). Not only does the unconscious constitute an unspoken "inner speech" that only fragmentarily surfaces in the rhetorical tropes of "oneiric discourse," but it also constitutes an Other language of the Self, an ex-centric language that is articulated only through rhetorical repressions and tropological displacements onto other (floating) signifiers whose diffractions seep into the discourse of consciousness. In other words, the internally dialogic operations of the language(s) of the unconscious speak of a knowledge of the Self, which, however, the Self cannot master. Lacan (1977,

169) explains in a truly Bakhtinian manner a diversity of psychological "defense mechanisms" by equating them to a series of literary tropes and stylistic figures. The exploration and understanding of this "ex-centric knowledge" requires an Other: "In language, our message comes to us from the Other, in a reverse form" (p. 9) and, "The Unconscious is that discourse of the Other by which the subject receives, in an inverted form, his own forgotten message" (Lacan, quoted in Felman 1987, 124). As a result, the psychoanalytic dialogue between analyst and analysand offers the opportunity for a recursive unfolding of the evocative resonances of unconscious discourse in which both analyst and analysand, in turn and simultaneously, listen and speak by means of the heteroglot voices of their own unconscious (hi)stories (see also Schafer 1980). As such, " 'the Other' thus stands in the psychoanalytic dialogue both for the position of the analyst, through whom the subject hears his own unconscious discourse, and for the position of the subject's own unconscious, as other to his self (to his self-image and self-consciousness)" (Felman 1987, 124).

Conclusion

Lacan's transformation of Freud is not necessarily anti-Freudian, though it is still early to evaluate the impact it may have had on psychoanalysis (cf. Leavy 1977, 1979). The practice of psychoanalysis, however, has been developing in interesting directions, such as the analysis of transference (Gill 1982), analysis as an exercise in the construction and deconstruction of narratives, Bakhtinian architectonics, and Gadamerian interpretation. The task of the analyst is "not to inform [the analysand about his own intrapsychic processes] but to evoke" (Lacan 1977, 86) his own unconscious reactive and activated voices as well as the internal polyphony of the unsaid played behind the spoken utterances of the session. As such, Lacan heralds the credo of "indeterminate negation" (Gadamer), the knowledge of not knowing, and reinstates the structural dynamic of dialogue as the primordial condition of knowing: knowing not of what is said and uttered, but of what remains unsaid. Moreover, the message of Socratic dialogue is not lost for Lacan: only when the analysand understands the absurdity of his quest for his true, full, or healthy Self—an original or undistorted signifier—and recognizes the "kernel of non-sense" that grounds the sea of floating signification is therapy terminated and a cure effected. Only when the analysand accepts the value and the inescapability of ignorance and non-sense does he reach (Self) knowledge, which is the knowledge that ultimate knowledge cannot be obtained. This recognition marks the transit point of the therapeutic cure.

The search for the possibility of understanding one's life and being can be conducted through self-reflection (self-analysis), but since it needs an Other, it unfolds more productively in a dialogue situation with an external Other. Two ideals of dialogue can help us approximate psychoanalytic dialogue: the Socratic and the Dosto-evskian. The Socratic dialogue strives to unearth the goodness that lies buried in the soul of man. In its search it discovers that the excavation itself is the sought-for goodness. Nevertheless, the Socratic dialogue postulates a goal outside itself, and consequently, although the question and answer between Self and Other is important, it remains as a propaedeutic to an ethical bonus that, however ingrained in the practice, is elusive and always beyond grasp. The ethical bonus of therapy must be fulfilled at the end of the interaction between analyst and analysand. From a Socratic point of view the self-knowledge gained by the patient is trivial, but from a Freudian point of view it is existentially sound. In post-Enlighten-ment Freudian thinking, the being of man lost the metaphysical tallness it enjoyed in Plato's philosophy.

The second ideal of dialogue, the Dostoevskian, is not a means but an end in itself. "Dialogue here is not a treshhold to action, it is the action itself. It is not a means for . . . bringing to the surface the . . . character of a person; no, in dialogue a person not only shows himself outwardly, but he becomes for the first time that which he is" (Bakhtin 1984, 252). In this sense, "When dialogue ends, everything ends. . . . At the level of his religious-utopian world view Dostoevsky carries dialogue into eternity, con-ceiving of it as eternal co-rejoicing, co-admiration, con-cord" (p. 252). Such an ideal of dialogue appealed to the neo-Kantian Bakhtin, leading him to formulate his dialogical principle, which turned up everywhere, in language, in discourse, in the ballet be-tween Self and Other, mind and world, word and object, and in the intertextuality of utterances. As far as the Dostoevskian/Bakhtinian ideal is concerned, psychoanalytic dialogue should either become interminable or melt into the unending dialogue of everyday life. Lacan tried to approximate the two extremes of terminable and interminable dialogue, and it is for that reason that his ideas are so challenging and his school of psychoanalysis so frustratingly im-possible in the clinical context.

The therapeutic dialogue reaffirms the Bakhtinian movement of identification and exotopy: the analysand needs to address the Other (the analyst), whose surplus of seeing/being leads, upon return, to a reappreciation of (the language[s] of) the Self. Radical alterity grounds not only the ethical dimension of addressivity and response-ability, but also the epistemological dimension of self-understanding, which, in a Gadamerian sense (*Dasein* is understanding), spills over into the ontological realm as a proliferation of being. Moreover, the therapeutic dialogue implies a dialectical exchange with (one's own) history: "What we teach the subject to recognize as his unconscious is his history" (Lacan 1977, 52). Consequently, the therapeutic process of "primary historization" refracts a dialectical reappropria-tion of the heteroglot languages of (un)conscious becoming (more my Self). As a result, the therapeutic dialogue reflects the hermeneutic "procedure" par excellence, which consists in the double movement of alienation and reidentification, of excursion and return (Gadamer), of transgredience and exotopy (Bakhtin), and of the eternal home-coming of the prodigal Self after each journey into *Bildung* ("cultural and linguistic conformation"). In surviving and transcending the texts of its existence, man rediscovers himself upon each return. The incompleteness of the psychoanalytic project lives out in the herme-neutical experience.

References

Bakhtin, Mikhail M. 1981. *The dialogic imagination.* Ed. Michael Holquist, trans. Caryl Emerson and Michael Holquist. Austin: University of Texas Press.

——. 1984. *Problems of Dostoevsky's poetics.* Ed. and trans. Caryl Emerson, intro. Wayne Booth. Minneapolis: University of Minnesota Press.

Clark, Katerina, and Michael Holquist. 1984. *Mikhail Bakhtin.* Cambridge: Harvard University Press.

Deleuze, G., and F. Guattari. 1977. *The anti-Oedipus: Capitalism and schizophre-nia.* New York: Viking.

Derrida, Jacques. 1978. Freud and the scene of writing. In *Writing and difference.* Chicago: University of Chicago Press.

Felman, Shoshona. 1987. *Jacques Lacan and the adventure of insight.* Cambridge: Harvard University Press.

Gadamer, Hans-Georg. 1975. *Truth and method.* New York: Continuum.

Gill, Merton. 1982. *Analysis of transference. Vol. I: Theory and technique.* Psychological Issues Monograph 53. New York: International Univer-sities Press.

Habermas, Jürgen. 1982. *Zur Logik der Sozialwissenschaften.* Frankfurt: Suhr-kamp.

Heidegger, Martin. 1971. *On the way to language.* Cambridge: Harper and Row.

Lacan, Jacques. 1977. *Ecrits: A selection.* New York: Norton.

Leavy, Stanley A. 1977. The significance of Jacques Lacan. *Psychoanalytic Quarterly* 46:201–19.

————. 1979. Review of *Ecrits* by Jacques Lacan. *Psychoanalytic Quarterly* 48:311–17.

Maranhão, Tullio. 1986. *Therapeutic discourse and Socratic dialogue: A cultural critique.* Madison: University of Wisconsin Press.

Schafer, Roy. 1980. Narration in the psychoanalytic dialogue. *Critical Inquiry* 7:29–53.

Spence, Donald P. 1982. *Narrative truth and historical truth: Meaning and interpretation.* In *Psychoanalysis.* New York: Norton.

Todorov, Tzvetan. 1984. *Mikhail Bakhtin: The dialogical principle.* Trans. Wlad Godzich. Minneapolis: University of Minnesota Press.

Voloshinov, V. N. 1976. *Freudianism: A Marxist critique.* Trans. I. R. Titunik, ed. intro. with Neal H. Bruss. New York: Academic Press.

9

Cybernetics of Dialogue:
A Conversational Paradigm
for Systemic Therapies

Bradford P. Keeney

This chapter presents a way of understanding psychotherapy, particularly systemic therapies, as conversation and dialogue. Systemic therapies are depicted as the construction and management of "semantics" and "politics" (see Keeney and Ross 1985; Keeney and Silverstein 1986). Semantics is used here as the name of a communicational frame of reference wherein meanings are requested and constructed. For example, the following conversation episode characterizes a semantic frame of reference:

T: Why have you come for therapy?
C: I suffer from depression.
T: What do you mean by "depression"?
C: I really get down sometimes.

In this conversational episode, meaning is requested and constructed by the therapist and client. Politics, on the other hand, is used as the name of a communicational frame of reference that principally attends to the specification of "who is doing what to whom when, where, and how." For example, the following interchange demonstrates requests and constructions that emphasize politics:

T: What's the first thing you do when you know you're starting to get depressed?
C: If I'm at work, I say I'm not feeling well and I go home.
T: What happens when you get home?
C: I go to bed.
T: Does anyone else try to help you?

Any construction of meaning always implies political consequences, and any specification of politics carries with it particular meanings. If the meaning of symptomatic behavior is defined in terms of social relationship systems rather than an individual's endocrine system, the politics of therapy will be markedly different. From the other direction, when a therapist responds politically to an individual's complaints about migraine headaches by suggesting that the whole family should come to therapy, the meaning of the headaches will probably be transformed. Semantics and politics are therefore two sides of the same conceptual coin: they suggest two ways of viewing human communication. Stated differently, human communication may be viewed through a semantic frame of reference that emphasizes meanings or a political frame of reference that emphasizes the social organization of communication.[1]

The relation of semantic and political frames of reference may be confused with another distinction, sometimes called "content and relationship" (see Keeney and Ross 1985). This latter distinction refers to the dual characteristics of a single message. For instance, a client's statement, "I have hallucinations about twice a day," can be seen as describing a client's experience (content) as well as proposing that the therapist do something about it (relationship). Knowing the conversational context of this message requires looking at its broader frame of reference. If the client's statement followed a therapist's request that the client define why he came to therapy, it would be seen as arising out of a semantic frame of reference. Note what happens, however, when the client's statement is seen as arising out of the following conversation:

T: How often do you have these hallucinations?
C: I have hallucinations about twice a day.
T: Who else knows about these hallucinations?

This conversation indicates a political frame of reference that emphasizes the sociopolitical organization of the problem behavior rather than its meaning.

Suppose that we, as observers of a particular therapeutic conversation, propose that a therapist is joined more with the wife than with the husband. Categorizing this description as a semantic or political frame of reference is a different order of categorization than framing therapist-client discourse. Take the following example of therapeutic conversation:

T: (to wife) Why does your husband continue harassing you?
W: He doesn't understand me.
T: Why doesn't he understand you?
W: Because he doesn't care.
T: (to husband) Why don't you care about your wife?

---

1. The distinction between semantics and politics is similar to Bateson's distinction between classification of form and description of process (see Keeney 1983). It may also be loosely compared to the distinction between hermeneutics and praxis.

Since this conversation involves requests and responses about the meaning of husband and wife's interaction, we can say that it specifies a semantic frame of reference. An observer from behind a one-way mirror might say, however, that this conversational episode indicates the political frame, that the therapist is joined more with the wife than with the husband. If we were to ask this observer how that conclusion was reached, he or she might point out that the therapist is sitting closer to the wife and making more eye contact with her than with the husband. In addition, the observer might say that the therapist's questions are more responsive to the wife's view and that the husband is not invited to present his own view.

These descriptions, however, are not descriptions that were constructed by the therapist, husband, or wife—they were constructed by an observer from behind a one-way mirror. The descriptions of this observer, however, can be seen as indicating a political frame of reference, but within the observational domain of the observer's discourse about his or her observations (and not the domain of therapist-client discourse).

Similarly, an observer of a session might inquire how the therapist uses affective experience to organize therapy. Although discourse about one's own affective experience may be more reliable, an outside observer is always free to make hypotheses about a client's or therapist's feelings and inner experience. Discourse about affective experience, from whatever observational domain, may again be classified as part of a semantic or a political frame of reference: For instance, the following discourse suggests a political frame of reference: "I get angry when she tells me to take out the trash; I then tell her she is 'queen of the naggers'; subsequently she gets angry, and then I feel hopeless." The following conversation, however, is more suggestive of a semantic frame of reference: "How do you feel about your behavior with your wife?" "It makes me depressed."

Note that these semantic and political frames pertain to the domain of discourse constructed by clients and therapists in a session. An outside observer, as I suggested, could also make inferences about the client's (and therapist's) affective experience, such as, "The wife gets more anxious when the husband describes himself as depressed." This discourse about affective experience, within the domain of discourse constructed by an outside observer, could in turn be distinguished as principally pertaining to either semantics or politics.

These examples illustrate how we can track a diversity of communicational domains involved in analyzing a therapeutic reality. The distinction between political and semantic frames of reference provides us with a view of the basic building blocks that are used to construct therapeutic realities. Clients present therapists with semantic and political frames that are then utilized in such construction. The semantic frames clients initially present sometimes involve defining their problems as well as explaining their origin. To effectively help a troubled system, a therapist must be able to introduce other semantic and political frames that are of a different order of abstraction from the simpler frames clients present. These frames give new meanings to clients' problems or attempt to shift the politics organizing problems, or both.

Recursive Dialectic of Semantics and Politics

The variety of semantic and political frames that may be used for constructing therapeutic realities is summarized in figure 1. The right-hand column of the figure, "politics," indicates three orders of description corresponding to simple action, interaction, and social choreography. These may be understood as different levels of magnification. At the microscopic level in this descriptive system, we see simple actions such as "pointing a finger," "loud shouting," "fast breathing," or "jumping up and down." At the next level of magnification, our view is widened so that simple actions are seen as part of a sequence of interaction that typically includes the participation of another individual. Here the arguing of one person may be viewed as linked to the arguing of another person.

As we look at this larger slice of their interaction, we may discern the alternating pattern $arguing_A-arguing_B-arguing_A$ $arguing_B$, and so on. This pattern indicates a symmetrical relationship where the more A argues, the more B argues. Moving up to the macroscopic level of magnification, descriptions of social choreography, we further widen our view to see how patterns of interaction (which indicated the patterning of simple actions) are themselves patterned. Here we might find that a particular symmetrical interactional episode is part of a more encompassing pattern that includes the participation of a third person. For instance, A's symmetrical arguing with B may be seen as part of a social triadic relation involving A, B, and C. A and B's argument might be about C, or C's behavior may result in some form of shift in the interaction between A and B.

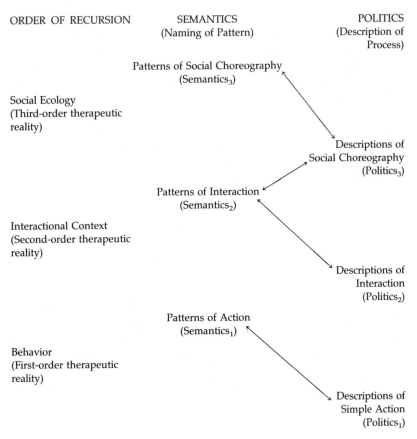

ORDER OF RECURSION   SEMANTICS   POLITICS
                          (Naming of Pattern)   (Description of
                                                          Process)

                      Patterns of Social Choreography
                              (Semantics₃)

Social Ecology
(Third-order therapeutic
reality)
                                                    Descriptions of
                                                   Social Choreography
                                                      (Politics₃)

                          Patterns of Interaction
                              (Semantics₂)

Interactional Context
(Second-order therapeutic
reality)

                                                    Descriptions of
                                                      Interaction
                                                      (Politics₂)

                          Patterns of Action
                              (Semantics₁)

Behavior
(First-order therapeutic
reality)

                                                    Descriptions of
                                                     Simple Action
                                                       (Politics₁)

Figure 1. Recursive dialectic of semantics and politics in the social domain.

As we ascend these levels of magnification or recursion, the
terms we use to build descriptions of politics change. While
discussing simple action, we referred to finger pointing, shouting,
and other descriptions of behavior. We subsequently gave meaning to
these actions by naming them "arguing." This construction of
meaning moved us to the domain of semantics, which in turn gave us
a new order of terminology for describing the politics of interaction.
Our description of interaction, in this example, was the alternation of
arguing$_A$– arguing$_B$– arguing$_A$– arguing$_B$, and so on. To give meaning
to this interaction (swinging to semantics) we named the pattern,
organizing it as a "symmetrical relationship." And finally, this order
of terminology enabled us to swing back to politics and build

descriptions that concerned the more encompassing patterns of social choreography.

Such a description of social choreography might involve a married couple's escalating argument (repetitive symmetrical interactions of arguing$_A$–arguing$_B$) until, say, the husband experienced a panic attack. At such a moment, the relationship shifts to complementarity, where the wife now seeks help for her symptomatic husband. In this example she calls her sister-in-law and asks her what to do. This leads to further arguments with the sister-in-law over who is to blame—the husband or wife. The more the wife argues that it was her husband's fault for precipitating his symptom, the more the sister-in-law defends her brother. We now have a new pattern of symmetrical interaction that in turn will lead to subsequent patterns of interaction. Note that we have built a view of the choreography of interactional patterns involving the participation of three people. Giving meaning to this example of social choreography could be in terms of discussing a social structure with a coalition of the brother and the sister joined against the brother's wife.

Another example for analysis is the "one-up husband" "one-down wife" relationship scenario. We begin by describing and giving meaning to simple actions. A husband's verbal behavior with its accompanying body movement (politics$_1$) may be given the meaning of "one-up" or "macho behavior" (semantics$_1$), while a wife's head nodding and limited verbal behavior (politics$_1$) may be given the meaning of her displaying a "one-down" position (semantics$_1$). These meanings (semantics$_1$) provide the bridge toward a higher-order analysis where we shift to analyzing interaction (politics$_2$). This political frame specifies an alternation between one-up and one-down positions (a description of interaction) that in turn may be given the meaning or classification of a "complementary relationship" (semantics$_2$). Subsequently, this higher-order meaning (semantics$_2$) provides a bridge toward building a view of social ecology. Here the couple's escalating complementary interaction may be calibrated by complaints from the wife's feminist friends, the husband's having an ulcer, or a child's becoming asthmatic. Given this view of social choreography (politics$_3$), we may proceed to give meaning to the participation of others in terms of a structure of social triadic relations (semantics$_3$).

This example again illustrates that any description of politics requires using some semantic frame to specify it and vice versa—any construction of meaning requires a political frame to which to ascribe

a name, classification, form, pattern, or meaning. We have thus far
described the relation of semantics and politics as a movement
upward from behavior to interaction to social ecology. Relations may
be constructed in other ways. For instance, if someone asked what we
meant by a symmetrical relationship, we could back up and give a
description of an interactional sequence in terms of A directing,
followed by B directing, with more directing by A, and so on. If
someone then asked what we meant by "directing," we could back
up a step further and say that we have chosen to name a particular
ensemble of simple actions (standing up, pointing a finger, and
speaking loudly) "directing." Of course, someone might then ask
how we know that someone is pointing a finger. We could then point
to a level of semantics (semantics$_0$) that names classes of neuromus-
cular movements that in turn could be seen as linked to simple
descriptions of body position and movement (politics$_0$). The conceptual scheme of figure 1, however, begins with descriptions of simple
action and assumes that an observer is clear about what these
descriptions mean.

Problems sometimes arise when statements about politics are
confused with statements about semantics and vice versa. To discuss
a one-down position (semantics) as if it were a description of a simple
action (politics) is a mistake in categorization or logical typing.
Similarly, to discuss a description of simple action such as "head
nodding" (politics) as if it were a category of behavior such as a
one-down position (semantics) is a category mistake. This is not to
say that the term "one-down" pertains solely to a semantic frame of
reference. As we have seen, this term can be used to construct a
political view of interaction. At this level of observation it is
impossible to see one person being one-down without seeing another
person engaged in a series of actions that fits with it. Thus, the
interactional view sees a one-up/one-down interactional system. To
mistake the term "one-down" as a description of simple action might
lead to describing people as one-downers or possible one-uppers
without paying attention to the interactional patterns from which
these names were abstracted.

Orders of Distinction

There are a variety of therapeutic strategies that prescribe particular
ways of attending (and not attending) to behavior, interaction, and
social ecology. For example, problem-solving approaches to therapy

utilize semantic frames about simple action (S_1) to construct a view of "problems" and attempted solutions. By asking clients to present a "problem" for treatment, these therapists request that some description of simple action become categorized as a problem. In other words, the term "problem" is not a description of a simple action—it is a name that gives meaning to a system of simple actions.

Treating marital fighting as a problem involves addressing multiple semantic frames. For example, a description of some sequence of behavior involving a husband and wife is named fighting, which in turn is classified and named as a problem. Imagine that a couple goes further and proposes that the real problem in their fighting involves the wife's losing control and breaking dishes. They then contract with the therapist to work on correcting that particular action.

On the level of simple action, we can observe that such a therapeutic contract prescribes a fundamental distinction that will begin to construct and organize a particular therapeutic reality. Namely, all subsequent communication will revolve around the distinction presence of dish breaking/absence of dish breaking. Continued reports about the wife's breaking dishes will be taken as an indication that the problem still exists, while any report suggesting less dish breaking may indicate a move toward problem alleviation.

From the perspective of interaction, we are immediately reminded that the wife's dish breaking is only one instant of an interactional pattern involving the participation of both the husband and the wife. Here it becomes more obvious that any effort solely to extinguish the wife's form of contribution to their interaction could result in what appears to be a countermove by the husband or the wife. If, following an intervention to stop the wife's dish breaking, the interactional pattern now includes the wife's throwing knives rather than merely breaking dishes (or the husband's beginning to throw furniture), we could easily propose the semantic frame that the attempted solution maintained (and perhaps escalated) their problem interaction.

What appears at the political level of simple action as a battle between opposite sides of a distinction—for example, "dish breaking/no dish breaking"—can be seen at the next level of politics as a pattern of interaction. This idea follows Bateson's (1979) theory of double description, where the interplay of two views of the same logical type results in a view of higher logical type. For example, the

contrast of two two-dimensional drawings may result in the perception of a three-dimensional (stereoscopic) image. For our purposes,
distinctions at one level of politics that appear to be related through
an either/or logic of negation (i.e., A/not A) can be seen at the next
level of politics as one side of a more encompassing distinction where
the two sides are now recursively related; for example, each side is
derived out of the other:

$$\frac{\text{pattern of organization}}{(\text{A/not A})}.$$

Consider the example we've been using:

$$\frac{\text{husband-wife interaction}}{(\text{dish breaking/no dish breaking})},$$

where the difference between the wife's breaking dishes and not
breaking dishes contributes to the organization of marital interaction.

    In particular, the wife's dish breaking is simply a behavior this
interactional system utilizes to calibrate itself—for example, to
change from an escalating symmetrical relationship to one of
complementarity. The so-called behavioral problem is therefore a
solution to an interactional problem. Eradicating the woman's dish
breaking requires that another form of calibration be introduced. As
I suggested, it is possible to eradicate her dish breaking and find that
the couple's interaction becomes calibrated by even more violent
behavior. The goal of therapy is to construct a more adaptive and
useful form of calibrating their interaction rather than compounding
their problem situation.

    From the perspective of interaction, the therapist's view of the
problem to be treated is different from the client's view. Specifically, clients see their problems from the level of simple action
(e.g., presence of problem behavior/absence of problem behavior),
whereas the therapist may see the problem as an interactional pattern.

    The general idea that what on one level appears as an either/or
distinction is at another level a pattern of organization gives us some
insight into how therapeutic realities can be structured. I have already
mentioned an example of this relation. Specifically, I discussed the
relation across interaction and simple action:

$$\frac{\text{interaction (level 2)}}{\text{simple action (level 1)}} \quad \frac{\text{pattern of interaction}}{\text{(problem behavior/no problem behavior)}'}$$

where an either/or relation at the level of simple action (e.g., problem behavior/no problem behavior) becomes the right-hand side of the more encompassing recursive distinction between interaction and simple action:

$$\text{interaction/simple interaction,}$$

which for this particular case is defined as:

$$\frac{\text{pattern of interaction}}{\text{(problem behavior/no problem behavior)}}.$$

Either/or relations at the level of interaction can also be seen as one side of the more encompassing recursive distinction between social ecology and interaction. For example:

$$\frac{\text{social ecology (level 3)}}{\text{interaction (level 2)}} \quad \frac{\text{pattern of social choreography}}{\text{(problem interaction/no problem}'} \\ \text{interaction)}$$

where the either/or relation at the level of interaction becomes one side of the distinction between social ecology and interaction, as is spelled out below:

$$\frac{\text{pattern of social choreography}}{\text{(problem interaction/no problem interaction)}}.$$

Stability and Change

This general view of the structure of therapeutic realities suggests a wide variety of ways of working with troubled systems. Most clients believe they are stuck at the level of trying to eradicate a particular problem behavior. With the view presented here, a therapist may choose to join with the clients' efforts and come up with other ways of trying to directly alleviate the problem behavior. Or the therapist may jump to the levels of interaction or social ecology and find alternative sets of choices for intervention.

Clients typically communicate, directly or indirectly, that a problem behavior needs to be changed while implying that the absence of the problem should be stabilized:

$$\frac{\text{stabilize absence of problem}}{\text{change presence of problem}}.$$

A therapist may organize therapy to stabilize a so-called behavioral problem while attempting to change an interactional pattern. Such a strategy may subsequently result in problem alleviation, which from the level of simple action may appear paradoxical. Recall that the distinction "stabilize problem absence/change problem presence" is conceptualized from the perspective of behavior. From an interactional view, this distinction becomes articulated as:

$$\frac{\text{stabilize interactional advantage of the problem behavior}}{\text{change interactional disadvantages of the absence of problem behavior}}.$$

The classic family therapy example concerns the problem behavior of a child that provides a way of getting the parents together through their joint efforts to help their "disturbed child." Whether the so-called problem is seen as a disadvantage or an advantage is determined by one's perspective. On the level of simple action, it is more clearly a "problem" or "disadvantage," while on the level of interaction it may appear as an "advantage" or "solution."

Using symptoms as a means of eradicating symptoms appears paradoxical only if viewed from the level of simple action. A therapist who prescribes a symptom as a means of stabilizing the interactional advantages it provides constructs a context wherein it is possible for the system to evolve an alternative form of organization.

An interactional pattern also may be stabilized while change is attempted at the level of social choreography. This social ecological strategy may subsequently result in both interactional and behavioral change, which from the perspective of interaction and behavior appear as indirect (and perhaps paradoxical) consequences of the therapeutic strategy.

In summary, therapy involves addressing the change and stability of semantic and political frames over the recursive levels of behavior, interaction, and social ecology. Any particular strategy of therapy prescribes particular ways of addressing (and sometimes ignoring) these different orders of politics and semantics.[2]

In a previous work (Keeney and Ross 1985), I described major approaches to systemic family therapy in terms of the key distinctions and patterns they construct. For example, a Mental Research Institute (MRI) therapeutic reality prescribed by Watzlawick, Weakland, and Fisch (1974) emphasizes understanding a problem situation (semantic frame from the therapist) in terms of the complementary relation between problems and attempted solutions. To change problem situations, they often prescribe the following political pattern for organizing therapy:

$$\frac{\text{stabilize problem definition}}{\text{change class of solution}}.$$

For instance, a client complaining of a speech phobia might be instructed to announce to an audience that he has a speech phobia, that he has tried every possible solution, and that nothing works. He is then to ask the audience to bear with him and not be shocked

2. Now the choice of the terms "semantics" and "politics" may be more fully addressed. In choosing names for what is proposed as the most basic distinction in understanding communication, "semantics" was an obvious choice for one side of the distinction. It clearly indicates the understanding of communication as requests and constructions of "meaning." However, to name the paradigm, approach, or understanding of communication that is not principally intended to specify meaning is immediately problematic. Namely, to specify or name it is an exercise invoking semantics. The name of the communicational frame of reference that is not about semantics requires a semantic frame of reference for indication. I avoided the term "action," since it too easily obscures orders of social process beyond simple action, particularly interaction and social choreography. The term "politics" more easily suggests a class of social processes, spanning action, interaction, and social choreography.

For therapists, "politics" is most identifiable with behavioristic orientations. With the shift to interactional and triadic social patterns, largely brought about by the field of family therapy, "politics" is particularly appropriate as the choice of reactions of other people. With this recursive view of interaction, it is no surprise that cybernetics has been influential in theories of family process. In this regard, "politics" may be taken as a way of indicating family therapy's efforts to develop an understanding of the cybernetic organization of human relationship systems.

The etymological connections between "politics" and "cybernetics" are interesting to note. In *Euthydemus* and *Cleitophon*, Plato uses "cybernetics" to denote "the art of steering men." In *The Republic* he uses it to specify the idea of "governability." Similarly, Ampere uses "cybernetics" to describe the concept "politique proprement dite." In other words, "the very art of governing and choosing in every case both what can be and what must be done" (Mihram, Mihram, and Nowakowska 1977, 411). Clearly, the correspondence between "politics" and "cybernetics" is historically rooted.

should he break out in a sweat or possibly faint. The structure of this intervention addresses stability by defining the problem as speech phobia while prescribing a change in the class of solution—in this case a solution that declares publicly that he has given up all solutions.

Jay Haley's (1976) strategy for constructing therapy prescribes a different way of understanding problem situations (semantic frame for the therapist). He begins by emphasizing the complementary relation between a problem and the repeating social sequence that embodies it. He then often prescribes political interventions that incorporate the following design:

$$\frac{\text{stabilize problem definition}}{\text{change social structure}}.$$

In one classic case, the problem was a child who set fires. The therapist stabilized this definition of the problem and attempted to make a social structural change by getting the mother and the problem child more involved. This was accomplished by having the mother set aside time each day for teaching the child how to light a safe fire.

Returning to our recursive dialectic of semantics and politics (fig. 1), all therapies can be seen as prescribing a semantic view of how to understand a troubled situation as well as politically prescribing a pattern for how to act and intervene in order to help effect therapeutic change. Therapists organize themselves to stabilize or change the meaning or politics, or both, of social choreography, interaction, or simple action. Problem-focused therapies, for instance, typically focus on stabilizing the semantics of simple action in terms of what problem behavior is being addressed. Some go on to address change with respect to changing political patterns of interaction through addressing the class of simple action that is regarded as solution behavior (e.g., Watzlawick, Weakland, and Fisch 1974). Others, however, may emphasize political change of social choreography through a strict focus on problem behavior (e.g., Haley 1976).

Silverstein's approach (see Keeney and Silverstein 1986) and that of the Milan team (see Keeney and Ross 1985) turn things upside down by introducing and stabilizing a semantic frame regarding the meaning of a family system's social choreography that attempts to change the meaning or connotation of problem behavior and interaction, which in turn leads to political changes. For example, they may prescribe stability of a couple's presenting interaction with the rationale that it serves intergenerational family loyalty. This latter explanation provides a change in semantics about family politics that enables the connotation of the couple's behavior and interaction to change from "problem" to "solution." With this shift, the couple may be more likely to construct alternative, less painful political patterns for maintaining family loyalty.

As can be seen, any school of therapy or any particular session of a case can be examined as to how it constructs and manages semantics and politics. In this way an understanding of the diverse ways therapeutic realities are constructed may be acquired.

Therapeutic Outcomes

Independent of a therapist's goals and intentions for a therapeutic reality, a wide variety of outcomes are possible for any given case. The classes of therapeutic outcomes are summarized as follows:

1. semantics same/politics same
2. semantics change/politics same
3. semantics same/politics change
4. semantics change/politics change.

The old yarn about the client who after ten years of intensive psychoanalysis reports, "I still have the same problem, but now I really understand it" exemplifies the category of outcome where the semantics change but the politics remain the same. As all therapists know, sometimes clients demonstrate no semantic or political change (outcome$_1$), while other clients may demonstrate both semantic and political changes (outcome$_4$). Therapists themselves sometimes emphasize trying to create certain forms of outcome. Strategic therapists occasionally demonstrate how it is possible (and perhaps even desirable) to focus on changing the political patterns organizing problem behavior with no accompanying change in the clients' understanding of their situation (semantics). Other therapists attempt to create changes in both semantics and politics. As I suggested, the work of Silverstein and the Milan associates emphasizes changing family politics through a change in family semantics.

Patterns of Intervention

Therapeutic realities are thus built out of the construction and management of particular semantic and political frames. In a nutshell, the therapist's work involves prescribing change or stability of the semantic and political frames that are presented in therapy. The pattern organizing the semantic and political building blocks of any approach to therapy directs how the therapist politically prescribes to clients what should change and what should remain stable. The way such prescriptions and interventions are packaged and delivered usually requires some form of explanation or rationale for the clients. This rationale or explanation is a semantic frame of reference about the therapist's political prescriptions. The general structure of therapeutic interventions can be depicted as follows:

$$\frac{\text{prescription for stability}}{\text{prescription for change}}.$$

$$\frac{\text{politics}}{\substack{\text{prescriptions given through some} \\ \text{semantic frame of reference}}}.$$

Semantics

"Semantics" has been called "meaningful noise" (see Keeney and Ross 1985; Keeney 1983) to indicate that the packaging of an intervention should be meaningful to clients (and therefore meaningful to the therapist), but it is noise in the sense that any possible meaning may be constructed out of it.[3]

The recursive organization of stability and change is the general pattern that therapy attempts to change. Changing the way a system changes in order to more effectively and adaptively stabilize its stability is one way of defining the purpose of therapeutic change. This change of change and stability of stability is indicated as follows:

$$\frac{\text{(stability/change)}}{\text{meaningful noise}}.$$

where (stability/change) refers to stability of a whole system's autonomy, identity, and existence, while meaningful noise refers to the construction of alternative ways of achieving such stability through change. I have discussed this definition more fully in previous works (Keeney 1983; Keeney and Ross 1985; Keeney and Silverstein 1986).

Figure 2 presents a summary of the possible patterns for or-

3. In addition, the term "meaningful noise" was chosen to indicate the two components of stochastic process—a source of the random ("noise") and some process of selection (an observer constructing "meaning"). This definition prescribes the political side of meaningful noise, indicating that it comprises the very process of adaptive change itself—stochastic process.

PERIODIC TABLE OF THERAPEUTIC INTERVENTIONS

SIMPLE ACTION				INTERACTION				SOCIAL ECOLOGY			
Semantics 1		Politics 1		Semantics 2		Politics 2		Semantics 3		Politics 3	
Stabilize	Change	Stabilize	Change	Stabilize	Change	Stabilize	Change	Stabilize	Change	Stabilize	Change
S_1/P_1*	P_1/S_1	P_1/S_1	S_1/P_1	S_2/S_1	S_1/S_2	P_2/S_1	S_1/P_2	S_3/S_1	S_1/S_3	P_3/S_1	S_1/P_3
S_1/S_2	S_2/S_1	P_1/S_2	S_2/P_1	S_2/P_1	P_1/S_2	P_2/P_1	P_1/P_2	S_3/P_1	P_1/S_3	P_3/P_1	P_1/P_3
S_1/P_2	P_2/S_1	P_1/P_2	P_2/P_1	S_2/P_2	P_2/S_2	P_2/S_2	S_2/P_2	S_3/S_2	S_2/S_3	P_3/S_2	S_2/P_3
S_1/S_3	S_3/S_1	P_1/S_3	S_3/P_1	S_2/S_3	S_3/S_2	P_2/S_3	S_3/P_2	S_3/P_2	P_2/S_3	P_3/P_2	P_2/P_3
S_1/P_3	P_3/S_1	P_1/P_3	P_3/P_1	S_2/P_3	P_3/S_2	P_2/P_3	P_3/P_2	S_3/P_3	P_3/S_3	P_3/S_3	S_3/P_3

*(S_1/P_1) = (stabilize semantics$_1$/change politics$_1$)

Figure 2. Periodic table of therapeutic interventions.

ganizing therapeutic interventions. A therapist may prescribe stability or change of semantic or political frames for three orders of recursion—simple action, interaction, and social ecology. In this scheme, MRI therapeutic interventions often take the following form:

$$(S_1/P_2)/\text{meaningful noise,}$$

where a semantic frame of simple action (the constructed problem to work on) is stabilized, while change is directed at the class of simple action (e.g., class of attempted solutions) or, more accurately, a pattern of interaction. The rationale for prescribing this change in politics (meaningful noise) arises from explanations that relate the assigned task to being a way of solving the problem.

A major form of intervention for a Haley therapeutic reality follows:

$$(S_1/P_3)/\text{meaningful noise,}$$

where, like MRI, a problem definition is stabilized while change of the social ecology is attempted through directives that are explained to the family (meaningful noise) as related to solving the problem. Minuchin and Fishman's (1981) strategy principally differs from Haley's in that there is no rigid constraint on stabilizing a problem definition (see Keeney and Ross 1985). Minuchin and Fishman allow the semantic frame that is stabilized to drift. They accept the family's definition of what is going on (S_1, S_2, and S_3) while attempting to change their social structure (P_3). Minuchin and Fishman's form of intervention is thus defined as follows:

$$(S_1\text{–}S_2\text{–}S_3/P_3)/\text{meaningful noise.}$$

The Milan approach (Selvini-Palazzoli et al. 1978) is sometimes a mirror image of Haley's strategy:

$$(P_1/S_3)/\text{meaningful noise,}$$

where stability of the presenting problem behavior is prescribed and explained as a consequence of the therapist's alternative semantic interpretation of the meaning of their patterns of social choreography (S_3). Silverstein's approach to systemic therapy (see Keeney and Silverstein 1986), similar to the Milan strategy, is:

$$(\text{stabilize } P_1 \text{ and } P_2/\text{change } S_3)/\text{meaningful noise,}$$

where her emphasis is on prescribing stability of interactional patterns that are explained through an alternative semantic interpretation of their social ecology.

Construction of a Systemic Therapeutic Reality

The structure of music provides a metaphorical way of talking about the construction of a therapeutic reality. In music, individual notes can be discriminated as well as heard in sequential patterns—the melodic line. Notes themselves, however, may be combined into chords, resulting in the experience of harmony or cacophony. And finally, a melodic line and its underlying harmony are coupled to give rise to repetitive themes and movements that combine into the whole system of music. In the construction of a systemic therapeutic reality, the individual notes have to do with specific political frames of reference that spell out the sequential organization of action in a social context. These sequential patterns of organization are themselves organized by patterns of social interaction and coalition structure—in a manner analogous to building chords in music. These structures, in turn, are experienced and described in terms of particular semantic frames of meaning. And finally, the coupling of these political and semantic frames gives rise to repetitive themes and stories that lead to a whole therapeutic reality.

Systemic therapy can be seen as involving a series of stages with each stage corresponding to a jump in the dialectical ladder between semantics and politics. The beginning stage involves the therapist's gathering simple-order semantic and political frames. The therapist will organize information in such a way that only those building blocks that offer a way of building up a higher-order view will be emphasized and discussed. With these simple-order frames, the systemic therapist can begin moving toward the middle stage of therapy. Here the therapist attempts to build and work with a view of interactional patterns and meanings. At this stage the different actions of people are seen as related and connected. In particular, the connection of problem behavior to more encompassing patterns of interaction will be underscored. When this higher-order view is firmly established, the therapist can proceed to the final stage of systemic therapy. At this stage, diverse patterns of interaction are connected in a way that emphasizes the social choreography of a whole social ecology.

One way of looking at the construction of a systemic therapeutic reality is that most client systems come to therapy stuck in a simple-order view of their situations. Most of their initial descriptions center on the politics and meanings of simple action. The therapist accepts these simple-order semantic and political frames and leads the family to higher-order realities, where their behavior is experienced as organized in a way that connects each of them as parts of a more encompassing system.

This account of systemic therapy may seem to suggest that therapeutic change requires clients to achieve some form of "systemic insight." An alternative view is that it is the therapist who requires a "systemic insight" to be useful to a troubled situation. Namely, the therapist must construct a higher-order view of the situation to be able to have access to the systemic patterns organizing problem behavior. Of course, the therapist's higher-order views are always only hypotheses that heuristically suggest higher-order ways of intervening. The outcomes of a therapist's interventions, usually described in simple-order terms, help maintain, polish, and correct the therapist's ongoing hypotheses.

Therapeutic Circles: Feedback Patterns

Another way of discussing therapeutic process involves describing the different patterns of *feedback* involved in its different stages of development. Feedback, the central idea of cybernetics, can be simply defined as utilizing the results of one's communication to help shape one's subsequent communication.

In the beginning state of developing systemic therapy, the therapist constructs feedback between simple-order semantic and political frames of reference. In particular, a semantic frame offered by a family member will often precipitate the therapist's asking a question about the political frame she assumes the semantic frame is contextualizing. For instance, consider the following therapeutic conversations:

Daughter: She's in outer space.

Therapist: How often do your mother and father go out together?

Daughter: Never. Well, maybe once every two months.

Therapist: Where are you when they go out?

In this conversation, the daughter proposes a semantic frame that the therapist hypothesizes as being about the politics of the mother and father's relationship. The daughter's response enables the therapist's subsequent response to extend her focus to include the daughter's own political participation.

In effect, a semantic frame introduced by a family member directs the therapist's questions about a political frame. The family's response is then used by the therapist either to scrap, to modify, or to elaborate her present line of inquiry. In this way feedback is established. This order of feedback is sketched in figure 3.

This sketch indicates four general categories of political frame that systemic therapists often address in their work:

P_1 = sequential organization of behavior
P_2 = problem-solving behavior including involvement of
     referring contexts
P_3 = social coalitions
P_4 = past and future descriptions of family politics.

The presentation of a particular semantic frame by a family member thus directs the therapist to address one of these classes of political frames. The family's response subsequently organizes which frame she addresses next. In this way the beginning stage of systemic therapy involves a feedback relation between simple-order semantic and political frames.

The next stage of therapy moves up to a different order of feedback (see fig. 4). Here the therapist begins connecting the political information derived from the family with her own theory of hypothesis about family politics. Any established therapeutic approach specifies a theory about how to understand the client's problem situation. This view of how to observe a system has been associated with simple cybernetics, the cybernetics of how to observe and understand systems (see Keeney and Ross 1985).

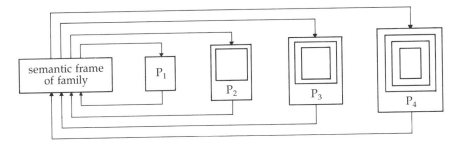

Figure 3. First-order feedback in systemic therapy.

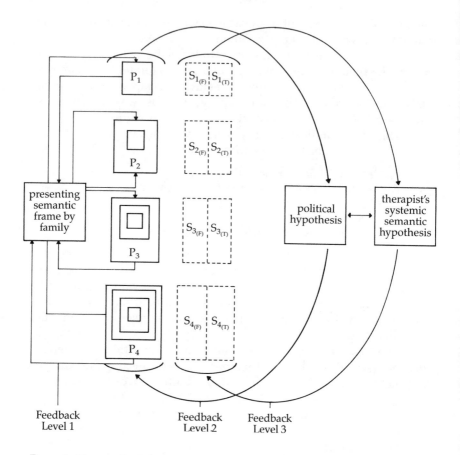

Figure 4. Therapeutic circles.

For instance, MRI proposes that client situations be understood as feedback relations between the experience of problems and repeated efforts to solve them. Haley's orientation understands the client's situation as the embeddedness of problems in repeating social interactions involving at least three people. Milan more generally understands client situations as metaphorical communications about configurations of family politics.

These theoretical prescriptions for understanding client situations are used to organize the second feedback level connection of simple semantic and political frames. In this way therapists (usually unknowingly) construct their interaction with clients in ways that verify their theoretical understanding of client situations. MRI therapists thus help shape MRI client systems that fit the MRI worldview. Haley creates Haley families, and so forth. Client systems that do not cooperate in becoming a particular form of experience for the therapist are often dismissed as "resistant," "noncompliant," or some other categorization that subsequently enables them to fit into the therapist's theoretical schema.

And finally, the last feedback stage of building a therapeutic reality involves building a systemic story, explanation, hypothesis, or directive that embodies the family's and the therapist's semantic frames as a way of articulating the therapist's political hypothesis. The emerging story is constructed through the feedback connection between the therapist's political hypothesis and the various semantic frames that the therapist and family have previously constructed about family politics. These latter semantic frames can be seen as metaphors about "partial arcs" of family politics (see Keeney and Ross 1985). For instance, the father's problem behavior may be explained as providing a solution for a problem of the mother. This view, however, is from the perspective of only one side of the relationship. We can therefore refer to this view as indicating a "partial arc" of the whole circular relationship.

In the last stage of this therapeutic approach, partial arc hypotheses become connected in a way that leads to a well-formed systemic hypothesis, that is, one that includes the participation of all relevant members of the social ecology. For instance, this might involve demonstrating how Mother's own problem behavior is complementary to Father's problem behavior and provides a solution for Father. In addition, Mother and Father's form of complementarity might be depicted as fitting into more encompassing patterns of social organization that include the behavior of their children as well as participation from other generations.

The therapist's systemic semantic hypothesis is derived from what is sometimes called cybernetics of cybernetics, the cybernetics of how to participate in cybernetic systems. These hypotheses correspond to what was previously called the periodic table of interventions. Here we find the way a therapeutic orientation politically prescribes how to present and manage interventions in a problem situation.

The second and third levels of therapeutic feedback correspond to what has been traditionally known as the relation of theory and practice or, more accurately, clinical understanding and clinical strategy. Figure 5 indicates this relation for three systemic therapies, MRI, Haley, and Milan. Simple cybernetics prescribes a way of understanding client situations, which as the figure indicates may be specified as a recursive complementary relationship. These recursive relations define a way of understanding client systems in terms of cybernetic feedback organization (see Keeney and Ross 1985).

The therapist, however, needs more than a view of the simple cybernetic organization of a troubled system. To help transform a troubled system requires direction for calibrating feedback. Each therapeutic orientation prescribes a way of constructing "feedback of feedback." This second-order pattern suggests how the therapist is to participate in therapy. Here we find the prescriptions for particular forms of therapeutic interventions.

In conclusion, I have demonstrated how dialogues between semantics and politics construct systemic therapeutic realities. The context of these dialogues is a conversation between therapist and clients. As Szasz has suggested, psychotherapy is to be understood not in terms of medical interventions, but in terms of the structure of rhetoric. Systemic therapy fully utilizes the rhetorical structure of therapy and builds upon the understanding that therapy is primarily within the domain of discourse.

In systemic therapy, what emerges are stories and stories about stories. Stories reveal how people construct their world and therefore provide clues for knowing their epistemological premises. In general, therapy is a process of weaving stories between therapist and client systems. Attending to symptomatic communication is one way of hearing a story. To paraphrase Bateson, the therapist must be cut down to fit the Procrustean bed of the client's stories. The therapist then builds her own story in response to the one she has been told. From a cybernetic perspective, when an exchange of stories is structured in terms of feedback, self-correction and adaptive change become possible.

NAME OF SYSTEMIC THERAPY	SIMPLE CYBERNETICS (Cybernetics of Observing)	CYBERNETICS OF CYBERNETICS (Cybernetics of Participating)
MRI	(Attempted solution/problem)	(S_1/P_2)/meaningful noise
Haley	(repeating social sequence/problem)	(S_1/P_3)/meaningful noise
Milan	(Family politics/presenting metaphor)	(P_1/S_3)/meaningful noise

Figure 5. Cybernetic patterns in systemic therapies.

The stories people live as well as their stories about those stories are all a therapist has to work with. In this sense, therapy is indeed a conversation, an exchange of stories. As Szasz (1978, 11) summarizes, "Seeing therapy as conversation rather than cure thus requires that we not only consider the error of classifying it as a medical intervention, but that we must also look anew at the subject of rhetoric and assess its relevance to mental healing."

It should be no surprise that poets are well aware of these concerns. Gary Snyder (1979, 29), for instance, describes poetry as "a hook; a net to trap, to clutch, and present; a sharp edge; a medicine, or the little awl that unties knots." This provides a tidy metaphor for systemic therapy, where knots of description are embodied in the stories clients and therapists construct and deconstruct.

Systemic therapy suggests a radically different understanding of what we regard as "problems" and "outcomes." For the systemic therapist there are no "real problems" that can be counted, weighed, measured, or quantified. Rather there are "constructed problems" that in turn have "constructed consequences." As a demonstration, imagine asking a client about his or her problem. Independent of the client's particular response, imagine the therapist subsequently responding with the question, "Please, what is your *real* problem?" More than likely, the client will offer a different semantic frame. As a further step, consider the therapist then responding with the question, "As I now speak to your unconscious mind, what is your deepest and most basic problem?" Again, it is likely that the client will construct an entirely different semantic definition of the problem. The question for an observer of this scenario is: "Which of the client's responses indicates the 'real' problem?"

Similarly, views of therapeutic outcomes are constructed and deconstructed. Asking a client what happened in therapy can always be followed by asking what really happened, and so on. In this way, clients and therapists coconstruct and codeconstruct the meanings and subsequent political consequences of their situation. Systemic therapy sidesteps these naive ontological traps by fully accepting and utilizing the client's own choice of semantics.

As I have implied throughout this discussion, systemic therapists organize their responses with a view of complementarity. This suggests, for example, that the question, Has the family changed? is always incomplete. The more systemic question is, How is the family stabilizing and changing? Similarly, in the beginning of therapy, the systemic therapist is interested in knowing about more than the family's problem. The systemic therapist is interested in knowing about their problems and their solutions, as well as the disadvantages and advantages accompanying each.

In sum, a systemic view of complementarity enables all responses of a client system to be utilized in a generative fashion. Knowing that any particular response can be seen as a description about part of a more encompassing pattern enables the therapist to address the implied parts. In this way, dialogue in therapy is generated. As I mentioned previously, systemic therapy has nothing to do with medicine—it is within the domain of rhetoric, dialogue, and conversation. Rather than offering cures and solutions, an alternative reality is built that transforms the meaning and politics of the people who are part of it, including family members, therapists, theorists, writers, and readers.

References

Bateson, G. 1979. *Mind and nature: A necessary unity.* New York: E. P. Dutton.

Haley, J. 1976. *Problem-solving therapy.* San Francisco: Jossey-Bass.

Keeney, B. 1983. *Aesthetics of change.* New York: Guilford Press.

Keeney, B., and J. Ross. 1985. *Mind in therapy: Constructing systemic family therapies.* New York: Basic Books.

Keeney, B., and O. Silverstein. 1986. *The therapeutic voice of Olga Silverstein.* New York: Guilford Press.

Mihram, D., G. Mihram, and M. Nowakowska. 1977. The modern origins of the term "cybernetics." In *ACTES: Proceedings of the Eighth International Congress on Cybernetics.* Namur, Belgium: Association Internationale de Cybernétique.

Minuchin, S., and C. Fishman. 1981. *Family therapy techniques.* Cambridge: Harvard University Press.

Selvini-Palazzoli, M., G. Cecchin, G. Prata, and L. Boscolo. 1978. *Paradox and counterparadox.* New York: Jason Aronson.

Snyder, G. 1979. Poetry, community, and climax. *Field* 20:21–36.

Szasz, T. 1978. *The myth of psychotherapy.* New York: Anchor Books.

Watzlawick, P., J. Weakland, and R. Fisch. 1974. *Change: Principles of problem formation and problem resolution.* New York: W. W. Norton.

part v

Dialogical Anthropology

10

On Dialogue

Vincent Crapanzano

> And there stand those stupid languages, helpless as two bridges that go over the same river side by side but are separated from each other by an abyss. It is a mere bagatelle, an accident, and yet it separates.
>
> Rainer Maria Rilke

Rilke wrote these words to his wife Clara from Paris on 2 September 1902. He had been visiting Auguste Rodin and was describing the difficulties he had had talking to the sculptor. Rodin "asked and said many things, nothing important," Rilke wrote. "The barrier of language is too great." He showed the sculptor his poems, and Rodin leafed through them. "The format surprised him, I think," Rilke noted.

Rilke's image of two bridges is striking. It describes many of the field situations in which the anthropologist finds himself. Rilke probably knew French better than most anthropologists know the language of the people they study. Rodin knew no German.

Rilke's words serve as an epigraph to this chapter. I will be treating "bridges" and "bagatelles"—languages, separations, and on occasion (conventional) comings together. I will be concerned with dialogue and its representations.

In the past few years there has been much talk about dialogue in anthropological circles. Some of it has a distinctly messianic tone; it heralds a new paradigm. An anthropology sensitive to dialogue will provide an escape from—a solution to—the present crisis (whatever that is) in anthropology. The talk, and the writing, is often confusing. "Dialogue" is bandied about with little concern for its meaning, its permissible metaphorical extensions, its dynamics, its ideology. Philosophical, linguistic, literary, and psychological approaches are conflated. Scant attention is given to levels of meaning. Dialogue, "dialogue," and " 'dialogue' " are confused.

The Ideology of Dialogue

Dialogue is a culturally and historically specific way of conceiving of certain verbal transactions and as such has considerable rhetorical force. In recent anthropological discussions, "dialogue" seems at times to substitute for "participant observation." It evokes a sentimentality that is associated with the participational pole of anthropology's traditional oxymoronic badge of methodological uniqueness and little of the anguish that centers on the observational pole—the anguish about the alienating effect of observation. It suggests friendship, mutuality, authenticity—an egalitarian relationship. So understood, dialogue not only describes such relations but *can* create the illusion of such relations where they do not exist. I am talking here not about bad faith—that can of course occur—but about the possibility of blindness inherent in the (dialogical) situation in which the anthropologist finds himself. *Dialogue*, then, not only reveals but conceals —often enough the power relations and the desires that lie behind the spoken word and, in other contexts, the recorded and distributed word. Power and desire can contradict the amity that dialogue connotes.

Anthropologists often use "dialogue" so broadly as to include just about any verbal communications, even endopsychic ones. Dennis Tedlock (1983a), who is one of the principal advocates of a dialogical anthropology, understands dialogue, for example, simply as "a speaking alternatively" or "a speaking across." Determined to call attention to the dialogical grounding of all fieldwork, a grounding that is masked in conventional, in Tedlock's terms, analogical ethnographies, Tedlock recognizes that anthropologists "do much more than engage in dialogues." They watch people hunt, gather, herd, hoe, shuck corn, and perform rituals. But, Tedlock asserts, the moment they talk about these practices they enter the realm of "human interobjectivity." They enter into dialogue, into conversation.[1] "The anthropological dialogue creates a world, or an understanding of the difference between two worlds, that exists between persons who were indeterminately far apart, in all sorts of different ways, when they started out in their conversation" (Tedlock 1983a, 323).

Tedlock overprivileges the anthropological field experience. It is in fact difficult to see why an anthropological dialogue should be distinguished from any other when it is understood in his terms. We are always "far apart"—"in all sorts of different ways"—when we

---

1. Tedlock and other dialogue theorists use "dialogue" and "conversation" interchangeably.

start out on a conversation or a dialogue. Otherwise there would be no conversation, no dialogue, just a kind of phatic affirmation of a shared view.

Phenomenological Perspectives

Even in Tedlock's minimalist view of dialogue one discerns something more than a mere alternation of speakers. The dialogue "creates a world" or at least "an understanding of differences between two worlds," and it seems to bring people who were far apart closer together. There is here an implicit phenomenological orientation, one that stresses the constitution of a shared world, a shared understanding, a coming together. Such a phenomenological-existential perspective is rather more explicit in the works of other anthropologists who advocate a dialogical anthropology. Steven Webster (1982) argues, for example, that the "dialogue is the foundation of ethnographic authenticity rather than an impediment to proper understanding," and he proposes an epistemological stance in which both subjectification and objectification are seen as extrapolations from the ground of mutual understanding upon which any encounter must begin insofar as its participants recognize themselves as human beings.

There is, as Gerhard Bauer (1969, 2) notes, a strong ethical dimension in the dialogical orientation of phenomenology. The integrating function of conversation is emphasized, and the differentiating function is neglected. The integrating function privileges —hypostatizes—a morally charged, an authentic, relationship that transforms the partners in a conversation from a *you* to a *thou*. Romantic, ideologically powerful, resonating, the psychoanalyst might maintain, with a desire to regain the pre-Oedipal, the Edenic unity, of mother and child, the emphasis on integration mystifies, certainly simplifies, the dynamics of dialogue. Agonism gives way to an often saccharine communion, and it is this communion that fits —How shall I say?—so nicely into the anthropologist's (often patronizing) idealization of his relationships—his friends—in the field. The Other (and pari passu the anthropologist) ceases to be a You, as realistically he ought to be, in traditional ethnology at least, and becomes a Thou. So strong is the desire for integration that an anthropologist like Kevin Dwyer (1982) sees in the very possibility of rupture the anthropologist's vulnerability. It is with some relief that we remember that in the *Laches* Plato took ironic pleasure in the breakup of a conversation devoted to the meaning of friendship! The German philosopher Hans-Georg Gadamer has given one of the fullest accounts of dialogue, or conversation. His principal work, *Truth and Method* (1975), reflects the ethical orientation and the romantic mode that Bauer notes. He discusses the nature of language but does not examine critically (or ironically, for that matter) his own use of language and the way his theory—his descriptions—reflect *that* language. As such, despite its claims to universality, his work has to be read as an expression of a culturally and historically specific ideology of language—one that many anthropologists, like Steven Webster, find particularly compelling.

Language, the medium of conversation, is ultimately the medium for all understanding, Gadamer argues. Conversation is ideally a process through which two people come to understand each other. Understanding the Other has three modes, according to Gadamer. In the first, we try to understand human nature—what is typical and predictable of the Other's behavior. This mode would correspond to the understanding sought by human biologists, students of national character, and role theorists. In the second mode we understand the Other as a person, but understanding is still in the form of self-relatedness. This is a dialectical—a reflective—relationship but, if I understand Gadamer correctly, not an immediate one. "To every claim, there is a counter claim," he writes (1975, 270). This mode would correspond to the understanding most anthropologists achieve when they begin to feel at home in an alien society. The third mode is immediate, open, and authentic. Unlike the second, in which the claim to understand the Other creates a distance, there is in this third, open mode no distance. The speakers are aware, though, of their own historical situation—their prejudices and preunderstandings—and are thus open to their interlocutor's questions and claims. This third understanding is, I believe, rare in anthropological research (precluded in part by the researcher's scientific intention and required observational stance), though it is longed for by those anthropologists who feel that *something* is missing in their understanding of the people they study.[2]

2. See Maranhão (1986) for a discussion of three operations of understanding—comprehension, acceptance, and appropriation—and the fragility of understanding within a dialogical context. For Maranhão, understanding is never complete without appropriation, and insofar as dialogue does not aim at producing texts, which are easily appropriated, understanding in a dialogical context remains always incomplete—and critical. I would argue, more cynically perhaps, that in many verbal transactions that pass for dialogue, there is in fact a struggle for—and insistence on—a particular, potentially textualized understanding that can—must—be appropriated by each of the partners to the dialogue.

For Gadamer, true conversation is one in which this third level of understanding occurs. Conversation requires that "the partners to it do not talk at cross purposes," that they are "with" one another, and that they allow themselves "to be conducted by the object" of conversation (1975, 33) and not to conduct the conversation (1975, 345). In true conversation something new to, and somehow independent of, its participants emerges (1975, 331, 489).

There is, then, a difference for Gadamer between "conducting a conversation"—a fixed interview, for example—and "falling into conversation." (Free association and the open-ended interview are usually compromises between the two.) In the one instance, I suggest, all we come up with are data, which can be arranged into a picture. In the second, we have understanding—"the creative fact; the fertile fact; the fact that suggests and engenders" that Virginia Woolf (1942) writes about in her study of biography. Such understanding can easily degenerate into mere knowledge of human beings; the "creative," the "fertile" fact can easily become a mere datum.

A South African Example

Let me illustrate these three modes of understanding with South African examples. I shall not make immediate use of my own understanding in the field but shall use that of a white South African I have called Peter Cooke (Crapanzano 1985, 88–90, 252–54). Peter Cooke was unusual. Unlike most whites in South Africa, he tried from time to time to take the perspective of the black and coloured.

White South Africans give bits of information about people of other races to any visitor to their country. This information resembles the bits of knowledge one brings away from a museum of natural history or from reading an old-fashioned manners-and-customs ethnography. "A Zulu will never greet you first. You must greet him. He is not being impolite. He is being polite in terms of his own tradition," a white will tell you. Or, "Blacks have to learn a job step by step. They think serially. They have no sense of the whole." Peter Cooke often made such remarks, but at times he tried to understand nonwhites in their own terms. He described a discussion over pay he had with one of his coloured farm workers.

> I said, "Let's talk about it!" He explained that he couldn't afford to buy his child a birthday present. I said, "Henry, that's terrible." We chatted a bit about the kids' birthdays, and then I asked him if he had bought

any wine the previous weekend. . . . He said he had. "And the weekend before?" I asked. He said he had. And then I asked him if he would rather buy wine for himself or a birthday present for his kid. Silence. I explained to him that when you need something special, you have to save for it. "If I want to go on holiday, Henry," I said, "I have to save for it. I have to do without other things. If I want to buy a motor car, I've got to put away for it. It means sacrificing other things." You see, he would never think of giving up his wine for his kid's birthday present. That just doesn't register being important. I made my point, but it was totally lost. (Crapanzano 1985, 252–53)

Peter added that his disillusionment with coloured workers came from trying to understand them according to his own standards. Peter tried to reckon, with whatever *méconnaissance*, with the other as a subject. There was here the beginning of a dialectical relation. Peter in his subjectivity was different from Henry in his subjectivity whatever that was for Peter. Peter's understanding—or lack of it—corresponds to Gadamer's second mode.

On another occasion Peter described his friendship with an Xhosa boy when they were both adolescents. Peter had been invited to the Xhosa's initiation. When I asked Peter is his relationship to the Xhosa changed after the initiation, he answered,

As children we could play together, throw balls at each other; but then suddenly there comes a time when all that stops [Peter grew silent, and then after a few saddened moments he said, without, I think, realizing the irony:] I remember once, after my friend had become a man, jogging down to his hut in the evening. I said I'd race him to a tree, as we had often done in the past, and he refused. "I am a man, and I must walk with dignity. I can jog but I can't run." He could no longer carry a knobkerrie around. He had to carry a staff. (Crapanzano 1985, 88–89)

There is here, I believe, a glimmering of Gadamer's third—immediate and open—mode of understanding, if only through the absence of understanding.

There are many kinds of encounters in the field, and how we respond to them depends upon our own assumptions about the significance of the encounter, the meaning of language, and the nature of understanding. When Peter talked to me about how blacks think, I listened, took notes, and had my data. When he described his experience with Henry, I listened with fascination. I engaged with Peter. And when Peter told me the story of his Xhosa's friend's refusal to run, I—so much of a romantic am I—felt a certain authenticity in his words. I could respond to him with a sympathetic silence. My experience of Peter's words seems to parallel Peter's experience of the exchanges he recounted. I suppose my account of my exchanges with Peter, as he recounted his exchanges with Henry and his Xhosa friend, serve a similar function in my exchange with you, the reader.

The Dialogue as a Model for Interpretation

Understanding a text is, for Gadamer, like the understanding that is achieved in a live conversation. A common language, which is more than "a tool for the purposes of understanding," has to "coincide with the very act of understanding and reaching an agreement." The meaning of a text cannot be "compared with an immovably and obstinately fixed point of view"; it emerges—over time—through a delicate conversation that, if it is to be authentic, demands of the interpreter an openness to his prejudices and preunderstanding (1975, 350). The interpreter has, however, a burden that the conversationalist does not: to give expression to his "conversational partner's"—the text's—meaning.

Conversation romantically, incantatorily, is more than a metaphor (stretched to the limit, I would say) for describing the work of interpreting a text. For Gadamer, who despite his concern for history seems never to be *critically* concerned with the effects of the recontextualizations that occur with the interpreter's expression or reexpression of the text's meaning, the hermeneutical conversation becomes a sort of memory, restoring "the original communication of meaning" (1975, 331).

Tedlock also suggests a dialogical model for interpretation—for the armchair sequelae of the field experience. The dialogue in the field does not stop, he maintains, when the anthropologist leaves the field (1983a, 324). But, like Gadamer, he does not discuss the new status of field recordings, the problems of their decontextualization and recontextualization—of their appropriation—in what I call secondary, or shadow, dialogues (Crapanzano, n.d.). Simply put, for the moment, a shadow dialogue is one a speaker has—silently, for the most part—with others, embodied say in his colleagues, who are not present at the primary dialogue. The primary dialogue becomes the theme of the shadow dialogue, and the partners in the primary dialogue become figures in this new dialogue that bypasses them.

To assume as Tedlock and others do that the interpreter can engage in a dialogue with his recordings, texts, and other materials is to err on three counts: (1) by taking a metaphorical relationship (the interpretation of a text is like a dialogue) nonmetaphorically; (2) by failing to recognize that the *dialogue* with which the interpreter is now dialoguing is no longer a dialogue but a "dialogue"—the theme of another dialogue; and (3) by granting the interpreter what has to be regarded as a superhuman ability to bracket off secondary dialogues and their languages.

Spoken Genres

Dialogue comes from the Greek *dialogos*. *Dia* is a preposition that means "through," "between," "across," "by," and "of." It is akin to *dyo* and *di-*, "two." As a prefix in English *dia* suggests a "passing through" as in diathermy, "thoroughly" or "completely" as in diagnosis, "a going apart" as in dialysis, and "opposed in moment" as in diamagnetism. *Logos* comes from *legein*, "to speak." It may also mean thought as well as speech—thought, as Onians (1951, 76 n. 9) points out, that is conceived materially as breath, spirit, *pneuma*. Hence, etymologically, a dialogue is a speech across, between, through two people. It is a passing through and a going apart. There is both a transformational dimension to dialogue and an oppositional one—an agonistic one. It is a relationship of considerable tension.

The dialogue is opposed, at least today in anthropological circles, to the monograph. "Monograph" also comes from the Greek. *Monos* means "alone" and is perhaps akin to *manos*, "thin." As a prefix in English *mono* means "alone," "single," or "one." Graph, *graphe*, from *graphein*, means a "representation by lines," a "drawing," a "painting" as well as "writing." *Graphe* is something written or drawn. *Graphein* was used, according to Onians (1951, 417), to describe the tapestry or pattern embroidery of the Moirai, or Fates, and even to mean fate. A monograph is then a writing, a drawing, or a painting alone: a writing that stands alone—as a fatality, perhaps. It is pictorial—representational—without inherent tension.

Etymologically, at least, there is an immense difference between a dialogue, a speech passing between two who are in some way opposed, and a mongraph, a writing, a text, that stands alone and is fated or embodies fate. The one is agonistic, live, dramatic; the other is pictorial, static, authoritative. At least since Plato's *Phaedrus*, the two have been understood in opposition to each other and have been defined as such.

The pitting of dialogue against monograph has probably led to an oversimplification of both. Certainly a minimalist definition of dialogue like Tedlock's is not adequate to the many modes of human communication. It seems that an awful lot of speaking occurs that is not dialogical insofar as dialogue is conceived as a crossing, a reaching across, a sharing if not a common ground of understanding than a common communicative presumption, a "coming together," a fusion. Is the recitative a dialogue? Are people who "talk at each other" engaged in a dialogue? Is there dialogue in a nasty argument? In a verbal exchange between a master and a servant? In a seduction as opposed to lovemaking? Indeed, Rilke's two bridges separated by an abyss seems an accurate model for many verbal exchanges even when the speakers speak the same language.

The point is that there are many genres of spoken as well as written communication with different implications, even within a single culture (Bakhtin 1986; Todorov 1984), and these genres can be distinguished not only through linguistic and stylistic analysis but more immediately, though not necessarily explicitly, by members of the culture themselves. As Alasdair MacIntyre (1984, 211) suggests, comprehension may well depend upon our ability to allocate conversation to one genre or another. The ill mastery of these genres of social conversation is the outsider's—the anthropologist's— Achilles' heel. Mikhail Bakhtin (1986, 80) has observed that frequently a person who has an excellent command of speech in some areas of cultural communicaton, such as delivering a scholarly paper, is very awkward in conversation because he does not have command of the appropriate genre of social communication. The ability to master a repertoire of genres is not, in my view, fully coordinate with linguistic competence "taken abstractly."

The genres of oral discourse determine the course of any utterance. "We choose words according to their generic specifications," Bakhtin (1986, 87) writes. Genres, for the Russian critic (p. 87), "correspond to typical situations of speech communication, typical themes, and, consequently, also to particular contacts between the *meanings* of words and actual concrete reality under certain typical circumstances." They are collective and demand completion through the *responsive understanding* of the speaker's interlocutor (p. 68).

The conventions of dialogue have varied in Western literary tradition, as has their presumed influence on nonliterary communication. We have, as Roger Deakins (1980) notes, "dialogue" and "familiar talk" in the sixteenth century; the "conference" and "meeting" in the seventeenth century; the eighteenth century's "conversation," the "colloquy" of the nineteenth century; and of course the "interview" of our own century. Such dialogue genres may give the illusion of an open-ended conversation or may suggest a highly conventionalized, closed-ended communication, say, between diplomats or courtiers. They may serve as a vehicle in which the author expresses his views through one character—a sort of dialogically masked monologue—or they may offer a range of current and competing views, without the author's own position being explicitly given. Or they may even suggest in some theater-of-the absurd manner mere banter that "never really goes anywhere." Presumably these different conventions have affected the way Westerners have engaged with non-Westerners—a point that has not been given sufficient attention by historians of anthropology and travel—and it has certainly affected the way such engagements have been reported and interpreted in the literature.

The genres of oral discourse are intimately related to these literary genres and, as Greg Urban has argued in this volume, to ritual genres as well. Urban suggests that the ceremonial dialogues characteristic of many Indian groups in South America not only imitate ordinary conversation but provide a model for such conversation. More limited stylistically, and pragmatically, than ordinary conversation, the ceremonial dialogue becomes a sign vehicle for dialogue itself, directing attention, however, not only to linguistic exchange but to social coordination and solidarity. It could of course be argued that all dialogue, and not just such privileged dialogue as the ceremonial or the literary, serves as a model for itself. Such, presumably, would be Gregory Bateson's (1972) position: by participating in a dialogue the participant learns what a dialogue is and how to participate in it.

Negotiating Dialogical Conventions

Whatever effect indigenous dialogue models have on the dialogues anthropologists witness and engage in the field, the anthropologist's own models also affect them and his understanding of them. The "negotiations of reality" that take place in the field are concerned not only with what "reality" is but, perhaps more significantly, with its expression (Crapanzano 1980). There is always a struggle between the anthropologist and the people he works with over the appropriate forms of discourse.

Given the power relations in the field situation, the native often succumbs to—or appears to succumb to—the ethnographer's insistent genre, the interview, where every "short" question demands a long, sincere, and relevant answer. Exotic, unexpected content can blind the ethnographer to the native's surrender to the anthropologist's form of expression as the native understands it. All too often, where the effect of genre and convention are recognized, they are justified—or dismissed—on dubious methodological grounds.

We must not assume, however, that even where a native appears to have acquiesced to the conventions of the interview, he has understood them as the anthropologist does and accepted them as the anthropologist desires. Faqir Mohammed, for example, a Moroccan farmer whom Kevin Dwyer (1982) interviewed over several months, seems to have accepted the conventions of Dwyer's ethnographic interview, that is, until Dwyer (1982, 219) asked him to reflect on their relationship and what they had been doing.

> K.D. And what do you think that I think about you? What might I say to myself about you?
>
> F.M. You're the one who understand that. Why am I going to enter into your head?
>
> K.D. But you can't enter the sheikh's head, or Si Hasan's, yet you said something about what they might think of you.
>
> F.M. I don't know. That—I don't know about it. I don't know about that.
>
> K.D. All right.

Dwyer notes that the faqir "would not be drawn into an answer." Clearly, the faqir found Dwyer's demand for self-reflection disturbing because such reflection went against *his* "construction" of the interview, against his sense of propriety and etiquette, and presumably against his motivations (whatever they were) for participating in it. Direct questions about the relationship threaten the relationship by formulating and objectifying it. The relationship—the conversation, however extraordinary from a Moroccan's point of view—would lose its subtlety and flexibility, which are highly valued in Morocco.

Being in the Dialogue

The dialogues that Tedlock, Dwyer, and other dialogical anthropologists write about are primarily those in which the anthropologist is one of the participants. They do not adequately consider, in my view, the implications of this "position" on their understanding of dialogue. Although they acknowledge the role the anthropologist plays in eliciting and formulating his "objective" data, they do not recognize the peculiar authorial (if I may use the word in both a literal and a metaphorical way) presumption in their participant-observational stance: a presumption that permits them to be both engaged in the field encounter (to the point even of determining its direction) and removed from it, rather like an otiose deity contemplating its creation in order to observe, record, and interpret it. The *real* problem so often hidden in anthropological discussions of participant observation that focus on the participation is how to extricate oneself from all the participation—how to observe, how to find an external vantage point, and how to recognize the legitimacy and the limitations of that vantage point. (I shall have more to say about this later when I discuss shadow dialogues. Let me note here that the anthropologist in his objectivist mode can aspire to the otiose—and feel all the pains and pangs of guilt that come from such separation—but he is no autonomous deity and can never achieve that end, his objectivity, without the help of another, an authoritative interlocutor whom, such is his presumption, he so often fails to acknowledge.)

Anthropologists often attempt to resolve the problems of extrication by clinging uncritically to some theoretical perspective or another—one that gives them, so they maintain, an appropriate distance—or to some methodological strategy that is "independent" of their research encounter. Many folklorists and anthropologists (Darnell 1974; Barre 1969) interested in oral literature have succumbed to the illusion that with appropriate instruments they can obtain a near-perfect rendition of what took place and thereby either extricate themselves from the encounter or adequately appraise their role in it. We await impatiently the multiperspective, gustatotactico-olfactory holograph sensitive to body heat, heartbeat, brain waves, sexual arousal . . . and the evolution of a being capable of comprehending all its data from a universally acceptable vantage point, but until that day we have humbly to make do with our perceptual and interpretive limitations. We have to recognize that we are *inextricably* involved in our research encounters and that any attempt to extricate ourselves from them, theoretically, methodologically, or technically, will have to be justified by our research—and other—interests (which are not totally independent of the encounters themselves) and not by fantasies of theoretical, methodological, and technical perfection, which keep us from acknowledging our own insufficiency.

Tedlock takes great pains to show that the anthropologist cannot be eliminated from the ethnographic encounter. In "The Story of How a Story Was Made" (1983b), he describes several ways his presence affected the narratives he heard. In one tale Tedlock collected from the Zuni, he—his tape recorder, at any rate—forced an anticipation of the decontextualization that would occur in the playback, transcription, and publication of the narrative. It "dampened" the audience's response and prevented the performer from "entangling" members of the audience in the story (1983b, 302). On another occasion the absence of the tape recorder, as Tedlock sees it, though it may well have been a different attitude the Zuni perceived in Tedlock without his tape recorder, "bared the conversational ground not only between the performer and the audience but also between the performer and the fieldworker" (1983b, 302). We see in Tedlock's writing, and in the writing of many other anthropologists who make use of the recording devices, a tendency to symbolize the ideologically constituted split between participant and observer in terms of the "fieldworker" and the "tape recorder." They do not appear to recognize the symbolism and its implications for their studies.

Despite all the concern anthropologists show for language, they tend to regard their own language as transparent. They do not always appreciate the difference between themselves and their interlocutors in the immediate field situation and in various renditions and representations, including the endopsychic ones, that occur in retrospection and remembrance. Here they become characters in some secondary conversation or dialogue. Tedlock talking to the Zuni is no longer Tedlock but "Tedlock." This situation should be obvious, though it is not always so, when the anthropologist describes the field situation and his role in it. We succumb to what can be called an *autobiographical illusion* and ignore the literary strategies—the generic constraints and conventions—by which an author represents himself.[3]

---

3. The autobiographical illusion is socially necessitated. Imagine the havoc our legal system would be in were we to recognize the quotation marks around witnesses and the people they talk about in their testimonies! We would then have to recognize them as *characters* in highly conventionalized, dramatic performances that are taken to be merely representations of what occurred. Rather than judging them in terms of their "truth value," as we do traditionally, we should have to judge them in terms of their persuasiveness. It seems, however, that the quotation marks have to be recognized in any endeavor that pretends to be science even if that recognition risks subverting its traditional scientific claim.

It is of course less obvious that the anthropologist has become a character in a tape recording or a transcription of a tape recording, but despite the differences between recording an event and describing it, the recording, like the description, is not the event. It is a peculiarly evaluated, closed-ended, repeatable rendition of the event that has been framed, even despite the concurrence of its participants, in a way that bypasses it. It has become the theme of a second dialogue. The participants become characters in this second dialogue just as they do in the descriptions of the recorded event, and any character-ization or evaluation will reflect their symbolic status. We see this clearly in Dwyer's preambles to his conversations with Faqir Moham-med and in his comments on specific exchanges. When Dwyer (1982, 228) agrees, for example, with the faqir's comment that "there is talk women shouldn't hear"—the faqir explaining why he does not eat with his family—Dwyer has to add a bit defensively a footnote: "I agree with the Faqir here, although I certainly would not if the conversation were with someone from New York!"

Much has been written about the interview in methodological treatises that could be considered in literary terms to be as prescrip-tive of genre and convention as, say, the rules of prosody and unity were for French classical theater. We cannot of course know to what extent such rules are followed in the field. We do know, however, that they affect the way information collected in the field (by whatever means) is reported. Indirectly, for example, data tend to be presented in a manner that does not focus on the role of the ethnographer in their elicitation, thereby creating an objectivist, timeless aura that marks the data as data, the investigation as science. Directly, the effects of methodological prescription can be seen in the reports of such interviews. Granting even the accuracy of reportage (a possibility that can be contexted, as I have suggested, on a number of grounds other than those of the reporter's sincerity and honesty), we find, if any, only truncated reports of what happened before and after the "interview," of how first contact was established, how the interview was explained, what trial runs, if any, were conducted, what comments were made afterward, what excerpting and editing rules were followed. A pseudoformalism that betrays the lived field experience but meets the criteria of scientific investigation is thereby created. It is clear that such presentations of what occurred are determined not just by what took place in the field but by the shadow dialogues the ethnographer has with his colleagues and theoretical positions.

Even in works as sensitive to the dynamics of the exchange as Dwyer's, the dialogues seem removed from their original context. Dwyer and Faqir Mohammed become cardboard figures in some minimalist drama that could be taking place almost anywhere, were it not for their "Moroccan content" that serves deictically to play them in a highly stylized—an ethnographic—Morocco.[4] Is it this minimalism that renders the exchanges as "vulnerable" as Dwyer would have them? Although the exchanges are at times metadiscursive—that is, they become their own subject matter—more often they are concerned with "external matters" that are not explained or described in a way that gives even an inkling of the pragmatically creative dimension of the exchange. Those indexical locutions that do not refer immediately to the exchange itself, that are not shifters in Jakobson's (1963) sense, seem to reflect a flattened context (affirmed by an authoritative ethnographic introduction) that has none of the presumable "warmth," "character," or "texture" of the original exchanges. They leave the reader, and the ethnographer, with the feeling that something vital has been left out.

Dialogical ethnographies *represent* dialogues. They may create the illusion of immediacy, but they are in fact subject to all sorts of representational constraints. The most notable of these I call radical pragmatic reduction and radical pragmatic reorientation. By *pragmatic reorientation*, I refer to the inevitable recontextualization—the appropriation —of the dialogical utterance, any repeated utterance for that matter, that occurs with its representation and participation in secondary dialogues. Pragmatic reduction leads to the flattening I mentioned earlier, and pragmatic reorientation vivifies the secondary dialogues that appear at times to betray (for the ethnographer, at least) the lived field encounter.

Contextualization

Henry James (1984), who had written several dialogical novels, came to regard the dialogical novel as inadequate because it lacked what he called "medium" or, as I believe we would say, context. We have to recognize that what constitutes a satisfactory medium is in fact culture specific. Traditional ethnographies—Tedlock would call them

4. Of course each dialogue is elaborately contextualized in terms of Dwyer's theoretical reflections. It is never altogether clear when and where these reflections occurred.

analogic—piece together bits of sociocultural material according to a model or paradigm that is methodologically or theoretically rationalized in such a way as to deny its literary conventions and the constraints they impose. Society, culture, becomes a container in which certain rarely particularized events—abstract sociocultural processes—are enclosed. There is minimal narrative (historical) movement, and where such movement occurs it is frequently framed as a case study that exemplifies the abstract processes and legitimates their frame. We might say, following Bakhtin (1981, 84–258), that in such traditional ethnographies the spatial dimension of the chronotope (literally, time-space, the way time and space, the "world," are characteristically organized in a particular genre) dominates the temporal dimension, which is highly elaborated in narrative literature. The "camp," the "village," the "slum," the "market," the "hearth," and the "ritual precinct"—the *horm* in Arabic—are the principal chronotopes of traditional ethnography. Perhaps because their temporal dimension is minimally and abstractly elaborated, they tend to be lifeless.

In dialogical ethnographies, or in those ethnographies that are sensitive to the dialogues that gave birth to them, the representation of context presents particular problems. As Jiri Veltrusky (1977, 128) observed in his discussion of dramatic dialogue, dialogue unfolds in both time and space. The "here and now" keep changing. Through deixis and other indexical locutions, the extralinguistic situation is constantly highlighted. But more important, not only is there no unchanging context, there is no single context. The dialogue has minimally two interpenetrating contexts, those of each of its participants (Mukarovsky 1977; Veltrusky 1977). Insofar as they are opposed to each other, their dialogue is characterized by "sharp semantic reversals" at the borderline between their individual speeches. (One has only to think of the exchanges between Kevin Dwyer and Faqir Mohammed I quoted above.) What unity occurs derives from the subject matter or theme (Mukarovsky 1977). In other words, if I may elaborate, the essentially agonistic dimension of the dialogue (articulated pragmatically through the constitution of competitive contexts, including the personnel) is marked by a semantically understood theme whose pragmatic effect—to create unity or the illusion of unity—is concealed by its very semanticity. It is precisely this paradox, that for a theme to be pragmatically effective its pragmatic capacity has to be concealed behind a semantic veil, that makes the discussion of the theme so fraught with tension. It may also account

for the banality of most discussions, where the conventional preserves the phatic function, the coming together, of the exchange. And
it may also account for the particular vulnerability that participants,
anthropologists and others, experience in cross-cultural dialogues.

The tensions between several contexts and their continual
change is reflected in Gadamer's discussion of the fusion of horizons.
"Every encounter with tradition that takes place within historical
consciousness," Gadamer (1975, 273) writes, "involves the experience
of the tension between text and present."

> The hermeneutic task consists in not covering up this tension by
> attempting a naive assimilation but consciously bringing it out. . . .
> Historical consciousness is aware of its own otherness and hence
> distinguishes the horizon of tradition from its own. On the other hand,
> it is itself, as we are trying to show, only something laid over a
> continuing tradition, and hence it immediately recombines what it has
> distinguished in order, in the unity of the historical horizon that it thus
> acquires, to become again one with itself.

Here, as so often in Gadamer and the other phenomenologists, we
see how conversational—dialogical—exchanges are reflected, refracted perhaps, in their theory—a theory that, despite its interest in
language, as I have noted, does not recognize the effects of that
language on itself. The result is a confusion of description and
prescription. Gadamer's discussion, which points at once to the
agonistic dimension of dialogue and to its dissolution in "tradition,"
exemplifies the unifying function of the theme in a process that can
only be called mystifying. A pseudotemporality—from awareness of
the tensions between contexts to fusion—conceals the contempora-
neity of the pragmatically constituted separation of contexts (horizon,
vantage point) and the pragmatically constituted (though semantically veiled) union (fusion, coincidence) of the theme. Whatever
"reality," whatever "significance" the theme may have in itself, it
also serves an ideological, a mystifying function.

If the extralinguistic situation of the dialogue is constantly
changing (if not fully, then at least in part), how is it possible to
describe that context in a way that does justice to it? (And insofar as
the representation of dialogue and its context, however described, is
itself dialogical, then how is it possible to describe its changing
context of representation?) Clearly, we have to face the limitations of
our descriptive capacity. However we depict the context, however

acceptable our choice of contextual features, however sensitive to the dialogical movement of the here and now, our contextualizations will always clash with the reality we are depicting. If we are participants in the dialogue, as most anthropologists are in the dialogues they represent, then the choice of context (whatever its claim to objectivity) will always weight the struggle for context in favor of the anthropologist. (Such a position is of course intolerable to those proponents of dialogical anthropology who have been conned by the egalitarian ideology, the "mutuality" of dialogue [Clifford 1983].) If we depict a dialogue we have witnessed but have not participated in, we create a "third" context even when we wish to appropriate the context of one of the speakers. We cannot ask the parties to the dialogue to describe the context, because they will then be engaged in a dialogue with us in which their particular retrospective contextualizations will serve pragmatic functions in their talk with us and will be modified accordingly, even with the best of wills.

In narrative literature, particularly in third-person accounts, all sorts of conventions for describing changing contexts have been developed: descriptions of the verbal exchange itself, of expressions and gestures, of the object of indexical locutions, of the unstated perceptions and thoughts of the characters, of "objective" features of the surroundings as they are highlighted. Such conventions usually imply some sort of omniscient or partially omniscient, certainly disengaged, narrator. They have not been acceptable in those sciences that so privilege the recorded word that they ignore the imaginative context it will necessitate if one is not given. And even then . . .

Whatever their objective claims, contextualizations are never neutral. They always have an imperative function; they tell us how the exchange they "enclose" is to be read. They confirm, thereby, the theoretical underpinning of—the rationalizations for—such instruction. The circle—theory–instruction–context–theory—is never full (except in the most reductive social descriptions). It is, up to a point, always responsive to the pragmatic struggle of the enclosed exchange.

In the primary dialogue the anthropologist and his informants struggle to determine the context of the dialogue. In the secondary dialogue—the anthropologist's description of the context of the primary dialogue—he is responsive to both the primary struggle and the secondary one, with outside authorities. Insofar as there is a tension between the primary dialogical contextualization and the secondary anthropological contextualization, the latter does not fully dominate—does not reduce the sitution to a mere confirmation of its theoretical claims.[5] Of course to acknowledge such a tension can be disquieting and produce all sorts of conservative reactions, ranging from the denial of the tension to an overestimation of the worth of the theoretical legitimation of the contextual choice.

Appropriation

To argue that the reproduction of the field dialogue gives an independent voice to the participants to the dialogue—the native and the ethnographer—is to deny the ethnographer's power (Clifford 1983; Tyler 1981; Crapanzano 1980; see also Maranhão 1986). It is the ethnographer who appropriates the word through both representation and contextualization; and as any gossip knows, he who has the word has the power of the word. Such is the tyranny of quotation. Writing has drastically extended the range of quotation and the power inherent in the word's appropriation. Subject of course to political and economic considerations, which should not be so exaggerated as to remove responsibility from the ethnographer, it is the ethnographer who, in his ethnographies, even his dialogical ones, has final control over the word. It is he who decides to select, to edit, to publish, to provide the "appropriate" context and theoretical orientation. So much is obvious.

But what do we mean when we say the ethnographer has control over the word? We must not grant him an irrealistic omnipotence. Like the people he converses with, the ethnographer engages in a verbal transaction that, whatever his power, he cannot completely control. Gadamer (1975, 343) would argue that any participant's control over a verbal exchange precludes its being an authentic conversation. A conversation has, in his words, a spirit of its own that escapes the will of its participants. We do not have to invoke conversational spirits and risk their reification to recognize that the conversation, the dialogue, and many other verbal exchanges (perhaps all exchanges, including the set questionnaire) are independent of their participants if only because, insofar as they are engaged in the exchange, the participants have no external vantage point from

5. In my paper "On Self-Characterizing," I have suggested that a similar struggle occurs between a character in a novel and the narrator who, though creating the character, is responsive to his "creation" once it is launched.

which to control it. (I am of course excluding consideration of the aleatory in such encounters.) Certainly the participants to the encounter (except perhaps when they are swept up by the flow of the encounter) are able to disengage themselves and evaluate it. Such disengagements and evaluations are attested both experientially and through the presence of shifters and other reflective and evaluative locutions in the exchange itself. But such disengagements, as I have suggested, are never complete. There can be no fixed vantage point. Rather, the process of disengagement depends upon the participation over time in shadow dialogues that may be so authoritative for the participants that they fall under the illusion that they have a fixed, a timeless, "an objective" vantage point. The ethnographer's—anyone's—participation in these shadow dialogues, with a colleague, for example, an important theoretical position, or a symbolically significant person, real or imagined, in his world, provides him with a position external to the immediate exchange, though never fixed or timeless, that enables him to reproduce the exchange and offer an interpretation of it. I should hasten to add that the other participants to the dialogue are also engaged in shadow dialogues that afford them external vantage points and that enable them to reproduce and interpret the dialogue when they choose.

The recognition of such shadow dialogues, as one converses, is always disturbing. It is as though a third party were observing and evaluating what one says. We become aware of their possibility when our interlocutor uses, for example, a stylistic register that appears inappropriate. He may appear distracted; he may appear to be addressing someone else; he makes "asides"; he speaks automatically; he "edits" what he has to say according to standards that have nothing to do with the occasion as we understand and assume he understands it. Revealing the existence of such shadow dialogues or at least their possibility is not without its effect. I can intimate an invisible presence. Think, for example, of the hushed tones, as though someone were listening, in a church. It can suggest a special relationship one's interlocutor has with supernatural powers (Crapanzano 1980). It can also give an aura of power to one's interlocutor. Think of the eloquent professor of philosophy who in his introductory lectures appears to be addressing those others, the great minds of history, as he lectures his students.

Often we come to embody the secondary interlocutor and suffer a sort of cognitive vertigo. We don't know who we really are: our conventional selves or whoever it is we embody for our interlocutor. It is an old shaman's trick and one that Hamlet himself uses as he attempts to discover the truth about his father's death (Crapanzano, n.d.). Most often, however, we converse with others in such a way as to conceal our shadow, our evaluative, dialogues from them.

Thus far I have used *shadow dialogue* loosely to refer to those dialogues that one partner to the primary dialogue has with an interlocutor, real or imaginary, who is not present at the primary dialogue. Such dialogues are "silent," "mental," "quasi-articulate," "beneath consciousness," though capable, at least in part, of becoming conscious. They are analogous to "thought" when it is conceived as a conversation (Vygotsky 1962). We have in fact to distinguish between at least two types of shadow dialogue. The first occurs during the primary dialogue; the second is after the fact, "in the armchair," interpretive.

In the first type, the absent interlocutor gives at least the illusion of a more-or-less stable, external vantage point to the primary dialogue and thereby permits those reflective moments, conscious or not, that are marked by shifters and other metadiscursive locutions. The absent interlocutor is a symbolically complex "figure" that is never so fixed, so defined, so immutable (except perhaps for the paranoid, the obsessive) as the "real" interlocutors one encounters in primary discourse. Reflection radically recontextualizes the dialogue. It places it and its participants in quotation marks. The primary dialogue becomes the theme of the shadow dialogue; its participants become its characters. They—the dialogue and its characters—are appropriated. Given the pressures of the ongoing conversation, such an appropriation is transitory but affects the conversation.

In the second type of shadow dialogue—the interpretive dialogue—the interpreter engages with the primary dialogue, now a text of some sort or another, dialogically. The dialogue, now in quotation marks, is appropriated and oriented toward an interlocutor who is wholly external to the primary dialogue and who provides *the* interpretive vantage point. (I should note the instability of this secondary interlocutor and the consequent "shiftings" of perspective that occur in even the most rigorous interpretations.) This shadow dialogue seems to have escaped the critical attention of the proponents of a dialogical approach to interpretation. To be sure, insofar as Gadamer recognizes community, tradition, preunderstandings, and prejudices, he can account for some of the "pressures" produced by a significant, an empowered, interlocutor in the shadow dialogues, but "community," "tradition," "preunderstanding," and "prejudices" are too monolithic, too stable, in my opinion, to provide a subtle enough basis for understanding the complex plays of power and desire in the production and reproduction, the representation and interpretation of dialogues. We have to remember that whatever the resistance of those we converse with, they are always a bit our creation, as we are their creation. That empirical fact perhaps marks the limit of our empiricism.

References

Bakhtin, Mikhail. 1981. *The dialogic imagination.* Austin: University of Texas Press.

———. 1986. *Speech genres and other late essays.* Austin: University of Texas Press.

Barre, Tolkein. 1969. The "pretty languages" of Yellowman: Genre, mode, and texture in Navajo Coyote narratives. *Genre* 2:211–35.

Bateson, Gregory. 1972. Social planning and the concept of deuterolearning. In *Steps to an ecology of mind*, 159–76. New York: Ballantine.

Bauer, Gerhard. 1969. *Zur poetik des Dialogs: Leistung und Formen der Gesprachsfuhrung in der neueren deutschen Literatur.* Darmstadt: Wissenschaftliche Buchgesellschaft.

Clifford, James. 1983. On ethnographic authority. *Representations* 1:118–46.

Crapanzano, Vincent. 1980. *Tuhami: Portrait of a Moroccan.* Chicago: University of Chicago Press.

———. 1985. *Waiting: The whites of South Africa.* New York: Random House.

———. 1988. Self-characterizing. Working Papers and Proceedings of the Center for Psychosocial Studies, Chicago.

———. n.d. Maimed rites and wild and whirling words: The restoration of meaning in *Hamlet.* Manuscript.

Darnell, Regna. 1974. Correlates of Cree narrative performance. In *Explorations in the ethnography of speaking*, ed. Richard Bauman and Joel Scherzer, 315–36. Cambridge: Cambridge University Press.

Deakins, Roger. 1980. The Tudor prose dialogue: Genre and anti-genre. *SEL* 20:5–25.

Dwyer, Kevin. 1982. *Moroccan dialogues: Anthropology in question.* Baltimore: Johns Hopkins University Press.

Gadamer, Hans-Georg. 1975. *Truth and method.* New York: Continuum.

Jakobson, Roman. 1963. Les embrayeurs, les catégories verbales et le verbe russe. In *Essais de linguistique générale*, 161–75. Paris: Editions de Minuit.

James, Henry. 1984. The lesson of Balzac. In *Literary criticism: French writers, other European writers, the Prefaces to the New York Edition*, 115–39. New York: Library of America.

MacIntyre, Alasdair. 1984. *After virtue.* 2d ed. Notre Dame: University of Notre Dame Press.

Maranhão, Tullio. 1986. *Therapeutic discourse and Socratic dialogue.* Madison: University of Wisconsin Press.

Mukarovsky, Jan. 1977. *The word and verbal art.* New Haven: Yale University Press.

Onians, Richard. B. 1951. *The origins of European thought about the body, the mind, the soul, the world, time, fate.* Cambridge: Cambridge University Press.

Rilke, Rainer Maria. 1969. *Letters of Rainer Maria Rilke, 1892–1910.* New York: W. W. Norton.

Tedlock, Dennis. 1983a. The analogical tradition and the emergence of a dialogical anthropology. In *The spoken word and the work of interpretation,* 321–38. Philadelphia: University of Pennsylvania Press.

———. 1983b. The story of how a story was made. In *The spoken word and the work of interpretation,* 302–11. Philadelphia: University of Pennsylvania Press.

Todorov, Tzvetan. 1984. *Mikhail Bakhtin: The dialogical principle.* Minneapolis: University of Minnesota Press.

Tyler, Stephen. 1981. Words for deeds and the doctrine of the secret world. In *Proceedings of the Chicago Linguistics Society,* 34–57. Chicago: University of Chicago Press.

Veltrusky, Jiri. 1977. Basic features of dramatic dialogue. In *Semiotics of art: Prague school contributions,* ed. Ladislav Matejka and I. R. Titunik, 128–33. Cambridge: MIT Press.

Vygotsky, L. S. 1962. *Thought and language.* Cambridge: MIT Press.

Webster, Steven. 1982. Dialogue and fiction in ethnography. *Dialectical Anthropology* 7:91–114.

Woolf, Virginia. 1942. *Death of a moth.* London: Hogarth Press.

11

Ode to Dialog on the Occasion of the Un-for-seen

Stephen A. Tyler

Dialogue is a complex figuration in Western discourse. It is not so much a form of discourse, though that too is part of our image of it, as a *forma formans*, a *usus disputandi* that uses and makes the participants who use and make it. It is already then an ethos expressed as a literary genre, a means of communication, a structural definition of thought, and the autobiography of the autonomous self.

As a literary genre emerging out of the Renaissance reinvention of the mood of the classical discourses of Plato, it has a simple form, consisting of a brief introduction describing participants, the setting, and the purposes and course of the conversation, followed by an account of what different speakers said in response to one another.[1] The form was meant to convey the impression of a documentary, to be a factual account of what someone said to someone in a particular setting about a particular topic. Too prolix for modern taste, it recorded the digressions, the flattery, the self-effacing modesty, the citations of ancient authority, and all the means of speaking employed in order to persuade. Typically it had a chance beginning in the conversation of a circle of civilized participants where different speakers would take up different positions on a topic until some sort of consensus emerged. The *dialogue*, when written, would then be circulated both within and outside the circle of original participants and would itself become a topic for further discussion. The fragment of the *dialogue*, a small part of a continuously emerging, never-completed discourse, and even though the originating *dialogue* ended in consensus, that consensus was only temporary, something to be

1. The following fiction of Renaissance *dialogue* owes much to dialogues with students and faculty at the Institut für Ethnologie and Afrika-Studien, at Gutenberg University in Mainz, West Germany, in the summer of 1987. I especially acknowledge Paul Drexler, who broached the topic and made me think and talk about it.

part of another *dialogue*. Consensus was not a final totalization or a sublation of opposing voices.

Throughout there is a sense of a real world, of real speakers, grappling with real issues that had a bearing on daily life. Unlike the rather contrived relevance of their Platonic predecessor, they seem to be authentic expressions of concerns active in a world outside the circle of discussants. And this is surprising because we modern readers know that these Renaissance discussants were only playacting, imitating a form of life evoked through the medium of the Greek texts that had captured their imaginations. In contrast to these Greek originals whose written artifice suggests a world of oral discourse merely "scribed," Renaissance dialogues are both transcriptions of *dialogue* and translations of texts and do not fully recapture the original story of "writing down," as the movement from orality to literacy. They are not in that way a *meta hodes*, a way beyond, a writing on writing, but are instead a writing on.

That complex of themes, that interplay of fragment, chance, supplement, consensus, and telos so familiar to modern minds emerges here, but one characteristic that makes Renaissance *dialogue* contrast with current uses of *dialog* in anthropology is the way it marginalizes its textualization. It deemphasizes the role of the literary document of the *dialog* as a representation or reproduction of the originating *dialogue*. Textualization is only one realization of a complex of movements from oral-to-written-to-oral-to-written. It is only a recurrent moment of the *dialogue* rather than its telos and totalization. It is not just a neutral change in the medium of expression, a movement from speech to writing, but is rather the permutation of speaking/writing, writing/speaking. Oral and literary are complementary here in a way they cannot be when the text is valued primarily as a representation and repository. For us, by contrast, the text of a *dialog* is a data base, a record of facts that can be removed from their originating context and put to new uses in other places. Here the role of representation is paramount and the text, as a repository of fact, usurps its oral contexts and undermines their function. This hegemony of the text arises because the text is valued as a reliquary of fact and as an aid to memory rather than as a contemplative object stimulating further discourse realized not just as another supplementary text, but as a continuing *co-lection* of text and talk.

The text of a *dialog* serving as a neutral resource within a universalized textual discourse, as in the case of ethnography as *dialog*, transforms *dialogue* from *ethos* to *logos*, from ethics to epistemology. The participatory and ethical context that grounds the *dialogue* is surpassed in the movement from particular to universal, the movement to *episteme* that in itself expresses the Western *episteme*. This image of textualization recapitulates the story of the sensorium as the movement from sensory-impression-to-symbolic-representation-to-symbolic-expression, which is also the movement from a grounding individual experience to a universalized symbolic representation seemingly derived from individual experience but always alienated from it. This textualization thus repeats as well the allegory of separation and alienation as the story of the symbol, the means of representation and universalization that makes universal representations only by destroying what it represents and universalizes. It is the story of epiphany deferred to the *logos* of some final, surpassing text entombing the corpus of a dead and dismembered discourse.

Here *dialog* is the death of one discourse in the birth and sustenance of another. Its image is "X," the coming-together-of-the-crossing-getting-across-crossing-over-crossing-out, the chiasmus within the *logos* conjuring at one and the same time a bright vision of reason, agreement, consensus, communion, unity, harmony, and mutuality and a darker picture of resistance, disagreement, *disensus*, opposition, antagonism, and raised voices. Its telos is the crossing out, the dying out of the *dia-* by the *logos*, the triumph of *logos* over *dia-* by means of *dia-* in the movement from agonism and dissent to consensus and agreement, from life to death. *Dialog* is discourse already infected by the disease of the *logos*, by the desire for transcendental resolution, demonstration, conclusion, QED, *the end* and death. This is *dialog* without the "you" in it.

Dialog is a creature of writing, dissembling its literary character in a semblance of speech. It is a literary form masquerading as speech, bending speech to the yoke of epistemology, harnessing it to the chariot of the *logos*. A method of knowing that pretends to persuade by reason alone, it needs still the aura of the *communis* to ground its movement to symbol in the guise of participation. It pretends to be a participatory means where the contesting voices of the *communis* are reconciled. The community of participants, that concrete image of the face to face, is conjured by the literary device of signatured speeches ligatured, of voices signed and dubbed in. *Dialog* is writing posing as speech in order to ground itself in the already constituted ethic of communication. It legitimizes its alienation from participants by invoking a context of seeming participation, thus giving itself an ethical foundation in the *communis* without the participation of the *communis*.

Plato: "Yes, as I've said many times, writing's a tricky business, but there is spoken dialog . . ."

Aristophanes (interrupting): "only in plays dahling."

   That aside, we do sometimes say "I'm having a dialog with X," or even "we are dialoging" as a way of characterizing our oral discourse with another, and we speak of having a dialog with a text as if it responded to our questions and answers, and even sometimes think of texts as having a dialog with one another. So, we have a literary genre—the text as *dialog*—and a genre of speech-talk organized dialogically, but what holds these different usages together, and what does it mean to say that talk is "organized dialogically"? Isn't the notion of "organization" here already a literary trope, pointing back to rhetoric and the idea that talk has an order in the arrangement of its parts, in the complementarity of participant roles, in the opposition and alternation of speaker/hearers, in its telos, and in its ethos? Does it not presuppose that talk is purposeful and that speaker/hearers mutually agree to the genre conventions of consensual truth in expressing their intentions? It would be odd, in other words, to say "we're dialoging here about nothing and for no particular reason," for "her idea of dialogue is she talks and I listen," or "we're having a dialogue even though we're not talking about the same thing." There are also borderline oddities, such as: "we're dialoging even though I can't understand a word you're saying" or "the three of us are having a dialogue." The first example is possible in situations where speaker/hearers seem to be alternating speaker/hearer roles even though they do not understand one another. The case is not far-fetched, since we might well say this of a mother interacting with her newborn baby when mother and child respond to each other by vocalization, gaze, gesture, and posture. The second case is odd because it goes against our catachrestic understanding of *dia-* as *di-*, meaning "two," which though etymologically incorrect has the great merit of capturing our sense of the face-to-face character of *dialog*. Face to face implies mutual diectic orientation, eye contact, or other indications of mutual attention. It also assigns third parties to the margins, "out of the corner of the eye" or as present but invisible participants, or as "onlookers," or other varieties of universalizing Peircean "thirds."
   One image of dialogue then evokes the seeming priority of oral discourse, of two participants who see one another or as we might say as if metaphorically, "have mutual regard," and by a mutual speaking

and listening, which need not be by prior necessity exclusive alternates, talk about somethings for some purposes not necessarily known in advance. In this image talk is not mediated by textuality. It does not begin with a problem set by textual interpretation or by a desire to textualize speech. It is neither speech about text nor text about speech and thus cannot be said to have "genre conventions"—in the sense of textual genres—that are other than those of the *con-mumus,* the *con-municating con-munity.* Isn't this just a phenomenology of *dialog* of the sort carried out in part in sociolinguistics, the ethnography of speaking, ethnomethodology, conversation analysis, speech-act theory, and pragmatics in an attempt to create or describe an ontology of *munus* ("exchange") by capturing the *con-mun* sense practice of *dialog* as different *con-munities?* That is to say, it is an attempt to illustrate an ontology-as-practice, showing the essence of *dialog* as an instrument of exchange that is also the *ur*-image of exchange itself as a picture of concrete, participatory instruments fully present in the face-to-face-give-and-take-of-talk-in-order-to. The ontology of *dialog* is the technology of discourse. It is a practice, a means, a method for doing the work of the world. That is, of course, the consequence, but the paradox of this phenomenology of *orality* is that is recapitulates the contemporary *episteme* of reason captured in a style of *writing* that we can identify either as modern, in that vague sense of everything since Descartes, or as "plain style." Its "white reason" is exemplified in the work of speech-act theorists such as Austin, Grice, and Searle, who tell the tale of the speaker as a rational agent working his will on the world by giving appropriate outer expression to his inner intentions. His speaking is the instrument of his will and the means of his intentions. Here is an image of the speaker who knows his mind and speaks it with clarity, economy, and planned execution, whose foreknowledge of intents, means, and effects of words conjures ready recognition of these intents, means, and effects in the minds of complicitous hearers. Faces suffused with the glowing light of reasonable reason, cooperation, consensus, harmony, and agreement speech acts are reason itself as expressions of the *communis fidelium* seeking truth in *conmun* purpose by the *conmun* means of *conmun* sense. Austin, Grice, Searle, and Habermas understand communication as the action of reason itself, as the form that removes obstacles, clarifies thought, and moves others to good works that secure utopian outcomes. It sounds more and more like scientific method, or perhaps a revision of the Cartesian rules for meditation or an unintended parody of "plain talk makes good deeds." There is about it a cloying Franklinesque sense of smug self-righteousness, of a slick, unproblematic ego self-satisfied in its unreflective assurance of how-one-ought-to-talk-in-order-to, a kind of braying colonial authoritarianism wrapped in the flag of undistorted communication.

This monologic of domination invokes *dialogue* in order to conjure images of symmetry, egalitarianism, mutuality, harmony, agreement, of an ethic of instrumental reason founded in the truth and totalization of a transcendent utopian community—the society of the saved. It is the story of the slaying of the beast of unreason.

Obscured here beneath these purple robes of sanctimony is rhetoric, the dark twin of sweet reason, whose black instrumentality is the means of the speaker's domination of the hearer. Not through reason, but by stirring the emotions, the trickster's bent and twisted truth persuades and convinces without belief in order to gain some illegitimate advantage over unwary listeners. Rhetoric is the untruth of unfair means, of selfish, evil ends or pretense, and false belief that rouses our animal spirits and moves us to unreasonable acts. Rhetoric is the demon passion, the emotion *dialog* overcomes in its heroic struggle against the dark animal powers of unreason.

This is the persuasive fiction *dialog* tells monologically, a tale that reminds us, without seeking to, of what is suppressed in this triumph. It speaks of another world where distortions of meaning, subversions of truth, subterfuges, strategies, hedges, vagueness, ambiguity, polyvocality, equivocality, misunderstanding, conflicting interests, dispute, antagonism, opposition, and domination are the norm. *Dialog* implicates rhetoric as its this-worldly counterpart. They are as inseparably linked in correlative antithesis as up/down, before/after, good/evil, or speaker/hearer. Rhetoric is the Other of *dialog*. They are joined in common desire, united in their pursuit of a form of expression that constrains the hearer's belief and understanding by making her a willing accomplice in the domination that suppresses her voice by invoking a unity of desire in which opposing voices sing in complicitous harmony as a single voice. *Dialog* incorporates the pathos of rhetoric, for the unity of souls is the instrument of its seduction. Just as rhetoric undermines and subverts poetry's evocation of ethos, *dialog* displaces the pathos of rhetoric, making it the means of *logos*.

So this narrative of rhetoric vanquished is also the tale of the dialectical overcoming of *dialogue* by logic. The crossing over of *dia-*, which has its source of rhetorical pathos, is the bridge for the *logos* that crosses over *di-/dia-* and leaves only the mono-logy of the *logos*/logic as the overcoming-surpassing-repressing-double-crossing of dialectical resolution.

Chorus: Oh Evil of Evils!

Return once more to the Renaissance, where *dialogue* was reinvented within a fully textualized culture as a kind of nostalgic recreation of an oral past. *Dialogue* was recuperated through rediscovered texts, and it recreated in part by unwitting design the story, mood, and circumstances of that "originating" textualization of *dialogue* as *dialog*. As in that "first" Greek story, Renaissance *dialogue* eschewed justification in practical reason and was not, at least at first, a technology of discourse or a means of instrumental reason or a method for evaluating future outcomes of possible courses of action in civil society. Renaissance dialogue could contribute to the *vita activa*, but that was not its first or principal calling. It neither legitimized itself as an instrument of practical action nor followed the Greek example of legitimizing itself in the emergent *logos* as *dialog*. For Renaissance *dialogue* neither practical action nor the *logos* was sufficient justification, and it attempted instead to ground itself in the *vita contemplativa*, which was a mode of being rather than a mode of action or a means of knowing. It did not, of course, exclude the possibility that *dialogue* might lead to a course of action or to an emergent *logos*, but these utilitarian piacularities were neither determinate nor necessary palliatives. This *vita contemplativa* was justified neither by theory nor by practice. It was not evaluated performatively within the scope of an economy of production, for, except indirectly, it was not meant to produce actions whose consequences could be judged. It was an *ethos*, part of what it meant to be a civilized participant in Renaissance society and culture. Its universalism was not given by the allegory of the symbol, with all its attendant alienation from participation, but was the implicate of a participatory *communis* that understood itself to be already a participant in a universal *ethos* deriving from the classical tradition whose conversation it recovered, allegorically reenacted, and continued.

Though Renaissance *dialogue* was in this sense ethical rather than ontological or epistemological, it did not thereby give up all epistemic and ontic claims, for it was thought to be the very structure of thought itself. Thought was simply the inner form of the outer *dialog*, and any civilized person engaged in thinking was doing within himself the same thing two civilized persons would do in external *dialogue*. There is here no separation between inner and outer discourse; they are only different loci of the same activity. Neither the romantic image of the lonely, alienated thinker torturing himself in private communion nor the isolated Cartesian ego thinking its own being by itself has meaning here, where thinking is not an activity separating one from another but is the continuation in another place of a public communion with dialogical others. Just as external *dialogue* is reason arguing with itself in public performance, internal *dialogue* is reason arguing with itself in anticipation or in memory of public performance. This imagery is, as we know from Derrida, especially vocal, the interiorization of outer voices speaking aloud within us, and indeed this participatory imagery deflects the imagination from imagining images of wordless thoughts, pure concepts, and symbolic calculi as the means of universalization.

The art of talking and the art of thinking were the same logic, not as the mono-logic of deduction and syllogism, assertion, and statement, but as a dialogic of *e-duction*, discourse, and question and answer. Textual monologism was possible only within the larger con-text of dialogue. No external Archimedean locus privileged the Cyclopean ay's ranting *logos*-locutions. It was only a single voice submerged in a murmurous multitude.

Even so, *dialogue* is already compromised by the *logos* it comprises, for it is an onto-logy, the self's story of itself, the auto-bio-graphy of the self's auto-nomy, the *selflectedself*. The *dialogue* that makes thought is also the *dialog* that makes the self. The Self conjures itself in the eye and word of the Other in the difference it posits to make its own identity. The Self discovers itself in the Other, in what it is not, just as the sign knows itself as the mirror of what it is not. The Self is the sign of the Other. The Self knows itself, as we say, by reflection, as it is mirrored in its own distortions of the Other. Self-consciousness *sees* the Other not as independent and different but as the reflection of itself and recognizes itself in that negative unity. Its ontology is the overcoming of the id-entity-threatening resistance of the Other. Singing here, as if in harmonious unison, the voices of the self-discovered Cartesian cogito, the Freudian Narcissus, Lacan's mirrored ego, Sartre's ego-in-the-look-of-the-other, and Piaget's egocentric child hymn and irenic other, Bardesanist bards minstreling the master narrative that governs *physis*, *bios*, and *psyche*, cosmos, civilization, and self in unending remugience.

This panegyric dialectic of desire, of the "master and the slave"

part VI

The Ontological and Ethical Dimensions of Dialogue

12

A Critique of Habermas's
Diskursethik

Alessandro Ferrara

In the past six or seven years, Habermas has considerably developed and systematized his views on ethics. Up till 1979, ethics was not a central concern for him and was of interest only because certain related concepts were crucial for the grounding of a universalist stance in philosophy and social theory (concepts such as the ideal speech situation, communicative action, and presuppositions of argumentation). A passing mention of a "universalistic ethic of speech" and of "communicative ethics" can be found in *Legitimation Crisis* (1975). However, the systematic formulation of the *Diskursethik* has been undertaken by Habermas only more recently. Thus, only now has it become possible to attempt an overall assessment of his ethical position.

The Project of a Cognitivist Diskursethik

Habermas's conception of ethics unfolds in the confutation of seven skeptical objections against universalistic ethics. First Habermas spells out which phenomena are going to constitute the domain of ethics. Then he tries to show that practical questions bear a relation to truth, albeit not the same kind of truth associated with descriptive statements. Third, he deals with the skeptic's contention that the irreducible pluralism of ultimate values (Weber's "warring gods") often prevents the achievement of rational consensus in moral matters. More specifically, Habermas responds to this objection by introducing a "bridge principle" of universalization that should enable us to generate rational consensus whenever the validity of a norm is thrown into question. Fourth, Habermas takes up the objection that the proposed principle of universalization merely absolutizes Western intuitions about morality; he responds by offering a transcendental-pragmatic grounding of such a principle.

Fifth, Habermas deals with renewed objections against the proposed transcendental foundation by modifying Apel's grounding of the principle of universalization in the direction of a *Diskursethik*. Sixth, he confronts the skeptic's attempt to thoroughly challenge universalistic morality, namely the skeptic's dropping out of argumentation altogether. Habermas tries to show that the option of stepping in or out of moral argument and of communicative action is not a real choice for any social actor, let alone entire communities. Finally, he comes to terms with the charge of ethical formalism.

As for the first two points, noncognitivist approaches to ethics such as Stevenson's *emotivism* or Hare's *prescriptivism*, as well as metaethical positions such as Moore's *intuitionism*, miss the phenomena that form the specific core of ethical reflection. Either they assimilate normative expressions to the expressions that describe reality (particularly the inner reality of feelings and preferences), or they assimilate normative expressions to *imperatives* uttered by speakers in the name of principles and values that are both ultimate and arbitrary, or they treat normative validity as a predicate to be attributed to sentences according to given rules. Thus, all the noncognitivist ethical theorists translate ethical experience into the vocabulary of some other order of experience, be it volitions, preferences, disguised utility, or power, and in so doing they fail to account for the moral experience par excellence—that is, the distinct perception that something (a norm or a principle of action) is *right* and for that reason alone *ought* to be the case, regardless of all considerations of expedience, utility, feelings, or preferences and regardless of what the community believes. But then what is it for a norm to be valid? What is it for an action to be justified? Those who ask such questions must presuppose that the possible answers are neither randomly valid nor completely arbitrary. They must presuppose, on the contrary, that right norms can be distinguished from unjust ones. The task of philosophical ethics is, according to Habermas, to reconstruct and spell out the principles that guide us in deciding what counts as normatively valid and what does not.

Although emotivist and prescriptivist approaches to ethics fail to do justice to the basic intuition that there is a sense in which norms *are* right, some overly cognitivist approaches fail to do justice to the fact that "being right" cannot be reduced to, although it resembles, the "being true" of factual statements. The asymmetries that set the *normative validity* of norms apart from the *truth* of assertions are discussed by Habermas in the second part of his essay. Whereas in the sphere of cognition assertions qua speech acts are the only entity about which truth or falsity can be predicated, in the sphere of morality normative rightness can be attributed primarily, but not exclusively, to norms. In fact, it can be attributed also to the speech acts through which those norms are expressed. Habermas then mentions a second asymmetry, linked with the ambiguity of normative validity. In the realm of morality a distinction must be made between the social fact that a given norm is recognized as valid and its being normatively valid, that is, its *deserving* recognition. These two aspects of validity may go together in specific cases, but they may also come apart. Nothing analogous to this twofold character of validity can be found in the realm of cognition. There we can find a relation between the existence of states of affairs and the truth of the statements that describe them, but not between the existence of states of affairs and the *expectation* that the corresponding statements *could* be shown as true. Rather, this is the case only with norms. The factual recognition of a norm by a community says nothing about the rightness of the norm. It only suggests that the norm *could* be shown to be valid. From these asymmetries, according to Habermas, we should conclude that the inner logic of moral argument is more crucial to answering the question, When is a norm valid? than the logic of scientific discourse is to answering the question, When is a statement true?

In terms of logic of argumentation—Habermas's third confutation—true statements are produced neither through pure deduction nor through mere fact gathering. The different procedures of induction acknowledged within the various disciplines can be seen as argumentive devices capable of bridging the gap between single observations and general hypotheses in an intersubjectively binding but still nontautological way. In the practical realm, when the rightness of a norm is questioned, a similar function is played by the *principle of universalization* (henceforth referred to as U). This principle ensures the possibility of generating rational consensus about the validity of a norm even in the face of a conflict of opinion or interest. This principle has been understood by all the proponents of a cognitivistic ethic from Kant to Rawls as the idea that those norms are right or valid that embed a truly general will or respond to a truly general interest. In the provisional version that Habermas chose as his point of departure, every valid norm must satisfy the condition that "the effects and side-effects which presumably follow from the *general* observance [of U] in the interest of *any* individual can be

accepted (and preferred to the consequences of the known alternatives) by *all* those concerned" (Habermas 1983, 75–76). With the
introduction of U Habermas closes his discussion of the skeptic's
point that even though one could conceive of the rational adjudica-
tion of the validity of norms, nevertheless the plurality of values
present in society might well put a conclusive and rational consensus
beyond the reach of otherwise good-willed actors.

Habermas's fourth confutation opens with the skeptic's objection that U, far from being a universally acceptable principle, merely
projects on a philosophical plane the moral intuitions of Western
culture. Habermas's strategy here is to avoid a *semantic* derivation of
U from the truth of some higher-order axiom—a move that would
expose him to Albert's *"Münchhausentrilemma"*[1]—and to have recourse to a *pragmatic* grounding of U. Habermas justifies our
acceptance of U because we know no other sensible way of
conducting a moral argument about the validity of a norm. This
transcendental-pragmatic grounding of U draws on Apel's work
(1973, 358–435), but Habermas modifies Apel's argument in one
important respect. Both Apel's and Habermas's transcendental
derivations of U hinge on the notion of a performative contradiction.
A semantic contradiction is one in which both one element and its
negation appear in the propositional content of a speech act; the
contrast in a performative contradiction typically occurs between
what is expressed at the semantic level and what is presupposed at
the pragmatic level.[2] Apel makes use of this notion in his claim that
the skeptic, by challenging the universal validity of U through an
argument, *implicitly* accepts some presuppositions of argumentation
that entail U among other things, and whose validity he then wishes
to deny *explicitly*. As Habermas points out, in this form Apel's
reasoning remains open to one important criticism. Namely, a skeptic
might counter that the "unavoidable presuppositions of argumentation" are binding only to the extent that one remains bound to the
context of moral *argument*. It is not clear how these presuppositions
can lay claim to universal validity when the regulation of *social action*
through norms becomes the issue.

1. The trilemma consists in having to choose one of three equally unacceptable
options: to enter an infinite regress, to break the chain of deduction at some arbitrary
first principle, or to argue in a circular way.
2. Some examples of utterances that involve a performative contradiction are "It
rains but I don't believe it rains"; "Tell me what day it is but I know it"; "I promise you
$100 but I don't intend to give you any money."

In the fifth confutation of the skeptic, Habermas tries to meet this new objection by giving up the attempt to derive U directly from the content of the presuppositions of discourse, as Apel does. Following Alexy (1978), Habermas specifies these presuppositions as *semantic* presuppositions (linked with consistency), *pragmatic* presuppositions (which have to do with sincerity), and *procedural* presuppositions (which prescribe an unlimited access to discourse, the equality of chances to raise and challenge points, and the equal chance to express attitudes, desires and needs). Furthermore, Habermas introduces a second premise in his grounding of U, to the effect that we consider valid only those norms that regulate social action in the common interest of all those concerned.[3] Habermas's argument can be summed up in the following way: If (1) whoever engages in argumentation must take for granted such procedural presuppositions as "No one concerned should be excluded from discourse" and "All participants should have an equal chance to raise and criticize claims and to express their needs," and if (2) only those norms are valid that regulate social matters in the common interest of all those concerned, then whoever honestly tries to evaluate within discourse any claim to normative validity commits himself or herself to procedural conditions that amount to the acceptance of the following principle: A contested norm is right (valid) if the effects that foreseeably follow from its *general* observance in the interest of any individual can be accepted by all *without coercion* (Habermas 1983, 103).

Habermas's argument is set up in such a way that the first premise implies U and the second makes it apply to the evaluation of the norms that regulate nondiscursive action. The status of U is for Habermas that of a general rule of moral argumentation, which enables moral actors to generate rational consensus whenever a divergence of interest or opinion arises. As such, it must not be confused with other principles and norms of conduct that may also be quite general and abstract but remain the object of moral discourse. Nor must it be confused with the procedural presuppositions of argumentation, whose significance extends beyond the scope of moral discourse (to theoretical and aesthetic discourse) and that *ground* the validity of U. The *content* of U is what each philosophical ethic tries to spell out in a different way. Habermas's own suggestion

3. By introducing this second premise, Habermas falls into a *petitio principii*. The central feature of U, that is, that the validity of norms is tied to their embodying a general interest, is surreptitiously introduced—as a minor premise—within the demonstration. See Wellmer (1985, 52).

is that it can best be specified in the direction of a *Diskursethik*, which would adopt as a core principle hereafter referred to as D: "Validity can be claimed only by those norms that meet (or could meet)—within the context of a practical discourse—the consensus of all those concerned" (Habermas 1983, 103).

Two additional considerations close Habermas's fifth confutation. First, the status of D is not to be construed as the intimation of a moral principle valid a priori. The foundation provided above is by no means an ultimate foundation. Rather, it is a *quasi-transcendental* one. The content of the first premise must remain open to the possibility of empirical falsification (Habermas 1983, 103). In this respect, the moral philosopher who renounces the claim to ultimate foundations is in the same position as the linguist who tries to make a case for a given grammatical rule by examining examples and counterexamples. The second consideration is that, in contrast to Rawls and other cognitivist theorists, the *Diskursethik* allows philosophers no privileged access to the operation of their own conceptual machinery. All substantive pronouncements on the validity of single norms must originate in *real discourses* or, alternatively, in discourses undertaken in an advocatory way (see Habermas 1983, 104; also Brumlik 1985). Philosophers cannot anticipate the outcome of these real discourses. When they try to do so, as Rawls (1971) does, their substantive prescriptions must be understood as *contributions* to a public discussion on the matter and, as such, open to dispute.

In the sixth confutation Habermas's imaginary partner, the skeptic, adopts an entirely different strategy. The skeptic now refuses to argue at all in order to take the wind out of Habermas's sails. Should this silent but eloquent objection remain unchallenged, a decisionistic residue would creep into Habermas's quasi-transcendental grounding of U. His grounding would be compelling for those who have already decided to step into rational argumentation but meaningless to those who decide otherwise. Moreover, the necessity of deciding in favor of rational argument could not itself be rationally grounded. Habermas's strategy here is to renounce a counterattack and settle for a long and patient blockade, as it were. You may refuse to argue now—he says to the skeptic—but sooner or later you will. The idea of a long-term withdrawal from discourse is only a Robinsonade, because the presuppositions of argumentation are also embedded in the structures of communicative action and thus are part of the everyday contexts of interaction in the lifeworld. Dropping out of the communicative aspects of the lifeworld is possible in the long run only at the price of severe mental disturbances and loss of identity. Even though a single individual could, in principle, choose to commit suicide or to drive herself insane to prove a philosophical point, such a refusal to enter argumentation could not be adopted by any community. For the symbolic structures of this community's lifeworld can be reproduced only in the medium of communicative action (Habermas 1981, 2: 212–28; 1982, 227). Thus the long-term rejection of U would prove self-destructive.

Finally, in the seventh confutation, the skeptic raises the charge of ethical formalism against the *Diskursethik*. It must be said that here Habermas fails to do justice to the real force of his opponent's objection. At times it is even hard to see how he imagines the objection to be exactly formulated. But since I intend to criticize the Diskursethik from what I understand to be a similar standpoint, for the time being I will just summarize Habermas's response to the "umbrella" accusation of formalism. In his reply, he stresses six points.

1. The *Diskursethik* has no substantive ethical orientations to offer, but only a procedure for choosing among competing orientations, that is *discourse*. In this sense it is correct to characterize it as a *formal* ethic.

2. Discourse, however, always takes place within a given lifeworld, that is, against the background of certain already made value choices. The *Diskursethik* can generate consensual choices about valid norms within one horizon of values but should not be expected to help us choose *between* one horizon of values and another. In this sense it offers no solution to the problem of the plurality of values (see Habermas 1983, 114; 1981, 1:41).

3. Prima facie, what is stated in point 2 seems to restrict the validity of ethical choices made under the guidance of the *Diskursethik* only to the horizon of values, within which the discussion has taken place. Habermas sees this as undeniable yet trivial. In fact, he argues, this holds only from an objectivating perspective. From the first-person standpoint of the actor who takes up in earnest the question of the validity of a norm, this validity is necessarily seen as extending beyond the limits of one's context (see Habermas 1983, 114; 1982, 255; 1984a, 229).

4. Insofar as the assessment of inner needs comes to be a crucial element in certain moral decisions, ethical discourse comes to interweave with aesthetic and therapeutic modalities of argument. These two modes of argument, however, differ from the "harder" quality of ethical discourse in that they do not share the presupposi-

tion that, in principle, a final consensus can *always* be reached (see Habermas 1981, 1:42–44, 70–71). Thus, when it happens that the "harder" ethical discourse must, in some concrete case, incorporate the results of argumentations of the "softer" kind, then the capacity of U to generate consensus under all conditions is also weakened.

5. Ethical discourse is inherently more vulnerable to the influence of social conflict than either theoretical or aesthetic forms of argument.

6. Practical discourses can be seen as islands (always at risk of being submerged) in the ocean of a praxis where the model of the consensual reconciliation of conflicts by no means prevails. Understanding is always threatened by power. Thus every action oriented to ethical principles must come to terms with the strategic imperatives that may support its effectiveness. This means that the *Diskursethik* must always incorporate the Weberian ethic of responsibility as a component.

The Hegelian-oriented skeptic—contends Habermas—wishes to dramatize these obvious but innocuous limitations of any formal ethic and tries to turn them into something that would undermine the validity of U. Rather, beneath these difficulties are to be recognized the complex problems generated by Western modernity and by the differentiation of the value spheres. The modern separation between the lifeworld and the specialized value spheres results, as far as the sphere of the practical is concerned, in a fateful differentiation of *questions of justice,* answerable along the universalistic lines of a cognitivist ethic, and *questions about the good life,* to be answered only from within the horizon of one life-form and with no guarantee (but only the possibility) of intersubjective agreement. One of the positive consequences of this process is the rationality gain that stems from the "decontextualization" of questions of justice. For now the validity of norms can rest on rational consensus, as opposed to authority, and conflict can be converted into consensus. The price to be paid is an increased need for *mediation* between principled ethics and the community's mores. Not only are the questions that come under ethical scrutiny decontextualized, but the answers that postconventional morality gives to these questions are *demotivated.* These answers have lost the motivational immediacy of the concrete prescriptions embedded in the mores of the community. Whenever they have to be *applied* to a concrete context of action, a special hermeneutic sagacity will have to be used to mediate between abstract principles and concrete constellations of needs, feelings, and meanings. However, Habermas insists it cannot be the task of the philosopher to specify this mediating faculty. Rather, this prudence must be seen in psychological terms, as part of the cognitive abilities of any postconventional moral actor.

The Problems of a Cognitivist Diskursethik

Before addressing the weak points of Habermas's *Diskursethik*, let me briefly recall the several strong and valuable aspects of his program. Borrowing the idea of McCarthy (1982), I will characterize these positive aspects as emphases on either Kantian or Hegelian themes. Overall, Habermas's position in ethics is that of one who is aware of Hegel's critique of the Kantian ethic and wishes to strengthen Kant's case in three ways: (a) by using psychological evidence (Kohlberg and Piaget) to substantiate the plausibility of a transhistorical universalization underlying the conduct of a mature modern personality (Habermas 1984a, 226, 230); (b) by clearly detaching norms (to which U applies) from values and forms of life, on which philosophical ethics must keep silent; and (c) by incorporating the systematic consideration of consequences of action into the factors of moral judgment in order to avoid the pitfalls of an ethic of ultimate ends (Habermas 1984a, 229). The first move is designed to counter Hegel's attack on the poverty of Kant's moral psychology and especially on the cleft between reason and feeling that pervades Kant's conception. The second move responds to Hegel's contention that the categorical imperative—or U, for that matter—helps us to discriminate good norms from bad ones only if we already know what we value most. The third move is designed to counter Hegel's contention that any formal ethic based on an abstract principle is bound to remain a self-righteous but ineffectual ethic of good intentions. The significance and worth of Habermas's program cannot be overestimated, especially if one considers that over the past 150 years philosophical thought oriented toward emancipation has always privileged the Hegelian priority of constructing "the state with good laws" over the Kantian priority of never treating others as means. The problem, however, is that in his critical rescue of the Kantian leitmotif Habermas keeps closer to Kant than is really necessary for his purposes. As I will argue below, from this fact stem many of the problems that haunt his *Diskursethik*.

Let us go back to the merits of Habermas's program. The first two are Kantian emphases. Habermas has an exceptional ability, just as Kant did, to aim his ethical theory precisely at the core of the ethical problem, that is, what it means to feel that a norm is *right*. His account of rightness, however, mitigates Kant's views in one important respect. In lieu of the a priori cogency of the categorical imperative, Habermas offers a principle of universalization whose cogency rests on an empirically falsifiable reconstruction of the presuppositions of argumentation. Habermas again plays a Kantian theme when, in spite of his acknowledgment that ethical action must "come to terms" with the strategic imperatives of the world as it is, he insists on distancing the *Diskursethik* from all political Machiavellianism, including that motivated by the desire for emancipation. Within the framework of the *Diskursethik* no one can legitimately play the role that Hegel assigned to the world-historical individual. Even though it is part of Habermas's program to integrate the systematic consideration of the consequences of action within ethical judgment, he pushes on the Kantian pedal of intention as the key determinant of right conduct. However, the solipsistic intention of the Kantian subject is transformed, in Habermas's account, into a process of discursive will formation. There are prices to be paid, to be sure. One of them is the much lamented lack of a "Habermasian politics" and the difficulty of deriving one. This difficulty he shares once more with Kant, because for both of them strategic action can never be justified in its own right but can at most be tolerated as an unfortunate second best. Yet the yields to be gained make it a price worth paying.

The last two strong points of Habermas's *Diskursethik* strike Hegelian chords. When he retorts against the skeptic that only in an "abstract" sense can we choose between stepping in and keeping out of rational argument, because no form of life or identity can survive without recourse to communicative action, Habermas is speaking in a Hegelian tongue. In that context "abstract" means, as it did for Hegel, "senseless because arbitrarily detached from the whole." Finally, even though U is meant to be as transhistorical a criterion as Kant's categorical imperative and is also grounded on transhistorical considerations (the unavoidable presuppositions of discourse), Habermas in a Hegelian way does not detach the emergence of this principle from the developmental process that has led to the rise of Western modernity. The fixed universalism of the Kantian ethic gives way to a dynamic approach that does not renounce universalism.

Let me now turn to the problems with Habermas's approach to ethics. Benhabib (1982, 57–59) and Wellmer (1985), among others, have recently offered valuable critiques of the foundations of the

Diskursethik. Benhabib has pointed to a circularity implicit in Habermas's use of the notion of "ideal speech situation." On the one hand, such requirements as an unrestricted access to dialogue and the equality of chances to raise and challenge claims are thought of as features of the ideal speech situation. On the other hand, the normative cogency of such requirements could be established—as with all other validity claims—only through general consensus in the ideal speech situation. Wellmer criticizes Habermas for his failure to differentiate, in his attempt to ground U as an *ethical* principle, between what it means for a *maxim of conduct* to be morally mandatory and what it means for a *norm* to be valid or legitimate. According to Wellmer, although Habermas intends to reconstruct the principle underlying our intuitions about the ethical appropriateness of modes and maxims of conduct, in the end he gives us only a (disputable) account of our intuitions on the legitimacy of norms. Furthermore, Wellmer revives against Habermas the objection from which Habermas tried to rescue Apel: that the ethical cogency of the presuppositions of discourse does not extend beyond the boundaries of argumentation. The presuppositions of discourse, far from implying anything at the level of conduct, for Wellmer have rather the status of *constitutive rules* for the language game: moral argument. No one can violate them without falling into a performative contradiction, just as no one can move a knight diagonally and still claim to be playing chess. Yet these presuppositions can no more orient our choice of a line of conduct than chess rules can orient our action outside the context of the game.

However, let us set aside these lines of criticism and give the benefit of the doubt to the *Diskursethik.* Let us assume that Habermas's grounding of U in transcendental-pragmatic terms could be strengthened and made invulnerable to these and other criticisms (which I am not sure is the case). Still the project of the *Diskursethik* as it is formulated now would be doomed to failure by its excessive formalism.

As we have seen above, against the skeptic's contention that the pluralism of values does in most cases prevent ethical questions from being rationally set one way or another, Habermas introduces U as a rule of argumentation capable of generating rational consensus. Later he qualifies the efficacy of this move when he admits that rational consensus about the validity of norms can be achieved only from within an already made choice of values, and that about such a choice between competing values the *Diskursethik* has little to say. However, the intersubjective assessment of the validity of a norm when all the participants are agreed on the values they wish to further is not really the issue. At least it is not the objection that any sensible skeptic would raise. Rather, the problem is that the pluralism of values is a sociological fact of modern society. *More often than not* our discussions about the validity of norms take place within contexts where the proponents of different theses also refer to different and competing value choices. Then, unless Habermas subscribes in his heart to the unlikely supposition that underlying society there exists one set of ultimate values recognized by all, it is hard to see how his *Diskursethik* can deal with the reality of contemporary moral life. As it stands now, his adoption of a formalistic perspective risks making the *Diskursethik* formally sound but irrelevant with regard to the lifeworld, because the conditions under which the *Diskursethik* can best generate rational consensus never (or very seldom) occur and, instead, in the most frequent cases of moral conflict it must remain silent. Furthermore, in Habermas's response to the skeptic's seventh objection one gets the irritating impression that he tends to minimize problems that are devastating for his account of ethics. For instance, in the space of just a few paragraphs he liquidates the issue of value choice, the fact that whenever inner needs come into the picture the "softer" forms of aesthetic and therapeutic argument "weaken" the *Diskursethik's* capacity to generate consensus, and also the fact that sometimes ethical principles must be balanced against strategic considerations. Habermas deals with these issues as though they simply represented innocuous "limitations" of the *Diskursethik* and were not, instead, the crucial problems to which the *Diskursethik* (or any other procedural ethic, for that matter) has so far failed to give a satisfactory solution. I would like to pursue this discussion with reference to a concrete example: Let me introduce a case of moral conflict I consider to be fairly representative of the kind of conflicts faced by contemporary moral actors; I will apply the *Diskursethik* to it, and, finally, I will discuss the results.

> *A moral dilemma:* A moral actor we will call Jones has borrowed some money from Bob, a friend he has known since high school. Bob holds a good job, and over the past few years has saved some money to buy a sports car. But the same morning that Bob is about to visit a dealer, Jones comes to see him and asks to borrow almost precisely that amount of money. Jones's father is seriously ill and needs immediate surgery. Jones reassures his friend that the debt will be paid back in two years.

At the time this takes place Jones barely has enough money for his rent and meals. He plans to finish in a few months the score of a symphony that is already scheduled for recording, and on this he places his hopes for a substantial improvement of his financial situation. The operation does not help Jones's father, who dies a few weeks thereafter. After this event, Jones suffers several breakdowns. Since he is unable to concentrate on his musical work, his chance for recording his symphony falls through. The prospect of completing the symphony becomes increasingly remote, and with it also Jones's chances for any reliable return from his musical work.

After the two years elapse, Bob wants his money back. This poses a gruesome alternative for Jones: either to take a secure job, negotiate a mortgage, pay his friend back, and then pay the loan back to the bank in fifteen years or, if Bob refuses another deferment, simply to postpone repayment until some better time that in fact may never arrive.

Jones is repelled by the second alternative but, on the other hand, knows himself well enough. Fifteen years of work at a full-time dull job most likely will spell the end of his aspirations of becoming a composer, no matter how hard he tries. Furthermore, the idea of giving up his artistic career frightens him. In the context of therapy, Jones has learned to see his interest in composing music as more than just the pursuit of an ambitious goal. From therapy Jones has gained the insight that his depression and his inability to enjoy life, which once led him to seek help, stem from the precariousness of his inner equilibrium. He oscillates between recurrent fears of self-dissolution and compensatory fantasies of omnipotence. The cultivation of his gift for music has become for Jones, toward the end of his therapy, a good way of practicing a mature and realistic relation to the world and to himself. It has become the solid ground on which he builds his sense of continuity, purpose, and cohesion. He fears that no other activity, let alone a clerical job, could replace music in this respect.

On the other hand, Bob wants his money back. He feels that by patiently waiting for months and months he has given Jones a more than fair chance to work out some way to pay. Bob likes to think of himself as a down-to-earth and realistic person who has been wise enough to give up his youthful fantasies and get started on a solid career as soon as possible. He is now manager of the local branch of a large bank, and with the money that he makes every year Bob can afford many things, which constitute for him a compensation for the dullness of his workday routine. One of these things was a sports car he once test drove and has dreamed of ever since. Bob firmly intends not to let a daydreamer like Jones spoil his chance to buy that car. Also, Bob thinks that to grant Jones a deferment, with no guarantee that it will really be the last, would only encourage Jones to indulge his childish fantasies.

Thus when Jones calls one last time, Bob flatly refuses to consider any alternative to quick payment.

The ethical question is then: Under these conditions, should Jones pay his debt?

I take this example to be representative of the kind of dilemma faced by contemporary moral actors in two respects. First, the values that direct Bob's life are not the same as the ones that appeal to Jones, even though the two characters live in the same society and perhaps even in the same social class. Second, the impact of one line of conduct on the self-identity of an actor is part of what should be decided before we take a stance. But Habermas could retort, it is unfair to test the *Diskursethik* on this moral dilemma. For value choice and the evaluation of the balance of identities necessarily take place within a "softer" form of argument, where eventual consensus cannot be guaranteed (Habermas 1983). The adequacy of the *Diskursethik* should be tested on cases where conflict or disagreement touches on the validity of norms, not on the appropriateness of values. This objection, however, loses much of its poignancy if one reflects on the following facts.

First, the conflict between Bob and Jones is about whether the circumstances of Jones's life justify a suspension of the general norm that debts should be paid back. Bob and Jones (presumably) agree on the validity of the norm in general but disagree on whether it should apply in Jones's case. They disagree because they apply the norm in the light of different values or in the light of different conceptions of the good life. This kind of conflict is far more common than the symmetric one, which involves complete agreement on values but disagreement on the norms that should implement them. To be sure, sociological observations cannot settle philosophical arguments, but nonetheless they can shed light on the context within which philosophical constructs must make sense. From recent studies on the cultural trends of advanced industrial societies (Inglehart 1977; Yankelovich 1981), it emerges that about 20 percent of the population of those societies subscribes to what has been called "postmaterialist" values, another 20 to 25 percent remains tied to the old life-style of possessive individualism and acquisitiveness, and the remaining 50 to 60 percent falls somewhere in between. Under these conditions one can be fairly confident that the conflicts between two or more social actors will almost always involve people who subscribe to different sets of values.

Second, the evaluation of the impact of conduct on the identity of people is not an isolated "special case" sometimes impinging on the capacity of U to generate consensus. Rather, it is the norm for a postconventional moral actor. The evolution of the modern personality also points in the direction of a greater and more refined ability to perceive one's own and others' inner needs. Then the "softer" forms of argument, which are linked with the interpretation of needs and identities, are *always* going to be in the picture of moral judgment and not just in certain "limit" cases. If this is true, how worthy is an ethic that can generate consensus only in those cases where no identity or inner need is at stake—such as perhaps general questions of fairness in political, legal, and administrative matters—but has little to say in the everyday contexts of moral decision?

In light of these considerations, it makes sense to test the *Diskursethik* in the Bob and Jones case. For one thing, from the difficulties of the *Diskursethik* one can learn in which direction to move in order to conceive a philosophical ethic that—as Habermas rightly requires—does not fall behind Kant, is universalistic and cognitivist, but is also *relevant* in the most common cases of moral choice. Then let us consider the question: What would Jones do if he adopted the *Diskursethik?* The first indication he would draw from Habermas's ethic is to try to convince Bob to acknowledge his good reasons and thus to allow him a deferment. Bob's consent would close the incident. But suppose that, just as happens with Kohlberg's druggist who refuses a lifesaving drug to somebody in order to make more money (Kohlberg 1981), Bob turns a deaf ear. Then Jones has to make up his mind "monologically," and things begin to get complicated. The next best thing to obtaining Bob's consent in a *real* discourse, according to the *Diskursethik*, is to instantiate this discourse in one's mind and see if Bob—now imagined as able to see through his interests and neurotic compulsions and as no longer angry at Jones or strategically motivated—would freely consent to a deferment. Here the question raised by Lukes, and never convincingly answered by Habermas, receives its proper place (Lukes 1982; Habermas 1982). That is, in such a case, how real must this imagined Bob be? Should we imagine an ideal discussion with a character as he in fact is? Then the result can only be negative. Bob imagined as Bob really is would still say no. On the other hand, Bob imagined as he *could* be if only he were not blinded by self-interest, neurosis, or whatever, could say yes. But then to what extent is this new Bob still Bob? We could imagine Bob as a liberated, rational, and sensitive person and be almost certain that he would then agree to a deferment. Yet this imagined character would no longer bear a meaningful resemblance to the real Bob. Where are we to stand between these two extremes, according to Habermas?

Now let us turn to the easy case. Bob decides to talk things over and agrees to meet Jones and discuss the matter with complete openness. Assume that both Bob and Jones are motivated by the best intentions and that their conversation comes as close as is humanly possible to the ideal speech situation. Still the *Diskursethik* would run into difficulties, even on the most favorable terrain. In fact, for Habermas the source of the normative validity of a correct moral judgment is the force of the best *argument*, not the plausibility of the best *ethical intuition*. To be sure, moral arguments express our ethical intuitions. But they do so by degrees of approximation. They are not *identical* with intuitions. There may be gaps between the far-reaching quality of one's intuition of what is right to do in a given situation and the contingent limitations of one's ability to express this intuition in the abstract and the reflexive language of practical reason. Even in the ideal speech situation, such limitations may exist owing to age, education, psychological states, or relative distribution of argumentative ability. Sometimes the historical context is such that there exists a whole stock of developed ideas that make it easy to make the best argument in support of one intuition; on the other hand, a relative lack of a similar background may make it difficult to make "the best argument" in favor of the correct intuition. Instead, Habermas makes it true *by definition* that the argument accepted as the best in the ideal speech situation always embeds the best intuition about the matter at hand. This strikes me as too strong an assumption, even by Habermas's standards. Such an assumption introduces a rationalist bias into Habermas's ethic, in that reflexive constructs (in this case arguments) come to be valued more than the intuitions for which they are the vehicle, and this is bound to generate further difficulties. Assume that Jones is subjectively certain of the collapse of his identity if he has to give up music. Yet Bob, unconvinced, makes the best argument about Jones's ethical duty to abide by his commitments and Jones, as a conscientious follower of the *Diskursethik*, pays the money. Later he does collapse and attempts suicide a few times; he survives, but his life becomes totally meaningless. In this case Bob need not feel guilty. Of course, he may feel sorry for his mistake and thereby win some of our sympathy, but strictly speaking no one can reproach him if he does not. For no one is under an obligation to feel guilty for doing what is right. On the other hand, if Jones unilaterally refuses to pay even though Bob has made the best argument, he is doing something wrong. If we independently consult his therapist and the therapist assures us that, to the best of his knowledge and professional experience, Jones could not withstand the loss of his artistic activity without collapsing, this is still irrelevant for the *Diskursethik*. At most we can invite Bob for another round of discussion and see if the new piece of evidence impresses him, but we cannot retrospectively say that Jones *ought* to have done what he did—refuse to pay when the best argument suggested that he should pay.

More difficulties arise if we consider our example from a third-person perspective, that is, from the standpoint of a moral philosopher who tries to separate rigorously the moment of normative rightness from the broader frame of questions about the good life and values. Two implications of the *Diskursethik* are of interest here: (a) from an *ethical* point of view, Bob's claim for his money is right, normatively valid; from an *aesthetic* standpoint we are free to say that we do not like his personality or that we like Jones's personality and life plan better; and (b) Jones must pay in all cases unless he obtains Bob's consent to a deferment. What problems arise from these conclusions? Habermas (1979, 1983) draws extensively on Kohlberg's work (1981) without ever taking distance from the various applications of Kohlberg's moral theory to concrete examples. It is then fair to assume that Habermas does not disagree with Kohlberg on the most important example, Heinz's dilemma. In this dilemma Heinz's wife needs a particular drug, produced by a druggist who is determined to profit from his discovery and would not sell it for less than his price. The woman will not survive without the drug, and Heinz has no way to raise the amount of money demanded by the druggist. The question is: In such a situation should Heinz steal the drug? Kohlberg assumes that every postconventional moral actor should answer positively. My dilemma is constructed in an analogous way, except for one feature: what is at stake is not physical life but identity, not Jones's physical survival but his ability to remain the same person. Although Kohlberg discusses the druggist's claim to his property and the woman's claim to her life as *rights* rather than norms, it is apparent that these rights are much closer to values in their scope and generality. The relevant way to phrase Kohlberg's question is: Should human life take precedence over property? It is hard to see this as a choice between two norms implementing the same value. Thus when Habermas insists that a modern universalistic ethic can answer only questions about the validity of norms, it is also hard to see how this claim can be reconciled with Kohlberg's substantive claim of a life-over-property hierarchy. Furthermore, if Kohlberg's solution to the Heinz dilemma can be vindicated within Habermas's conception of ethics, it is even harder to see how the *Diskursethik* could side with a property-over-identity hierarchy in the Bob-and-Jones example. For if we allow that Heinz has a right to steal the drug, how are we to deny Jones's right to "force" a deferment upon Bob? One could say, perhaps, that we can never be so certain about identities as with physical life. In other words, it is easier to know if one would die without a drug than to know whether one would become another person if deprived of a cherished activity. But this is far from true. The statements of medical science are also probabilistic and based on experience, just as the statement of an analyst is. Only a matter of degree separates the certainty with which a physician can say that under certain conditions someone is going to die from the certainty with which a psychoanalyst can say that under certain conditions someone will break down. The difference is not to be seen in terms of probability. Rather, it consists in the fact that the knowledge of medical science is nomothetic and the knowledge psychoanalysts rely on is based on understanding. But do we want to say that this nomothetic quality makes the prediction a better one? Do we want to say that *this* makes Heinz more justified in stealing the drug than Jones in not paying his debt? On the other hand, one could say that the difference between surviving and dying is clear enough to anyone in a way that the difference between remaining oneself and becoming another is not. Or, in other words, that survival is an all-or-none endeavor whereas identities can be altered by degrees. Again, this objection rests on a misunderstanding. If we modify Kohlberg's example to the effect that Heinz's wife will not die but is at risk of being paralyzed, we could still find a general consensus on Heinz's being justified in stealing the drug. But what if his wife risks only a partial paralysis or indeed a very minor one? Where would we draw the line between an impairment of life that is serious enough to override the claims of property and one that is not? If one sees death as the ultimate and irreversible impairment of life, then the impression that moral questions are easier to solve when they concern physical life rather then identity problems is quickly dispelled.

Another difficulty has to do with the idea of a distinction between *questions of justice,* capable of receiving a universally and intersubjectively valid answer, and *evaluative questions,* usually answered either in terms of subjective preference or in terms of the value orientations embedded in cultural identities and life-forms. Although considered at an abstract level the distinction makes sense, in the context of a concrete moral choice Habermas's expectation that the two orders of questions can be kept separated seems too optimistic. For one thing, actions are interpretations of doings from a given perspective. Depending on the description under which it is considered, an action then may or may not fall within the scope of the *Diskursethik*. For example, when Bob utters the sentence by which he claims his money, he can be seen as performing several acts, such as (at least) a locutionary act, an act of reference, an illocutionary act (a request), and a perlocutionary act. Under one description, from an illocutionary perspective, what Bob does is request that his money be given back to him, and as such his action would fall within the class of actions about which it is possible to decide intersubjectively whether they are justified. Under another description, however, what Bob does can be seen as an instance of somebody's using the normative weight of legal right to obtain the satisfaction of a desire at the cost of a friend's identity. Yet under this description what Bob does would rather fall into the realm of those outlooks on life that can be evaluated only in terms of subjective preference. In other words, the problem of the plurality of values that Habermas tried to solve by introducing his distinction between questions of justice and questions about the good life has merely been shifted onto another plane. Now we have a criterion U for rationally deciding whether an action is justified, but we do not have a criterion for rationally choosing between various descriptions of the same action. In order for the distinction between questions of justice and questions about the good life to play its role, one has to presuppose that moral actors always know, and always agree on, the category their actions fall into. Again, this seems too optimistic an assumption.

The listing of the shortcomings of the *Diskursethik* could continue, but at this point it would add little to the specification of the common pattern that underlies all the problems linked with Habermas's ethical views. This common pattern can best be described as an excessive residue of Kantianism. In spite of his attempt to prop up Kant's weak moral psychology with Piaget's and Kohlberg's empirical generalizations, and to preempt the accusation of self-righteous sterility by requiring the systematic consideration of consequences and rebuke the Hegelian charge of bogus contentlessness by detaching norms from values, it is still ironic that Habermas's *Diskursethik* should reproduce many of the same weaknesses of the Kantian ethic. For example, Habermas recognizes that the certainty of reaching rational consensus diminishes when the evaluation of self-identities is introduced into the picture of moral judgment, but he fails to draw the proper conclusion. That is, if one also realizes that most ethical dilemmas require the evaluation of the impact of alternative courses of action on identities, and if it belongs to the notion of a mature postconventional actor that he or she always addresses such orders of problems, then one should accord a more central place to empathy, taste, and reflective judgment. Instead, Habermas tends to restrict the meaning of ethics to reduce the significance of this element of *phronesis* or taste to a matter of application and to the psychology of moral actors. Competent moral actors are generally able to mediate abstract norms and concrete cases, but the principles underlying this competence (i.e., the inner logic of the judgment of taste and the potential for universalism contained therein) are not seen as part of ethics and thus are not worked out adequately within the *Diskursethik*. This I take to be a weakness of Habermas's conception of ethics and, moreover, one that stems from quite the same reasons as do the weakness of Kant's moral psychology. Both Habermas and Kant tend to overlook the *real* conditions under which ethical judgment takes place and consequently fail to take these conditions into account on a philosophical plane.

The same "unrealistic" flavor of the Kantian approach to ethics can be felt when Habermas dismisses as "trivial" the questions raised by the Weberian version of an ethic of responsibility or when he considers the temporal and motivational limitations inherent in every real discourse to be "trivial requisites of the institutionalization of discourse" that "by no means contradict the partially counterfactual content of the presuppositions of discourse" (Habermas 1983, 102). Precisely because these trivial requisites are not adequately taken into account, the *Diskursethik*'s counterfactual standard cannot provide much guidance for action. We are left, as in the case of Bob and Jones, with questions: What is a just solution short of consensus? Which criteria should I adopt if consensus cannot be reached? The invocation of the counterfactual criterion does not solve the problem. Can we say that from the counterfactual specification of the ideal speech situation it follows that the longer a discussion has gone on the more likely it is the agreed solution will be just? Or that the less restricted the access to the discussion the more likely it is the resulting agreement will be rational? Neither of these criteria seems a convincing guide for action.

Furthermore, if the context creates a tension between all the criteria derivable from the ideal speech situation, the *Diskursethik* proves even less able to orient action. Suppose that the available resources require us to choose between allowing more time for the discussion and having more participants for a shorter time, or between having more participants with more strategic motivations discussing for a longer time and very few good-willed actors with very little time for reaching agreement. What indication could we draw from the *Diskursethik* in this case? What would be best for us to do? Again, it is hard to derive a convincing answer from the *Diskursethik*. The only possible solution could be to balance all the various factors (time, participation, and motivation) in such a way as to best approximate the ideal speech situation.[4] But this is easier said than done. In fact, neither Habermas's concept of the ideal speech situation nor Apel's complementary principle of application contains any a priori specification of the relative weight of the various aspects of the ideal speech situation (time, participation, motivation, reciprocity of role taking, etc.), nor is it easy to see how they could. Unless Apel is able to ground convincingly some a priori priorities—for example, "it is better to lose two points on the dimension of unrestricted participation if one point can be gained on the dimension of nonstrategic motivation"— his complementary principle will not take us far. The *balancing* of all the relevant elements that determine which of two alternative courses of action will bring us closer to the ideal speech situation still will have to be based on that kind of prudence or *phronesis* about whose inner logic the *Diskursethik* has little to say (see Benhabib 1982, 70–72).

Habermas tries to counter the skeptic's objection (that the supposedly contentless procedure for generating consensus about the *rightness* of norms presupposes a common vision of the *good* and that because the latter is culture specific so is the former) by limiting

---

4. In fact, this is the solution suggested by Apel (1985); he tries to formulate a general principle underlying the correct application of U. According to this principle, we should apply the *Diskursethik* in such a way as to reduce as far as possible the gap between the ideal speech situation and the actual communicative contexts. This principle of maximizing communicative patterns should for Apel render superfluous the neo-Aristotelian concept of *phronesis*. Also, Habermas has recently turned his attention to the question of the principles underlying the *impartial application* of the *Diskursethik*. See Habermas, (1985). Prima facie it seems doubtful that such attempts to extend the morality-as-impartiality approach also to the problems of "application" can really solve difficulties that stem in the first place from the separation of issues of "grounding" and problems of "application." However, Habermas's attempt to develop an answer along these lines is only at its beginning.

the validity of this objection to a third-person approach to the issue. From the perspective of a moral actor directly involved in deliberation (Habermas argues), the issue of the relativity of the value horizon within which one operates simply does not arise. Just as every scientist trying to explain some phenomenon assumes the position of the last scientist and every historian takes on the epistemic role of the last historian, so every moral actor deliberates from the standpoint of the last judgment. While this is certainly so, it is not clear what we are to make of it. Why not call it an *illusion*, albeit a necessary one, to which moral actors may succumb to various degrees? In fact, ethical competence has to do not only with the capacity for correctly applying the universalization procedure, but also with the ability to distance oneself from as large a section as possible of the horizon of values within which one operates. Thus, for example, we understand Kant's views on excluding women from suffrage as an almost inevitable reflection of the limitations of his historical situation. Yet his defense of the death penalty as the only adequate punishment for a murderer strikes us as somewhat less justified. Even more unjustified appears to us his idea that there is nothing wrong with killing an illegitimate child because, being born outside marriage, this child "is also outside the protection of the law" (Kant 1965, 106). In all three cases Kant offers a consistent application of his moral theory. Where then does our increasing repulsion for his first, second, and third conclusions come from? It comes from our perception that to an increasing extent in all three cases he *could* have distanced himself from his value horizon and yet failed to do so. We hold *him* more responsible for his views on infanticide than for his views on women's rights, because we imagine it should have been easier to see through the time-boundness of the values underlying leniency toward infanticide than through the discriminatory quality of patri- archal values. From this perspective, the fact that in the first-person attitude moral actors forget the relativity of their background values and claim universality for their applications of U should be cause for alarm rather than rejoicing. Our reaction to Kant's three conclusions shows that alongside the correct application of the universalization procedure there exists another dimension on which we evaluate the soundness of moral judgment. This other dimension has to do with actors' ability to question as much as possible of the vision of the good that underlies their judgment about the right. And in a society where the diversity of value orientations is large, it has to do also with the ability to mediate, without compromising, different visions of the good. But the *Diskursethik*, just like Kant's ethics, can offer only a peripheral place to this dimension of *phronesis*. Suppose that in eighteenth-century Königsberg Kant is summoned as a member of the jury at a trial where somebody is accused of infanticide and the defense pleads "not guilty" on account of the child's illegitimacy. Suppose that the discussion within the jury comes sufficiently close to the ideal speech situation. Someone has the vague intuition that every child should be equally protected by the law, but needless to say Kant makes the best argument. One could say that if only the debate had gone on longer, in the long run Kant would have been convinced. But let us suppose that none of the participants felt any pressure and all felt satisfied with ending the discussion at the point they did, with the agreement that the man should be acquitted. There is no way of saying, within the framework of the *Diskursethik*, that the jury's decision was wrong or unjust at the time it was made. There is no way of saying that the intuition of the other members of the jury represented a more *prudent* or *wiser* stance toward the values of the time and as such deserved at least as much consensus as Kant's more articulate argument. Leaving open for the moment the question of the grounds on which we can now say that the jury's decision was *then* unjust, the inability to say so is one of the most serious consequences of Habermas's reducing prudence or *phronesis* to a mere psychological quality of the actor.

Furthermore, Habermas shares with Kant the disputable assumption that morality has to do with following a law. There are important differences between them, to be sure. Kant saw the "moral law" as something that could introduce into the evaluation of human action the same kind of unbending certainty that he associated with the synthetic a priori basis of natural science. Habermas softens this tone very much when he speaks of a principle of universalization that is rooted in the presuppositions of discourse and that is to be used for a dialogical solution of moral conflicts. Yet for both Habermas and Kant to act ethically evokes the image of following a rule or a procedure that alone can put us beyond reproach. At least this image is evoked more readily by their moral views than by the alternative images of acting ethically because of virtue, prudence, or empathy. No sheer reversal of these priorities is advocated here, but rather a true mediation of the procedural and prudential aspects of ethics.

Finally, as much as Habermas wishes to distance himself from the Kantian notion of two distinct "realms" (Habermas 1985, 16), that of necessity and that of freedom, his ethical and social views have not completely broken away from Kant's rigid dualism. Rather, Habermas's thought seems to reproduce the Kantian opposition of the phenomenal and the intelligible world under the new categories of the system and the lifeworld, of instrumental and communicative action. The limitations of this approach become clear in connection with the role of conflict (social and moral) within Habermas's views. On the one hand, Habermas wants to retain a positive role for conflict as a motor for the development of society. Yet on the other hand, in a legitimate social order (Habermas 1981) presumably the system will be kept in check by the lifeworld, and its role in social reproduction will be limited to those dealings with outer nature that are necessary for the maintenance of society. However, one gets the impression that once the current excess of systemic influences on the lifeworld has been eliminated, there will be no place from which conflict can arise. A lifeworld that reproduces its symbolic structures entirely and solely through communicative action—as *ought* to be the case for Habermas—is bound to be a thoroughly pacified lifeworld. The illusory perspective of a conflict-free society, or of a society where conflict has been reduced to irrelevant quarrel, has been eradicated from Habermas's social theory.[5] A parallel tension traverses his conception of ethics. Here Habermas often plays two dissonant themes. When he explicitly addresses the evaluation of life-forms or the plurality of values, he rightly acknowledges that values and cultural identities come only in the plural. Yet when he discusses other aspects of his moral theory, one again receives the impression that for Habermas moral conflict originates only in the clash of strategic, and thus illegitimate, motivations and that if only we could rid ourselves of the undue pressure of system imperatives and act communicatively throughout, there would be no moral conflicts but only a harmonious process of communal will formation. Habermas seems to waver between two perspectives, neither of which is really viable for him. In fact, if moral conflict is imported into social interaction only through the undue influence of the system, then a Habermasian ideal society where interaction is undistorted cannot be distinguished from the Kantian "realm of ends." As in Kant's fictional

5. For a detailed criticism of Habermas's transformation of his conceptual distinction of instrumental and communicative action into the misleading image of society as de facto split between the corresponding spheres of the system and the lifeworld, see Honneth (1985, chaps. 5 and 6). Also, in chapter 9 Honneth offers an interesting reconstruction of the single theoretical decisions that have led Habermas to this new formulation of his theory of society.

world, also in Habermas's there would be no room for *real* diversity among moral actors and thus no real individuation either (Wellmer 1985, 27; Benhabib 1982, 71–72). On the other hand, if Habermas wishes to maintain that even if the system was perfectly kept in check there would nonetheless be moral conflict (because moral actors would continue to interpret their needs and life circumstances in the light of different and sometimes competing values), then his ethical theory appears somewhat off balance. In fact, Habermas should then recognize that the questions of how one can validly choose between values and of what constitutes prudence in this kind of choice are crucial issues. If even in the good society there will be moral conflicts, then the essential moral quality will still be that *phronesis* whose role Habermas tries to downplay.

To sum up, the problems of a recurrent overlooking of the real conditions under which moral judgment takes place, of an excessive emphasis on rules and procedures at the expense of *phronesis* or taste, and of a relative inability to orient human action, so typical of Kant's ethics, continue to haunt Habermas's *Diskursethik*. Habermas's most recent tendency has been to accentuate this formalistic, but in his opinion more justifiable, approach and to abandon altogether his earlier overtures to what potentially could have developed into a more substantive (but not metaphysical) view of ethics. Here the memory of stage 7 looms large. When Habermas spoke of a seventh stage of moral reasoning, beyond the six outlined by Kohlberg, he characterized this stage as marking the transition from a "formalistic ethic of duty to a universal ethics of speech" (Habermas 1979, 93). One of the features that differentiated the proposed stage 7 from Kohlberg's stage 6 was the fact that "need interpretations are no longer assumed as given" but are drawn into the process of discursive will formation through their being rendered "communicatively fluid and transparent." Furthermore, the values through which needs are shaped and interpreted would also come to be questioned. The guiding idea underlying morality in stage 7 was a "freedom that limits itself in the intention of reconciling—if not identifying—worthiness with happiness" (Habermas 1979, 94). It is unfortunate that this promising attempt to overcome a purely formalistic view of ethics has subsequently been given up by Habermas, who no longer considers stage 7 a stage on its own and also questions the distinction between Kohlberg's stage 6 and stage 5. No one can deny the boldness of Habermas's suggestion: rather than dreaming of solving the problem of the plurality of values, the problem of the intersubjective validity of aesthetic interpretations, or the problem of "dirty hands," it is wiser for a postconventional moral actor to learn how to live with them. However, when Habermas suggests that nothing really meaningful can be said about these problems, he is probably going too far. If he accuses the skeptic of overdramatizing these limitations of moral judgment, he himself seems to exceed on the opposite dimension of a complacent optimism. No ethic can "live with these problems" and retreat into the invulnerable fortress of the transcendental-pragmatic foundation of U. For in so doing such an ethic would lose the ability to orient action and would thereby unwillingly vindicate Hegel's verdict, that any formalistic ethic is bound to remain an ingenious exercise of the intellect, irrelevant to life. The problem with Habermas's rescue of Kant's approach to ethics is that he has succeeded in *immunizing* Kant's case against Hegel's critique but has so far failed to make Kant's ethic more relevant to life.

Toward a Nonformalistic Diskursethik

If the diagnosis sketched above is correct, what remedy could be adopted against the excessive formalism of the *Diskursethik?* We want a view of ethics that does not retreat into metaethical considerations and remains procedural and universalistic but at the same time is better able than the *Diskursethik* as it stands now to orient our action in the world. This last requisite I take to imply that this ethic not only must contain a specification of rightness or justice, but must also say something about the good. Yet this is problematic. Habermas is right when he claims that today no metaphysical grounding of the good life could be convincing and when he points to the dangers of Hegel's recourse to a "futurized community" as a standpoint from which reason can then legislate upon the validity of life-forms. From this, however, he draws the dubious conclusion that a sound ethic should remain silent altogether on the subject of the good life. Thus Habermas's *Diskursethik* comes to occupy a peculiar position within contemporary moral philosophy. Compared to Rawls's ethic, for instance, Habermas's approach provides a more convincing account of the right, but because Rawls's theory also embeds a theory of the good—which Habermas lacks entirely—on the whole Rawls's ethic appears more relevant to life and more capable of orienting action. Why not try, then, *to incorporate a theory of the good* into Habermas's *Diskursethik,* in spite of his protestation that one cannot do so?

The project of correcting the formalistic flavor of the *Diskursethik* through adding a theory of the good meets with a basic difficulty. How are we to reconcile our modern diffidence toward all "positive" intimations of good values or good life-forms with the desire to avoid the pitfalls of formalism? I suggest that we take a "negative" approach to the good and combine it with proceduralism. That is, we will not specify what the good is but will use only a formal notion of the good to keep in check the normative force of the best argument. We may never know what the good life is, but we can be in a position to say that certain ways of life, and the values that pervade them, are less conducive to the good than others.[6] Something similar occurs within aesthetic theory. Namely, the difficulty of providing a positive specification of the beautiful does not prevent us from pointing out how concrete works of art are more or less distant from emboding beauty. But is it not contradictory to maintain that one way of life is less conducive to the good than another and at the same time to say that nobody can spell out what the good is? To say that X is less good than Y, must one not know already what the good is? No contradiction arises if one conceives the good in formal terms. One can conceive the good as the ability to live one's life as fully as one can, which I take to mean—in contrast to other interpretations according to which it would mean "to live by the instant"—to undergo a succession of states and events, from birth to death, that can at any point be reconstructed as coherent narrative, whatever its specific content. It is part of the notion of a coherent narrative that it must include a protagonist and that this protagonist possesses, among other things, a quality called *autonomous agency*, exercised in the process of achieving certain goals. A narrative where the protagonist accomplishes no action whatever is only an avant-garde experiment, not really a narrative. This vision of the good does not imply that one should look for money, power, glory, pleasure, recognition, good intimacy, or any other specific thing. It does include the idea, however, that—as is the case with narratives—the fuller and worthier one's life, the larger the number, extension, and intricacies of the subplots and parallel themes that enrich the core without subtracting from the coherence of the whole. The telos of each individual's life narrative is the acquisition of what is good for that person. The good life for man, then, is the life spent seeking the good

6. Recently Habermas has attenuated his rejection of the idea that modern ethics might have anything to say about the worthiness of values or life-forms. Now he acknowledges the possibility of investigating the *necessary* conditions of a good life. See Habermas (1986).

life (MacIntyre 1981, 204). It is up to the individual to determine which concrete goals to pursue, but at the same time not all choices are equally conducive to the attainment of the good. We could say, for instance, that a certain pattern of life is less conducive to the expression of a certain identity than another way of life, on the grounds that the former life-style may undermine the autonomy of the person or is more likely to fragment the person's life narrative into a series of unconnected subplots. The inner logic of this kind of judgment has been worked out by Kant in his discussion of aesthetic judgment (1951, 30–33) and further elaborated along hermeneutic lines by Gadamer (1975, 33–55). The key feature of this type of judgment is its "soft" universalism. That is, its validity does not depend on the factual agreement of other people, but rather points to what everybody *ought* to think; yet on the other hand its cogency can only be made plausible, not *demonstrated*. What is the *ethical* relevance, in terms of a theory of right, of this new vantage point that allows us to pass judgment, albeit with the "soft" cogency of aesthetic judgment, on the relative worthiness of values and ways of life? We must carefully avoid being misled by some tempting, yet erroneous, conclusions. In particular, we must avoid the conclusion that from the superior quality of somebody's life plan follows any consequence —positive or negative—regarding that person's ethical claim to something. For example, we cannot say that what justified Jones's refusal to pay back his debt is the fact that his life project is worthier than Bob's. That on a separate dimension of judgment indeed we can say that Jones's life plan is better than Bob's is not really the reason he can be exempted from paying his debt. Rather, the reason is that, if Jones loses his potential to become a musician, his chance to attain the good life (as he defines it) is going to suffer a more devastating blow than Bob's will if he has to renounce his sports car. On this basis we can say that, in the particular circumstances of our example, Jones ought to be granted an exemption from the general norm that debts should be paid back. It is against this kind of judgment, based on *phronesis* or taste as it applies to a vision of the good life, that the outcome of the ideal speech situation has to be balanced. But before going any further into the matter, we should deal with one important objection.

A defender of ethical formalism could raise the question: What if Bob protests that the car is as important to him as being a composer is to Jones? The question can be handled without difficulty from the perspective I have tried to develop. In fact, two cases should be distinguished. In the first case Bob is right in his claim. Imagine, for instance, that becoming a champion of car racing has long been Bob's secret dream and that buying the car was to him a first step in this direction. Then of course, under *these* conditions, Jones ought to pay. However, by raising this question and imagining Bob's self-perception as basically correct, the defender of formalism implicitly modifies our example in the sense of increasing the salience of the car to Bob's identity. As a consequence, in a condition of equal salience of what is to be lost, Jones's claim to an exemption from the norm is no longer justified. But this in turn shows with great poignancy that the decisive element in the whole matter is precisely the impact of one course of action or another on the identities of those involved and not the abstract claim to his money that Bob can ground on the *Diskursethik*. Let us consider the second case. Bob *says* that the car is that important to him, but in fact it is not. Then why should we be impressed by his claim? Why should Bob's protestation impress us more than, for instance, a possible protestation from Kohlberg's druggist that money is as important to him as his wife's survival is to Heinz?

To sum up, to make use of a formal notion of the good in order to keep in check the normative force of the best argument does not mean that we bring our evaluation of the relative worthiness of life plans to bear on questions of justice. It means, in a much weaker sense, that we balance the discourse-ethical standard of the best argument against the standard of the least disruptive impact on the identity needs of all those concerned. That is, if even after the ideal speech situation has come to a satisfactory close one still feels that the best argument has failed to do complete justice to identity needs that one is not able to advocate with the best argument, then one is justified in disregarding the outcome of the ideal speech situation and acting on one's best intuition.

Perhaps more problems are raised by such a formulation than we can hope to solve. Nor can I hope to address them all in this context. Rather, I would like to develop a few considerations that are immediately brought to mind. First, what is the basis for such a decision? As we have seen, the basis on which we decide whether and to what extent the needs crucial to an identity are met by a given course of action is taste, or *phronesis*, as it applies to the actor's own vision of the good life. We want to judge a form of life not from without but only from within, in terms of its chance to bring the actor as close as possible to the attainment of the good life. The relevant question that the actor endowed with *phronesis* asks about the best argument in the ideal speech situation is, Does the course of action prescribed by the best argument deprive someone of something that is crucial to the chance to live a full life? And how crucial is this thing to the attainment of the good life? If we admit that such a question is part of ethics, alongside the universalization principle, and constitutes a substantive counterweight with which we can further scrutinize and, if necessary, appeal the outcome of the procedural component, then we can see the Königsberg jury example in a different light. Although Kant's suggestion to acquit the child murderer constitutes, by the uncoerced agreement of all the jury members, the best argument, the jury members could all *justifiedly* vote against Kant's verdict even if they had no counterargument but only the feeling or intuition that the irreversible loss suffered by the child should take precedence over all other considerations and orient the verdict. By incorporating a theory of the good into ethics, we come to emphasize a parallel set of qualities alongside the truthfulness and autonomy of judgment emphasized by procedural approaches to the right. These other qualities include the willingness and ability to take as much distance as possible from the horizon of values in which one lives; the willingness to acquire as much self-knowledge as possible; the courage to act on one's intuitions; and above all the ability to balance the "right theoretic" intimation to live a life beyond reproach against the "good theoretic" intimation to express as much as one can of one's identity.

Second, an ethics that includes a theory of the good alongside the discourse-ethical component allows for a better comprehension of moral *change*. The conflict between a valid norm and a feeling, need, or desire that could become a new norm in a just society yet to come constitutes a difficulty for all formalistic ethics, but in particular for the *Diskursethik*. Norms specify values. If the conflict occurs in a situation where we have on one hand the accepted values, embodied in valid norms, and on the other hand the mere feeling that something somehow does not work, and if this feeling anticipates the creation of a new value or a substantial modification of the old values, then it is hard to see how, in an ideal speech situation taking place within the lifeworld of the time, anybody could make *the best argument* about a new norm based on value choices yet to be made. Not only is it then difficult to explain how moral innovation comes about, but moral innovation is bound to appear, from this perspective, as a break with morality. Rousseau, in his novel *Julie, ou La nouvelle Heloise*, offers a good example of this predicament. At one point in the plot

Julie is faced with the following dilemma: either she flees her oppressive family to live with her lover, thereby throwing her old father into despair, or she gives up a relationship crucial to her identity and later contract a marriage to her father's liking, thereby jeopardizing her own chance to attain the good life. In the novel Julie, who does not share her father's values about family and marriage, decides to give up her relationship on the Kantian ground that a state of happiness acquired at the expense of someone else's despair would not be a *deserved* happiness but would be tainted with guilt. As a result of her disregard for her own identity needs, Julie's life loses coherence, her self-perception becomes more shallow and fragmented, and in the end she acknowledges that for her to die means only to "die once more." Again, it is easy *for us*—two centuries later—to say that the claim of Julie's father to a right to arrange a marriage for his daughter is void and creates no obligation for Julie and no problem for the moral philosopher. The point is, however, that the innovative act of the first person who no longer regards that claim as valid, on the ground that it sacrifices too much on the side of the good, is bound to appear immoral from the standpoint of all ethics oriented solely to the right. It is the inadequacy of her own ethics—a powerful anticipation of the Kantian categorical imperative—that prevents Julie from *legitimately* playing that innovative role and ultimately condemns her to self-destruction. Nor could the *Diskursethik*, as it is formulated by Habermas, legitimate Julie's playing that role (Ferrara 1984, 334–37). When not outright immoral, moral innovation is likely to appear as sentimentalism or sophistry to a conscience that reduces the practical to the right. In fact, Kant uses these two notions to characterize Beccaria's argument on the ethical indefensibility of capital punishment (1966, 162–63). Instead, an ethic that includes a theory of the good may be in a better position to account for moral change. Though in a sense different from the one Bernard Williams (1981, 20–39) attributes to the expression "moral luck", the view of ethics I wish to suggest does not purport to eliminate luck from ethical judgment. Moral actors may find themselves in situations where it is sensible, *prudent*, to bet that the innovative value choices implicit in their course of action will become the accepted choice at a later time. In a sense, their being right today depends on something's being the case tomorrow. A formal but nonformalist ethic must be able to accommodate this possibility and must specify what precisely is shared by all the situations where it is *prudent* for the actor to make this bet.

Third, in a still procedural but nonformalist version of the

Diskursethik, the outcome of the ideal speech situation (the line of conduct suggested by the best argument) has to be balanced against one's considered judgment as to the least possible disruption of the identity needs of those concerned. I have mentioned the role of *phronesis* and of a formal notion of the good life in this judgment. Following Gadamer, we can reinterpret the Aristotelian concept of *phronesis* in the light of Kant's analysis of reflective judgment. Also, we can reframe the theory of the good life, as we have seen, in terms of the properties that every life history must possess, no matter which concrete values pervade it. This knowledge about the general properties of the good life is no longer rooted in an ontology, but is based on the fallibilistic kind of knowledge provided by some disciplines, such as Freud's metapsychology or post-Freudian psychoanalytic theory or cultural anthropology. If in lieu of Kant's grounding of the principle of universalization in the noumenal aspect of man's nature we can accept a quasi-transcendental grounding of the same principle in an empirically falsifiable reconstruction of the presuppositions of discourse, why not accept, in lieu of Aristotle's metaphysics, an empirically falsificable theory of the psychic requirements of a person's well-being? Just as the "linguistic turn" based on the theory of speech acts has allowed a rescue of Kant's transcendentalism, in my opinion the developments in psychoanalytic theory allow today a parallel "psychological turn," which can lead to a rescue of the Aristotelian doctrine of the good life along new, and fully modern, lines. For example, the notion of *eudaimonia* as the quality of a life pattern where several partial *goods* are combined within the totality of a person's pursuits in accordance with their proper weight and role can be reinterpreted, on the basis of a psychoanalytic theory of self-identity, as the global coherence of an identity where all the crucial inner *needs* of a person are given their proper place.

Fourth, the two components of our ethical theory (the *Diskursethik* and the theory of the good) are centered on two moral qualities: autonomy and authenticity. Autonomy is the quality that philosophers such as Kant, Habermas, and Rawls present as the key virtue of the moral actor. In their view, autonomy is defined by the actor's courage to stand by ethical intuitions (and to act on them) even in the face of adverse opinion on the part of the community. Authenticity, on the other hand, could be taken to mean, in a psychological sense, the complete and spontaneous coincidence of feeling and duty or the total transparency of motives to oneself. But here authenticity, as a moral quality, is defined as the actor's courage to stand by ethical intuitions (and act on them) even in the face of a contingent inability to work them out adequately in the language of abstract reflection. These two qualities of the moral actor, which represent the paramount moral virtues respectively in early and in contemporary modernity, are not mutually exclusive but complementary. Autonomous actors may acquire authenticity, and actors endowed with authenticity necessarily have autonomy in the Kantian-Habermasian sense. However, situations such as the Bob and Jones dilemma, or Julie's choice, or the Königsberg jury, may give rise to a tension between what we must regard as the best argument and the solution that will satisfy more, or disrupt fewer, of the identity needs at stake. Then, if this is the case, the qualities of autonomy and authenticity also come into tension, along with the ethical conceptions that emphasize each of them. Philosophers who privilege the right and autonomy over the good and authenticity advise us, in case of conflict, to side with our reflective constructs (be they monological generalizations or arguments in real discourses), because in the end there is no way of knowing which intuitions are good other than by testing them in the light of reason. Do not take a step—runs the advice—beyond what you can justify in terms of rational discourse. This alone will put your conduct beyond reproach and free you from guilt. Philosophers who privilege the good and the authentic, instead, do not simply equate ethical conduct with "putting oneself beyond reproach." They admit that furthering the good sometimes may not silence the claims of the right but nonetheless should take precedence. Today's good is often tomorrow's right, but not vice versa.

The fifth and final consideration concerns the different relation of our theory of the good life to the public sphere and to the private realm. From Machiavelli to Hegel to Weber, philosophers and social theorists have tended to accord politicians a greater leeway than other citizens, when judgment has to balance the good against the principled expressions of the right. For instance, Weber's ethic of responsibility can be seen as an ethic of authenticity with its domain of validity restricted to the public sphere alone. Hegel's conception of world-historical individuals allows those who act in the public sphere access to a higher standard of morality that will justify their trampling the right if they really contribute to move history toward the good. In my opinion, we should take the opposite path. Only in the private sphere are moral actors allowed to legitimately disregard the best argument if the best argument fails to meet their intuitions about the good in their circumstances of choice. In the public sphere, precisely because the stakes and the risks are so much higher and often involve unaware (and obviously unconsenting) others, moral actors in general—and in particular politicians, who are entrusted with the destiny of many others—should never step beyond the limits of what can be validated by consensus in the ideal speech situation. In this sense the *Diskursethik* can receive its proper place within the realm of the practical. It should not be seen—as Habermas sometimes presents it—as an exhaustive reconstruction of our ability to correctly evaluate norms and conduct in all spheres of *life*, but as a specification of the standards for legitimate decision making in the public sphere of a participatory democracy.

References

Alexy, R. 1978. Eine Theorie des praktischen Diskurses. In *Normenbegrund-ung, Normendurchsetzung*, ed. W. Oelmüller. Paderborn.

Apel, K. O. 1973. Das Apriori der Kommunikantionsgemeinschaft und die Grundlagen der Ethik. in *Transformation der Philosophie*. Frankfurt: Suhrkamp.

———. 1985. Kann der post-kantische Standpunkt der Moralität noch einmal in substantielle Sittlichkeit "aufgehoben" werden? Das Anwendungs-problem der Diskursethik zwischen Utopie und Regression. Paper presented at the Conference on Moralität und Sittlichkeit, J. W. Goethe-Universität, Frankfurt, 18–22 March.

Benhabib, S. 1982. The methodological illusions of modern political theory: The case of Rawls and Habermas. In *Neue Hafte für Philosophie* 21:47–74.

Brumlik, M. 1985. Über die Ansprüche Ungeborener und Unmündiger—Wie advokatorisch ist die diskursive Ethik? Paper presented at the Confer-ence on Moralität und Sittlichkeit, J. W. Goethe-Universität, Frankfurt, 18–22 March.

Ferrara, Alessandro. 1984. Autonomy and authenticity, Ph.D. diss., University of California, Berkeley.

Gadamer, H. G. 1975. *Truth and method.* New York: Continuum.

Habermas, J. 1975. *Legitimation crisis.* Boston: Beacon Press. Originally published as *Legitimations probleme im Spätakpitalismus.* Frankfurt: Suhrkamp, 1973.

———. 1979. *Communication and the evolution of society.* Boston: Beacon Press.

———. 1981. *Theorie des kommunikativen Handelns.* 2 vols. Frankfurt: Suhrkamp.

———. 1982. A reply to my critics. ed. J. B. Thompson and D. Held, In *Habermas: Critical debates,* 219–83. London: Macmillan.

————. 1983. Moralbewusstsein und kommunikatives Handeln: "Diskursethik—Notizen zu einem Bugründungsprogramm. In *Moralbewusstsein und kommunikatives Handeln*. Frankfurt: Suhrkamp.

————. 1984a. Über Moralität und Sittlichkeit—Was macht eine Lebensform rational? In *Rationalität*, ed. H. Schnadelbach, 218–35. Frankfurt: Suhrkamp.

————. 1984b. Wahrheitstheorien. In *Vorstudien und Erganzungen zur Theorie des kommunikativen Handelns*, 127–83. Frankfurt: Suhrkamp.

————. 1985. Moral und Sittlichkeit: Treffen Hegels Einwande gegen Kant auch die Diskursethik zu? Paper presented at the Conference on Moralität und Sittlichkeit, J. W. Goethe-Universität, Frankfurt, 18–22 March.

————. 1986. Questions and counterquestions. *Praxis International* 4(3): 229–49.

Honneth, A. 1985. *Kritik der Macht*. Frankfurt.

Ingelhart, R. 1977. *The silent revolution*. Princeton: Princeton University Press.

Kant, I. 1951. *The critique of judgement*. New York: Hafner.

————. 1965. *The metaphysical elements of justice*. Part 1 of the *Metaphysics of morals*. Indianapolis: Bobbs-Merrill.

————. 1966. *Metaphysik der Sitten*. Hamburg: Meiner.

Kohlberg, L. 1981. Indoctrination versus relativity in value education. In *Essays on moral development*, I:6–28. San Francisco: Harper and Row.

Lukes, S. 1982. Of gods and demons: Habermas and practical reason. In *Habermas: Critical debates*, ed. J. B. Thompson and D. Held, 134–48. London: Macmillan.

McCarthy, T. 1982. Rationality and relativism: Habermas' "Overcoming of Hermeneutics." In *Habermas: Critical debates*, ed. J. B. Thompson and D. Held, 57–78. London: Macmillan.

MacIntyre, A. 1981. *After virtue*. Notre Dame, Ind.: University of Notre Dame Press.

Rawls. 1971. *A theory of justice*, Cambridge: Harvard University Press.

Wellmer, A. 1985. Moral und Recht: Zur Rekonstruktion der Diskursethik. Paper presented at the Conference on Moralität und Sittlichkeit, J. S. Goethe-Universität, Frankfurt, 18 –22 March.

Williams, Bernard. 1981. *Moral luck*. Cambridge: Cambridge University Press.

Yankelovich, D. 1981. *New rules*. New York: Random House.

13

Dialogue and Text:
Re-marking the Difference

Steven G. Crowell

When Heidegger argued that "the meaning of phenomenological description as a method lies in interpretation (Heidegger 1962, 61), he was not simply proposing a revised conception of the philosophical procedures circumscribing the always tenuous unity of the "phenomenological movement." To claim that phenomenological method is interpretive was to insist that what it describes are unities of meaning, that is, such themata as must be *understood* before they can be "seen." Since for Heidegger, as for Husserl, meaning is what is always already at work in our scientific and prescientific dealings within the world, since it is "that wherein the intelligibility of something maintains itself" (Heidegger 1962, 193), interpretation will be our specific access to the lifeworld before being made thematic as a question of method. Interpretation is first of all neither an art nor a science, but our basic way of being in the world.

It is hardly surprising, then, that the "universal" claim of hermeneutics, the claim that all access to meaning of whatever sort is interpretive, should bring the question of language to the center stage of phenomenological concern. Where the task is to provide a philosophical account of the hermeneutic situation, the coordinates of which condition the experience of intelligibility as such, the emphasis of the older hermeneutics on "empathy" and "divination" (Schleiermacher), and even the "psychology of worldviews" (Dilthey), proves one-sided. It is rather in the play of language itself that one finds the horizon for a universal theory of interpretive understanding.

But a reflection that turns to linguistic phenomena for instruction concerning that *Sinnvollzug* that is equivalent to being in the world, a reflection that does not approach the phenomena a priori with a speculative (or positive-methodological) conception of language, encounters at the outset two equiparadigmatic forms in which language presents itself: as written, in the experience of reading, and as spoken, in the experience of hearing. These two forms of linguistic experience have yielded two distinct metaphors for approaching the general question of the understanding of meaning—the metaphor of the *text* and the metaphor of the *dialogue*. To speak here of metaphors is to indicate that the structural-hermeneutic moments disclosed in a reflection, for example, reading, on texts, have been "carried over" to nontextual engagements with intelligibility such that one comes to refer to paintings, the plastic arts, actions, institutions, and finally nature itself as "texts." So also for dialogue, where the dynamics of face-to-face speaking and hearing, question and answer, are turned to account for our experience of everything from the claim of the nonverbal arts to the highly mediated "voice" of tradition.

No doubt the encounter with texts and the dynamics of dialogue both belong within the scope of a general hermeneutics. The only question is how the two are to be coordinated. There seem to be three possible ways to approach the moment of interpretation embedded in textual and dialogical situations. First, the hermeneutical situation of text interpretation might be understood by way of dialogical structures; reading would then be construed in terms of the "logic of question and answer." Second, the dialogical situation might be "inscribed" in the "graphic" of textuality; orality would then become subject to the dissemination of reading. Finally, the two may be held apart according to their *essential* difference, reflecting what I will call the twofold "ground" of intelligibility, the ethical and the ontological.

That both ontological and ethical questions—questions of truth and being, on the one hand, and questions of justice, on the other —will be encountered by hermeneutic reflection follows from the very idea of a "philosophical" hermeneutics, that is, one that presents itself not as a regional art of interpretation, but as a universal account of meaning. Yet the way ethical and ontological problems are integrated into hermeneutic reflection, the relative weight accorded each in the theory of meaning, seems tied to the question of how textual and dialogical hermeneutics are coordinated. To suggest some of the difficulties involved in coordinating the fourfold constellation of dialogue and text, ethics and ontology, I will examine in outline three current hermeneutic strategies illustrating the three possible approaches indicated above: Gadamer's attempt to resolve textual into dialogical hermeneutics by way of ontological considerations, Derrida's attempt to reduce dialogue to textual structures by way of a critique of ontology, and Levinas's re-marking of dialogue by recovering and emphasizing the primary ethical dimension it manifests.

Within this project Gadamer's work will receive the most sustained critical attention. This is not only because it is the most powerful articulation to date of the idea of a philosophical (or universal) hermeneutics, but also because his position regarding the connection between dialogue and text interpretation clearly involves both ethical and ontological considerations. I wish to emphasize at the outset that Gadamer, no less than Levinas, is attuned to the ethical import of dialogue and seeks explicitly to draw out its implications for hermeneutics. Yet because his approach to language is essentially an ontological one ("Being that can be understood is language" [Gadamer 1975, 432]), the ethical dimension of the dialogical situation is subordinated to its disclosive function as a way toward "truth." Thus, as I will argue, Gadamer's altogether legitimate concern with the ontological problem of truth in hermeneutics exerts a distorting influence on his phenomenology of dialogue such that, ironically enough, dialogue comes to be entangled in text-hermeneutic implications.

Gadamer's position is thus exposed, its deepest intentions notwithstanding, to the criticisms of poststructuralists such as Derrida who represent the opposite movement of an ontological skepticism grounded in an explicit claim for the "textuality" of dialogue. However, here too one finds that the concern with ontology leads to an *effacement* of the difference between dialogue and text, an effacement that can be criticized only by a phenomenology of dialogue in which the ethical dimension is brought to the fore. Since the ethical moment is indeed implicit in Gadamer's conception of hermeneutics, and of dialogue in particular, a phenomenology that holds fast to the difference between dialogue and text offers the possibility of enriching, rather than undermining, Gadamer's claim for the universality of hermeneutics and of making more perspicuous the kind of "truth claim" at issue in his invocation of the "conversation that we ourselves are" (Gadamer 1975, 340). To indicate this I will conclude by suggesting how Levinas's phenomenology of dialogue allows us to resituate some of the central notions of Gadamer's hermeneutics on the terrain of the primordial ethical significance of orality, of speech as speaking and address.

Gadamer: The Text as Voice

Is there any essential difference between the hermeneutic situation of textual and of dialogical interpretation? Gadamer's work provides the best example of a project that seeks to minimize any such difference by emphasizing the dialogical moments in text interpretation. But this project presupposes a suitable account of dialogue. Gadamer's account highlights those aspects of dialogue that appear to have analogues in the experience of reading, with the result that what is peculiar to the dialogical situation, as a situation of face-to-face orality, is minimized though not altogether overlooked. The reason for this is found in Gadamer's point of departure for developing a universal hermeneutics, namely, the problem of interpretation as it appears in *philology*.

As Gadamer reminds us,[1] *Truth and Method* was born of the desire to recover the genuine philosophical ground of primarily philological inquiry, that is, inquiry in the "historical human sciences" (*Geisteswissenschaften*) such as history, art criticism, and literary studies. Following Dilthey, Gadamer argued that what distinguishes these inquiries from the natural sciences is their concern for the irreducible *individuality* of their objects. This concern for individuality precludes adoption of the "generalizing" methods of the natural sciences, for which individuality is but a vanishing moment. On the other hand, Gadamer criticized what he took to be Dilthey's "historicist" response to the problem of individuality, whereby historical individualities (events, persons, artworks, etc.) were to be taken as objects to be reconstructed according to their place within the horizon or general cultural coordinates of an age, a *Weltanschauung*. This view of philological inquiry yields a methodologically produced "alienation" from the works themselves, as though they were to be approached like museum curios: "Ultimately, this view of hermeneutics is as foolish as all restitution and restoration of past life. What is reconstructed, a life brought back from the lost past, is not the original. In its continuance in an estranged state it acquires only a secondary, cultural, existence. . . . [A] hermeneutics that regarded understanding as the reconstruction of the original would be no more than the recovery of a dead meaning" (Gadamer 1975, 149).

Gadamer's universal hermeneutics begins as an effort to overcome such methodological, historicist alienation by rethinking the

1. Two loci among many others: Gadamer (1975, xiii, 1976, 18).

notion of *truth* underlying our concern with philology. This concern is finally one of *self*-understanding achieved by way of explicit appropriation of that "tradition" that bears us along prior to any scientific thematization and that is partially constituted by the very texts that subsequently come under philological scrutiny (Gadamer 1975, 87, 207). From this perspective, establishing the text "in itself" (by way of source criticism, historical reconstruction, manuscript editing, and the like) is at best a propaedeutic to philological understanding, the truth of which depends upon the interpreter's coming to confront for herself the "matter" or "issue" (*die Sache*) the original text is "about." To understand Plato's *Republic* is not simply to reconstruct what Plato actually wrote, not *simply* to understand Plato as he understood himself, but rather to be brought to think further about the "issue(s)" by means of the encounter with Plato's text. The identity of the text, the philological "object," is therefore established and fixed not by the reconstruction of the context (psychological, cultural, etc.) of its origin, but by its truth claim, that *Sache* that is addressed and glimpsed through the text, serving as its measure for any subsequent interpreter.

I shall return to these issues below. The point here is simply that Gadamer's hermeneutic appeal to dialogue emerges from essentially philological motives, and that means, ultimately, from a concern with the interpretation of *texts*. This philological emphasis has been attacked by those who believe that a universal hermeneutics projected on such a basis conceals the achievements and emancipatory potential of the social sciences, properly so called, in which non-hermeneutical methods may legitimately be employed not for *recovering* the "truth claim" of an effective tradition, but for criticizing it.[2] Gadamer himself has admitted that the philological perspective of *Truth and Method* may have distorted some of his conceptions.[3] But even so the philological emphasis upon texts as the paradigm of interpretive concern remains. Although for the philologue "the text . . . is given like a fixed quantity," while the historian "must first reconstruct his basic text, history itself" (Gadamer 1986c, 20), it is still with texts that we have to do in both cases. Indeed, Gadamer's notion of "tradition" is not that of some "collective subjects" but is "simply the collective name for what is in each case an individual text (and this

2. Cf., for example, Habermas (1980).
3. For example, retracting what he had said in *Truth and Method*, p. 304, Gadamer now asserts that "history is not philology writ large" (cf. Gadamer 1986c, 20).

in the widest sense of text, so that a painting, a building, indeed even a natural event is contained in it" (Gadamer 1986a, 370; my translation). The ease with which Gadamer extends the notion of text to cover the most diverse phenomena reflects the "philologism" built into his universal conception of hermeneutics. *Reading* remains the paradigmatic hermeneutic activity: "Reading itself is already interpretation of what is meant [*des Gemeinten*]. Thus reading is the general basic structure of *all* accomplishing of meaning [*Vollzug des Sinnes*]" (Gadamer 1986a, 19).

Given this paradigmatic status of reading within the theory of interpretation as *Sinnesvollzug*, one might begin to wonder why conversation or dialogue takes on the importance it has within Gadamer's hermeneutics. Yet there is no doubt that in fact Gadamer's philosophical recovery of the truth claim of the tradition depends on marking dialogue as "the original phenomenon of language (Gadamer 1986b, 332; my translation), thereby enabling one to construe the text as a "partner" in that dialogue constituted on the other side by the interpreter's (reader's) interrogative activity. The text is not primarily an object for reconstruction; its individuality (*Sinneinheit*) is to be preserved by hearing it as a "voice" in the conversation of tradition. Such a privileging of dialogue is made possible by Gadamer's ontological approach to language, the horizon in which the phenomenon of dialogue is taken up and described.

Any differences between the hermeneutics of hearing and the hermeneutics of reading (and Gadamer certainly knows of them) are absorbed in principle by the ontological view of language underlying Gadamer's metaphorical transference of the notion of "voice" to the sphere of what is written. A text may be treated as a dialogical partner because both spoken and written forms of discourse repose in, and are governed by, the "ideality of the word" (Gadamer 1975, 352, 354). That is, both are to be understood finally not as "expressions of life" (with the full indexicality this implies), but as "truth claims" that derive their sense from what is spoken or written *about*. Interpreting texts can be dialogical because dialogue itself is founded in the ideality of the referential intention, an ideality that written discourse (as nonindexical, as the absence of the moment of utterance) only makes explicit. Though both spoken and written discourse depend upon the "ideality of the word," dialogue takes on preeminence as the "original phenomenon of language" because the ideality of the word is simply an indication that language is being conceived from the perspective of "truth"—that is, from the ontological perspective of an openness to the "world," to the *Sache*, that any given instance of discourse, spoken or written, can address, indicate, "disclose," or conceal but can never dispense with. Because dialogue appears to illustrate most clearly this ontological function of language, this openness to what is, Gadamer employs it as a metaphor for all interpretation.

To see why, one must recall what it was that attracted Gadamer to the idea of dialogue as a model for hermeneutics. Above all it was the example of the Socratic dialogue, of the "logic of question and answer," that suggested the way truth comes to be at issue as that "toward which" the partners in a dialogue are oriented through discourse. What appealed to Gadamer in the Socratic model was the essential *symmetry* of the dialogical relation between (equally "ignorant") inquirers. Dialogical inquiry would involve an essential "selflessness" of the partners, that is, a freedom from purely rhetorical intentions of persuasion, a mutual readiness to place at risk the fundamental prejudices for taken-for-granted (truths) that are nevertheless held fast as enabling initial approach to "the issue." The expression for such selflessness, this putting oneself into play at risk, is the dialectic of question and answer. The movement of question and answer is governed neither by the purely individual interests of conversation partners nor by the essentially asymmetrical authority relation of teacher to student, but by the "thing itself" in terms of which the partners come at last to understand one another, that is, in terms of which they achieve a (perhaps provisional) "fusion of horizons" (Gadamer 1975, 273, 337). It is *die Sache* that "poses questions" (Gadamer 1986c, 6), and all genuine understanding of a discourse must place itself in relation not only to "what is said," but to what is "spoken about." In this particular—the pivot of Gadamer's universal hermeneutic theory—"*Schriftlichkeit* as such alters nothing" (Gadamer 1986c, 6).

Thus, preserving the truth claim of the text means inserting it as a partner into a form of the dialogical I-Thou relation. But it is an I-Thou relation of a particular sort, one whose ground lies in the search for truth (Gadamer 1975, 321). That the text, unlike the reader, is not *free* to raise questions of its other—that the Thou, but not the text, can change the subject or refuse to speak—is an obvious point against any dialogical construal of the hermeneutics of texts. Gadamer seeks to overcome such objections by treating the text as an answer to a question: "We must attempt to reconstruct the question to which the transmitted text is the answer. . . . The reconstruction of the question to which the text is presumed to be the answer takes place itself within a process of questioning through which we seek the answer to the question that the text asks us. . . . [T]he reconstruction of the question, from which the meaning of a text is to be understood as an answer, passes into our own questioning" (Gadamer 1975, 33 ff.). Since the question *precedes* the text, it does not refer to the "freedom" of either partner. Both are equally addressed, thus preserving dialogical symmetry. But this means that in Gadamer the ontological ground of dialogue, *die Sache,* asserts its priority over the ethical, the I-Thou encounter, the *freedom* involved in the face-to-face orality of dialogue.

Gadamer's insertion of the text into a dialogical relation with the interpreter thus depends upon a particular way of marking the phenomenon of dialogue, a particular thematic emphasis within the phenomenology of dialogue. I shall mention here only a few implications of this marking for Gadamer's conception of dialogue. First, although any phenomenology of dialogue must begin with a face-to-face relation, Gadamer's interest in truth leads him to fix upon a kind of *symmetry* as the defining feature of genuine dialogue, namely, the condition that neither party "reflect herself out" of the relationship in order to manipulate the direction of discourse for purposes that would not be at issue in the discourse itself. Thus, as is familiar from Gadamer's long-standing debate with Habermas, the asymmetrical therapeutic situation would be dialogical only to the extent that the explanatory schema or filter by which the analyst interprets the analysand's discourse is simultaneously an issue for both. Such symmetry at the level of "validity claims" may be bad therapy, but Gadamer insists that it is an essential structure of dialogue. Persuasion, explanation, deep-structural translation, and the like all supervene on dialogue and thus alter it into something else.[4]

This symmetry also implies that dialogue is never a process of translation but already presupposes it. Dialogue demands "listening" —an attention to what the Other is saying, not to its mode of expression. To understand another through dialogue is to come to an understanding *about* something; it is not simply to come to understand language. Thus in a certain sense dialogue always presupposes a shared language.

In another sense, however, dialogue is the constitution of a

4. See Gadamer (1976, 41–42).

shared language. The language of the Other is always *surprising*, revelatory, to the extent that he is other. Whether or not the participants in a dialogue belong to the same "tradition," each approaches the other from a perspective, a horizon of prejudgments or "prejudices," that is always in an irreducible sense "mine." Because there are always two horizons at risk in the dialogical situation, there is always *emergent* meaning, the possibility of mutual enrichment of the idiolect.

Linguistically the situation might be described as follows: even where the partners share a common language (*langue*), meaning is constituted in the moment of discourse (*parole*) where the abstract-logical "semantic fields" of individual words are concretized each time in a *particular* way by each partner individually. Such semantic fields do not, however, exist as sets of determinations present at hand in the mind of a speaker; what it is possible for a word to mean can be determined only negatively, by exclusion or refusal of what it cannot mean. And this, in turn, can be determined only dialogically, by the emergence of discursive conflict. Stated otherwise: Even where individuals with equal "communicative competence" are using the same term, they may be using it "differently" in that one would be willing to allow it to figure in predications that would be negated or denied by the other. In this sense the function of dialogue would consist in a "coming to terms" with the other, that is, in discovering, through question and answer, the particular ordering of the semantic field that governs the "sense" of the other's judgment (predication) —an ordering that, if not made explicit through dialogue, can undermine any apparent "agreement" so that it is in fact a misunderstanding.[5] This linguistic issue of coming to terms by becoming mutually attuned to the respective orderings of the semantic field is at the core of what Gadamer calls the "fusion of horizons," the need for which becomes evident in the experience of any collapse of agreement, that is, in that "disagreement" that is paradigmatically present when one partner challenges the *truth* of what the other is saying.

Gadamer provides this dialogical phenomenon of coming to terms with an ontological ground by seeing in it a "becoming clear about" (or "fixing") the referent, *die Sache*, which, by "posing

---

5. Here I am appropriating the general semantic approach laid out by Simon (1978, 35–87). I do not presume that Simon would necessarily agree with the consequences I infer from this situation.

questions," conducts both participants and appears "at issue" as the horizon of their respective semantic orderings: "The goal of all communication and understanding is agreement concerning the object" (Gadamer 1975, 260). Since dialogue is said to consist in the symmetrical movement toward a fusion of horizons between reciprocally self-effacing participants who "risk" inherited prejudices within a common interrogative orientation toward the truth, we do not so much conduct a conversation as we are "conducted by" it, by the momentum of a disclosure that is in the freedom of neither participant (Gadamer 1975, 345). But this assumes a particular resolution of the struggle involved in coming to terms, one in which the ethical moments governing the approach of I to Thou are subordinated to an ontological dimension conceived in its ideality as the "common concern" of the participants. Hence the ease with which the notion of dialogue is transferred to textual hermeneutics. But it is an indication of the complexity of this situation that the ontological ground Gadamer relies upon in constituting "agreement" appears as the essence of dialogue only because experiences appropriate to the hermeneutics of texts have been smuggled into an account of the dialogical situation.

This is suggested already by the notion of a fusion of horizons. Can one really speak of "fusion" as the *telos* of the dialogical project of coming to terms with the Other? Paradoxically, Gadamer can use the notion of "fusion" to describe the dialogical situation because he has one eye on the interpretation of *texts*.[6] Even if the text is in some sense a Thou with its "own" horizon, it is still the reader who inevitably provides both horizons in her reanimation of "expressions fixed in writing" (Gadamer 1975, 349). Thus a "fusion" is altogether possible. The world of the text contains only as many surprises as the reader's own horizon *can* allow it; any challenge to the reader's self-conception has already been prepared by that very self-conception. The most "open" reading can risk only what it is already prepared to modify or abandon, for only that will be "audible" to it in the text.

The textual aspects of Gadamer's notion of dialogue can be seen in other elements of his theory of meaning as well, above all in the regulative idea of a "unity of meaning" (*Sinneinheit*), correlate of the "anticipation of meaning" (*Sinnvermutung*) (Gadamer 1986b, 340 and passim) that underwrites Gadamer's hermeneutic principle, the

---

6. As is shown by the context in which Gadamer introduces the term (cf. Gadamer 1975, 373 ff.).

"fore-conception of completion" (Gadamer 1975, 261). Such determinations seem to derive from the experience of texts in reading, not from an original reflection on the dialogical situation. For one thing, the very idea of the "unity" and "identity" of a discourse appears to derive from the fact that texts, of whatever length, come to an end. Even if the text involves an "outer horizon" that renders its interpretation interminable, there are still the graphological conventions (the period, the paragraph, the blank "end paper") that provide the experience of reading with a relative closure not found in dialogue and that sustain a certain sense in talk of the text as an "identity," as a "fixed quantity," as a "unity of meaning." In dialogue, on the other hand, it makes no sense to speak of such a unity. Any actual conclusion to question and answer is utterly provisional; even under the guise of ideal "agreement" it is threatened from the outset by the freedom of either participant to raise "just one more small point," to happen onto new and unsuspected paths. Any identity relevant to the dialogical situation is one not to be presupposed, but to be achieved.

Of course for Gadamer the identity of the text cannot simply be a matter of orthographic conventions. Indeed, his notion of "effective history" is designed to show how the identity of the text is inseparable from its interpretations, from its "effect" on readers who, in the dialogue of question and answer, draw out of the text its "unspoken" implications. Still, the principle of identity governs this whole procedure. The text faces us as a "firm point of orientation opposed to the questionable, arbitrary, or at any rate multiple possibilities for interpretation directed toward the text" (Gadamer 1986b, 340). In contrast, it seems that dialogical discourse is never definitive, is never a fixed point of reference for interpretation. Nevertheless, Gadamer insists that this moment can be found in dialogue too, as when one demands of the Other a "binding formulation" (Gadamer 1986b, 340) of her idea ("Are you sure this is how you want to put that?"). However, though it is undeniable that one frequently tries to resolve in this way the open-ended ambiguity involved in dialogical coming to terms, the unpredictability of question and answer in face-to-face dialogue, grounded in freedom, undermines any attempt to repose in the illusion of "binding formulations."

Thus the guiding notions of Gadamer's hermeneutics—fusion, foreconception of completion, unity of meaning, identity of the text, and so on—all reveal their origin in a fundamental tendency that has its motivation in the experience of reading, namely, a tendency toward "wholeness" and plenitude. Indeed, the textual principle of the "foreconception of completion" is explicity exalted to "a formal condition of all understanding," that "only what constitutes a unity of meaning is intelligible" (Gadamer 1975, 261). In the language of Levinas, Gadamer's hermeneutics is governed by the ontological principle of "totality." To be sure, this principle does not function for Gadamer as it did for Hegel, as a speculative concept that would be sufficient for the constitution of meaning. Despite his deep appreciation of Hegel's achievement, Gadamer is convinced that Hegelian claims to speculative knowledge must be tempered by phenomenological insights into the *finitude* of the interpreter, and so of all understanding (Gadamer 1975, 253 ff.). Gadamer even asserts that, against Hegel, philosophical hermeneutics seeks to be the theory of the "bad infinite," that is, the Heideggerian opening out upon truth without the methodological guarantees provided by possession of the "speculative concept."

The principle of totality and the related notions of fusion, unity, and so forth, thus take on the characteristics of "regulative ideas," while the notion of truth becomes that of a continually renewed interpretive "uncovering" of *die Sache* in which temporal and other "distances" play a productive role. Gadamer is perfectly aware that the relative totalities involved in interpretation are *projections*, guiding ideas, open horizons rather than speculatively "completed' givens. Thus he is clear that the fusion of horizons is never complete (Gadamer 1986c, 14, 16), that a "unity of meaning" cannot always be found, that the identity of a discourse is always problematic, constituted by its "effective history," and so on. But finally Gadamer does not question that such unities and totalities lie at the basis of *all* intelligibility and provide the indispensable criteria for *any* interpretation. One need only recall here the oft-stated maxim that, in the case of conflicts of interpretation, "the wider context decides" (Gadamer 1986b, 359; cf. Gadamer 1975, 272). Particular elements are to be interpreted as parts of a whole, and the "better" interpretation will be one that can encompass more elements coherently within its projection of the meaning of the whole. I certainly do not intend to impugn this hermeneutic maxim, which I hold to be a genuine description of what we do when we read, and as such to be indispensable. I want only to indicate how Gadamer's commitment to it guides his appropriation of dialogue and so in a certain sense conceals the difference between dialogical and textual hermeneutics.

The problem arises already in examining the systematic significance Gadamer attributes to dialogue, as the answer to the phenomenological problem of intersubjectivity. On the one hand, Gadamer
admits that his hermeneutics takes its stand (against the later
Heidegger and, in another sense, against Derrida) on the principle of
self-consciousness understood (with Husserl) as a field of "intentional immanence" rather than (with Hegel) as a dialectical process of
mediation (Cf. Gadamer 1975, xxv; Gadamer 1986c, 10). This "immanence," reflected in the hermeneutic circle of all interpretation, "is
nothing but the description of what understanding is (Gadamer
1986b, 335). On the other hand, Gadamer realizes that appeal to
immanence raises the crucial question whether "understanding" can
thereby "preserve the otherness of the Other, rather than suspending
it" (Gadamer 1986c, 5), that is, rather than reducing it to what is
merely "my own" (which would mean not a *fusion* of horizons, but a
collapse of the Other's horizon into mine). This problem—the
hermeneutic equivalent of Husserl's perplexity in the fifth *Cartesian
Meditation*—is the site at which the systematic significance of dialogue
shows itself.

Dialogue points toward that which limits the autonomy of
immanence without being estranged from it, that which belongs to all
experience of *Sinnvollzug* without being reducible to the immanent
interpretive processes of the partners between whom such *Vollzug* is
achieved. For the "experience of dialogue" is "not limited to the
sphere of giving reasons and counterreasons, in whose exchange and
unification the meaning of every conflict can find its end." Rather,
there is "still something else" found in such experience, "so to speak
a potentiality for being-other which lies over and beyond any coming
to terms by way of what is in common [*Verständiguing in Gemeinsa-
men*]" (Gadamer 1986b, 336). Now, as we have seen, for Gadamer this
"potentiality for being other" that transcends my/our immanence
belongs to *die Sache*, and dialogical openness (beyond the closure of
argumentive agreement) toward *die Sache* appears to preserve the
"totalizing power of truth (above all, its power to establish a
nonviolent relation between me and the Other) without making
appeal to it as a speculatively given principle. Hermeneutics seeks,
"against the ontological self-domestication that belongs to dialectic, to
indicate a way into the open [*ins Freie*]" (Gadamer 1986a, 367). For
Gadamer this hermeneutic move appears necessary on the basis of an
ultimate philosophical either/or: either the "way from dialectic back to
dialogue and back to conversation," or the "complete dissolution of
all unity of meaning" (Gadamer 1986a, 368).

From Derrida to Levinas

This either/or is formulated by Gadamer as an explicit response to Derrida.[7] Nevertheless, Gadamer's own appropriation of the dialogical situation as the key to preserving the "unity of meaning" is at the very least in tension with the avowed "bad infinite" involved in any interpretation, especially the interpretation of texts. It is this tension that Derrida can exploit by emphasizing the caustic side of the "bad infinite"; it is here that the poststructuralist critique of the concept of truth, displacement of the Gadamerian notion of *die Sache*, can take hold. This it does by taking the concept of text as primary, by focusing on the "graphic" of textuality, and so calling into question the assumed privilege of dialogue as "the original phenomenon of language," as the "plentitude of discourse": "The exteriority of the signifier is the exteriority of writing in general, and . . . there is no linguistic sign before writing" (Derrida 1974, 14).

Even without going into the details of Derrida's position, it is clear that it moves in a direction precisely opposite that of Gadamer. Instead of construing reading ultimately in terms of dialogue, it begins with reading and refuses to acknowledge any essential difference in the interpretive *Sinnvollzug* of reading and dialogue. For Derrida reading is not conducted with one eye toward an extratextual *Sache;* it is structured behind its back by the intertextual dissemination of the sign. This point is underlined by Derrida's distinction between the "book" and the "text" (Derrida 1974, 18):

> The idea of the book is the idea of a totality, finite or infinite, of the signifier; this totality of the signifier cannot be a totality, unless a totality constituted by the signified preexists it, supervises its inscriptions and its signs, and is independent of it in its ideality. The idea of the book, which always refers to a natural totality, is profoundly alien to the sense of writing. . . . If I distinguish the text from the book, I shall say that the destruction of the book, as it is now under way in all domains, denudes the surface of the texts.

Reading points only toward other readings, never toward that moment within dialogue that I have called "coming to terms." The horizon of the text is another text; the Gadamerian "agreement

---

7. Materials pertaining to the so-called "Gadamer/Derrida encounter," including translations of essays referred to in this chapter, are included in Michelfelder and Palmer (1989).

concerning the object," the "presence" of a "transcendental signified" that would constitute the ontological principle for a fusion of
reader-horizon is *permanently* deferred.

This means that whereas Gadamer's hermeneutics emphasizes
the regulative role of the *semantic* dimension of discourse (as that
which prevents a perspective from becoming a prison), Derrida's
challenge arises through an *elision* of the semantic dimension. By
thematizing the interweave of signifiers themselves, the linguistically
"deferring" character of writing becomes paradigmatic for the
interpretation of *all* discourse (Derrida 1974, 7):

> In all senses of the word, writing thus *comprehends* language. Not that
> the word "writing" has ceased to designate the signifier of the signifier,
> but it appears, strange as it may seem, that "signifier of the signifier"
> no longer defines accidental doubling and fallen secondary. "Signifier
> of the signifier" describes on the contrary the movement of language: in
> its origin, to be sure, but one can already suspect that an origin whose
> structure can be expressed as "signifier of the signifier" conceals and
> erases itself in its own production. There the signified always already
> functions as a signifier.

Interpretation becomes a mapping of the oppositional character
governing the generation of significance in a text, while the semantic
or "validity" level is itself but an echo of this very project of
interpretation. It is a semiotic absence that undermines or refuses any
putative fusion of horizons. Interpretation of texts, on this view, is
not an attempt to awaken the question to which the text is an answer,
but to demonstrate the law of its structural composition and the sites
of its self-immolation or failure to say/be "about" anything. At its
extreme such a strategy aims at inscribing "textuality" into the
spoken dialogue itself by showing that the apparent indexicality of
the face-to-face dialogue is an illusion, that *no* context (and thus no
face-to-face consensus or fusion of horizons) can "saturate" discourse
so as to bring a halt to the "undecidability," the deferrals, of
signification. Thus, whereas Gadamer suggests that the dialogical
context allows for the "possibility of overcoming" the "foreignness
that always pops up between man and man and produces always
new confusions," that is, whereas he holds that in dialogue oriented
toward a common theme I can "seek and find the word that can reach
the Other" (Gadamer 1986a, 364) and so "build a common language"
(p. 365), Derrida's criticism of the illusion of phonocentrism implies

that "no meaning can be determined out of context, but no context permits saturation" (Derrida 1979, 81). "What I am referring to here," continues Derrida, "is not richness of substance, semantic fertility, but rather structure: the structure of the remnant or of iteration. . . . Nomination is important, but it is constantly caught up in a process that it does not control" (p. 81).

Derrida's criticism is grounded in his critique of the ontological truth concept and so pertains to Gadamer's hermeneutics of dialogue to the extent that this is oriented toward the concept of truth. If the semantics of *die Sache* cannot serve any regulative role in disambiguating discourse, oral or written, then either one faces the implications of a "permanent deferral" of meaning (in Gadamer's terms, the "dissolution of all unity of meaning"), or one achieves "agreement" through nonhermeneutic means—"closure" achieved either by dogmatic principles or by "violence" (Levinas), the domination of one voice by the other.

At this point one must ask whether the poststructuralist critique of Gadamer's *ontological* grounding of his central hermeneutical notions (fusion of horizons, unity of meaning, identity of texts, etc.) really applies equally to dialogical and textual hermeneutic situations. Since both Gadamer and his deconstructive critics proceed by minimizing the importance of orality in dialogue, subordinating it to an ontological conception of meaning (and of language) that plays itself out indifferently in spoken and written discursive contexts, it may be that this neglected "orality" involves more than what can be prescribed by its ontological significance. May not its *ethical* moment yield clues for understanding what is really at issue in Gadamer's description of "coming to terms," while avoiding the totalizing assumptions that expose Gadamer to deconstructive criticism?

If Gadamer's assimilation of textual to dialogical hermeneutics cannot be maintained, it is not, I think, because dialogue is subject to the law of the text. Rather, it is because even though Gadamer properly seeks to ground dialogue on the I-Thou relation, he overlooks the genuine sense in which it *is* a ground. Because he has his eye on the ontological structure of the dialogue (the disclosure of *die Sache* in question and answer), Gadamer does not always attend to the ethically irreducible meaning of the face-to-face dimension of spoken dialogue and so occasionally overlooks hermeneutically relevant differences between orality and textuality. If it is the textual hermeneutics of the "book" (Derrida) that suggests the totalizing assumption of a shared orientation toward *die Sache*, dialogue is instead grounded in what *resists* this assumption. Thus, for example, the textualist moment of "symmetry" with regard to validity claims ought not to be read into the intersubjective foundation of dialogue, which is essentially *asymmetrical;* nor is "coming to terms" anything but a preservation of that asymmetry. In facing the Other, dialogue is our condition for a mutuality that, in its asymmetry, eludes ontology.

This does not mean that Gadamer has gone astray in insisting on the difference between dialogue and all forms of rhetoric, therapy, and critique. But by locating this difference in the ontological symmetry of the dialogical situation as regards *truth claims,* Gadamer conceals, without altogether binding us to, the asymmetry in which alone I can encounter the Other; namely, as the one who makes a claim on me prior to the assertion of truth claims, as one who challenges my self-sufficiency and thus is encountered "above" me—not as partner but as teacher. Such is the ethical (not ontological) asymmetry that distinguishes dialogue from the "rhetorical strategies" that rest on it, and so also from the texts with which it may be confused.

By suggesting that dialogue is founded not in mutual orientation toward *die Sache,* but in the irreducible dynamics of the face-to-face, not in an ontology of the referent but in an ethics of the face, I am appealing to the basic insight of Emmanuel Levinas upon which he seeks to reverse the traditional hierarchy that subordinates ethics to ontology, justice to truth. Here I must restrict myself to suggesting certain theses that bear on the issues of dialogue, textuality, and orality as they have been developed so far. Still, these hints may allow us to see how the genuine insights of Gadamer's hermeneutics can be retained through an interpretation that, putting the accent elsewhere, recovers ontology as the issue of an original ethical relation. Since for Gadamer, too, the symmetry or "goodwill" of the dialogical partners is the precondition for that common orientation toward *die Sache* that distinguishes dialogue from other forms of discourse, Levinas's position may be seen as providing a necessary reminder of the ethical dynamics that underlie the Gadamerian *presupposition* of symmetry and goodwill. It is at the ethical level alone that dialogue shows itself to be the "plentitude of discourse."

Levinas's phenomenology of dialogue begins by charting the excess or remainder that resists the reduction to meaning in Husserl's transcendental philosophy, namely, the "absolute exterior" or "separation" of the Other, and pursues this resistance in post-Husserlian (dialectical and existential) attempts to bring the Other into the ontological fold. For Levinas all such transcendental or neo-Hegelian attempts to locate the Other within a totalizing theory collapse under the weight of the "infinity" revealed in self-expression, the presence of the Other. To speak of such a "presence" is to speak exclusively in ethical terms; it is to recognize the presence of a claim prior to all truth claims, a claim not subject to the dialectic of argumentation; it is to assert the priority of justice over knowledge in the "foundation" of truth. From the vantage point of this "primacy of the ethical," Levinas pursues a phenomenology of the origin of language that challenges both Gadamer and his critics. Dialogue is neither a fusion of horizons nor a site of endless deferrals, but the creation of commonplaces governed by justice, or the giving-welcoming of the Other as stranger (Levinas 1969, 39 ff.).

Why does Levinas insist on the irreducibility of the face-to- face? The answer lies in his conception of the face as "expression": "The face is a living presence; it is expression. . . . The face speaks. The mainfestation of the face is already discourse" (Levinas 1969, 66). This view of language already announces the crucial difference between Levinas's and Gadamer's appropriation of the phenomenological notion of immanence. For whereas Gadamer struggled with the question of how the standpoint of immanence could avoid reducing the Other and his discourse to a function of "my" horizon, Levinas describes the ethical emergence of the Other as itself a kind of "expression" that breaks in on immanence as an "absolute experience." This is because the Other "expresses himself" in the face, that is, reveals himself as that absolute excess or exteriority that would not *need* to be disclosed or constituted from a "point of view" (Levinas 1969, 67). Even if all ontology depends on the conditions for disclosure and constitution of entities contained in my immanent horizon as being-in-the-world, the Other is no entity, and her "presence," as ethical claim, as "expression," is meaningful without reference to the factual and projective "foreconceptions" that govern my experience of meaningful *things*. Not that these latter are lacking even here—but they are *irrelevant* to the experience. It is in this absolute experience, a signifying not dependent on the "borrowed light" of a subjective horizon, that Levinas locates the origin of "truth." Truth is not a product of the correlation of the I and the Other but a function of the *impossibility* of such a correlation, as a closer look at Levinas's conception of what we have called the phenomenological sphere of immanence will illustrate.

Levinas describes the sphere of the "I" as a sphere of autonomy and freedom, of need and enjoyment (happiness) playing itself out in the an-archic circle of the Self, of the in-significant, the egoistic plenitude of economic existence (Levinas 1969, 60). Into this autarchic system of need the irruption of the Other, the absolute exterior, constitutes desire. Phenomenologically, this movement is crucial. For in opposition to the Platonic tradition Levinas conceives desire as altogether other than a "lack": "Desire is an aspiration that the Desirable animates; it originates from its object; it is a revelation— whereas need is a void of the Soul, it proceeds from the subject" (Levinas 1969, 62). That dialogue seeks truth (Gadamer) is grounded in this revelation of the Other as the exterior, the desireable: "Truth is sought in the other, but by him who lacks nothing" (Levinas 1969, 62). At the same time this irruption of the Other is the origin of language: "The separated being is satisfied, autonomous and none-theless searches after the other with a search that is not incited by the lack proper to need nor by the memory of a lost good. Such a situation is language. Truth arises where a being separated from the other is not engulfed in him but speaks to him" (Levinas 1969, 62).

Speech indicates the absolute excess present in the presence of the Other. Because its *arche* is not the void of "need," its *telos* is not found in the satisfaction of need, in the Gadamerian fusion of the Other with the "own." The deepest root of dialogue lies not in overcoming separation and exteriority, but in *establishing* them by calling into question the autonomy (the an-archy) of need. It is this, I might suggest, that underlies Gadamer's idea that symmetry is a precondition for dialogue. Symmetry would thus be a function of that original asymmetry that, as an ethical challenge, demands that I relinquish my anarchic autonomy. Dialogue takes place only in the maintenance of that asymmetry, which is equivalent to the establish-ment of what is irrevocably exterior, or separated from me. It is born in a "traumatism of astonishment," in the desire for instruction in the presence of the "absolutely foreign" (Levinas 1969, 73). Discourse, dialogue, is born of asymmetry, where the "common plane" of community between the two terms of the relation "is wanting or yet to be constituted" (Levinas 1969, 73). It is ethically, not ontologically, distinguished.

By re-marking the foundation of dialogue in this "ethical" way Levinas develops a view that has more affinities with the anthropol-ogist's hermeneutical situation than with the philologist's. Since Gadamer's problem was particularly that of "historical distance" (historicism), he could conceive of dialogical interpretation as being mediated by that "tradition" shared by both the text and its interpreter. The I-Thou relation was seen as supported by a tradition—however, open—to which both belonged. For the anthropologist struggling with "cultural distance" such an assumption is not always available. On Levinas's view, however, this ethnographic situation of confronting the radically (culturally) "other" only makes explicit the foundation of *all* dialogue: "the strangeness of the other, his very freedom" (Levinas 1969, 73).

As we know, Gadamer locates the priority of dialogue over writing in that reciprocity of question and answer wherein meaning comes to be constituted through the criticism of truth claims. For Levinas, however, this does not capture what is genuinely peculiar to the dialogical nature of language: "The 'communication of ideas,' the reciprocity of dialogue, already hides the profound essence of language . . . for language can be spoken only if the interlocutor is the commencement of his discourse, if, consequently, he remains beyond the system, if he is not *on the same plane* as myself" (Levinas 1969, 101). In writing, on the other hand, this disparity between me and the Other is concealed. In written discourse I confront not another freedom but a theme, a proposition, a "given"—something "past" (Levinas 1969, 96).

Here "reciprocity" is possible, since the Other is absent; I can speak of a fusion of horizons with the text because *it* can become *my* theme within the spontaneity of my freedom, my "interiority." But for Levinas, in essential agreement here with the poststructuralists, such a fusion is "an-archic," the pro-position of a world that is never original. "The signified is never a complete presence; always a sign in its turn, it does not come in straightforward frankness" (Levinas 1969, 96). The thematized, "pro-posed" world of the text (like the world contemplated "theoretically," as spectacle, landscape, or still life) is the world from which the signifier (speaker) has fled. It is the "silent" world, the "mocking" of the evil genius; the Other who "gives a sign but declines every interpretation" (Levinas 1969, 91).

In contrast to written discourse, with its silent semantic root indistinguishable from illusion, its *deus malignus* "undecidability," the nonreciprocal situation of speech or genuine dialogue, as a discourse that is a "relation to exteriority," is grounded in the "face," the "presence" of the Other whose speech is first of all a *self*-signification. Here too there is thematization, the pro-posal of a world, but it is carried by the self-revealing of the Other: "The Other, the signifier, manifests himself by proposing the world, by *thematizing* it" (Levinas 1969, 96). Such thematization gains an advantage over the an-archic thematization of the essentially "past" or "written" fact-world: "The presence of him who speaks" inverts "the inevitable movement that bears the spoken word to the past state of the written word" (Levinas 1969, 69). The presence of the Other renders signification present by bringing to the word "what the written word is already deprived of: mastery" (Levinas 1969, 69). Such mastery is not, however, to be construed epistemologically as a final cognitive disambiguation or referential Archimedean point, but is an act of "giving" (thematizing, the "given") in which the signifier does not absent himself from the "sign he delivers" but rather "comes to the aid" of his discourse, "attends" his own manifestation, "comes to the assistance" of the word in an "ever recommended effort of language to clarify its own manifestation" (Levinas 1969, 97).

Thus in the text, though not in dialogue, we can speak of "fusion of horizons," while in dialogue, though not in the text, we can "come to terms" with the Other. However, just as the fusion of horizons is not the consequence of an ontological/semantic foundation in *die Sache,* so the dialogical "coming to terms" does not depend on a mastery of signification that would presuppose the prior "disclosure" of a referent world. It is true that dialogue, as opposed to writing, constitutes for Levinas a "plenitude of discourse," but it is not one that would be grounded ontologically in the mediating presence of the referent. It is instead an *ethical* plenitude that challenges the autonomy or freedom of the an-archic self: "A proposition is maintained in the stretched field of questions and answers. A proposition is a sign which is already interpreted, which provides its own key. The presence of the interpretive key in the sign is precisely the presence of the Other in the proposition, the presence of him who can come to the assistance of his discourse, the teaching quality of all speech. Oral discourse is the plenitude of all discourse" (Levinas 1969, 96).

The "interpretive key" of the sign is the presence of the Other, not as one who "knows," but simply as Other. In the dialogical "assistance" she can render her sign lies the opportunity of coming to terms with, or "understanding," the Other. This would not be grounded in a prior relation toward a common *Sache* but would be the act that begins to establish such commonality, the creation of commonplaces. The speech of plenitude, face-to-face, "first founds community by *giving*, by presenting the phenomenon as given; and it gives by thematizing" (Levinas 1969, 99). Such "giving" is measured not in the neutrality of the validity claim it grounds (truth depends on justice) but in the "absolute relation"—the presence of the Other who speaks and so *judges* my "murderous freedom" (appropriation). Such judgment is the "supremacy" of the Other that "posits him in himself, outside of my knowing, and it is by relation to this absolute that the *given* takes on meaning" (Levinas 1969, 101).

The plenitude of speech, the "saturation" of dialogical discourse, is thus not of an epistemological or ontological order, but of an ethical order. Dialogical hermeneutics, coming to terms with the Other, is guided not by *knowledge*, but by *desire*, an encounter with another freedom that would not, for Levinas, be redeemable in the speculative dialectic of reciprocal recognition, not yet mediable by a presupposed "common theme," but would "call forth" the abolition of "the inalienable property of enjoyment" (the an-archic silence of *theoria* as landscape and *contemplatio*), laying the "foundations for a possession in common" (Levinas 1969, 76). To come to terms with the Other, to engage in dialogue, is to prepare the way for sharing the world given in speech.

References

Derrida, Jacques. 1974. *On grammatology*. Trans. G. C. Spivak. Baltimore: Johns Hopkins University Press.

———. 1979. Living On. In *Deconstruction and criticism*. New York: Seabury Press.

Gadamer, Hans-Georg. 1975. *Truth and method*. Trans. Garrett Barden and John Cumming. New York: Seabury Press.

———. 1976. On the scope and function of hermeneutic reflection. In *Essays in philosophical hermeneutics*, trans. David E. Linge. Berkeley: University of California Press.

———. 1986a. Destruktion und Dekonstruktion. In *Gesammelte Werke*, Vol. 2. Tubingen: J. C. B. Mohr.

———. 1986b. Text und Interpretation." In *Gesammelte Werke*, Vol. 2. Tubingen: J. C. B. Mohr.

———. 1986c. Zwischen Phanomenologie und Dialektik, versuch einer Selbstkritik. In *Gesammelte Werke*, vol. 2. Tubingen: J. C. B. Mohr.

———. Habermas, Jürgen. 1980. The hermeneutic claim to universality. In *Contemporary hermeneutics*, ed. Josef Bleicher, 181–211. London: Routledge and Kegan Paul.

Heidegger, Martin. 1962. *Being and time*. Trans. John Macquarrie and Edward Robinson. New York: Harper and Row.

contributors

Mehdi Abedi recently received his Ph.D. from the Department of Anthropology at Rice University.

Vincent Crapanzano is professor of anthropology at the Graduate Center of CUNY.

Steven Crowell is associate professor of philosophy at Rice University.

Sven Daelemans recently received his Ph.D. in human development and family studies from Texas Tech University.

Alessandro Ferrara is assistant professor of sociology at the University of Rome.

Michael Fischer is professor of anthropology at Rice University.

R. Lane Kauffmann is associate professor of Spanish language and civilization at Rice University.

Bradford Keeney is professor of systemic therapy at Nova University.

Werner Kelber is professor of religious studies at Rice University.

Richard McKeon was Charles F. Grey Distinguished Professor of Classics and Philosophy at the University of Chicago.

Jochen Mecke is assistant professor of romance literature at the University of Heidelberg.

C. Jan Swearingen is professor of rhetoric in the English Department at the University of Texas, Arlington.

Stephen Tyler is professor of anthropology at Rice University.

Greg Urban is associate professor of anthropology at the University of Texas, Austin.

index

Aban ibn Taghlib, 129
Abdullah ibn Abbas, 128–29, 138, 142
Abedi, Mehdi, 9, 13
Abelard, Peter, 133
Abraham, 131–32, 139
Abrogated verses of Qur'an, 136–37
Abu Bakr, 128, 133
Abu Lahab, 124
Abul-Qasem, Muhammad, 133
Academica (Cicero), 51
Academy, Greek, 31–32
Acceptance, 272 n
Achuar, 100, 102, 104-9, 111–16
Ackrill, J. I., 57, 58
Adam, 131–32, 137
Addressivity, 226, 234, 240
Adorno, Theodor W., 160, 180, 211
Aesop's fables, 168–69
Aesthetics, 5; and Bakhtin, 224, 227; and Habermas's *Diskursethik*, 309–10, 314, 330
Akhbaris, 143–44
Alan of Lille, 37
Alcohol, consumption of, 137
Alexy, R., 307
Algar, Hamid, 147
'Ali, 126, 128, 132, 141, 147
Allen, R. E., 58
Alter, Robert, 77
Alterity. *See* Self/Other
al-Amil, Shaykh Hurr, 145

Anaxagoras, 35
Angels, in Qur'anic dialogues, 131–32
Anglo-American analytic philosophy, 52–54
Animals, as Other, 168–91
Ansari, Mortada, 143
Ansari, Shaikh Morteza. 144
Answerability, 224–28, 232
Anthropology, 2–4, 6, 267–90; Bakhtin's philosophical, 229, 230; and democratization of dialogue, 48–49; and identity, 206; and Levinas's phenomenology, 356–57; logic in, 53; and Other question, 159–89; Renaissance dialogue versus *dialog* in, 292–300
Apel, Karl-Otto, 2–3, 304, 306–8, 313, 323, 323 n
Aphorisms, biblical, 78–87
Apology (Plato), 35
Appropriation, 272 n, 287–90
Aquinas, Saint Thomas, 39
Arcesilas, 31
Aristotle, 35, 37, 40, 57; dialectic of, 7–8, 28–29, 50–51, 59, 61, 62, 66; on division of sciences, 39; grammar of, 54, 55, 57–59; *logos* in, 60; and *phronesis*, 334
Atomists, 8, 35–36
Auerbach, Erich, 76–77
Augustine, Saint, 29, 54
Authenticity, 334–35

363